THE BIOGRAPHICAL DICTIONARY OF SCIENTISTS

Mathematicians

THE BIOGRAPHICAL DICTIONARY OF SCIENTISTS

Mathematicians

General Editor
David Abbott PhD

PETER BEDRICK BOOKS
New York

First American edition published in 1986 by
Peter Bedrick Books
125 East 23 Street
New York, NY 10010

7-87 Publ 3500

Copyright © 1985 David Abbott

93 92 91 90 89 88 87 86   1 2 3 4 5 6 7 8 9

Published by agreement with Muller, Blond & White Ltd., London

Library of Congress Cataloging-in-Publication Data
Main entry under title:

The Biographical dictionary of scientists. Mathematicians.

  Includes index.
  1. Mathematicians—Biography. I. Abbott, David, 1937–
QA28.B54   1986   510′.92′2   85-20011
ISBN 0-87226-008-9

Manufactured in the United States of America
Distributed in the USA by Harper & Row
and in Canada by Book Center, Montreal

Printed on acid-free paper

Contents

Acknowledgements

Many people are involved in the creation of a major new series of reference books. The general editor and the publishers are grateful to all of them and wish to thank particularly the contributing authors: Gareth Ashurst; Jim Bailey; Mary Basham; Alan Bishop; William Cooksey; David Cowey; Michael Darton; Valerie Neal; Adam Ostaszewski; Mary Sanders; Robert Smith; Robert Stewart; Christopher Tunney and David Ward. Our thanks are also due to Mick Saunders for his artwork and to Bull Publishing Consultants Ltd, whose experience in the development of reference books has made a significant contribution to the series: John Clark; Kate Duffy; Nikki Okell; Martyn Page; Hal Robinson and Sandy Shepherd.

Historical introduction

Most ancient civilizations had the means to make accurate measurements, to record them in writing, and to use them in calculations involving elementary addition and subtraction. And for many of them that was apparently sufficient. It seems, for example, that the ancient Egyptians relied on simple addition and subtraction even for calculations of area and volume – although their number system was founded upon base 10, as ours is today. They certainly never thought of mathematics as a subject of potential interest or study for its own sake.

Not so the Babylonians. Contemporaries of the Egyptians, they nevertheless had a more practical form of numerical notation and were genuinely interested in improving their mathematical knowledge. (Perversely, however, their system used base 10 up to 59, after which 60 became a new base; one result of this is the way we now measure time and angles.) By about 1700 BC the Babylonians not only had the four elementary algorithms – the rules for addition, subtraction, multiplication and division – but also had made some progress in geometry. They knew what we now call Pythagoras's Theorem, and had formulated further theorems concerning chords in circles. This even led to a rudimentary understanding of algebraic functions.

The ancient Greeks

Until the very end of their own civilization, the ancient Greeks had little use for algebra other than within a study of logic. After all, to them learning was as interdisciplinary as possible. Even Thales of Miletus (*fl.*585 BC), regarded as the first named mathematician, considered himself a philosopher in a school of philosophers; mathematics was peripheral. The Greeks' attitude of scientific curiosity was, however, to result in some notable advances in mathematics, especially in the endeavour to understand why and how algorithms worked, theorems were consistent, and calculations could be relied on. It led in particular to the notion of mathematical proof, in an elementary but no less factual way. Pythagoras (*fl.*530 BC), having proved the theorem now called after him, imbued mathematics with a kind of religious mystique on the basis of which he became a rather unsuccessful social reformer. Others became fascinated by solving problems using a ruler and compass, in which an outline of the concept of an irrational number (such as π) inevitably appeared. Further investigations of curves followed, and resulted in the first suggestions of what we now call integration. Such geometrical studies were often applied to astronomy. A corpus of various kinds of mathematical knowledge was beginning to accumulate.

The man who recorded much of it was Euclid (*fl.*300 BC). His work *The Elements* is intended as much as a history of mathematics as a compendium of knowledge, and was massive therefore in both scope and production. It contained many philosophical elements (as we would now define them) and astronomical hypotheses, but the exposition of the mathematical work was masterly, and became the style of presentation emulated virtually to this day. Euclid's geometry, especially, became the standard for millennia: mathematicians still distinguish between Euclidean and non-Euclidean geometry. He included even discussion and ideas on spherical geometry. Unfortunately, some of *The Elements* was lost, including the work on conic section.

Conic sections seem to have been a source of fascination to many ancient Greek mathematicians. Archimedes (*c.*287–212 BC), one of the most-practical men of all time, used the principle of conic sections in an investigation into how to solve problems of an algebraic nature. A little later, Apollonius of Perga (*fl.*230 BC), wrote definitely of the subject, in great detail, adducing a considerable number of associated theorems and including relevants proofs. The significance of part of this extra material was established only at the end of the nineteenth century.

The Romans and their successors

After about 150 BC, the study of astronomy dominated the scientific world. Consequently, for a while, little mathematical progress was made except in the context of the cosmological theories of the time. (There was accordingly some significant research into spherical geometry and spherical trigonometry.) It was then too that Roman civilization briefly flourished and began to recede – again with little effect on the

1

status of mathematics. Surprisingly, however, after about 400 years, the Alexandrian Diophantus (*fl.c.* AD 270-280) devised something of extreme originality: the algebraic variable, in which a symbol stands for an unknown quantity. Equations involving such indeterminates - Diophantus included one indeterminate per equation, needing thus only one symbol - are now commonly called Diophantine equations.

Alexandria thus became the centre for mathematical thought at the time. Very shortly afterwards, Pappus (*fl.* 320) deemed it time again for a compilation of all known mathematical knowledge. In *The Collection* he revised, edited and expanded the works of all the classic writers and added many of his own proofs and theorems, including some well-known problems he left unsolved. It is this work more than any other that ensured the survival of the mathematics of the Greeks until the Renaissance about a thousand years later.

In the meantime the initiative was taken by the Arabs, whose main sphere of influence was, significantly, farther east. They were thus in contact with Persian and Indian scientific schools, and accustomed to translating learned texts. Both Greek and Babylonian precepts were assimilated and practised - the best known proponent was Al-Khwarizmi (*fl.c.*840), whose work was historically important to later mathematicians in Europe. The Arabs devised accurate trigonometrical tables (primarily for astronomical research) and continued the development of spherical trigonometry; they also made advances in descriptive geometry.

It was through his learning in the Arab markets of Algeria that the medieval merchant from Pisa Leonardo Fibonacci (or Leonardo Pisano; *c.*1180-*c.*1250), brought much of contemporary mathematics back to Europe. It included - only then - the use of the "Arabic" numerals 1 to 9 and the "zephirum" (0), the innovation of partial numbers or fractions, and many other features of both geometry and algebra. From that time, hundreds of translators throughout Europe (especially in Spain) worked on Latin versions of Arab works and transcriptions. Only when Europe had regained all the knowledge and, so to speak, updated itself could genuine development take place. The effort took nearly 400 years before any truly outstanding advances were made - but may be said to be directly responsible for the overall updating and advance in science that then came about, known as the Renaissance.

The sixteenth century

One of the first instances of genuine progress in mathematics was the means of solving cubic equations, although acrimonious recriminations over priority surrounded its initial publication. One particularly charismatic contender - Niccolo Fontana (*c.*1499-1557), usually known as Tartaglia - besides being a military physicist, remained an inspirational figure in the propagation of mathematics. The means of solving quartic equations was discovered soon afterwards.

Within another 20 years, the French mathematician François Viète (1540-1603) was improving on the systematization of algebra in symbolic terms and expounding on mathematical (as opposed to astronomical) applications of trigonometry. It was he, if anyone, who initiated the study of number theory as an independent branch of mathematics. At the time of Viète's death, Henry Briggs (1561-1630) in England was already Professor of Geometry; a decade later he combined with John Napier (1550-1617), the deviser of "Napier's Bones", to produce the first logarithm tables using the number 10 as its base, a means of calculation commonly used until the late 1960s but now outmoded by the computer and pocket calculator. Simultaneously, the astronomer Johannes Kepler was publishing one of the first works to consider infinitesimals, a concept that would lead later to the formulation of the different calculus.

The seventeenth century

It was in France that the scope of mathematics was then widened by a group of great mathematicians. Most of them met at the scientific discussions run by the director of the convent of Place Royale in Paris, Fr Marin Mersenne (1588-1648). To these discussions sometimes came the philosopher-mathematician René Descartes (1596-1675), the lawyer and magistrate Pierre de Fermat (1601-1675), the physicist and mathematician Blaise Pascal (1623-1662), and the architect and mathematician Gérard Desargues (1591-1661). Descartes was probably the foremost of these in terms of mathematical innovation, although it is thought that Fermat - for whom mathematics was an absorbing but part-time hobby - had a profound influence upon him. His greatest contribution to science was in virtually founding the discipline of analytical (co-ordinate) geometry, in which geometrical figures can be described by algebraic expressions. He applied the tenets of geometry to algebra, and was the first to do so, although the converse was not uncommon. Unfortunately, Descartes so much enjoyed the reputation his mathematical discoveries afforded him that he began to envy anyone who then also achieved any kind of mathematical distinction. He therefore regarded Desargues - who published a well-received work on conics - not only as competition but actually as retrogressive. And when Pascal then publicly championed Desargues (whom Descartes had openly ridiculed), putting forward an equally accepted form of geometry now known as projective geometry, matters became more than merely unfriendly.

In the meantime, Fermat took no sides, studied both types of geometry, and was in contact with several other European mathematicians. In particular, he used Descartes' geometry to derive an evaluation of the slope of a tangent, finding a method by which to compute the derivative and thus being considered by many the actual formulator of the differential calculus. Part of his study was of tangents as limits of secants. With Pascal he investigated probability theory, and in number theory he independently devised many theorems, one of them now famous as Fermat's Last Theorem.

It is now known that at about this time in Japan, a mathematician called Seki Kowa (c.1642-1708) was independently discovering many of the mathematical innovations also being formulated in the West. Even more remarkably, he managed to change the social order of his time in order to popularize the subject.

Three years after Pascal died a religious recluse haunted by self-doubt, Isaac Newton (1642-1727), was obliged by the spread of the plague to his university college in Cambridge to return home to Woolsthorpe in Lincolnshire and there spend the next year and a half in scientific contemplation. One of his first discoveries was what is now called the binomial theorem,which led Newton to an investigation of infinite series, which in turn led to a study of integration and the notion that it might be achieved as the opposite of differentiation. He arrived at this conclusion in 1666 - but did not publish it. More than seven years later, in Germany, Gottfried Leibniz (1646-1716) - who had possibly read the works of Pascal - arrived at exactly the same conclusion, and did publish it. He received considerable acclaim in Europe, much to Newton's annoyance - and a priority argument was very quickly in process. Naively, Leibniz submitted his claim for priority to a committee on which Newton was sitting, so the outcome was a surprise to no one else - but it was in fact Leibniz's notation system that was eventually universally adopted. And it was not until 1687 that Newton's studies on calculus were published within his massive *Principia Mathematica*, which also included much of his investigations into physics and optics. Leibniz went on to try to develop a mathematical notation symbolizing logic, but although he made good initial progress it met with little general interest, and despite his energy and status he died a somewhat lonely and forlorn figure.

Another who died in even worse straits was an acquaintance of both Newton and Leibniz: Abraham de Moivre (1667-1754), a Hugenot persecuted for his religious background to the extent that he could find no professional position despite being a first-class and innovative mathematician. He met his end broken by poverty and drink - but not before he had formulated game theory, reconstituted probability theory, and set the business of life insurance on a firm statistical basis.

Leibniz's work on calculus was greatly admired in Europe, and particularly by the great Swiss mathematician family domiciled in Basle: the Bernoullis. The eldest of three brothers, Jakob (or Jacques; 1654-1705), actually corresponded with Leibniz; the youngest, Johan (or Jean; 1667-1748), was recommended by the physicist Christiaan Huygens to a professorship at Groningen. Both brothers were fascinated by investigating possible applications of the new calculus. Unhappily, their study of special curves (particularly cycloids) using polar co-ordinates proceeded independently along identical lines and resulted in considerable animosity between them. When Jakob died, however, Johan succeeded him at Basle, where he educated his son Daniel - also a brilliant mathematician - whose great friends were Leonhard Euler (1707-1783) and Gabriel Cramer (1704-1752).

The eighteenth century

Euler may have been the most prolific mathematical author ever. He had amazing energy, a virtually photographic memory and a gift for mental calculation that stood him in good stead late in life when he became totally blind. Not since Descartes had anyone contributed so innovatively to mathematical analysis - Euler's *Introduction* (1748) is considered practically to define in textbook fashion the modern understanding of analytical methodology, including especially the concept of a function. Other works introduced the calculus of variations and the now familiar symbols π, e and i, and systematized differential geometry. He also popularized the use of polar co-ordinates, and explained the use of graphs to represent elementary functions.

It was his friend Daniel Bernoulli (1700–1782) who had originally managed to secure a position for him in St Petersburg. When, in 1766, Euler returned there from a post at the Prussian Academy, his place in Berlin was taken by the Frenchman Joseph Lagrange (1736–1813) whose ideas ran almost parallel with Euler's. In many ways Lagrange was equally as formative in the popularizing of mathematical analysis, for although he might not have been so energetic or outrightly creative as Euler, he was far more concerned with exactitude and axiomatic rigour, and combined with this a strong desire to generalize. The publication of his studies of number theory and algebra were thus models of precise presentation, and his mathematical research into mechanics began a process of creative thought that has not ceased since. One immediate result of the latter was to inspire his friend and fellow-Frenchman Jean le Rond d'Alembert (1717–1783) to great achievements in dynamics and celestial mechanics. It was d'Alembert who first devised the theory of partial differential equations.

Towards the end of Lagrange's life, when he was already ailing, he became Professor of Mathematics at the institution which for the next 50 years at least was to exercise considerable influence over the progress of mathematics; the newly-established École Polytechnique in Paris. Two of his contemporaries there were Pierre Laplace (1749–1827) and Gaspard Monge (1746–1818). Laplace became famous for his astronomical calculations, Monge for his textbook on geometry; both were acquaintances of Napoleon Bonaparte – as was Joseph Fourier (1768–1830), the physicist who demonstrated that a function could be expanded in sines and cosines through a series now known as the Fourier Series.

It was one of Gaspard Monge's pupils – Jean-Victor Poncelet (1788–1867) – who first popularized the notion of continuity and outlined contemporary thinking on the principle of duality. And it was one of Laplace's colleagues (whom he disliked), Adrien Legendre (1752–1833), who took over where Lagrange left off, and researched into elliptic functions for more than 40 years, eventually deriving the law of quadratic reciprocity and, in number theory, proving that π is irrational.

The nineteenth century

Legendre's investigations into elliptic integrals were outdated almost as soon as they were published by the work of the Norwegian Niels Abel (1802–1829) and the German Karl Jacobi (1804–1851). Jacobi went on to make important dis-coveries in the theory of determinants: he was a great interdisciplinarian. The tragically short-lived Abel has probably had the longer-lasting influence, in that he devised the functions now named after him. He was unlucky, too, in that his proof, that in general roots cannot be expressed in radicals was discovered simultaneously and independently by the equally tragic Evariste Galois (1811–1832), who only just had time before his violent death to initiate the theory of groups. Further progress in function theory was made by Augustin Cauchy (1789–1857), a prolific mathematical writer who in his works pioneered many modern mathematical methods, developing in particular the use of limits and continuity. He also originated the theory of complex variables, based at least partly on the work of Jean Argand (1767–1822), who had succeeded in representing complex numbers by means of a graph.

By this time, however, the centre of mathematics in Europe was undoubtedly Göttingen, where the great Karl Gauss (1777–1855) had long presided. Sometimes compared with Archimedes and Newton, Gauss was indisputably not only a mathematical genius who made a multitude of far-reaching discoveries – particularly in geometry and statistical probability – but was also an exceptionally inspirational teacher who inculcated in his pupils the need for meticulous attention to proofs. Late in his tenure at Göttingen, three of his pupils/colleagues were Lejeune Dirichlet (1805–1859), Bernhard Riemann (1826–1866) and Julius Dedekind (1831–1916). There could not have been a more influential quartet in the history of mathematics: the work of all four provides the basis for a major part of modern mathematical knowledge.

Gauss himself was most interested in geometry. Jakob Steiner (1796–1863) in Germany was trying to remove geometry from the "taint" of analysis as propounded by the French, but Gauss went further and decided to investigate geometry outside the scope of that described by Euclid. It was a momentous decision – made almost simultaneously and quite independently by Nikolai Lobachevsky (1792–1856) and János Bolyai (1802–1860). Between them they thus derived non-Euclidean geometry. The ramifications of this were widespread and fast-moving. In Ireland William Hamilton (1805–1865) suggested the concept of n-dimensional space; in Germany Hermann Grassmann (1809–1877) not only defined it but went on to use a form of calculus based on it. But it was Gauss's own pupil, Riemann, who really became the arch-apostle of the subject. He invented elliptical hyperbolic geometries, introduced "Riemann surfaces" and redefined conformal mapping (transformations) explaining his innovations with such enthusiasm and accuracy that the modern understanding of time and space now owes much to his work.

Meanwhile Dirichlet - who succeeded Gauss when the great man died and himself became an influential teacher - and Dedekind concentrated more on number theory. Dirichlet slanted his teaching of mathematics towards applications in physics, whereas Dedekind was determined to arrive at a philosophical interpretation of the concept of numbers. Such an interpretation was thought likely to be of use in the contemporary search for a mathematical basis for logic. George Boole (1815-1864) had already attempted to create a form of algebra intended to represent logic that, although not entirely successful, was stimulating to others.

As the study of geometry expanded rapidly, the importance of algebra also increased accordingly. Riemann was influential; Karl Weierstrass (1815-1897) provided important redefinitions in function theory; but in algebraic terms development was next most instigated by the Englishman Arthur Cayley (1821-1895) who discovered the theory of algebraic invariants even as he carried out research into *n*-dimensional geometry. The principles of topology were being established one by one even though the branch itself was not yet complete. Sophus Lie (1842-1899) made important contributions to geometry and to algebra - and indirectly to topology - with the concept of continuous groups and contact transformations, and Cayley went on to invent the theory of matrices. Gaston Darboux (1842-1917) revised popular thinking about surfaces. Felix Klein (1849-1925) - an influential figure in his time - unified all the geometries within his Erlangen Programme (1872). But it was Felix Hausdorff (1868-1942) who is actually credited with the formulation of topology.

Dedekind finally achieved his goal and axiomatized the concept of numbers - only for his axioms to be (albeit apologetically and acknowledgedly) "stolen" from him by Giuseppe Peano (1858-1932). The axioms, however, may have inspired - among others - Hausdorff to conceive the idea of point sets in topology, and Georg Cantor (1843-1918) to define set theory (the basis on which most mathematics is taught in schools today) and transfinite numbers, and certainly caused a revival of interest in number theory generally. Immanuel Fuchs (1833-1902) reformulated much of function theory while attempting to refine Riemann's method for solving differential equations. His pupil, Henri Poincaré (1854-1912) - similarly fascinated by Riemann's work - made many conjectures that were later useful in the investigation of topology and of space and time, but less successfully spent years researching into what are now called integral equations, only to discover after they were finally axiomatized by Ivar Fredholm (1866-1927) that he had done all the work without perceiving the answer.

The twentieth century

A different result of the Peano axioms was a renewal of the quest to find a relationship between mathematics and logic. Another system of symbolic logic had been devised by Gottlob Frege (1848-1925), whose pride was turned to ashes when Bertrand Russell (1872-1970) pointed out to him an internal, and fundamental, inconsistency. Russell, with his pupil and friend Alfred North Whitehead (1861-1947), attended lectures given by Peano; together they then published a large work on the foundations of mathematics, entitled *Principia Mathematica*. It had an immediate impact, and remained influential. Other prominent figures in the philosophy of mathematics at the time included Hermann Weyl (1885-1935) and Jacques Herbrand (1908-1931).

The search for meaning in mathematics was not solely philosophical, however. One of Fredholm's pupils was David Hilbert (1862-1943), possibly the latest of the truly great mathematicians. A genuine polymath and an enthusiastic teacher, he expanded virtually all branches of mathematics, especially in the interpretation of geometric structures implied by infinite-dimensional space. He too was involved in the debate over the primary nature of mathematics, formal or intuitional. But all philosophical theories were dealt a heavy blow by the theorem formulated in 1930 by Kurt Gödel (1906-1978). This stated that the overall consistency (i.e. completeness) of mathematics cannot itself be proved mathematically - which means that the foundations of mathematics must forever remain impenetrable.

The days of debate were over; Hilbert went on with his work. Mathematics became gradually either more theoretical or more practical. Theoretically interest swung towards finding features in common between disparage mathematical structures. Henri Lebesgue (1875-1941) devised a concept of measure that contributed greatly to the theory of abstract spaces. Andrei Kolmogorov (1903-   ) and others not only related this to probability theory but thereby to problems of statistical mechanics and the clarification of the ergodic theorems provided by George Birkhoff (1884-1944) in 1932. In alge-

braic topology, René Thom (1923–) categorized surfaces. It is worthy of note that thereafter most modern mathematics has concerned
itself with such abstract mathematical structures
or concepts as fields, rings or ideals.

The study of statistics and probability was
also taken up with new enthusiasm for more
practical applications. Karl Pearson (1857–
1936) refined Gauss's ideas to derive the notion
of standard deviation. Agner Erlang (1878–
1929) used probability theory in a highly practical way to aid the efficiency of the circuitry of
his capital's telephone system. Alonso Church
(1903–) defined a "calculable function" and
by so doing clarified the nature of algorithms.

Following this, George Dantzig (1914–)
was able to set up complex linear programmes
for computers. Such progress is being maintained, sometimes now as a result of using the
machines themselves to devise further advances.

The applications of mathematics are also increasing. It is no longer possible to separate in
any real way, for example, mathematics and
physics. Even much theoretical physics can be
worked out mathematically – as has in fact been
done by Stephen Hawking (1942–), and the
same is true in many other sciences.

The trend will probably continue, although
the necessity for total computerization of data
and calculation then becomes almost inevitable.

A

Abel, Neils Henrik (1802-1829), was a Norwegian mathematician who, in a very brief career, became the first to demonstrate that an algebraic solution of the general equation of the fifth degree is impossible.

Abel was born at Finnöy, a small island near Stavanger, on 5 August 1802. He was educated by his father, a Lutheran minister, until the age of twelve, when he was enrolled in the Cathedral school at Christiania (Oslo). There his flair for mathematics received little encouragement until he came under the tutelage of Bernt Holmboe in 1817. Holmboe put Abel in touch with Euler's calculus texts and introduced him to the work of Lagrange and Laplace. Abel's imagination was fired by algebraic equations theory and by the time that he left school in 1821 to enter the University of Oslo he had become familiar with most of the body of mathematical literature then known. In particular he had, during his last year at school, began to work on the baffling problem of the quintic equation, or general equation of the fifth degree, unsolved since it had been taken up by Italian mathematicians early in the sixteenth century.

Because of his father's death in 1820, Abel arrived at the university virtually penniless. Fortunately, his talent was apparent, and he was given free rooms and financial support by the university. Since the university offered no courses in advanced mathematics, most of Abel's research was done on his own initiative. In 1823 he published his first paper. It was an unimportant discussion of functional equations, but another paper published in that year heralded the arrival of a highly original new mind in the world of mathematics, although it went unregarded at the time. In it Abel provided the first solution in the history of mathematics of an integral equation. All the while he remained obsessed by the problem of the quintic equation. During his last year at school he had sent to the Danish mathematician, Ferdinand Deger, his "solution" to the problem, only to receive from Deger the advice to abandon that "sterile" question and turn his mind to elliptic transcendentals (elliptic integrals). Deger was kind enough, even so, to ask Abel for examples of his solution and this request proved to be fruitful. For when Abel began to construct examples he discovered that it was no solution at all. He therefore wrote a paper demonstrating that a radical expression to represent a solution to fifth- or higher-degree equations was impossible. After three centuries a niggling question had been resolved. Yet when Abel sent his demonstration to Gauss he received no reply. Nor was anyone else much interested and Abel was forced to publish the paper himself.

In 1825, taking advantage of a government grant to enable scholars to study foreign languages abroad, Abel went to Berlin. There he met Leopold Crelle, the privy councillor and engineer much taken with problems in mathematics. Together they brought out the first issue of Crelle's Journal, which was to become the leading nineteenth-century German organ of mathematics. (The first issue consisted almost entirely of seven papers of Abel.) A year later Abel moved on to Paris, where he wrote his famous paper "*Mémoire sur une propriété générale d'une classe très-étendue de fonctions transcendantes*". It dealt with the sum of the integrals of a given algebraic function and presented the theorem that any such sum can be expressed as a fixed number of these integrals with integration arguments that are algebraic functions of the original arguments. Abel sent the manuscript to the French Academy of Sciences and was deeply disappointed when the referees – who alleged that the manuscript was illegible! – did not publish it. He returned to Berlin a disheartened man. Low in funds and unable to get a post at the university there, he accepted Crelle's offer to edit the journal. In 1827 he published the longest paper of his career, the "*Recherche sur les fonctions elliptiques*". He also suffered his first attack of the tuberculosis that was to kill him. At the end of the year he returned to Norway, where he lived in gradually deteriorating health until his death, at Froland, on 6 April 1829.

Abel, in addition to this work on quintic equations, transformed the theory of elliptic integrals by introducing elliptic functions, and this generalization of trigonometric functions became one of the favourite topics of 19th-century mathematics. It led eventually to the theory of complex multiplication, with its important implications for algebraic number theory. He also provided the first stringent proof of the binomial theorem. A number of useful concepts in modern mathematics, notably the Abelian group and the Abelian function, bear his name. Yet it was only after his death that his achievement was publicly acknowledged. In 1830 the French Academy awarded him the Grand Prix, which he shared with Karl Jacobi (1804-1851), the German mathematician who had (independently) made important discoveries about elliptic functions. And eleven years later the Academy finally came round to publishing the "illegible" manuscript of 1826.

Ackermann, Robert John (1933-   ), is an American philosopher whose most important work has been in logic.

Ackermann was born at Sandusky, Ohio, on 5 March 1933, and received his BA in Philosophy from Capital University in 1954, his MA from the University of Ohio in 1957, and his PhD from Michigan State University in 1960. He then embarked on an academic teaching career and since 1968 has been Professor of Philosophy at the University of Massachusetts. In 1964-1965 he was a Fulbright visiting lecturer at Exeter University in England.

Ackermann's most important work has been to investigate problems in logic, as described in his books *Non-deductive Inference* (1966), *Introduction to Many Valued Logics* (1967) and *Modern Deductive Logic* (1970). He has also published a contribution to the post-Kuhnian debate, the *Philosophy of Science* (1970). Although none of his work treats directly of mathematics it is, especially in its discussion of the distinctions between sentential logic (SL) and predicate logic (PL), of interest to mathematicians, particularly those working in the computer sciences.

Aiken, Howard Hathaway (1900-1973), was an American computer and data-processing pioneer who invented the Harvard Mark I and Harvard Mark II computers, the prototypes of modern digital computers.

Aiken was born at Hoboken, New Jersey, on 9 March 1900. He studied engineering at the University of Wisconsin and graduated in 1923. He then took a job with the Madison Gas and Electric Company, where he remained until 1927, when he went to Chicago to work for the Westinghouse Electric Manufacturing Company. In 1931 he left Westinghouse to take up a research post in the department of phyics at the University of Chicago. The rest of the decade he spent in research, both at Chicago and at Harvard. He received his PhD from Harvard in 1939 and was appointed an instructor in physics and communication engineering. He quickly rose to become a full professor in applied mathematics and remained at Harvard until 1961, when he was appointed Professor of

Information Technology at the University of Miami. He died at St Louis, Missouri, on 14 March 1973.

When Aiken began his research into computer technology in the 1930s the subject was still in its infancy. Simple, manual calculating machines had been in use since the mid-seventeenth century, but they were too elementary and too slow to meet the military and industrial requirements of the twentieth century. It was, indeed, the US Navy which started Aiken on the career for which he became world famous. His early research at Harvard was sponsored by the Navy Board of Ordnance and in 1939 he and three other engineers from the International Business Machines Corporation (IBM) were placed under contract by the Navy to develop a machine capable of performing both the four basic operations of addition, subtraction, multiplication and division and also referring to stored, tabulated results.

Aiken played the central role in the development for the US Navy of the first Automatic Sequence Controlled Calculator in the world, the Harvard Mark I, which was completed in 1944. It was principally a mechanical device, although it had a few electronic features; it was 15m long, 2.5m high and weighed more than 30 tonnes. Addition took 0.3 seconds, multiplication 4 seconds. It was able to manipulate numbers of up to 23 decimal places and to store 72 of them. Information was fed into the machine by tape or punched cards and produced output in a similar form. Its chief functions were to produce mathematical tables and to assist the ballistics and gunnery divisions of the military.

On the completion of the Mark I, Aiken was posted to the Naval Proving Ground at Dahlgren, Virginia, to begin working on improving his invention. There the Mark II was completed in 1947. It was a fully electronic machine containing 13,000 electronic relays. It was also much faster than its predecessor, requiring only 0.2 seconds for addition and 0.7 seconds for multiplication. Moreover it could store 100 10-digit figures and their signs.

For his great achievements, sufficient to earn him the name of the father of modern computers, Aiken was given the rank of Commander in the United States Navy Research Department.

Aleksandrov, Pavel Sergeevich (1896-   ), is a Soviet mathematician who is a leading expert in the field of topology and one of the founders of the theory of compact and bicompact spaces.

He was born in Bogorodsk (now Noginok), near Moscow, on 7 May 1896. He studied mathematics at Moscow University, graduating in 1917, and was appointed a lecturer there in 1921. Since 1929 he has been its Professor of Mathematics. From 1932 to 1964 he was President of the Moscow Mathematical Society. He has received five Orders of Lenin and was awarded the State Prize in 1942.

Although he began his career by studying set theory and the theory of functions, Aleksandrov has worked principally in the development of topology. He introduced many of the basic concepts of this relatively new branch of mathematics, notably the notion that an arbitrarily general topological space can be approximated to an arbitrary degree of accuracy by simple geometric figures such as polyhedrons. Of great importance, too, has been his investigations into that branch of topology known as homology, which examines the relationships between the ways in which spatial structures are dissected. He formulated the theory of essential mappings and the homological theory of dimensionality, which led to a number of basic laws of duality relating to the topological properties of an additional part of space.

Aleksandrov has always been greatly interested in the dissemination of mathematical knowledge and in broad collaboration in seeking it. Much of his topological work was done within a group of colleagues and students whom he gathered round him. Being one of the few Soviet scientists given great freedom to travel abroad, he has also, by his numerous visits to European universities, done much to carry new ideas back and forth between the East and the West. His passion for international co-operation led him to supervise the publication of an English-Russian dictionary of mathematical terminology in 1962.

Amsler-Laffon, Jakob (1823-1912), was a Swiss mathematical physicist who designed and manufactured precision instruments for use in engineering.

Amsler-Laffon was born Jakob Amsler at Stalden bei Brugg on 16 November 1823 and educated locally until the age of 19, when he went to Jena to study theology. Theology absorbed his interest for only one year, however, and in 1844 he went to the university at Könisberg to study mathematics and physics. He received his doctorate in 1848, after which he worked briefly at the observatory in Geneva. The next eight years were spent in teaching, first at the University of Zürich (1849-1851) and then at the Gymnasium in Schaffhausen. But in the middle of this period Amsler abandoned his interest in pure science and became involved in

the design of scientific instruments. He established a factory for the manufacture of his designs at Schaffhausen in 1854. In that year he also married Elise Laffon, the daughter of a drugs manufacturer, and added her surname to his own. He devoted himself to his factory for the rest of his life, until his death at Schaffhausen on 3 January 1912.

Amsler-Laffon's best idea was his first, the design for an improved tool to measure areas inside curves. This was his polar planimeter. Earlier models of tools to measure the surface of spheres had been based on Cartesian coordinates, but they were bulky and expensive. Amsler-Laffon's design, based on a polar co-ordinate system, was not only more delicate and more flexible than its predecessors, but was also much cheaper to manufacture. It could be used in the determination of Fourier co-efficients and was thus of particularly valuable use to shipbuilders and railway engineers. By the time he died, his factory had produced more than 50,000 polar planimeters.

Apollonius of Perga ($c.245$–$c.190$ BC) was the last of the great Greek mathematicians, whose treatise on conic sections represents the final flowering of Greek mathematics.

Apollonius was born early in the reign of Ptolemy Euergetes, King of Egypt (247-222 BC), in the Greek town of Perga in southern Asia Minor (now part of Turkey). Little is known of his life. It is thought that he may have studied at the school established by Euclid at Alexandria, especially since much of his work was built on Euclidean foundations.

Apollonius' fame rests on his eight-volume treatise, *The Conics*, seven volumes of which are extant. The first four books consisted of an introduction and a statement of the state of mathematics provided by his predecessors. In the last four volumes Apollonius put forth his own important work on conic sections, the foundation of much of the geometry still used today in astronomy, ballistic science and rocketry.

Apollonius described how a cone could be cut so as to produce circles, ellipses, parabolas and hyperbolas; the last three terms were coined by him. He investigated the properties of each and showed that they were all interrelated because, as he stated, "any conic section is the locus of a point which moves so that the ratio of its distance, f, from a fixed point (the focus) to its distance, d, from a straight line (the directrix) is constant". Whether this constant, e, is greater than, equal to, or less than 1 determines which of the three types of curve the function repre-

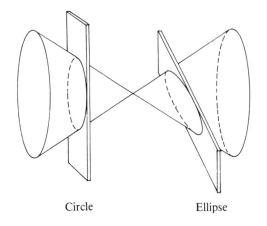

Circle   Ellipse

Hyperbola

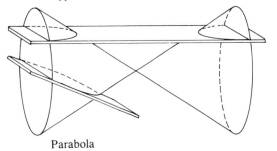

Parabola

Conic sections were studied avidly by Ancient Greek mathematicians. Archimedes in particular wrote several contemplative articles on the subject – but it was Apollonius whose work became the definitive description.

sents. For a hyperbola $e > 1$; for a parabola $e = 1$; and for an ellipse $e < 1$. At the time, Apollonius' discoveries lay in the realm of pure mathematics; it was only later that their immensely valuable application became apparent, when it was discovered that conic sections form the paths, or loci, followed by planets and projectiles in space.

Other than *The Conics*, only one treatise of Apollonius survives; it is entitled *Cutting off a Ratio*. It was found written in Arabic and was translated into Latin in 1706, but is of little mathematical significance.

Apollonius' brilliant concept of geometry was a milestone in mankind's understanding of mechanics, navigation and astronomy. Above all, his work on epicircles and ellipses played a major part in Ptolemy's working out of the cosmology which dominated western astronomy

from the second century to the sixteenth century.

Archimedes (*c*.287–212 BC) was probably the greatest mathematician and physicist of the ancient world. What little is known about his life comes from the writings of later Greek historians, and many of the stories told about him are at best apochryphal. Archimedes was born in about 287 BC in Syracuse in the then Greek colony of Sicily (the date is based on the belief that he was 75 when he died). He came of a noble family and his father was an astronomer called Phidias. In about 250 BC Archimedes went to Alexandria to study under Conon and other mathematicians who had been students of Euclid (who flourished *c*.300 BC). He then returned to Syracuse and continued his studies of mathematics, physics and mechanisms. The Romans laid siege to Syracuse in 215 BC, and Archimedes used his mechanical ingenuity to devise a series of weapons to combat the Roman fleet, but in 212 BC the attackers finally sacked the city and Archimedes was killed by a Roman soldier. Cicero discovered his tomb in 75 BC and fulfilled Archimedes' wish to have it inscribed with a cylinder enclosing a sphere and the formula for the ratio of their volumes, which Archimedes is said to have regarded as his greatest achievement. According to Plutarch, Archimedes thought highly only of his theoretical contributions to mathematics and physics, and disdained his practical inventions.

In mathematics Archimedes wrote many treatises, some of which still exist in (modified) Arabic translation. His approximation for π, the average of 223/71 and 220/70, is within three parts in 10,000 of the modern accepted value. He also devised a special notation for expressing very large numbers, it is said to present his calculation (equal to 10^{63}) of the number of grains of sand in the Universe.

Archimedes developed methods for solving cubic equations and for determining square roots by approximation. He also found formulas for the surface areas and volumes of various curved surfaces and solids (2,000 years before the invention of integral calculus). Like Euclid, he based his proofs on the methods of exhaustion and *reductio ad absurdum*, which were probably originally developed by Eudoxus of Cnidus early in the fourth century BC.

In physics, Archimedes made fundamental discoveries in statics and hydrostatics – many of his inventions made cunning uses of levers and pulleys. Perhaps one of his greatest contributions to science, however, was his use of experiment to test his observations and theories, which he then formulated mathematically. When his work, which had been preserved by Byzantium and Islam, became known in Europe from the twelfth century onwards, it had a profound effect on the development of science.

Argand, Jean Robert (1768-1822), was a Swiss mathematician who invented a method of geometrically representing complex numbers and their operations.

Argand was born in Geneva on 18 July 1768. Almost nothing is known of his life except that he was working in Paris as a bookseller and living there with his wife, son and daughter in 1806, the year in which he published his method. He appears to have been entirely self-taught as a mathematician and to have had no contact with any other mathematicians of any standing. By dint of his diligent pursuit of what was for him simply a hobby he hit upon a happy idea at just the right time in the history of mathematics. He devised his method in 1806 and thereafter did nothing again mathematically important. He died in obscurity at Paris on 13 August 1822.

The idea of giving geometric representation to complex numbers had already been worked out

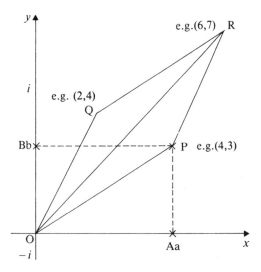

The Argand diagram is a graphic representation of the addition of complex numbers of the forms a + b*i, in which* a *and* b *are integral real numbers and* i *is the square root of* −1. *From* O, *the origin, and corresponding to each real number a point* Aa *or* Bb *is defined on the* x *or* y *axis, from which an intersection* P *is plotted. If* P = a + i b = α, *then to construct* α + β *in which* α ≡ P *and* β ≡ Q, *the parallelogram* OPRQ *is drawn. Then* R = α + β.

by the Norwegian mathematician Caspar Wessel (1745-1818) and by Gauss when, in 1806, an anonymous book, *Essai sur une manière de représenter les quantités imaginaires dans les constructions géométriques*, was published in a small, privately printed edition. But neither Wessel nor Gauss had published his idea, so that Argand, the anonymous author, deserves the credit for the system which the book propounded, sometimes wrongly attributed to Gauss, but properly known as the "Argand diagram". Yet Argand's name might never have come to light but for a curious set of circumstances. Before publishing his book he had outlined his ideas to Adrien Legendre. Some years later Legendre mentioned the system in a letter to the brother of J.R. Français, a lecturer at the Imperial College of Artillery at Paris. Français discussed the new system in a paper published in the journal *Annales de mathématiques* in 1813 and, acting from curiosity and kindness, asked the anonymous inventor of it to come forward and make himself known. Argand did so and a paper of his was published in a later issue of the *Annales* for that year.

In his book Argand adopted Descartes' practice of calling all multiples of $\sqrt{-1}$ "imaginary". That pure imaginary numbers might be represented by a line perpendicular to the axis of real numbers had been suggested in the seventeenth century by John Wallis. Argand went further, to demonstrate that real and imaginary parts of a complex number could be represented as rectangular co-ordinates. It had for some time been usual to picture real numbers - negative and positive - as corresponding to points on a straight line. Of the models studied by Argand, and discussed in his book, one used weights, progressively removed from a beam balance, to represent the generation of negative numbers by repeated subtractions. Another simply subtracted portions from a sum of money. Argand argued that these models showed that distance could be considered separately from direction in constructing a geometrical representation, such distance being "absolute". Furthermore, whether a negative quantity were considered as real or imaginary depended on the sort of quantity being measured. Argand was thus able to use these distinctions - between direction and absolute distance, and between real and imaginary negative quantities - to construct his diagram.

The diagram is a graphic representation of complex numbers of the form a + b*i*, in which a and b are integers and *i* is $\sqrt{-1}$. One axis represents the pure imaginary numbers (those belonging to the b*i* category) and the other the real numbers (those belonging to the a category); it is thus possible to plot a complex number as a set of co-ordinates in the field defined by the two axes.

Argand was an amateur and had a somewhat patchy knowledge of mathematics. It is clear, for instance, from his discussion of the central problem, whether all rational functions, f(a + bi), could be reduced to the form A + Bi, where i, b, A and B are real, that he understood the work of Lagrange, Euler and d'Alembert; but he also revealed that he did not know that Euler had so reduced $\sqrt{-1}\sqrt{-1}$, since he cited that expression as one that could not be reduced. It is also true that, had Argand never lived, his idea would have come to light through the work of Gauss at about the same time. It would nevertheless be a grave injustice to deny him his honourable, if minor, place in the history of mathematics.

Artin, Emil (1898–1962), was an Austrian mathematician who made important contributions to the development of class field theory and the theory of hyper-complex numbers.

He was born in Vienna on 3 March 1898, but his secondary education was at Reichenburg in Bohemia (now part of Czechoslovakia). His undergraduate study at the University of Vienna was interrupted when he was called up for military service in World War I; in 1919 he went to the University of Leipzig, where he received his PhD in 1921. From 1923 to 1937 he lectured at the University of Hamburg in mathematics, mechanics and the theory of relativity. He and his family emigrated to the United States in 1937. There Artin lectured at the University of Indiana (1938–1946) and Princeton (1946–1958). In 1958 he returned to Hamburg, where he died on 20 December 1962.

Artin's early work was concentrated on the analytical and arithmetical theory of quadratic number fields and in the 1920s he made a number of major advances in this field. In his doctoral thesis of 1921 he formulated the analogue of the Riemann hypothesis about the seroz of the classical zeta function, studying the quadratic extension of the field of rational functions of one variable over finite constant fields, by applying the arithmetical and analytical theory of quadratic numbers over the field of natural numbers. Then in 1923, in the most important discovery of his career, he derived a functional equation for his new-type L-series. The proof of this he published in 1927, thereby providing, by the use of the theory of formal real fields, the solution to Hilbert's problem of definite functions. The proof produced the general law of reciprocity – Artin's phrase – which included all previously known laws of reciprocity going back to Gauss and which became the fundamental theorem in class field theory. Between the statement of his theory in 1923 and its publication in 1927, Artin made two other important theoretical advances. His theory of braids, given in 1925, was a major contribution to the study of nodes in three-dimensional space. A year later, in collaboration with Schrier, he succeeded in treating real algebra in an abstract manner, defining a field as real-closed if it itself was real but none of its algebraic extensions were. He was then able to demonstrate that a real-closed field could be ordered in an exact manner and that, in it, typical laws of algebra were valid.

Although the fires of his genius burned less brightly after 1930, Artin continued to work at a high level. In 1944 his discovery of rings with minimum conditions for right ideals – now known as Artin rings – was a fertile addition to the theory of associative ring algebras, and in 1961 he published his *Class Field Theory*, a rounded summation of his life's work as one of the leading creators of modern algebra.

B

Babbage, Charles (1792–1871), was a British mathematician, one of the greatest pioneers of mechanical computation.

Babbage was born at Totnes, in Devonshire, on 26 December 1792. His father was a banker who left him a large inheritance, and throughout his life Babbage was financially secure. He developed an interest in mathematics as a young boy and in 1810 went to Cambridge University to study mathematics. There he became a close friend of the future astronomer, John Herschel (1792–1981), and, convincing himself that Herschel would be placed Senior Wrangler in the honours examinations, chose not to be placed second and took only a pass degree, in 1814. While at Cambridge Babbage, Herschel and other undergraduates founded the Analytical Society, and it was in the society's rooms one evening, that Babbage is recorded as saying (while looking over some error-filled logarithm tables) "I am thinking that all these mathematical tables might be calculated by machinery".

The year after he left Cambridge Babbage wrote three papers on "The Calculus of Functions" for publication by the Royal Society and in the following year, 1816, he was elected a Fellow of the society. Some time later, while making a tour of France, he examined the famous French logarithms which had been recently calculated and which were the most accurate tables then known. They had, however, required the combined efforts of nearly one hundred clerks and mathematicians. Mathematical tables of all kinds, including logarithmic tables, were of great use for astronomical, commercial and, especially, navigational purposes. On his return to London, therefore, Babbage set about to develop his ideas for a cheaper and more accurate method of producing tables by mechanical computation and automatic printing.

By 1822 he had ready a small calculating machine able to compute squares and the values of quadratic functions. It worked on the method of differences, an example of which involves subtracting one square from the preceding one to obtain a first difference, and then the first difference from the next above it to obtain a second difference, which is always 2.

By working backwards, adding the second difference to the first difference, and then adding the higher of the squares used in the subtraction which produced the first difference, the next square is always obtained. Using second-order differences of this kind Babbage's first machine could produce figures to six places of decimals.

With the backing of the Royal Society, Babbage was able to persuade the government to support his work to devise a much larger Difference Engine to calculate navigational and other tables. He was elected to the Lucasian chair of mathematics at Cambridge in 1826, a post which he held until 1835, but he continued to live in London and did not perform the usual professorial duties of lecturing and teaching. He devoted himself entirely to his machine, which he proposed to make work to sixth-order differences and 20 places of decimals. The construction of the large Difference Engine was a laborious and lengthy operation. New tools had to be designed to previously unknown tolerances, many of them being made for Babbage by the great pioneer of precision engineering, Joseph Whitworth (1803–1887). The project cost the government £20,000, but it was eventually abandoned, partly because of problems of friction (the arch-enemy of the engineer), partly because of personality clashes, but chiefly because before it was completed Babbage had hit upon a better idea.

That idea was the Analytical Engine. The Difference Engine could perform only one function, once it was set up. The Analytical Engine was intended to perform many functions; it was to store numbers and be capable of working to a programme. In order to achieve this, Babbage borrowed the idea of using punched cards from Joseph Jacquard, who had invented such cards in 1801 to programme carpet-making looms to weave a pattern. Babbage's machine, begun in 1833, was to have a mill to carry out arithmetical operations, a memory unit to store 1,000 numbers of 50 digits, and the programme cards, linked together to direct the machine. The cards were of three kinds: those to supply the store with numbers, those to transfer numbers from mill to store or store to mill, and those to direct the four basic arithmetical operations. In order to unite the programmes for his cards Babbage devised a new mathematical notation.

Babbage's machine had not been completed by the time of his death, on 18 October 1871. And although his son H.P. Babbage carried on the enterprise between 1880 and 1910, the fact is that its complexity was beyond the engineering expertise of the day and its very conception beyond the grasp of society to spend the amount of time and money required to build it. Nevertheless, it was Babbage's machine – although, being decimal, not binary, and requiring the use of wheels, not strictly digital in the modern sense – which Howard Aiken used as the basis for his development of the Harvard Mark I Calculator.

Babbage was a true representative of the Victorian age, the age of the steam-engine and the industrial revolution. He wished to harness science to the practical improvement of society. Hence, dissatisfied by the practical usefulness of the Royal Society, he had a hand in founding the Astronomical Society (1820), the British Association for the Advancement of Science (1831) and the Statistical Society of London (1834). The same passion for improvement led him to investigate the operation of the Post Office and, on finding that most of its costs derived from the handling of letters, not their transport, to recommend (what Rowland Hill introduced as the penny post) that it should simplify its procedure by introducing a single rate. But his greatest idea, the mechanical computation of tables, remained ahead of the practical possibilities of his time.

Baker, Alan (1939–   ), is a British mathematician whose chief work has been devoted to the study of transcendental numbers.

He was born in London on 19 August 1939 and studied mathematics at the University of London, where he received his BSc in 1961. He then did graduate work at Cambridge and was awarded a PhD in 1964. He remained at Trinity College, Cambridge, for the next ten years, as a research fellow (1964–1968) and as Director of

Studies in Mathematics (1968-1974). Since 1974 he has been Professor of Pure Mathematics in the university. He was elected a Fellow of the Royal Society in 1973. Visiting professorships have taken him to many parts of the United States and Europe. In 1978 he was honoured by the appointment as the first Turán lecturer of the János Bolyai Mathematical Society in Hungary and in 1980 he was elected a Foreign Fellow of the Indian National Science Academy.

Since his research days as a young man, Baker has been chiefly interested in transcendental numbers (numbers which cannot be expressed as roots or as the solution of an algebraic equation with rational coefficients). In 1966 he extended Joseph Liouville's original proof of the existence of transcendental numbers by means of continued fractions, by obtaining a result on linear forms in the logarithms of algebraic numbers. This solution opened the way to the resolution of a wide range of diophantine problems and in 1967 Baker used his results to provide the first useful theorems concerning the theory of these problems. He obtained explicit upper bounds to Thue's equation, $F(x,y) = m$, where F denotes a binary irreducible form and also to Mordell's equation, $y^2 = x^3 + k$. In 1969 he achieved the same result for the hyper-elliptic equation, $y^2 = f(x)$. For this work he was awarded the Fields Medal at the International Congress of Mathematicians at Nice in 1970.

Apart from individual papers, Baker's most important publication is *Transcendental Number Theory* (1975). Baker's work has greatly enriched the many branches of mathematics influenced by the development of transcendental number theory. It has led to an important new series of results on exponential diophantine equations: his theory provides bounds of 10^{500} or more and it has been shown that these are sufficient in simple cases to calculate the complete list of solutions. The theory has also been used to solve some classical problems of Gauss, to assist in the approximation of algebraic numbers by rationals (an investigation begun by Liouville in 1844), and to inspire new lines of research in elliptic and Abelian functions. Baker is thus at the very forefront of contemporary work on number theory.

Barrow, Isaac (1630-1677), was an English mathematician, physicist, classicist and Anglican divine, one of the intellectual luminaries of the Caroline period.

Barrow was born in London in October, 1630. His father, a linendraper to Charles I, sent him to Charterhouse as a day boy, but there he achieved little beyond gaining a reputation as a bully, and he was removed to Felstead School. In 1643 he was entered for Peterhouse, Cambridge, where an uncle was a Fellow, but by the time that he went up to university in 1645 his uncle had moved to Trinity College and it was there that Barrow entered as a pensioner. He received his BA in 1648 and a year later was elected a Fellow of Cambridge. In 1655 his former tutor, Dr Dupont, retired from the Regius Professorship of Greek; he wished Barrow, his former pupil, to succeed him. But the appointment was not offered to Barrow. His reputation then was more for mathematics than classics, and he was very young. Even so, it may be true that he was barred from the chair by Cromwell's intervention. Certainly Barrow had never concealed his royalist opinions and he was out of sympathy with the prevailing republican air of Cambridge. He decided to leave England for a tour of the continent and to help finance his trip sold his library.

He remained abroad for five years, returning to England only with the restoration of Charles II in 1660. Immediately he took Anglican orders and was elected to the Regius Professorship previously denied him. He was also appointed Professor of Geometry at Gresham College, London, and in 1663 became first Lucasian Professor of Mathematics at Cambridge. In 1669 he resigned the Cambridge Chair in favour of Isaac Newton and a year later was made a DD by royal mandate. During the 1660s his lectures on mathematics at Gresham College formed the basis of his mathematical reputation; thereafter his energies were devoted more to theology and preaching. He was made master of Trinity in 1675 and died two years later, on 4 May 1677.

In his time Barrow was considered second only to Newton as a mathematician. Now he is best remembered as one of the greatest Caroline divines, whose sermons and treatises, especially the splendid *Treatise on the Pope's Supremacy* (1680), have gained a permanent place in ecclesiastical literature. Certainly he was an admirable teacher of mathematics, and although it is not true that Newton was his pupil, Newton attended his lectures and later formed a fruitful friendship with him. His mathematical importance is slight, the *Lectiones mathematicae*, delivered at Gresham between 1663 and 1666 and published in 1669, being marred by his insistence that algebra be separated from geometry and his desire to relegate algebra to a subsidiary branch of logic. His geometry lectures were read by few and had little influence.

More important were his lectures on optics. Most of his optics was immediately eclipsed by

Newton's work, but there is no doubt that Newton was greatly inspired by Barrow's work in the field and to Barrow is due the credit for two original contributions: the method of finding the point of refraction at a plane interface, and his point construction of the diacaustic of a spherical interface. Barrow was a man of great powers of concentration and original thought. If he failed to reach the highest class of mathematics, the reason may well be that he spread his intellectual interests so broadly.

Beltrami, Eugenio (1835–1899), was an Italian mathematician whose work ranged over almost the whole field of pure and applied mathematics, but whose fame derives chiefly from his investigations into theories of surfaces and space of constant curvature, and his position as the modern progenitor of non-Euclidean geometry.

Beltrami was born at Cremona on 16 November 1835. From 1853 to 1856 he studied mathematics at the University of Pavia. After graduating he was engaged as secretary to a railway engineer, but in his spare time he continued his research in mathematics and in 1862 he published his first paper, an analysis of the differential geometry of curves. In the same year he was appointed to the Chair of complementary algebra and analytical geometry at the University of Bologna. The rest of his life was spent in the academic world: until 1864 at Bologna, from 1864 to 1866 as Professor of Geodesy at Pisa, at Bologna again from 1866 to 1873, as Professor of Rational Mechanics, at the new University of Rome from 1873 to 1876 (in the same Chair), and at Pavia from 1876 to 1891 as Professor of Mathematical Physics. In 1891 he returned to Rome, where he continued to teach until his death on 4 June 1899. A year before he died he was appointed President of the Accademia dei Lincei and was made a member of the Italian senate.

Beltrami's career may be divided into two parts. After 1872 he devoted himself to topics in applied mathematics, but in the earlier period he worked chiefly in pure mathematics, on problems in the differential geometry of curves and surfaces. Work had been done in this field earlier, notably by Saccheria a century before and by Nikolai Lobachevsky in the first half of the nineteenth century. But their work had had little influence, since their contemporaries were unimpressed by the possibilities of non-Euclidean geometry. The publication of Beltrami's paper, "*Saggio di interpretazione della geometria non-euclidia*" in 1868 is therefore a landmark in the history of mathematics. It advanced a theory of hyperbolic space that laid the analytical base for the development of non-Euclidean geometry.

In an earlier paper of 1865, Beltrami had shown that on surfaces of constant curvature (and only on them) the formula $ds^2 = E du^2 + 2F du dv + G dv^2$ can be written such that the geodisics are represented by linear expressions in u and v. For positive curvature R^{-2} the formula would be $ds^2 = R^2(v^2 + a^2)du^2 - 2uv du dv + (u^2 + a^2)dv^2 \times (u^2 + v^2 + a^2)^{-2}$, the geodisics behaving like the great circles of a sphere. In 1868 he went further and showed that by changing R to iR and a to ia, a new formula for ds^2 was obtained, one which defined the surfaces of constant curvature $-R^{-2}$ and which presented a new type of geometry for the geodisics of constant curvature inside the region $u^2 + v^2 < a^2$.

These demonstrations were not greatly different from what Lobachevsky had shown 40 years earlier, but what Beltrami did was to present the theories in terms which were acceptable within the existing Euclidean framework of the subject. He demonstrated that the concepts and formulae of Lobachevsky's geometry are realized for geodisics on surfaces of constant negative curvature. He showed also that there are rotation surfaces of this kind—and to these he gave the name "pseudospherical surfaces". He also demonstrated the usefulness of employing differential parameters in surface theory, thereby beginning the use of invariant methods in differential geometry.

After 1872 Beltrami switched his attention to questions of applied mathematics, especially problems in elasticity and electromagnetism. His paper "*Richerche sulle cinematics dei fluidi*" (1872) was an important development in the field of elasticity. But his lasting fame rests on his signal achievement in overcoming the prevailing mid-nineteenth-century suspicions of non-Euclidean geometry and, by bringing it into the mainstream of mathematical thought, opening wide-ranging fields of new inquiry.

Bernays, Paul (1888–   ), is a British-born Swiss mathematician who has been chiefly interested in the connections between logic and mathematics, especially in the field of set theory.

Bernays was born in London on 17 October 1888, but grew up in Berlin, where he attended the Köllnisches Gymnasium from 1895 to 1907. As an undergraduate he studied mathematics, philosophy and theoretical physics at the universities of Berlin and Göttingen. In 1912 he presented his post-doctoral thesis, called an *Habilitationschrift*, at Zürich, where he continued to do research until 1917. In that year he was invited to become David Hilbert's assistant at

Göttingen. In 1919 he received his *venia legendi*, or right to lecture in the university, at Göttingen and he remained there as a lecturer without tenure until 1933. In that year he became one of the early Jewish victims of the Nazi regime in Germany, when his *venia legendi* was withdrawn. Hilbert employed him privately for six months, but Bernays then decided to take advantage of his father's adopted Swiss nationality and move to Switzerland. For several years he had to make do with short-term teaching appointments at the Technical High School in Zürich, before that institute granted him a *venia legendi* in 1939. He became an extraordinary professor there in 1945 and joined the editorial board of the philosophical journal *Dialectica*. In the 1950s and 1960s he was several times a visiting professor at the University of Pennsylvania and the Princeton Institute for Advanced Study.

Bernays' early interests ranged over a wide area of problems in mathematics. His doctoral thesis of 1912 was on the analytic number theory of binary quadratic forms and his *Habilitationschrift*, later in the same year, dealt with function theory, in particular Picard's theorem. He then became interested in "axiomatic thoughts", and it was after hearing Bernays lecture on this subject at Zürich in the autumn of 1917 that Hilbert invited him to Göttingen as his assistant to work on the foundations of arithmetic. There he wrote his *Habilitationschrift* on the axiomatics of the propositional calculus in Bertrand Russell's *Principia Mathematica*; this was published in abridged form in 1926.

Bernays' most enduring work has been in the field of mathematical logic and set theory. He first presented his principles of axiomatization in a talk to the Mathematical Society at Göttingen in 1931, but hesitated to publish his opinions because he was troubled by the thought that axiomatization was an artificial activity. His fullest treatment of the subject was given in lectures at the Princeton Institute for Advanced Study in 1935-1936.

Bernays made a significant contribution to the theory of sets and classes. In his treatment of the subject, classes are not given the status of real mathematical objects. This represents a fundamental divergence from the theory of John von Neumann. Bernays modified the Neumann system of axioms to remain closer to the original Zermelo structure. He also used some of the set-theoretic concepts of Friedrich Schröder's (1841-1902) logic and some of the concepts of the *Principia Mathematica* which have become familiar to logicians. In Bernays' theory there are two kinds of individuals, "sets" and "classes": a "set" is a multitude forming a real mathematical object, whereas a "class" is a predicate to be regarded only with respect to its extension.

For all his own doubts about the validity of axiomatization, Bernays' arrangement of sets and classes is now widely believed to be the most useful, and by his study of the work of such men as Neumann, Hilbert and Abraham Fraenkel, he has made a major contribution to the modern development of logic.

Bernoulli, Daniel (1700-1782), was a Dutch natural philosopher and mathematician, whose most important work was in the field of hydrodynamics and whose chief contribution to mathematics was in the field of differential equations.

Bernoulli was born at Grönigen on 9 February 1700, the son of the mathematician Jean Bernoulli and nephew of the mathematician Jacques Bernoulli. As a young boy he first studied philosophy and logic, obtaining his baccalaureate by the age of 15 and his master's degree by the age of 16. He had also by then been given some mathematical training by his father and uncle, but in 1717 he went to Switzerland to study medicine. He received his doctorate for a thesis on the action of the lungs in 1721. His interest in mathematics seems then to have quickened. In 1724 he published his *Exercitationes mathematicae* and in 1725 he was appointed to the Chair of Mathematics at the St Petersburg Academy. Bernoulli left Russia in 1732 and in the following year became Professor of Anatomy and Botany at the University of Basle. He remained there, although after 1750 as Professor of Natural Philosophy, until his retirement in 1777. He died in Basle on 17 March 1782.

Bernoulli was a scientific polymath. During his career he won ten prizes from the French Academy, for papers on subjects which included marine technology, oceanology, astronomy and magnetism. His greatest work, *Hydrodynamica*, completed by 1733 but not published until 1738, gave not only a history of hydrodynamics but broke new ground by using Newton's laws of force together with the *vis viva* of Leibnitz to extend the understanding of the conservation of energy (as we would now put it) and the velocity of liquids.

In more strictly mathematical vein his interests probably stemmed, in part at least, from his close friendship with Euler and d'Alembert, who introduced him to problems associated with vibrating strings, in which connection Bernoulli did much of his work on partial differential equations. Perhaps his single most striking achievement in pure mathematics was to solve the differential equation of J.F. Riccati (1676–1754). Other achievements were to demonstrate how the differential calculus could be used in problems of probability and to do some pioneering work in trigonometrical series and the computation of trigonometrical functions. He also showed the shape of the curve known as the lemniscate $(x^2 + y^2)^2 = a^2(x^2 - y^2)$, where a is constant and x and y are variables.

Bernoulli was a competent mathematician and a first-rate physicist, and his use of mathematics in the investigation of problems in physics makes him one of the founding fathers of mathematical physics.

Bernoulli, Jacques (1654–1705), and **Bernoulli, Jean** (1667–1748), were Swiss mathematicians, each of whom did important work in the early development of the calculus.

They were sons of the mathematician Daniel Bernoulli and both were born at Basle, Jacques on 27 December 1654 and Jean on 7 August 1667. Although Jacques was originally trained in theology and expected to pursue a career in the Church, he made himself familiar with higher mathematics – especially the work of Descartes, John Wallis and Isaac Barrow – and on a trip to England in 1676 met Robert Boyle (1627–1691) and other leading scientists. He then decided to devote himself to science, became particularly interested in comets (which he explained by an erroneous theory in 1681) and in 1682 began to lecture in mechanics and natural philosophy at the University of Basle. During the next few years he came to know the work of Leibniz and to begin a correspondence with him. In 1687 he was made Professor of Mathematics at Basle and he held the Chair until his death, at Basle, on 10 August 1705.

Jean Bernoulli originally studied medicine, but he was instructed in mathematics by his elder brother, and before he received his doctorate for a thesis on muscular movement he had already spent some time in Paris (1691) giving private tuition in mathematics. In 1694, the year in which his doctorate was awarded, he was appointed Professor of Mathematics at the University of Gröningen, where he remained until 1705, when he succeeded his brother in the Chair at Basle. In 1730 he was awarded a prize by the French Academy of Sciences for a paper which sought (unsuccessfully, as d'Alembert was able to show) to reconcile Descartes' vortices with Kepler's third law. His son Daniel Bernoulli (1700–1782) became one of the first mathematical physicists. Jean Bernoulli died in Basle on 1 January 1748.

Both Jacques and Jean wrote papers on a wide variety of mathematical and physical subjects, but their chief importance in mathematical history rests on the work on the calculus and on probability theory. It is often difficult to separate their work, even though they never published together. Thus, for example, Jean's solution to the problem of the catenary, published in 1691, had been all but given in Jean's analysis of the problem in 1690. Jean's *Leçons de Calcul Differentiel et Integral* was written for his French pupil, G. de l'Hôpital (1661–1704) in 1691 and he was outraged when Hôpital later published the substance of Jean's teaching in his *Analyse des Infiniments Petits* without acknowledging his debt to his teacher. Jacques' most important papers were those on transcendental curves (1696) and isoperimetry (1700, 1701) – it is here that the first principles of the calculus of variations are to be found. It is probable that these papers owed something to collaboration with Jean. His other great achievement was his treatise on probability, *Ars Conjectandi*, which contained both the Bernoulli numbers and the Bernoulli theorem and which was not published until 1713, eight years after his death.

Together the two brothers advanced knowledge of the calculus not simply by their own work but also by giving spirited public support to Leibniz in his famous quarrel with Newton and thereby helping to establish the ascendancy of the Leibnizian calculus on the continent.

Bernstein, Jeremy (1929–   ), is an American mathematical physicist who is well known for his "popularizing" books on various topics of pure and applied science for the lay reader.

Bernstein was born at Rochester, New York, on 31 December 1929. He received his BA from Harvard in 1951 and his PhD from the same university in 1955. From 1957 to 1960 he was attached to the Institute for Advanced Study at Harvard. In 1962 he was appointed an associate professor in physics at New York University. Since 1967 he has been a Professor of Physics at the Stevens Institute of Technology at Hoboken, New Jersey. He has also for a number of years been a consultant to the Rand Corporation and to the General Atomic Company.

Bernstein's most important advanced work has been in the field of elementary particles and their currents. In particular he has sought to give a mathematical analysis and description to the behaviour of elementary particles. But although he is a competent mathematician who has worked at the very frontier of elementary particle theory, his greatest gift is the ability to write lucidly about difficult subjects for the non-specialist. Since 1962 he has been on the staff of the urbane magazine, *The New Yorker*. His best known publication for that magazine was "*The Analytical Engine: Computers, past, present and future*", a witty guide to the history and theory of computers. He has also published a general survey of the historical progress of scientific knowledge, *Ascent* (1965), and a biography of Albert Einstein (1973).

It is a rare day when a mathematician both conducts research at the highest level of specialist theory and writes clearly and entertainingly for the public, and Bernstein's singular achievement in this regard was suitably recognized when he was awarded the Westinghouse prize for scientific writing in 1964.

Betti, Enrico (1823–1892), was an Italian mathematician who was the first to provide a thorough exposition and development of the theory of equations formulated by Evariste Galois.

Betti was born near the Tuscan town of Pistoia on 21 October 1823. His father died when he was very young and he received his early education from his mother. After obtaining his BA in the physical and mathematical sciences at the University of Pisa, he taught for a time at a secondary school at Pistoia before being appointed to a professorship at Pisa in 1856; he held the professorship for the rest of his life. Betti was also much interested in politics. He had fought against Austria at the battles of Curtatone and Montanara during the first wars of Italian independence and in 1862 he became a member of the new independent Italian parliament. He entered the government as Under-Secretary of State for Education in 1874 and served in the senate after 1884. He died at Pisa on 11 August 1892.

Betti's early, and most important, work was on algebra and the theory of equations. In papers published in 1852 and 1855 he gave proofs of most of Galois' major theorems. In so doing he became the first mathematician to resolve integral functions of a complex variable into their primary factors. He also developed the theory of elliptical functions, demonstrating (in a paper of 1861) the theory of elliptical functions which is derived from constructing transcendental entire functions in relation to their zeros by means of infinite products. In thus providing formal demonstration to Galois' statements and in drawing out some of their implications, Betti greatly advanced the transition from classical to abstract algebra.

In 1863 a change occurred in Betti's mathematical interests. In that year the German mathematician Bernhard Riemann went to Pisa.

He had only three years to live, but he became a close friend of Betti and directed Betti's mind to mathematical physics, especially to problems of potential theory and elasticity. Betti studied George Green's methods of attempting to integrate Laplace's equation (the foundation of the theory of potentials) and applied them to the study of elasticity and heat. The result was the paper of 1878 in which he gave the law of reciprocity in elasticity theory which became known as Betti's theorem. Along the way, conducting research into "analysis situs" in hyperspace in 1871, he also did valuable work on numbers characterizing the connection of a variety, these later becoming known as "Betti numbers".

Betti also played a principal part in the expansion of mathematics teaching in Italian schools, in particular lending his enthusiastic advocacy to the restoration of Euclid to a central place in the secondary-school curriculum. His lectures at the University of Pisa also inspired a generation of Italian mathematicians, the most famous of them being Vito Volterra (1860–1940).

Birkhoff, George David (1884–1944), was one of the most distinguished of early twentieth-century mathematicians, who made fundamental contributions to the study of dynamics and formulated the "weak form" of the ergodic theorem.

Birkhoff was born at Overisel, Michigan, on 21 March 1884. He studied at the Lewis Institute (now the Illinois Institute of Technology) from 1896 to 1902, when he entered the University of Chicago. He then went to Harvard, where he received his BA in mathematics in 1905. In 1907 he received a PhD for his thesis on boundary problems from the University of Chicago. He taught at the University of Michigan and Princeton before being appointed an assistant professor at Harvard in 1912. He was a full professor at Harvard from 1919 until his death. Birkhoff was president of the American Mathematical Society in 1925 and of the American Association for the Advancement of Science in 1937. He was awarded the Bocher Prize in 1923 for his work on dynamics and the AAAS Prize in 1926 for his investigation of differential equations. He died at Cambridge, Massachusetts, on 12 November 1944.

Birkhoff's early work was on integral equations and boundary problems, and his investigations led him into the field of differential and difference equations. He developed a system of differential equations which is still inspiring research, while his work on difference equations was notable for the prominence which he gave to the use of matrix algebra.

Birkhoff's high reputation derives chiefly, however, from his investigation of the theory of dynamical systems such as the Solar System. After grounding himself thoroughly in Jules Poincaré's celestial mechanics, he began to examine the motion of bodies in the light of his work on asymptotic expansions and boundary value problems of linear differential equations. In 1913 - one of those exhilarating moments in mathematics - he proved Poincaré's last geometric theorem on the three-body problem, a problem with which Poincaré had grappled unsuccessfully. Birkhoff's formulation ran as follows: "Let us suppose that a continuous one-to-one transformation T takes the ring R, formed by concentric circles C_a and C_b of radii a and b ($a > b > 0$), into itself in such a way as to advance the point of C_a in a positive sense, and the point of C_b in a negative sense, and at the same time preserve areas. Then there are at least two invariant points."

With Johann von Neumann (1903-1957), Birkhoff was chiefly responsible for establishing, in the 1930s, the modern science of ergodics. He arrived, indeed, at the statement of his "positive ergodic theorem", or what is known as the "weak form" of ergodic theory, just before Neumann published his "strong form" of it. By using the Lebesque measure theory Birkhoff transformed the Maxwell-Boltzmann hypothesis of the kinetic theory of gases, which was undermined by the number of exceptions found to it, into a vigorous principle.

Birkhoff also made a number of valuable contributions to related problems in other fields to which he was led by his ergodic investigations. One such was his paper of 1938 "Electricity as a Fluid" which, although consistent with Einstein's special relativity, found no need of the general curvilinear co-ordinates of the general theory of relativity. Throughout his life Birkhoff continued to argue that Einstein's general relativity was an unhelpful theory and his 1938 paper did much to provoke thought and research on the subject.

Few twentieth-century mathematicians achieved more than Birkhoff and he was, in addition, the most important teacher of his generation. Many of the United States' leading mathematicians did their doctoral or post-doctoral research under his direction. His standing, generally acknowledged, as the most illustrious American mathematician of the early twentieth century is deserved.

Black, Max (1909-   ), is a Russian-born American philosopher and mathematician, one of whose concerns has been to investigate the question "What is mathematics?".

Black was born at Baku, in Azerbaijan, on 24 February 1909, and he received his higher education in England where he studied philosophy, gaining his BA at Cambridge University in 1930 and his PhD from London University in 1939. From 1936 to 1940 he was a lecturer at the University of London Institute of Education. He went to the United States in 1940 to take up a post in the department of philosophy at the University of Illinois. He became a naturalized American citizen in 1948. He moved from the University of Illinois to Cornell in 1946 and was Susan Lin-Sage Professor of Philosophy and Humane Letters there from 1954 to 1977, when he retired. In 1970 he was vice-president of the International Institute of Philosophy.

Black's analysis led him to describe mathematics as the study of all structures whose form may be expressed in symbols. Within that broad spectrum there are three main schools of mathematics: the logical, the formalist and the intuitional. The logical considers that all mathematical concepts, such as numbers or differential coefficients, are capable of purely logical definition, so that mathematics becomes a branch of logic. The formalist, rejecting the notion that all mathematics can be expressed as logical concepts, looks upon mathematics as the science of the structure of objects and concerns itself with the structural properties of symbols, independent of their meaning. The formalist approach has been especially fruitful in its application to geometry. The third school, the intuitional, by laying less emphasis on symbols and more on thought, considers mathematics to be grounded on the basic intuition of the possibility of constructing an infinite series of numbers. This approach has had most influence in the theory of sets of points.

Black has thus done little work in mathematics itself, but his writings, such as *The Nature of Mathematics* (1950) and *Problems of Analysis* (1954), have been a major contribution to the philosophy of mathematics.

Bolyai, Farkas Wolfgang (1775-1856) and **Bolyai, Janos** (1802-1860), were Hungarian mathematicians, father and son, the younger of whom was one of the founders of non-Euclidean geometry.

Wolfgang Bolyai was born at Nagyszeben, in Hungary (now Sibiu, Romania), on 9 February 1775. He studied mathematics at the University of Göttingen, where he fell into friendship with

Carl Gauss. For the rest of his life the elder Bolyai was a professional mathematician, teaching at the Evangelical Reformed College at Nagyszeben and then at the college at Marosvásárhely (now Tirgu-Mures, Romania) until his retirement in 1853. He died at Marosvásárhely on 20 November 1856.

János Bolyai was born at Koloszvár, in Hungary (now Cluj, Romania), on 15 December 1802. He was first taught by his father and at an early age showed a marked talent both for mathematics and for playing the violin. At the age of 13, by which time he had mastered the calculus and analytical mechanics, he entered the college at Marosvásárhely where his father was teaching. He remained there for five years, concentrating on mathematics, but also becoming an adept swordsman. Then, in 1818, against the wishes of his father (who wanted him to study under Gauss at Göttingen), he entered the Royal College of Engineers at Vienna. He graduated in 1822 and joined the army engineering corps, rising eventually to the rank of lieutenant, second class. Increasingly he fell victim to attacks of fever until, in 1833, he was retired from the army with a small pension. He returned to his father's house at Marosvásárhely and lived there, a semi-invalid, until his death on 27 January 1859.

The mathematical lives of the father and son were closely entwined. It was because of his son's growing interest in higher mathematics that Wolfgang was inspired to write the book on which his posthumous fame rests, the *Tentatem Juventum*, or *Attempt to Introduce Studious Youth into the Elements of Pure Mathematics*. Completed in 1829, but not published until 1832, it was a brilliantly suggestive survey of mathematics, although (and to Wolfgang's chagrin) overlooked by his contemporaries. Of greater importance for his son's future was Wolfgang's obsession with the hoary problem of finding a proof for Euclid's fifth postulate, that there is only one line through a point outside another line which is parallel to it, or, in layman's language, that parallel lines do not meet.

In 1804 Wolfgang thought that he had found a proof of the axiom. He sent it to Gauss, who pointed out a flaw in the argument and returned it. Undaunted Wolfgang continued his quest, and János caught his enthusiasm. By about 1820, however, János had become convinced that a proof was impossible; he began instead to construct a geometry which did not depend upon Euclid's axiom. Over the next three years he developed a theory of absolute space in which several lines pass through the point P without intersecting the line L. He developed his formula

relating the angle of parallelism of two lines with a term characterizing the line. In his new theory Euclidean space was simply a limiting case of the new space, and János introduced his formula to express what later became known as the space constant.

János described his new geometry in a paper of 1823 called "*The Absolute True Science of Space*". His father, unable to grasp its revolutionary meaning, rejected it, but sent it to Gauss. To the surprise of both father and son Gauss replied that he had been thinking along the same lines for more than 25 years. Gauss had published nothing on the matter, however, and János' paper was printed as an appendix to his father's *Tentatem* in 1832.

János' paper was a thorough and consistent exposition of the foundations of non-Euclidean geometry. He was therefore cast down when its publication received little attention and when he discovered that Nikolai Lobachevsky had published his account of a very similar geometry (also ignored) in 1829.

Deeply disappointed at their lack of recognition, the Bolyais retired into semi-seclusion. In 1837 the failure of their joint paper to win the Jablonov Society's Prize plunged them deeper into dejection. Thereafter Wolfgang did no serious mathematical research, and although János dabbled in problems connected with the relationship between pure trigonometry and spherical trigonometry, both died in relative obscurity. It was not until 30 years later that the work of Beltrami and Klein at last put into proper perspective János Bolyai's place as one of the fathers of modern mathematics.

Bolzano, Bernardus Placidus Johann Nepomuk (1781-1848), was a Czech philosopher and mathematician who made a number of contributions to the development of several branches of mathematics.

Bolzano was born at Prague, in Bohemia (now part of Czechoslovakia), on 5 October 1781. He went to the University of Prague, where he studied philosophy, mathematics and physics until 1800, when he entered the theology department. He was ordained in 1804. He did not abandon his mathematical interests, however, and in 1804 he was recommended for the Chair of Mathematics at the university. In 1805 he was appointed as the first Professor to the new Chair of Philosophy at Prague. For the next 14 years he lectured mainly on ethical and social questions, although also on the links between mathematics and philosophy. He was much admired by the students not only for his intellectual abilities but also for the forthright expression of liberal and Czech nationalist views. He became the Dean of the philosophy faculty in 1818. But by then his opinions were bringing him into disfavour with the Austro-Hungarian authorities and in 1819, despite the backing of the Catholic hierarchy, he was suspended from his professorship and forbidden to publish. A five-year struggle ensued, ending only in 1824 when Bolzano, resolute in his refusal to sign an imperial order of "recantation", resigned his Chair. He retired to a small village in southern Bohemia. He returned to Prague in 1842 and died there on 18 December 1848.

Owing to the opposition of the imperial authorities, most of Bolzano's work remained in manuscript during his lifetime. It was not until the publication of the manuscripts in 1962 that the range and importance of his research was fully appreciated. Early in his career he worked on the theory of parallels, based on Euclid's fifth postulate. He found several faults in Euclid's method, but until the development of topology nearly a century later, these difficulties could not be resolved. Bolzano also formulated a proof of the binomial theorem and, in one of his few works published in his lifetime (1817), attempted to lay down a rigorous foundation of analysis. One of the most interesting parts of the book was his definition of continuous functions.

During the 1830s Bolzano concentrated on the study of real numbers. He also formulated a theory of real functions and introduced the non-differentiable "Bolzano function". He was also able to prove the existence and define the properties of infinite sets, work later of much use to Julius Dedekind when he came to produce his definition of infinity in the 1880s.

Bolzano fell short of making any really fundamental breakthroughs in mathematics, but he was one of the most accomplished and wide-ranging of nineteenth-century mathematicians.

Boole, George (1815–1864), was a British mathematician who, by being the first to employ symbolic language and notation for purely logical processes, founded the modern science of mathematical logic.

He was born in Lincoln on 2 November 1815. He received little formal education, although for a time he attended a national school in Lincoln and also a small commercial school. His interest in mathematics appears to have been kindled by his father, a cobbler with a keen amateur interest in mathematics and the making of optical instruments. Boole also taught himself Greek, Latin, French, German and Italian. At the age of 16 he became a teacher at a school in Lincoln; he subsequently taught at Waddington; then, at

the age of 20, he opened his own school. All the while his spare time was devoted to studying mathematics, especially Newton's *Principia* and Lagrange's *Mécanique Analytique*. He was soon contributing papers to scientific journals and in 1844 he was awarded a Royal Society medal. In 1849, despite his lack of a university education, he was appointed Professor of Mathematics at the newly-founded Queen's College at Cork, in Ireland. He held the Chair until his death, at Cork, on 8 December 1864.

Boole's first essay into the field of mathematical logic began in 1844 in a paper for the *Philosophical Transactions* of the Royal Society. In it Boole discussed ways in which algebra and calculus could be combined, and the discussion led him to the discovery that the algebra he had devised could be applied to logic. In a pamphlet of 1847 he announced, against all previous accepted divisions of human knowledge, that logic was more closely allied to mathematics than to philosophy. He argued not only that there was a close analogy between algebraic symbols and those that represented logical forms but also that symbols of quantity could be separated from symbols of operation. These were the leading ideas which received their fuller treatment in Boole's greatest work, *An Investigation of the Laws of Thought on which are founded the Mathematical Theories of Logic and Probabilities*, published in 1854.

It is not quite true to say that Boole's book reduced logic to a branch of mathematics; but it did mark the birth of the algebra of logic, later known as Boolean algebra. The basic process of Boole's system is continuous dichotomy. His algebra is essentially two-valued. By subdividing objects into separate classes, each with a given property, it enables different classes to be treated according to the presence or absence of the same property. Hence it involves just two numbers, 0 and 1. This simple framework has had far-reaching practical effects. Applying it to the concept of "on" and "off" eventually produced the modern system of telephone switching, and it was only a step beyond this to the application of the binary system of addition and subtraction in producing the modern computer.

Later mathematicians modified Boole's algebra. Friedrich Frege (1848–1945), in particular, improved the scope of mathematical logic by introducing new symbols, whereas Boole had restricted himself to those symbols already in use. But Boole was the true founder of mathematical logic; it was on the foundations that he laid that Bertrand Russell and Alfred Whitehead attempted to build a rigidly logical structure of mathematics.

Borel, Émile Félix-Édouard-Justin (1871–1956),
was a French mathematician whose lasting
reputation derives from his rationalization of
the theory of functions of real variables.

Borel was born in Saint-Affrique on 7 January
1871. At an early age he showed such a strong
aptitude for mathematics that he was sent away
from his native village to a lycée at Montauban.
In 1890 he entered the École Polytechnique in
Paris, where he so distinguished himself that on
his graduation in 1893 he was appointed to the
faculty of mathematics at the University of Lille.
In 1894 he received his DSc from the École Normale Supérieure. For the next few years Borel
proved himself to be a prolific writer of highly
valuable papers and in 1909 the Sorbonne
created a Chair in Function Theory especially
for him. A year later he took on the additional
duty of becoming deputy director, in charge of
science, at the École Normale Supérieure.

Borel's professional career was interrupted by
World War I, during which he took part in
scientific and technical missions on the front.
The war also marked a turning-point in his life.
When it was over he took less interest in pure
mathematics and more in applied science. He
also became involved in politics. From 1924 to
1936 he was a Radical-Socialist member of the
national Chamber of Deputies, serving as Minister of the Navy in 1925. He was also in these
years one of the moving spirits behind the establishment of the National Centre for Scientific
Research (he received the institute's first gold
medal in 1955). He was, too, one of the founding members of the Henri Poincaré Institute,
serving as its first Director from 1928 until his
death. In 1936 Borel left active politics and four
years later he retired from his Chair at the Sorbonne. World War II drew him back into public
life: in 1940 he was taken briefly into custody by
the occupying German forces and on his release
he joined the Resistance movement. In 1945 he
was awarded the Resistance Medal. Thereafter
Borel lived in retirement until his death, in Paris,
on 3 February 1956.

Borel's first papers appeared in 1890 and it
was in the 1890s that he did his most important
work - on probability, the infinitesimal calculus,
divergent series and, most influential of all, the
theory of measure. In 1896 he created a minor
sensation by providing a proof of Picard's theorem, an achievement which had eluded a host of
mathematicians for nearly 20 years. In the 1920s
he wrote on the subject of game theory, before
Johann von Neumann (generally credited with
being the founder of the subject) first wrote on
it in 1928. But he will be remembered, above all,
for his theory of integral functions and his

analysis of measure theory and divergent series.
It is this work which established him, alongside
Henri Lebesgue (1875–1941), as one of the foun-
ders of the theory of functions of real variables.

Bourbaki, Nicolas, is the pseudonym taken by a
group of mathematicians, most of them French,
who began to publish collectively and anony-
mously in the late 1930s. The group, which at
any one time contained about 20 members, was
centred at the École Normale Supérieure in Paris.
A few Americans have at times been members.
The group's effort to persuade people that Bourbaki was a real person failed, most notably when
his application for membership of the American
Mathematical Society was rejected.

The origin of the pseudonym is not known
for certain, but it is believed to have been taken
from the French general, Charles Bourbaki
(1816–1897). During the siege of Metz in 1870
Bourbaki was duped by the Germans into going
to England to be present at the signing of peace
terms between Germany and France, and the
story of this trick was told in a pamphlet entitled
Quel est votre nom? It has been suggested that
the name "Nicolas" was intended to signify that
the group was bringing mathematical gifts to the
world.

The group's object was to provide a definitive
survey of mathematics or, at least, of those subjects worthy of the Bourbaki's transcendant talents. Their work appeared in instalments, the
first in 1939 and the thirty-third and last in 1967.
All their work was subjected to continual revision and updating. The work as a whole is
called *Elements of Mathematics*. It can be understood only by persons possessing expert
knowledge of higher mathematics and follows a
pattern markedly different from traditional in-
troductions to mathematics. The order of topics
dealt with is set theory, then (abstract) algebra,
followed by general topology, functions of a real
variable (including ordinary calculus), topological vector spaces and general theory of integration.

For a number of reasons the group's work
has been very influential. It gave the first systematic account of a number of topics that had
previously lain scattered in learned journals. The
precision of style and the order in which topics
were discussed recommended the work to
professional mathematicians. And there was
great interest in the group's axiomatic method
- a method that was at any rate gaining currency in the 1930s. Owing to the popularity of
the work, mathematicians had to learn "Bourbaki's" terminology and it is the mark of the
group's impact that many of the terms have

passed into the language of mathematical research.

Briggs, Henry (1561-1630), was an English mathematician, one of the founders of calculation by logarithms.

Briggs was born at Warley Wood, in Halifax, Yorkshire, in February 1561. He attended a nearby grammar school, and in 1577 went to St John's College, Cambridge. He was made a scholar in 1579 and received his BA in 1581. He was elected a Fellow of the college in 1588 and was appointed lecturer and examiner in 1592. It was a tribute to his rare abilities that, in an age when the universities paid scant attention to mathematics, he was appointed Professor of Geometry at the newly-established Gresham College, London, in 1596. He held the Chair until 1620, resigning it because a year earlier he had accepted the invitation of Henry Savile (1549-1622) to succeed him as Professor of Astronomy at Oxford. He was elected a Fellow of Merton College, where he died on 26 January 1630.

In 1616 Briggs wrote a letter to James Ussher, later Archibishop of Armagh, informing him that he was wholly absorbed in "the noble invention of logarithms, then lately discovered". Two years earlier John Napier had published his discovery of logarithms and as soon as Briggs learned of it he formed an earnest desire to meet the great man, for which purpose he travelled to Edinburgh in 1616. On this and subsequent visits the two men worked together to improve Napier's original logarithms which, having in modern notation $\log N = 10^7 \log_e \frac{10^7}{N}$, was in need of simplification. It seems most probable that the idea of having a table of logarithms with 10 for their base was originally conceived by Briggs. And although both men published separate descriptions of the advantages of allowing the logarithm of unity to be zero and of using the base 10, the first such logarithmic tables were published by Briggs in 1617. They were published under the title *Logarithmorum Chilias Prima*, and were followed in 1624 by the *Arithmetica Logarithmica*, in which the tables were given to 14 significant figures. In fact, the logarithms of Briggs (and of Napier) were logarithms of sines, a reflection of both men's interest in astronomy and navigation, fields in which accurate and lengthy calculations using that trigonometrical function were everyday matters. It is owing to the way that sines were then considered that the large factor 10^9 was important and that Briggs' 1624 tables took the form $10^9 \log_{10} N$.

For that reason Briggs' logarithms were one thousand million times "larger" than those in modern tables. Despite that, however, and despite the fact that many mathematicians (including Kepler) subsequently calculated their own tables, Briggs' tables remain the basis of those used to this day.

Bronowski, Jacob (1908-1974), was a Polish-born British scientist, journalist and writer, originally trained as a mathematician, who won international recognition as one of the finest popularizers of scientific knowledge in the twentieth century.

Bronowski was born in Poland on 18 January 1908, fled with his family to Germany when, in World War I, Russia occupied Poland, and moved in 1920 to England and became a naturalized British citizen. He studied mathematics at Jesus College, Cambridge, where he also edited a literary magazine and published some unremarkable verse, graduating as Senior Wrangler. He was awarded his PhD in 1933 and a year later was appointed Senior Lecturer at University College, Hull. He remained there until after the outbreak of World War II, when in 1942 he joined Reginald Stradling's Military Research Unit at the Home Security Office. His principal job was to forecast the economic effects of bombing. After the war he conducted statistical research at the Ministry of Works until 1950, when he was appointed Director of the National Coal Board's research establishment. From 1959 to 1963 he served as Director-General of Process Development for the board. During these years as a government official, he was continually extending the range of his intellectual pursuits. In particular he devoted himself to studying the development of Western science and thought. In 1953 he was visiting Professor of History at the Massachusetts Institute of Technology. His last appointment was a senior Fellow at the Salk Institute for Biological Studies in California, a post he took up in 1964. He died in San Diego on 22 August 1974.

Of his appointment to the Salk Institute Bronowski said that he was a "mathematician trained in physics, who was taken into the life sciences in middle age by a series of lucky chances". In fact he will probably be least remembered as a biologist. His true métier was for explaining to a large public the broad canvas of European intellectual history. His first published work of note was *The Poet's Defence* (1939) and at one time it might have been thought that he would come to specialize in literary subjects. After World War II he wrote several plays for radio, most memorably two in 1948, *Journey to Japan* and *The Face of Violence*, the latter of which won the Italia Prize in 1951 as the best radio play in Europe. He never lost his interest in literature (*William Blake and the Age of Revolution* appeared as late as 1965), but from the early 1950s his main interest turned towards broader intellectual and scientific themes.

The Common Sense of Science (1951) represented Bronowski's first attempt to bring the mysteries of science within the ken of non-scientific readers and was notable for the manner in which it displayed the history and workings of science around three central notions – cause, chance and order. In the early days of the Cold War he used the pages of the *New York Times* to discuss, in accessible language, both the technology of nuclear science and the moral question raised by the development of nuclear weapons. An extension of his newspaper articles was the book *Science and Human Values*, which was published in 1958.

Bronowski was deeply concerned about the general effects on society of the widening division between the arts and the sciences, a phenomenon given great publicity by the famous Leavis-Snow controversy, and he was at pains to do what he could to narrow the divide, while at the same time bringing the specialist conclusions of scholars in both the sciences and the humanities to a wide public. The result was two of his finest popularizing works, *The Western Intellectual Tradition* (1960), an illuminating survey of the growth of political, philosophical and scientific knowledge from the Renaissance to the nineteenth century written with Bruce Mazlish, and the brilliant 13-part BBC television documentary, *The Ascent of Man*, issued as a book in 1973.

When he was president of the British Library Association in 1957-1958, Bronowski said, in his inaugural address, that for public libraries to serve in the general expansion of a society's culture, writers must make the language of science comprehensible to the non-specialist. It is his great distinction that he practised, with great wit and erudition, what he preached.

Brouwer, Luitzen Egbertus Jan (1881-1966), was a Dutch mathematician who founded the school of mathematical thought known as intuitionism.

Brouwer was born in Overschie on 27 February 1881. He studied mathematics at the University of Amsterdam, and on receiving his BA was appointed an external lecturer to the university in 1902. He remained at that post until 1912, when he was appointed Professor of Mathematics, a Chair which he held until his retirement in 1951. His singular contribution to mathematics earned him numerous honours, most notably the Knighthood of the Order of the Dutch Lion in 1932. He died in Blaricum on 2 December 1966.

Brouwer's first important paper, a discussion of continuous motion in four-dimensional space, was published by the Dutch Royal Academy of Science in 1904, but the greatest early influence on him was Gerritt Mannoury's work on topology and the foundations of mathematics. This led him to consider the famous quarrel between Jules Poincaré and Bertrand Russell on the logical foundations of mathematics, and his doctoral dissertation of 1907 came down on the side of Poincaré against Russell and David Hilbert. He took the position that, although formal logic was helpful to describe regularities in systems, it was incapable of providing the foundation of mathematics.

For the rest of his career Brouwer's chief concern remained the debate over the logical, or other, foundations of mathematics. His inaugural address as Professor of Mathematics at Amsterdam in 1912 opened new ground in this debate, which had begun with the work of Georg Cantor (1843-1918) in the early 1880s. In particular Brouwer addressed himself to problems associated with the law of the excluded middle, one of the cardinal laws of logic. He consistently took issue with mathematical proofs (so-called proofs, as he saw them) that were based on the law. In 1918 he published his set theory which was independent of the law, explaining the notion of a set by the introduction of the idea of a free-choice sequence.

Having rejected the principle of the excluded middle as a useful mathematical concept, Brouwer went on to establish the school of intuitional mathematics. Put simply, it is based on the premise that the only legitimate mathematical structures are those that can be introduced by a coherent system of construction, not those which depend upon the mere postulating of their existence. So, for example, the intuitionist principle denies that it makes sense to talk of an actual infinite totality of natural numbers; that infinite totality is something which requires to be constructed.

Brouwer's work did not create an overnight sensation. But when, in the late 1920s, Kurt Gödel (1906-1978) broke down Hilbert's foundation theory, it gained great pertinence. The result of Gödel's work was the theory of recursive functions, and in that field of mathematics Brouwer's work was of such fundamental significance that his intuitional theories and analysis have continued to be at the very centre of research into the foundations of mathematics.

Burali-Forte, Cesare (1861–1931), was an Italian mathematician who is famous for the paradox named after him and for his work on the linear transformations of vectors.

Burali-Forte was born at Arezzo on 13 August 1861. He received his BA in mathematics from the University of Pisa in 1884 and then taught for three years at the Technical School in Sicily before being appointed extraordinary professor at the Academia Militare di Artiglieria e Genio in Turin. At Turin he lectured on analytical projective geometry. In the years 1894 to 1896 he served as assistant to Giuseppe Peano (1858–1932) at the University of Turin, and he later did much to make known Peano's work on mathematical logic, especially by his expanded edition (with his own interpolations) of Peano's *Logica mathematica*. He remained at the Academia Militare until his death, at Turin, on 21 January 1931.

Burali-Forte published his famous antimony in 1897: "To every class of ordinal numbers there corresponds an ordinal number which is greater than any element of the class". This discovery dealt a sudden, and severe, blow to the developing science of mathematical logic – that is, to the notion that mathematics (or at least its foundations) could be adequately expressed in purely logical terms. What Burali-Forte had done was to expose a contradiction in Georg Cantor's theory of infinite ordinal numbers, and in 1902 Bertrand Russell demonstrated that this contradiction was of a fundamental logical character and could not be overcome by minor changes in the theory. It was thus Burali-Forte who brought to the fore the threat which such antimonies posed to the foundations of mathematical logic.

Burali-Forte's chief interest, and major accomplishments, however, lay in the field of vector analysis. Much of this work was done in collaboration with Roberto Marcolongo. In 1904 they published a series of papers on the unification of vector notation, including in this work a comprehensive analysis of all the notations that had been proposed for a minimal system. Five years later they produced their own proposals for a unified system of vector notation. Having thus laid the groundwork, they began in 1909 to study the linear transformation of vectors. Of great importance was Burali-Forte's simplification of the foundations of vector analysis by the introduction of the notion of the derivative of a vector with respect to a point, which led to new applications of the theory of vector analysis and, in particular, to more efficient treatment of such operators as the Lorenz transformations.

In 1912–1913 Burali-Forte published more volumes on linear transformations and demonstrated their application to such things as the theory of mechanics of continuous bodies, hydrodynamics, optics and some problems of mechanics. His great ambition was to produce an encyclopaedia of vector analysis and its applications, but he did not live to complete this work. His last contribution, a paper on differential projective geometry, was finished in 1930, shortly before his death.

Burnside, William (1852–1927), was a British applied mathematician and mathematical physicist whose interest turned in his later years to a profound absorption in pure mathematics. In this field he was particularly prominent for his research in group theory and the theory of probability.

Burnside was born in London on 2 July 1852, and was orphaned when only a young child. He proved so gifted in mathematics at Christ's Hospital that in 1871 he won a scholarship to St John's College, Cambridge. He transferred to Pembroke College after two years, and graduated with high honours in 1875, winning the first Smith's Prize and being given the post of Fellow and Lecturer at the College. Apart from his normal lecturing duties, Burnside began to give advanced courses on hydrodynamics to other groups outside the College.

In 1885 he left Cambridge to take up the Chair of Mathematics at the Royal Naval College at Greenwich where, in addition to his teaching routine, he often accepted the responsibility of being an examiner for the Universities and the Civil Service. It was at this stage that his interests began to move towards group theory. Even as he formalized the institution of instruction at three different levels at the Royal Naval College, he was putting together his thoughts and his papers for a book that finally appeared in 1897. A revised form of that work is now regarded as a classic. A member of the Royal Society since 1893, Burnside served on the Society's Council from 1901 to 1903 and was awarded its Royal Medal. After World War I he began to reduce his scholarly output, and retired from the Royal Naval College in 1919. He continued to write on mathematical subjects, and a nearly completed manuscript on probability theory was found after his death and published posthumously. He died in West Wickham, Kent, on 21 August 1927.

Although it was well outside the scope of Burnside's undergraduate courses, his first publication (produced while he was at Cambridge) was in the field of elliptic functions. His study of elliptic functions led him, over the years, to study the functions of real variables and the theory of functions in general. One of his most influential papers, written in 1892, was a development of some work by Jules Poincaré on automorphic functions.

Burnside's lectures at the Royal Naval College were on a surprisingly wide range of subjects. He varied the content and the standard of his lectures according to whether he was addressing the Junior (ballistics), the Senior (dynamics and mechanics) or the Advanced (hydrodynamics and kinetics) Section of trainees.

His research interests in the meantime included differential geometry and the kinetic theory of gases. During the early 1890s, references to group theory began to enter his work, and by the middle of the decade his study of automorphic functions had brought him fully into the field. He became particularly concerned with the theory of the discontinuous group of finite order. In 1897 he published the first book on group theory to appear in English. The papers that he and other mathematicians wrote over the ensuing years produced such major advances in the subject that a revised edition was soon necessary. It was issued in 1911, and is today considered to be a standard work.

Work on the theory of probability began only in 1918, by which time Burnside had virtually ended his career. Nevertheless he was sufficiently interested in the subject to draft a manuscript on it which, although incomplete at the time of his death, was of so high a standard that it was published.

C

Cajori, Florian (1859–1930), was a Swiss-born American historian of mathematics. His books dealt with the history of both elementary and advanced mathematics, as well as the teaching of mathematics (including its importance in education). Cajori was also the author of biographies of eminent mathematicians.

Cajori was born on 28 February 1859 in St Aignan, near Thusius. At the age of 16 he emigrated to the United States, where he took up studies at the University of Wisconsin. He was awarded his bachelor's degree in 1883, and in 1885 was offered the position of Assistant Professor of Mathematics at Tulane University in New Orleans. There he continued his own studies in parallel with his teaching activities, earning his master's degree in 1886, and his PhD

in 1894. In 1889 Cajori moved to Colorado College at Colorado Springs in order to take up the position of Professor of Physics, but returned to Tulane University in 1898 to become Professor of Mathematics, a position he held until 1918. He served also as Dean of the Department of Engineering from 1903 until 1918. In that year Cajori moved to the University of California at Berkeley to take up the Chair of History of Mathematics, a post he retained until his death. He died at Berkeley on 14 August 1930.

Cajori's influence on the modern perception of the development of mathematics was profound, and his works are frequently quoted to this day. His reputation is founded mainly on his many books on the history of mathematics, although a number of his works – notably his edited version of Newton's *Principia Mathematica* (published posthumously) – have been subject to some criticism for their interpretation of historical material. His two-volume *History of Mathematical Notations* (1928–1929) is, however, still very much a standard reference text. He also compiled *A History of Physics* (1899).

Cantor, Georg Ferdinand Ludwig Philip (1843–1918), was a Danish-born German mathematician and philosopher who is now chiefly remembered for his development of the theory of sets, for which he was obliged to devise a system of mathematics in which it was possible to consider infinite numbers or even transfinite ones.

Cantor was born on 3 March 1843 to Danish parents living in St Petersburg (now Leningrad). The family moved to Germany when Cantor was 11, and he was educated at schools in Wiesbaden and Darmstadt, where he showed exceptional talent in mathematics. He then attended the Universities of Zurich and Berlin – obtaining his doctorate in 1867 – before moving to Halle University to take up a position as member of staff in 1869. He remained at Halle for the rest of his life, as Extraordinary Professor from 1872, and as Professor of Mathematics from 1879. He founded the Association of German Mathematicians, was its first President from 1890 to 1893, and was also responsible for the first International Mathematical Congress in Zurich in 1897. Although he received a few honorary degrees and other awards, he did not gain great recognition during his lifetime. Indeed, controversy over some of his work may have contributed to the deep depression and mental illness he suffered towards the end of his life, particularly after 1884. He died in the psychiatric clinic of Halle University on 6 January 1918.

Cantor's early work was on series and real

numbers, a popular field in Germany at the time. In a study on the Fourier series – a well known series that enables functions to be represented by trigonometric series – he extended the results he obtained and developed a theory of irrational numbers. It was in this connection that he exchanged correspondence with Richard Dedekind (1831-1916), who later became famous for his definition of irrational numbers as classes of fractions. With Dedekind's support, Cantor investigated sets of the points of convergence of the Fourier series, and derived the theory of sets that is the basis of modern mathematical analysis (now more commonly called set theory). His work, fundamental to subsequent mathematics and mathematical logic, contains many definitions and theorems that are now referred to in textbooks on topology. For the theory of sets, however, Cantor had had to arrive at a definition of infinity, and had also had therefore to consider the transfinite; for this consideration he used the ancient term "continuum". He showed that within the infinite there are countable sets and there are sets having the power of a continuum, and proved that for every set there is another set of a higher power – a realization that was of great importance to the continued development of general set theory. Cantor's definitions were necessarily crude; he was breaking new ground. He left refininements to his successors.

Some of Cantor's other ideas and studies were distinctly odd, particularly in the realm of physics. He considered metaphysics and astrology to be a science, for example – a science into which mathematics, and especially set theory, was capable of being integrated. As probably the last Platonist among serious mathematicians, he also insisted that the atoms of the Universe were countable.

Cantor's was in its way a unique contribution to the science of mathematics; he opened up a complete new area of research that at the same time was fundamental to basic mathematics.

Carathéodory, Constantin (1873-1950), was a German mathematician who made significant advances to the calculus of variations and to function theory.

Carathéodory was born in Berlin on 13 September 1873; his parents were of Greek extraction. He showed an aptitude for mathematics from an early age and attended the Belgian Military Academy from 1891 to 1895. He then worked in Egypt for the British Engineering Corps on the building of the Asyut Dam. Carathéodory returned to Germany in 1900, first attending the University of Berlin and then in

1902 moving to Göttingen University, where Felix Klein, David Hilbert and Hermann Minkowski had built up an excellent mathematics department.

Carathéodory was awarded his PhD in 1904 and qualified as a lecturer a year later. He taught at the University of Bonn for four years and then in 1909 was appointed to a professorship at the University of Hanover. In 1910 he transferred to a similar position at the University of Breslau (now Wrocław, Poland). In 1913 he moved back to Göttingen, and five years later he returned to the University of Berlin.

The Greek government invited Carathéodory to supervise the establishment of a new university and he went to Smyrna in 1920, but his efforts were destroyed by fire two years later. He took a post at the University of Athens, where he taught until 1924 before becoming Professor of Mathematics at the University of Munich. He remained there for the rest of his life, apart from one year (1936-1937) in the United States as Visiting Professor at the University of Wisconsin. He died in Munich on 2 February 1950.

Carathéodory's work covered several areas of mathematics, including the calculus of variations, function theory, theory of measure and applied mathematics. His first major contribution to the calculus of variations was his proposal of a theory of discontinuous curves. From his work on field theory he established links with partial differential calculus, and in 1937 he published a book on the application to geometrical optics of the results of his investigations into the calculus of variations.

One of Carathéodory's most significant achievements – also the subject of a book (1932) – was a simplification of the proof of one of the central theorems of conformal representation. It formed part of his work on function theory, which extended earlier findings of Picard and Schwarz. In measure theory he developed research begun in the 1890s by Émile Borel (1871-1956) and his student Henri Lebesgue (1875-1941), work which he summarized in 1918 in a text on real functions.

Carathéodory's interest also extended beyond pure mathematics into the applications of the subject, particularly to mechanics, thermodynamics and relativity theory. A mathematician of diverse talents, he can thus be seen to have enlarged the understanding of several disciplines.

Cauchy, Augustin-Louis (1789-1857), was a French mathematician who did important work in astronomy and mechanics, but who is chiefly famous as the founder, with Gauss, of the modern subject of complex analysis.

He was born in Paris on 21 August 1789 and received his early education from his father, an accomplished classical scholar and a barrister in the *parlement* of Normandy. When he was little more than an infant he was taken by his family to live in the village of Arceuil, where his father went to escape the terror of the French Revolution in 1793-1794. There he grew up with illustrious neighbours, the mathematician Pierre Laplace and the chemist Claude-Louis Berthollet (1749-1822), who together had established the famous Société d'Arceuil. The story runs that Lagrange, who also met the young Cauchy, quickly recognized the boy's scientific flair, but advised his father to give him a firm literary education before showing him any mathematical texts. True or not, Cauchy's first real introduction to mathematics was delayed until he entered the École Polytechnique, in Paris, in 1805. Two years later he entered the École de Ponts et Chausses to study engineering, leaving it in about 1809 to take employment first at the Ourcq Canal works, then at the Saint-Clou bridge, and finally (in 1810) at the Cherbourg harbour naval installations. In 1813 he returned to Paris, apparently for health reasons, and two years later he was appointed to the École Polytechnique, where he was made a full professor in 1816.

In the same year the restoration of the Bourbons to the French throne after the Napoleonic interlude brought a great change in his fortunes. Gaspard Monge (1746-1818) and Lazare Carnot (1753-1823), both of them republicans and Bonapartists, were expelled on political grounds from the Academy of Sciences and Cauchy was elected to fill one of the vacancies. In that year his paper on wave modulation won the Grand Prix of the Academy (renamed the Institut de France). That paper marked the real beginning of his fruitful years as a mathematician, years which gained the reward, some time before 1830, of his appointment to the Chair of the faculty of science at the Collège de France.

In 1830 Charles X was overthrown by the July Revolution, and when Cauchy refused to take the new oath of allegiance he was forced to resign his Chair. He went into exile at Fribourg, where he lived among a Jesuit community; they recommended him to the king of Sardinia and he was appointed to the Chair of Mathematical Physics at the University of Turin. From 1833 to 1838 he was tutor to Charles X's son at Prague. At last, in 1838, he returned to Paris to resume his professorship at the École Polytechnique. From 1848 to 1852 he was a professor at

the Sorbonne. He died at Sceaux, outside Paris, on 23 May 1857.

In 1805 Cauchy provided a simple solution to the problem of Apollonius, namely to describe a circle touching three given circles; in 1811 he generalized Euler's theorem on polyhedra; and in 1816 he published his award-winning paper on wave modulation. His best work, however, was all done in the 1820s and was published in this three great treatises, *Cours d'analyse de l'École Polytechnique* (1821), *Résumé des leçons sur le calcul infinitésimal* (1823) and *Leçons sur les applications de calcul infinitésimal à la géométrie* (1826-1828). Although he did other valuable research - in mechanics he substituted the concept of the continuity of geometrical displacements for the principle of the continuity of matter and in astronomy he described the motion of the asteroid, Pallas - his vital contributions were contained in these three treatises.

Cauchy made the principles of calculus clearer by developing them with the aid of limits and continuity, and he was the first mathematician to provide a rigorous proof for the famous theorem of Brook Taylor (1685-1731). Taylor's theorem, enunciated in 1712, expands a function of x as an infinite series in powers of x. Cauchy's proof was of great usefulness, because the theorem is extremely helpful in finding the difference columns in books of tables. More generally, Cauchy's work in the 1820s provided a satisfactory basis for the calculus. Perhaps even more important, for future pure and applied mathematicians alike, was his monumental research into the fundamental theorems of complex functions. He provided the first comprehensive theory of complex numbers (still, at the beginning of the nineteenth century, not accepted by all mathematicians) in his *Cours d'analyse*, and in doing so made a vital contribution to the development of mathematical physics and, in particular, to aeronautics.

During his lifetime Cauchy published seven books and about 800 papers. He has the credit for sixteen fundamental concepts and theorems in mathematics and mathematical physics, more than for any other mathematician. For both his creative genius and his prolific output he is remembered as one of the greatest of mathematicians in history.

Cayley, Arthur (1821-1895), was a British mathematician who was responsible for the formulation of the theory of algebraic invariants. A prolific writer of scholarly papers, he also developed the study of *n*-dimensional geometry, introducing the concept of the "absolute", and devised the theory of matrices.

Multiplication of matrices

To multiply the matrix $\begin{pmatrix} 3 & -2 & 8 \\ 1 & 0 & 5 \end{pmatrix}$ by 2,

all components must undergo transformations:

$$2\begin{pmatrix} 3 & -2 & 8 \\ 1 & 0 & 5 \end{pmatrix} = \begin{pmatrix} 6 & -4 & 16 \\ 2 & 0 & 10 \end{pmatrix}$$

because multiplication is scalar.

Matrix theory was to a large extent formulated by Cayley, although considerable investigation of the subject was undertaken by other mathematicians such as George Birkhoff and James Silvester.

Cayley was born in Richmond, Surrey, on 16 August 1821, the son of a merchant and his wife who were visiting England from their home in St Petersburg (now Leningrad). Cayley spent the first eight years of his life in Russia, and then attended a small private school in London, before moving to King's College School there. He entered Trinity College, Cambridge, as a "pensioner" to study mathematics and became a scholar in 1840. He graduated with distinction in 1842. Awarded a Fellowship at the College, he took up law at Lincoln's Inn in 1846 instead, prevented from remaining at Cambridge through his reluctance to take up religious orders - at that time a compulsory qualification. Cayley was called to the Bar in 1849 and worked as a barrister for many years before, in 1863, he was elected to the newly-established Sadlerian Chair of Pure Mathematics at Cambridge. He occupied the post until he died in Cambridge on 26 January 1895.

Cayley published about 900 mathematical notes and papers on nearly every pure mathematical subject, as well as on theoretical dynamics and astronomy. Some 300 of these papers were published during his 14 years at the Bar, and for part of that time he worked in collaboration with James Joseph Sylvester, another lawyer dividing his time between law and mathematics. Together they founded the algebraic theory of invariants (although in their later lives they drifted apart, until Cayley lectured at Johns Hopkins University, Baltimore, in 1881-1882 at Sylvester's invitation).

The beginnings of a theory of algebraic invariants may be traced first in the work of Joseph Lagrange (1736-1813), who investigated binary quadratic form in 1773. Later, in 1801, Karl Gauss (1777-1855) studied binary ternary forms. A final impetus was provided by George Boole (1815-1864) who, in a paper published in 1841, showed that all discriminants - special functions of the roots of an equation, expressible in terms of the coefficients - displayed the property of invariance. Two years later, Cayley himself published two papers on invariants; the first was on the theory of linear transformations. In the second paper he examined the idea of co-variance, setting out to find "all the derivatives of any number of functions which have the property of preserving their form unaltered after any linear transformations of the variables". He was the first mathematician to state the problem of algebraic invariance in general terms, and his work immediately attracted a lot of interest from other mathematicians.

Over the next 35 years he wrote ten papers on what he called "quantics" (which later mathematicians refer to as "form") in which he gave a lively account of the theory as it was being developed. He used the term "irreducible invariant" and defined it as an invariant that cannot be expressed rationally and integrally in terms of invariants of the same quantic(s) but of degree lower in the coefficients than its own. At the same time he acknowledged that there are many circumstances in which irreducible invariants and co-variants are limited. (His system was eventually simplified and generalized by David Hilbert (1862-1943).)

Cayley developed a theory of metrical geometry that could be identified with the non-Euclidean geometry of such mathematicians as Nikolai Lobachevski, János Bolyai and Bernhard Riemann. His geometry was the geometry of n dimensions. He introduced the concept of "absolute" into geometry, which links projective geometry with non-Euclidean geometry, and together with Felix Klein (1849-1925) distinguished between "hyperbolic" and "elliptic" geometry - a distinction that was of great historical significance. When Cayley's "absolute" was real, his distance function was that of hyperbolic geometry, and when "absolute" was imaginary, the formulae reduced to Riemann's elliptic geometry.

Cayley also created a theory of matrices which did not need repeated reference to the equations from which their elements were taken, and established the principles for forming general algebraic functions of matrices. He went on to derive many important theorems of matrix theory. He claimed to have arrived at the theory of matrices via determinants, but he always made great use of geometrical analogies in his algebraic and analytical work.

He also laid down in general terms the elements of a study of "hyperspace", and in 1860 devised a system of six homogeneous co-ordinates of a line. These are now more often known as Plücker's line co-ordinates because the same ideas were independently published – five years later – by Julius Plücker (whose assistant was Cayley's former collaborator, Felix Klein).

Cayley wrote on almost every contemporary subject in mathematics, but completed only one full-length book. He clarified many of the theorems of algebraic geometry that had previously been only hinted at, and he was one of the first to realize how many different areas of mathematics were drawn together by the theory of groups. Awarded both the Royal Medal (1859) and the Copley Medal (1881) of the Royal Society, generally in demand for both his legal and his administrative skills, Cayley played a great part in bring mathematics in England back into the main stream and in founding the modern British school of pure mathematics.

Cesaro, Ernesto (1859–1906), was an Italian mathematician whose interests were wide-ranging, but who is chiefly remembered for his important contributions to intrinsic geometry. His name is perpetuated in his description of "Cesaro's curves", first defined in 1896.

Cesaro was born on 12 March 1859 in Naples, where he grew up and completed the first part of his education. At the age of 14 he joined his brother in Liège, Belgium, and entered the École des Mines on a scholarship. After matriculation, he continued studying mathematics and published his first mathematical paper. On the death of his father in 1879, Cesaro returned to his family in Torre Annunziata for three years before going back to Liège on another scholarship. In 1883 he published a major mathematical paper, "*Sur diverses questions d'arithmétique*", in the *Mémoires de l'Academie de Liège*. After some sort of disagreement with the educational authorities in Liège, however, he entered the University of Rome in 1884. There he wrote prolifically on a wide range of subjects. Two years later he became Professor of Mathematics at the Lycée Terenzio Mamiani, but left after one month to fill the vacant Chair of Higher Algebra at the University of Palermo, where he remained until 1891. Finally he became Professor of Mathematical Analysis at Naples, and held this post until his untimely death on 12 September 1906 as a result of injuries he received in attempting to rescue his son from rough seas near Torre Annunziata.

Cesaro's most important contribution to mathematics was his work on intrinsic geometry. He began his study of the subject while in Paris, and continued to develop it for the rest of his life. His earlier work is summed up in his monograph of 1896, the *Lezione di Geometrica Intrinsica* in which, commencing with Gaston Darboux's method of a mobile co-ordinate trihedral (formed by the tangent, the principal normal, and the bi-normal at a variable point of a curve), Cesaro simplified the analytical expression and made it independent of extrinsic co-ordinate systems. He stressed the intrinsic qualities of the objects. In elaborating this method later, he pointed out further applications. In the *Lezione* Cesaro described the curves which now bear his name. He later included the curves devised by Koch (which are continuous but have no tangent at any point). The *Lezione* also deals with the theory of surfaces and multi-dimensional spaces in general. Much later on, Cesaro was able to emphasize the independence of his geometry from the axioms of parallels, and also established other foundations on which to base non-Euclidean geometry.

Cesaro's other work, particularly during his time at the University of Rome, covered topics ranging from elementary geometrical principles to the application of mathematical analysis; from the theory of numbers to symbolic algebra; and from the theory of probability to differential geometry. He also made notable interpretations of James Clerk Maxwell's work in theoretical physics.

Christoffel, Elwin Bruno (1829–1900), was a German mathematician who made a fundamental contribution to the differential geometry of surfaces, carried out some of the first investigations that later resulted in the theory of shock waves, and introduced what are now known as the Christoffel symbols into the theory of invariants.

Christoffel was born on 10 November 1829 in Montjoie (now Monschau), near Aachen. He studied at the University of Berlin, where he received his doctorate at the age of 27. Three years later he became a Lecturer at the University before, in 1862, becoming a professor at the Polytechnicum in Zurich. After seven years there, he returned to Berlin to take the Chair of Mathematics at the Gewerbsakademie. In 1872 he became Professor of Mathematics at the newly-founded University of Strasbourg, where he remained until his retirement in 1892. He died on 15 March 1900.

Christoffel's best-known paper annotated his investigation into the theory of invariants. Called "*Über die Transformation der homogen*

Differentialausdrücke zweiten Grades" and published in 1869, the paper introduced the symbols that later became known as Christoffel symbols of the first and second order. The series of other symbols of more than three indices, including the four index symbols already introduced by Bernhard Riemann, are now known as the Riemann-Christoffel symbols. (The symbols of an order higher than four are obtained from those of a lower order by a process called covariant differentiation.)

Christoffel is additionally remembered as the formulator of the theorem that also bears his name, and concerns the reduction of a quadrilateral form; the theorem was later incorporated by Curbastro Ricci (1853-1925) and Tullio Levi-Civita (1873-1941) in their tensor calculus.

Christoffel's contribution to the differential geometry of surfaces is contained in his *Allgemeine Theorie der geodätischen Dreiecke* (1868), in which he presented a trigonometry of triangles formed by geodesics on an arbitrary surface. He used the concept of reduced length of a geodesic arc, stating that when the linear element of the surface can be represented by

$$ds^2 = dr^2 + m^2 dx^2,$$

m is the reduced length of the arc r.

Inspired by Riemann - who was of a similar age - Christoffel's papers in 1867 and 1870 were on the conformal tracing of a simply connected area bounded by polygons on the area of a circle. In 1880 he showed algebraically that the number of linearly independent integrals of the first order on a Riemann surface is equal to the genus p. Later, in *Vollständige Theorie der Riemannschen θ-Function* (published posthumously), Christoffel gave an independent interpretation of Riemann's work on the subject.

In 1877, Christoffel published a paper on the propagation of plane waves in media with a surface discontinuity, and thus made an early contribution to shock wave theory.

Church, Alonso (1903-   ), is an American mathematician who in 1936 published the first precise definition of a calculable function, and so contributed enormously to the systematic development of the theory of algorithms.

Church was born on 4 June 1903. Completing his education at Princeton University, and obtaining his PhD there in 1927, he joined the University staff and remained at Princeton for 40 years, finally occupying the Chair of Mathematics and Philosophy. Since 1967 he has held a similar post at the University of California in Los Angeles. The author of many books on mathematical subjects, Church is a member of a number of academies and learned societies.

The concept of the algorithm, in the development of which Church played such a part, did not properly appear until the twentieth century. Then, as the subject of independent study, the algorithm became one of the basic concepts in mathematics. The term denotes an exact procedure specifying a process of calculation that begins with an arbitrary initial datum and is directed towards a result that is fully determined by the initial datum. The algorithm process is one of sequential transformation of constructive entities: it proceeds in discrete steps, each of which consists of the replacement of a given constructive entity with another. (Familiar examples of algorithms are the rules for addition, subtraction, multiplication and division in elementary mathematics.)

Luitzen Brouwer (1887-1966) and Hermann Weyl (1885-1955) did some tentative studies in the 1920s, and Alan Turing (1912-1954) later offered the first application of the algorithm concept in terms of a hypothetically perfect calculating machine. The solving of algorithmic problems involves the construction of an algorithm capable of solving a given set with respect to some other set, and if such an algorithm cannot be constructed, it signifies that the problem is unsolvable. Theorems establishing the unsolvability of such problems are among the most important in the theory of algorithms, and Church's theorem was the first of this kind. From Turing's thesis, Church proved that there were no algorithms for a class of quite elementary arithmetical questions. He also established the unsolvability of the solution problem for the set of all true propositions of the logic of prediction.

Since Church's pioneering work, much further progress has been made: Alfred Tarski (1902-   ), for example, has obtained some important results. Today, the theory of algorithms is closely associated with cybernetics, and the concept is fundamental to programmed instruction in electronic computers.

Clifford, William Kingdon (1845-1879), was a British mathematician and scientific philosopher who developed the theory of biquaternions and proved a Riemann surface to be topologically equivalent to a box with holes in it. His name is perpetuated in "Clifford parallels" and "Clifford surfaces". In his philosophical studies he was much preoccupied with theories of evolution.

Clifford was born on 4 May 1845 in Exeter, Devon. Educated locally, he went to King's College, London, at the age of 15. Three years later he won a small scholarship and entered Trinity College, Cambridge, where his academic progress was phenomenal. In 1868 he was made a Fellow of the College, and continued to live there until 1871, when he was appointed Professor of Applied Mathematics at University College, London. He was elected a Fellow of the Royal Society in 1874, and became a prominent member of the Metaphysical Society. In 1876, however, he developed pulmonary tuberculosis and was obliged to live first in Algiers, and then in Spain, for the sake of his health. But his condition continued to deteriorate and, although he was able to make several trips to England for short periods, he went finally to Madeira in 1879, and died there on 3 March of that year.

Despite his connection with the city, Clifford was one of the first mathematicians to protest against the analytical methods of the "Cambridge school". Primarily a geometrician, regarding geometry as to all intents and purposes a branch of physics, Clifford had as his fundamental aim in his teaching the compelling of his students to think for themselves. He did much to revolutionize the teaching of elementary mathematics, and was responsible for introducing into England the geometrical and graphical methods of August Möbius, Karl Culmann and others. It was through a generalization of the quaternions (themselves a generalization of complex numbers) formulated by William Hamilton that Church derived his theory of biquaternions, associating them specifically with linear algebra. In this way representing motions in three-dimensional non-Euclidean space, and together with his suggestion in 1870 that matter itself was a kind of curvature of space, Church may be seen to have foreshadowed in some respects Einstein's General Theory of Relativity.

Clifford continued his studies in non-Euclidean geometry, with reference particularly to Riemann surfaces, for which he established some significant topological equivalences. He further investigated the consequences of adjusting the definitions of parallelism, and found that parallels not in the same place can exist only in a Riemann space - and he proved that they do exist. He showed how a certain three parallels define a ruled second-order surface that has a number of interesting properties (which were subsequently examined by Bianchi and Felix Klein).

Clifford also achieved some renown as an agnostic philosopher.

Cocker, Edward (1631-1675), was an English engraver, calligrapher and amateur arithmetician, famous as the reputed author of *Cocker's Arithmetic*.

Very little is known of his life. He may have been born in Norfolk, but wherever he was born he was most probably a member of the Northamptonshire Cokers. It is known that by 1657 he was living in St Paul's Churchyard, London, then a centre for the publishing trade, and that he had set up there as a teacher of writing and arithmetic. In 1664 he advertised in the press for boarders to attend his school of writing and arithmetic. In the same year he is mentioned several times in Samuel Pepys' diary as a man excellently well read in the English poets. Cocker himself wrote passable poetry, some specimens of which he included in his anthology *Muses' Spring Garden* (1675). In 1665 Cocker lived for a time in Cheapside, but soon after he seems to have moved to Northampton and it is there, probably, that he died in 1675.

In his lifetime Cocker was best known as an engraver and he published many manuals for students on calligraphy. The most celebrated of them is *Daniel's Copy-Book, ingraven by Edward Cocker, Philomath* (1664), a copy of which is preserved in the British Museum. He may also have compiled an *English Dictionary* (1704), although it is probable that, despite the appearance of his name on the title page, the dictionary is the work of his friend, editor and publisher, John Hawkins. The same is believed to be true of his *Decimal Arithmetic* (1684). Cocker is remembered, however, for *Cocker's Arithmetic*, which was published in 1712 and subsequently ran through 112 editions. It was the first arithmetical text which addressed itself specially to men engaged in business and its accuracy came to be so relied upon that it gave rise to the saying, "according to Cocker". The length of time during which *Cocker's Arithmetic* held its high place may be gauged from the fact that the saying was not really popularized until 1756, when it was used by Arthur Murphy in his play, *The Apprentice*.

In 1847 Augustus de Morgan published a book entitled *Arithmetical Books*, in which he argued that *Cocker's Arithmetic* was a forgery, being written entirely by Hawkins. He added that the book's popularity was a misfortune, since it marked a decline from the existing standards of arithmetic and became a best-seller not by its merits but by its being continually puffed by Grub Street hacks. Morgan's arguments are, however, considered somewhat dubious. At any rate, whether Cocker was or was not the author (the answer will almost certainly never be known), Morgan was right to remark that "this Edward Cocker must have had a great reputation, since a bad book under his name pushed out the good ones".

Coolidge, Julian Lowell (1873-1954), was an American geometrician and a prolific author of mathematical textbooks in which he not only reported his results but also described the historical background, together with contemporary developments.

Coolidge was born to a prominent family in Brookline, Massachusetts, on 28 September 1873. Completing his education, he studied at Harvard University where in 1895 he was awarded his bachelor's degree with top honours. Two years later he travelled to Britain and took a degree in natural sciences at Balliol College, Oxford. He then returned to the United States to teach mathematics at the Groton School. (One of his pupils there was Franklin D. Roosevelt.) In 1900 he became an Instructor in mathematics at Harvard, and was made a member of the faculty in 1902. In that same year he was given leave of absence in which to continue his own studies, and returned to Europe, studying in Paris, Griefswald, Turin and Bonn. Having earned a PhD in 1904 at Bonn University, Coolidge went back to teaching at Harvard. Four years later he was made an Assistant Professor. His work was then disrupted by World War I, in which he served as a Major in the army. After the war he was a liaison officer in France, where he organized and taught courses at the Sorbonne for the benefit of American soldiers still stationed in the country.

In 1918 Coolidge had been made a full Professor of Mathematics at Harvard, and on his return from France he remained there until his retirement in 1940. Even then, however, as his own war effort, he again took to giving courses to military personnel. Many honours were awarded to Coolidge in recognition of his contributions to mathematics. He died in Cambridge, Massachusetts, on 5 March 1954.

Coolidge's work lay in the field of geometry and the history of mathematics. His early research for his PhD thesis and his first book (1909) were on non-Euclidean geometry, and were strongly influenced by the work of Segre and Study; in particular, Coolidge used Study's new method of approach to line geometry. He was especially interested in the use of geometry in the investigation of complex numbers.

Other areas of interest soon began to develop. Coolidge wrote his first paper on probability theory in 1909, in which he also examined certain problems in games theory. He produced several later studies on statistics, and all of this work was included in his 1925 book on prob-

ability – one of the first on the subject to be published in English, and as such it received considerable acclaim.

His first work on the algebraic theory of curves appeared in 1915. Stimulated by the topic, Coolidge elaborated on his initial investigation and eventually (1931) published a full-size book detailing his results. Work on two classical geometrical figures – the circle and the sphere – also led to the writing of a book published in 1916. Lectures given at the Sorbonne in 1919 on the geometry of the complex domain were expanded into book form and published in 1924. There were three further books: one in 1940 on geometrical methods, one in 1943 on conic sections, and the last a historical text in 1949. In addition to his books, Coolidge was also the author of many papers, the last of which was written in 1953.

Courant, Richard (1888-1972), was a German-born American mathematician who taught mathematics from a very early age, wrote several textbooks that are now standard reference works, and founded no fewer than three highly influential mathematical institutes.

Courant was born the son of a Jewish businessman on 8 January 1888 in Lublintz, in Upper Silesia (now in Poland). He attended schools in Glatz, and then Breslau (Wroclaw), where he showed exceptional talent and was soon teaching privately people who were several years above him at school. At the age of 16 Courant was earning so much money as a teacher that he remained in Breslau when his parents moved elsewhere; at school, however, he was told to give up his tutoring or be expelled. Instead, he left of his own accord, and began attending lectures unofficially at the university there. The following year, he entered the university on an official basis, but in 1907, on the advice of one of his friends, he moved on to the University of Göttingen, where he quickly distinguished himself. He became acquainted with David Hilbert (1862-1943), and tutored Hilbert's son, becoming also Hilbert's assistant – a position that allowed him to be at the centre of one of the most thriving contemporary mathematical communities. In 1910 he was awarded his doctorate for an investigation into Dirichlet's Principle. The following year he returned to Göttingen, married, and prepared the thesis to qualify him as a university teacher. During World War I, Courant served as an infantryman (being promoted to lieutenant) until he was wounded in 1915. At about this time he interested the military authorities in a device for sending electromagnetic radiation through the earth to carry messages; this was developed, and Courant spent the rest of the war involved with communications. He then returned to Göttingen for a few months before being appointed Professor of Mathematics at the University of Münster. However, he was soon recalled to the vacant Chair at Göttingen (which only a few years earlier had been occupied by Felix Klein).

Courant spent more than ten years at Göttingen, gradually building up the mathematics department into an autonomous unit, and raising funds for new buildings. He found his position untenable, however, as a Jew in Adolf Hitler's Germany, and after a visit to the United States in 1931-1932, settled there in 1934, joining the teaching staff at New York University. Neither the university nor his position were similar to that which he had been used to in Germany, but from these small beginnings he again built the mathematical department into a renowned centre of research; the success he achieved was even greater than that in Göttingen, in that he was Director of the Institute of Mathematical Sciences of New York University from 1953 to 1958, and in 1962 work was begun on a new Institute which was opened in 1965 as the Courant Institute of Mathematical Sciences. Courant retired in 1958 but still retained an interest in mathematics and mathematical education. He died in New Rochelle on 27 January 1972.

Much of what Courant achieved during his life was as a result of his great skill in administration and organization. At Göttingen, Felix Klein (1849-1925), although he had retired some years before, still enjoyed the privileged status of Emeritus Professor and wielded enormous influence in the structure of its mathematical teaching and organization. It was he who saw in Courant a worthy successor to himself as administrator. In his own characteristic way, Courant then set about developing the few rooms and the autonomous mathematical professors and other staff into a Mathematical Institute worthy of the reputation it already commanded throughout the world. By subtle changes (including that of the title on the stationery) he separated the mathematics department from the philosophical faculty. Then he persuaded the International Education Board to donate the money for a new building. It was unfortunate that after this was built and Courant appointed its first Director in 1929 that Hitler came to power, because four years later Courant, being of Jewish descent, was suspended from duty. Nevertheless, once in the United States, Courant managed to do it all over again, this time more by paying close atten-

tion to the nurturing of graduates, and by publicizing the fact that his courses dealt with applied, as well as pure, mathematics.

Courant was also a very able writer on mathematical topics. By treating many of the subjects developed by his mentor David Hilbert, he prepared a book, *Methods of Mathematical Physics* (now universally known as the "Courant-Hilbert"), which turned out to be just what was needed by physicists in their research on the quantum theory. The first volume was published while he was in Germany, the second after he had settled in the United States. Its influence on the scientific community has been so great that it is still in use today. Another book, *Differential and Integral Calculus*, also in two volumes, has been used for 40 years as a university textbook, and is still in use in an updated form. Like the Courant-Hilbert it was soon translated into English. Courant was also sole or part author of a number of books on more specialized areas of mathematics. One general book still of great interest, however, is his *What is Mathematics?*, written in conjunction with Herbert Robbins and published in 1941.

Cramer, Gabriel (1704-1752), was a Swiss mathematician who is now chiefly remembered for Cramer's Rule, Cramer's Paradox, and for the concept of utility in mathematics. He was, however, an influential teacher, personally acquainted with some of the great mathematicians of his age, and a prolific editor of other people's writings.

Cramer was born on 31 July 1704 in Geneva. It was there that he was educated, and there too - at the age of 20 - that he shared the Chair of Mathematics at the Académie de la Rive with his friend Calandrini (he taught geometry and mechanics, and Calandrini taught algebra and astronomy). In 1727 Cramer travelled to Basle, where he met Leonhard Euler (1707-1783) and his friend Daniel Bernoulli (1700-1782), and Daniel's uncle Johann Bernoulli (1667-1748) - all famous mathematicians. And for the next eighteen months he visited London, Leiden and Paris. (The next time he visited Paris, 20 years later, he took with him his pupil, the young Prince of Saxe-Gotha.) Cramer returned to Geneva, and in 1734 was appointed to the full Chair of Mathematics at de la Rive. In 1750 he was made Professor of Philosophy. In that year also, he published his major work, the *Introduction à l'analyse des lignes courbes algébriques*, in which 'Cramer's Rule' provided a method for the solution of linear equations. The following year, however, he had an accident, after which he was advised to go to the south of France and rest. The journey there was itself too much for him; he died on the way, on 4 January 1752.

Cramer's work was acclaimed by his contemporaries and he received many honours. He was made a member of the Royal Society in London, and of the Academies of Berlin, Lyons and Montpelier.

Although Cramer made a number of original contributions to mathematics, the two he remains famous for are, of course, Cramer's Rule and Cramer's Paradox. His Rule, published in 1750, was responsible for a revival in interest over the use of determinants. Determinants exist as part of a method to solve linear equations, and although the German mathematician Gottfried Leibniz - or Leibnitz - is most often credited with their discovery in 1693, there is some evidence that they were known to the Japanese mathematician Seki Kowa some years before. But despite the fact that they were also referred to in the major work of the Scotsman Colin Maclaurin in 1720, determinants had never received general attention until Cramer rediscovered them while working on the analysis of curves. The next year, Alexis Vandermonde (1735-1796) developed Cramer's work; his results were in turn extended by Pierre Laplace and Joseph Lagrange; later, the foundations of modern determinant theory were laid by Augustin Cauchy, Karl Jacobi and many others. Today, determinants are part of matrix theory, and are the means of classifying different systems of linear equations.

Cramer's Paradox revolves around a theorem formulated by Colin Maclaurin. He stated that two different cubic curves intersect at nine points. Cramer pointed out that the definition of a cubic curve - a single curve - is that it is determined itself by nine points. But although he attempted an explanation, his was inadequate, and it was Leonhard Euler and others who derived a proper elucidation later.

Cramer's concept of utility now provides a connection between the theory of probability and mathematical economics. (That this was not the only interest Cramer showed in probability is revealed in his correspondence with Abraham de Moivre.)

As an editor of historically mathematical works, Cramer was indefatigable. In the last ten years of his life, he edited and published the collected works of Johann Bernoulli (whom he had met) and his brother Jakob Bernoulli (whom he had not), two volumes of correspondence between Johann Bernoulli and Gottfried Leibniz, and five volumes of the *Elementa* of Christian Wolf.

D

D'Alembert, Jean le Rond (1717-1783), was a French mathematician and theoretical physicist who was a great innovator in the field of applied mathematics, discovering and inventing several theorems and principles - notably d'Alembert's Principle - in dynamics and celestial mechanics. He devised the theory of partial differential equations and contributed many of the scientific articles that went into the first editions of Denis Diderot's (1713-1784) *Encyclopédie*.

D'Alembert was a foundling, discovered on the doorstep of a Paris church on 16 November 1717. Evidently the illegitimate son of a courtesan, d'Alembert nevertheless grew up well provided for, his accommodation and education financed by the chevalier Destouches (who is therefore generally supposed to have been his father). Following schooling under the Jansenists at Mazarin College, he studied law and was called to the Bar in 1738. However, he then spent a year engrossing himself in medical studies before deciding to devote the rest of his life to mathematics. This he did very successfully, distinguishing himself greatly and becoming personally acquainted with many famous scientists and literary men of the time; in 1741 he was admitted as a member of the Academy of Sciences. He died in Paris on 29 October 1783.

D'Alembert's first mathematical work published was a paper on integral calculus (1739). The subject continued to fascinate him - in the next nine years he wrote two further papers published in the *Mémoires* of the Academy of Berlin which were fundamental to the development of calculus - and eventually led him to the discovery of the calculus of partial differences. Thereafter he applied his calculus to as many mathematical problems as he encountered.

Nevertheless, it is in the field of dynamics that d'Alembert remains best remembered. The principle that now bears his name was first published in 1743 in his *Traité de dynamique*, and was an extension of the Third Law of Motion formulated by Isaac Newton more than 50 years earlier: that for every force exerted on a static body there is an equal, opposite force from that body. D'Alembert maintained that the Law was valid not merely for a static body, but also for mobile bodies. Within a year he had found a means of applying the principle to the theory of equilibrium and the motion of fluids; previously, such problems had always been solved by means of geometrical calculations. Within a further three years, and by then using also the theory of partial differential equations, he carried out important studies on the properties of sound, of air compression, and had also managed to relate his principle to an investigation of the motion of any body in a given figure.

It was natural for him, therefore, to turn his attention to astronomy. From the early 1750s, together with other mathematicians such as Leonhard Euler (1707-1783), Alexis-Claude Clairaut (1713-1765), Joseph Lagrange (1736-1813) and Pierre Laplace (1749-1827), he applied calculus to celestial mechanics. The problem they set themselves was to determine the motion of three mutually gravitating celestial bodies; in solving it they brought Newton's celestial mechanics to a high degree of sophistication, capable of explaining in detail all the peculiarities of celestial movements shown by contemporarily increasing accuracy of measurements. In particular, d'Alembert worked out in 1754 the theory needed to set Newton's discovery of the precession of the equinoxes on a sound mathematical basis. He determined the value of the precession and explained the phenomenon of the oscillation of the Earth's axis. At about the same time he also wrote an influential paper in which he gave accurate calculations of the perturbations in the orbits of the known planets.

It was also at that time that d'Alembert was persuaded by his friend Denis Diderot to contribute to his *Encyclopédie* - a work that was to contain a synthesis of all knowledge, particularly of new ideas and scientific discoveries. D'Alembert duly wrote on scientific topics, linking especially various branches of science. After a few years, however (when at least one volume had already appeared), the Church in France denounced the project, and d'Alembert resigned his editorship. It may have been this, all the same, that spurred him into publishing no fewer than eight volumes of his mathematical investigations over the next 20 years.

Towards the end of his life, d'Alembert's friend Johann Lambert (1728-1777) announced that he had discovered a moon circling the planet Venus, and proposed that it should be named d'Alembert; he declined the honour very diplomatically - but whether because of (entirely justified) suspicions about the existence of such a satellite, or for other reasons, there is no means of knowing.

Dantzig, George Bernard (1914-   ), is an American mathematician who is an expert on (computer) linear programming and operations research. His work is now regarded as fundamental to many university courses in business studies, industrial engineering and managerial sciences.

Born the son of a well-known mathematician on 8 November 1914 in Portland, Oregon, Dantzig completed his education at the University of Maryland, gaining his BA in 1936. He then attended the University of Michigan as a Horace Rackham Scholar for a year, earning his MA. During the latter part of World War II he was with the Statistical Control Headquarters of the USAF as Chief of the Combat Analysis Branch where, from 1946 to 1952, he then became Mathematical Adviser. For the next eight years he was a Research Mathematician with the Rand Corporation at Santa Monica, California, transferring in 1960 to the University of California at Berkeley as Professor and Chairman of the Operations Research Center. Since 1966, among other consultative posts, his major position has been as C.A. Criley Professor of Operations Research and Computer Science at Stanford University, Palo Alto, California. The author of two influential books and many technical papers, Dantzig has received a number of awards and honorary degrees, including the National Academy of Sciences Award in Applied Mathematics and Numerical Analysis (in 1977).

A fundamental problem in economics involves the optimum allocation of scarce resources among competing activities - a problem that can be expressed in mathematical form. In 1947 Dantzig discovered that many such planning problems could be formulated as linear computer-programmes. He compounded this discovery in that at the same time he also devised an algorithm - known as the simplex method - that turned out to be remarkably efficient for the purpose. (His method is still the best way to resolve nearly all linear programmes of this type.) Moreover, Dantzig's discovery coincided with the development of the first successful computers, which meant that managers in industry were provided with a powerful and practical method for comparing a large number of interdependent alternative courses of action. Dantzig led the way in developing applications for the new linear programming approach. By 1972, a survey showed that a considerable proportion of all industrial organizations was using the simplex method of linear programming. The system has also had an impact on economics and statistics.

Subsequently, Dantzig has been involved in all the main areas of mathematical programming and other parts of operations research. He has worked on the development of techniques for dealing with large systems, and originated the "decomposition principle" for solving large systems with block-diagonal structure. In 1971 it was possible by this method, and using an IBM 370/165 computer, to solve a linear programme with 282,468 variables and 50,215 equations in $2\frac{1}{2}$ hours.

The development of linear programming in the 1950s enabled the mathematical science of decision-making to be developed into the discipline now known as operations research or management science. Most universities at present offer courses on operations research, nearly all emphasizing the importance of linear programming. Operations research is also important in the academic studies of many university departments of business sciences and industrial engineering.

Darboux, Jean Gaston (1842–1917), was a French geometrician who contributed immensely to the differential geometry of his time, and to the theory of surfaces. An innovator in much of his research, he was also an able teacher, a capable administrator, and an influential author in writing of his own studies. His name is perpetuated in the Darboux sums and the Darboux integrals.

Darboux was born on 13 August 1842 in Nîmes. Educated locally, at the age of 19 he sat the entrance examinations for both the École Polytechnique and the École Normale Supérieure in Paris. In both he came top; he chose to enter the École Normale. During his studies there, he wrote his first paper (on orthogonal surfaces, in 1864). Two years later he extended this work, for which he received his doctorate from the Sorbonne. Thereafter, Darboux taught at the Lycée Louis le Grand (1866 to 1872) before transferring to a similar post at the École Normale. From 1873 to 1878 he also held the Chair of Rational Mechanics at the Sorbonne, as an assistant to Joseph Liouville (1809–1882, from whom he may have gained his interest in differential geometry). He then became assistant to Michel Chasles, the author of a standard reference work on geometry, and in 1880 succeeded him as Professor of Higher Geometry. He held this post until he died, in Paris, on 25 February 1917.

Elected a member of the Paris Academy of Sciences in 1884 (and for many years later its secretary), Darboux was made a Fellow of the Royal Society in 1902. He also won several other awards and honours.

Darboux's research concentrated on geometry – the major interest throughout his life. Nevertheless, only five years or so after his doctoral thesis on orthogonal surfaces (a subject he returned to time and time again), he published a paper on partial differential equations of the second order. What was particularly novel in his approach was that in order to further his examination he had devised a new method of integration. Within another five years – during which he also formulated the theory of a specific class of surface called a cyclide – he managed to complete a proof of the existence of integrals of continuous functions that had defeated Augustin-Louis Cauchy (1789–1857) a generation before. Continuing his investigations, Darboux succeeded (in 1879) in defining the Riemann integral, in order to do which he derived the "Darboux sums" and used the "Darboux integrals".

Between 1887 and 1896 he published a collection of the lectures he had given at the Sorbonne, under the overall title *Leçons sur la théorie générale des surfaces et les applications géométriques du calcul infinitésimal*. The four volumes described all of his work to date, but dealt mainly with the application of analysis to curves and surfaces, and the study of minimal surfaces and geodesics. In a later work, *Leçons sur les systèmes orthogonaux et les coordonnées curvilignes*, published in 1898, Darboux applied the theorem on algebraic integrals formulated by the Norwegian Niels Abel (1802–1829) to orthogonal systems in n dimensions. Important among Darboux's other work were his papers on the theory of integrations, the theory of analytical functions, and his research into the problems involving the Jacobi polynomials.

Dedekind, Julius Wilhelm Richard (1831–1916), was a German mathematician, a great theoretician in some respects way ahead of his time, whose work on irrational numbers – in which he devised a system known as Dedekind's cuts – led to important and fundamental studies on the theory of numbers. A pupil and friend of outstanding mathematicians, he taught for many years and published some highly influential books.

Dedekind was born on 6 October 1831, the youngest son of a professional civil servant who worked at the Collegium Carolinum in Braunschweig (Brunswick). Educated locally, Dedekind showed aptitude in the sciences, particularly in physics. Nevertheless, at the age of 17, it was mathematics he went to study at the Collegium Carolinum for two years before entering the University of Göttingen, where he was taught by the ageing Karl Gauss (1777–1855). Having received his PhD in 1852, he remained as an unpaid lecturer at the university for a few years before taking up the post of Professor of Mathematics at the Zurich Polytechnicum. In 1862 he returned to Brunswick and became Professor at the Technische Hochschule - a position he held for the remainder of his life. He was Director of the Hochschule from 1872 to 1875, and retired (as Professor Emeritus) in 1894. Dedekind became a member of several academies and received a large number of honorary degrees and other awards. He died in Brunswick on 12 February 1916.

At Göttingen, Dedekind developed a friendship with Bernhard Riemann (1826-1866), who later became Professor of Mathematics there. He also met Lejeune Dirichlet (1805-1859) and, with Karl Gauss, the four of them formed a formidable mathematical quartet which profoundly influenced each other's ways of thinking. From Gauss Dedekind learned about the method of least squares (in lectures he was able to recall vividly after 50 years); probably through Riemann's influence, Dedekind's thesis concerned the theory of integrals devised by Leonhard Euler; and from Dirichlet - himself to succeed Gauss and precede Riemann as Professor of Mathematics at Göttingen - Dedekind learned about the theory of numbers, potential theory, definite integrals and partial differential equations. Both Riemann and Dedekind also gave lectures at the University, Riemann on Abelian and elliptic functions, Dedekind on the new beginnings of group theory (as advanced by Evariste Galois just before his death in 1832). Dedekind was no lecturer, however, and his seminars were very ill-attended.

He was nevertheless outstanding for his original contributions to mathematics. In 1858 he had succeeded in producing a purely arithmetic definition of continuity and an exact formulation of the concept of the irrational number. From this, and from his editing of Dirichlet's lectures in 1871 (to which he added a supplement establishing the theory of algebraic number fields), he derived the subject of the first of his three great publications, *Stetigkeit und irrationale Zahlen*, published in 1872. In it he defined and explained the use of what are now called Dedekind's cuts - a device by which irrational numbers can be categorized as fractions - a completely original idea that has since passed into general use in the real number system.

Number theory continued to fascinate Dedekind. In his second great work, *Was sind und was sollen die Zahlen?*, published in 1888, he elaborated on his attempt to derive a purely logical foundation for arithmetic, and devised a number of axioms that formally and exactly represented the logical concept of whole numbers. (The axioms were later wrongly attributed to the Italian mathematician of a generation ahead, Giuseppe Peano (1858-1932), by whose name they are still known.)

In his third great work, Dedekind returned again to one of his former interests in order to extend his previous research; he described the factorization of algebraic numbers using his new theory of the "ideal" - the modern algebraic concept. Published in two sections, in 1879 and 1894, the work was fundamental in that Dedekind later further developed his theory of the ideal (determining the number of ideal classes in a field) and the subject was taken up by others.

Dedekind was also responsible for the publication of papers on a variety of other mathematically oriented subjects such as time-relationships and hydrodynamics; in 1897 and 1900 he introduced the concept of dual groups, which was eventually developed (well after his death) into the modern lattice theory.

Dehn, Max (1878-1952), was a German-born American mathematician who in 1907 provided one of the first systematic studies of what is now known as topology - that branch of mathematics dealing with geometric figures whose overall properties do not change despite a continuous process of deform, by which a square is (topologically) equivalent to a circle, and a cube is (topologically) equivalent to a sphere.

Dehn was born on 13 November 1878 in Hamburg, the son of a Jewish family. He studied at Göttingen University under David Hilbert (1862-1943) and received his doctorate in 1900. He then became a teacher. At the outbreak of World War I he joined the army. After the war Dehn became Professor of Pure and Applied Mathematics at Frankfurt University, and remained there until 1935, when he fell victim to Adolf Hitler's anti-Semitism laws and he lost his position. Accordingly, he emigrated in 1940 to the United States, and occupied posts at the University of Idaho, the Illinois Institute of Technology, and St John's College, Annapolis. From 1945 Dehn worked at the Black Mountain College in North Carolina. He died there on 27 June 1952.

Influenced strongly by David Hilbert, Dehn's work was mainly concerned with a study of the geometric properties of polyhedra. His first major contribution was to demonstrate that whereas the postulate of Archimedes - that the sum of the angles of a triangle is not greater than two right-angles - is not provable, a generalization of the related theorem proposed by Adrien Legendre (1752-1833) - that the sum of the angles of any two triangles is identical - *is* provable.

In a famous address in 1900, David Hilbert presented 23 unsolved mathematical problems to the International Congress of Mathematicians. Dehn found a solution to one of them (concerning the existence of tetrahedra with equal bases and heights, but not equal in the sense of division and completeness).

In 1910 Dehn proved an important theorem on topological manifolds. The theorem came to be known as Dehn's lemma, but was later found not to apply in all circumstances. It nevertheless provided stimulation for considerable scientific discussion. Dehn continued to work on topological problems of transformation and isomorphism.

Dehn's later research concerned statistics and the algebraic structures derived from differently axiomatized projective planes. He also made a notable contribution with his published work on the history of mathematics.

De Moivre, Abraham (1667-1754), was a French mathematician who, despite being persecuted for his religious faith and subsequently leading a somewhat unstable life, pioneered the development of analytical trigonometry - for which he formulated his theorem regarding complex numbers - devised a means of research into the theory of probability, and was a friend of some of the greatest scientists of his age.

De Moivre was born on 26 May 1667 in Vitry-le-Francois, Champagne - a Huguenot (Protestant) in an increasingly intolerant Roman Catholic country. Although he first attended a local Catholic school, his next school was closed for being too evidently Protestant, and he then studied in Saumur, and finally (in 1684, at the age of 17) in Paris. With the revocation of the Edict of Nantes in the following year, however, he was imprisoned as a Protestant for twelve months; on his release he went immediately to England. In London he became a close friend of Isaac Newton (1642-1727) and the Secretary to the Royal Society, Edmund Halley (1656-1742). It was Halley who read de Moivre's first paper - on Newton's "fluxions" (calculus) - to the Royal Society in 1695, and saw to his election to the Royal Society in 1697. (Forty years later he was elected a Fellow of the Berlin Academy of Sciences, and no less than fifty years later - in the year of his death - to the Paris Academy of Sciences.) In 1710 de Moivre was appointed to the Grand Commission through which the Royal Society tried to settle the dispute over the priority for the systematization of calculus between Gottfried Leibniz (1646-1716) and Newton. Although de Moivre was a distinguished mathematician, he spent his whole life in comparative poverty, eking out a precarious living by tutoring and acting as a consultant for gambling syndicates and insurance companies. In spite of the fact that he had powerful friends, he never obtained a permanent position; no matter how he begged his influential associates to help him secure a Chair in Mathematics, particularly at Cambridge, it was without success. Finally, at the age of 87, he gave in to lethargy and spent 20 hours of each day in bed. He died nearly blind on 27 November 1754 in London.

While de Moivre was studying in Saumur, he read mathematics almost secretly, and studied Christiaan Huygens' work on the mathematics of games of chance. It was not until he went to Paris that he received any thorough mathematical instruction and studied the later books of Euclid under the supervision of Jacques Ozanam (1813-1853). But his first view of Newton's *Principia Mathematica* came even later, in London. Fascinated by it, it is said that he cut out the pages and read them as he walked along the street between tutoring one pupil and another.

He dedicated his own first book, *The Doctrine of Chances*, to Newton. (Subsequently, Newton - as he felt himself becoming more infirm with age - took to sending students to de Moivre.) A masterpiece, the work was published first in Latin in the *Philosophical Transactions* of the Royal Society, and then in expanded English versions in 1718, 1738 and 1758. Until 1711, the only texts on probability were the one by Huygens and another by Pierre de Montmort, published in Paris in 1708. When de Moivre first published, Montmort contested his priority and originality. Both men had made an approximation to the binomial probability distribution; now known as the normal or Gaussian distribution, it was the most important single discovery in the formulation of probability theory and was incorporated into statistical studies for the next 200 years. De Moivre was the first to derive an exact formulation of how "chances" and stable frequency are related. He obtained from the binomial expansion of $(1+1)^n$ what is now recognized as $n!$ (the approximation of Stirling's formula). With $n!$, de Moivre could sum the terms of the binomial from any point up to the central term. He seems to have been aware of the standard deviation parameter (σ) although he did not specify it. He also hinted at another approximation to the binomial distribution - which is now attributed to Siméon-Denis Poisson (1781-1840), a century later - but in this case he seems not to have realized its potential in probability theory.

Perhaps with regard to his own constant state of penury, de Moivre also took a great interest in the analysis of mortality statistics, and laid the mathematical foundations of the theory of annuities, for which he devised formulae based on a postulated law of mortality and constant rates of interest on money. He worked out a treatment for joint annuities on several lives, and one for when both age and interest on capital have equal relevance. First published in 1725, his work became standard in textbooks of all subsequent commercial application. Again, however, he had to fight for copyright with Thomas Simpson (1710-1761), who published a work on annuities in 1742, the year before de Moivre republished.

All his life, de Moivre published papers in other branches of mathematics; one of the subjects that particularly interested him was analytical trigonometry. In this field he discovered a trigonometric equation that is now named after him:

$$(\cos z + i \sin z)^n = \cos nz + i \sin nz.$$

It was first stated in 1722, although it had been anticipated by related forms in 1707. It entails or suggests a great many valuable identities, and became one of the most useful steps in the early development of complex number theory.

Sadly, de Moivre died a disillusioned man; much of his work was valued only long after his death.

De Morgan, Augustus (1806-1871), was a British mathematician whose main field was the study of logic, an interest that led him into a bitter controversy with his contemporary William Hamilton (1805-1865).

De Morgan was born on 27 June 1806 in Madura (now Madurai), India, the son of a colonel in the Indian Army. He entered Trinity College, Cambridge, in 1823 and graduated with a BA four years later. He disliked competitive scholarship and did not proceed to an MA degree nor did he become a candidate for a fellowship; neither would he comply with his parents' wishes that he should enter the Church. De Morgan considered a career in medicine but decided instead to become a barrister, and entered Lincoln's Inn to study for the bar. He changed his mind yet again and in 1828 applied for and obtained the position of the first Professor of Mathematics at the new University College, London, where he remained for 30 years. He died in London on 18 March 1871. After De Morgan's death, Lord Overstone bought his library of more than 3,000 books and presented them to the University of London.

De Morgan expended most of his energy on writing voluminous articles on mathematical, philosophical and antiquarian matters. A major controversy arose from his tract on "The Structure of the Syllogism", read to the Cambridge Philosophical Society in 1846 and subsequently incorporated into his book *Formal Logic*, published a year later. De Morgan had consulted William Hamilton on the history of Aristotelian theory, and Hamilton accused him of appropriating his doctrine of "quantification of the predicate" (and returned a copy of *Formal Logic* which De Morgan presented to him).

In logic the expression "every ... is" (or "all ... is") is treated as a single syntactically unanalysable term, which in concatenation (linked) with two noun expressions forms a proposition. Traditionally, however, it has been held that "every" (or "all") modifies the way in which the subject should be construed. Logicians therefore suggested a similar modification of the predicate. This idea was not new – it had been suggested by Aristotle, only to be abandoned later. Some of his early commentators worked out that such modification could generate 16 different propositions, but that is as far as they went. De Morgan recognized these restrictions and succeeded in expanding syllogistic when he developed a logic of noun expressions in *Formal Logic* and in his *Syllabus of a Proposed System of Logic*. He also extended his syllogistic vocabulary using definitions, so giving rise to new kinds of inferences, both direct (involving one premise) and indirect (involving two premises). He was thus able to work out purely structural rules for transforming a premise or pair of premises into a valid conclusion.

Inferences that appeared to illustrate principles belonging to the logic of noun expressions – but which could not be accommodated in syllogistic – had been known before. But De Morgan initiated and developed a theory of relations. He devised a symbolism that could express such notions as the contradictory, the converse and the transitivity of a relation, as well as the union of two relations. Together with George Boole (1815-1864), De Morgan can be credited with stimulating the upsurge of interest in logic that took place in the mid-nineteenth century.

Descartes, René (1596-1650), was a celebrated and influential French philosopher-mathematician whose work in attempting to reduce the physical sciences to purely mathematical principles – and particularly geometry – led to a

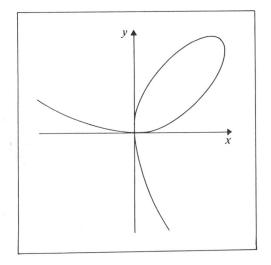

The folium is an algebraic curve discovered by Descartes that may be represented by the equation $x^3 + y^3 = 3xy$. The name probably derives from a supposed likeness to a leaf (folio).

fundamental revision of the whole of mathematical thought. So influential was his work that his astronomically erroneous description of the Solar System (in an endeavour not to offend the powerful Roman Catholic Church) held back astronomical research in continental Europe for decades.

Descartes was born at La Haye, Touraine, on 31 March 1596, the third son of Joachim Descartes, a Councillor of the Parliament of Rennes in Brittany. When René was 8, he was sent to the Jesuit College at La Flèche, where he spent five years studying grammar and literature and then three years studying science, elementary philosophy and theology; his favourite subject was mathematics. In 1612 he went to the University of Poitiers to study law and graduated four years later. Wanting to see the world, he joined the army of Prince Maurice of Nassau and used his mathematical ability in military engineering. A dream in November 1619 made him think that physics could be reduced to geometry and that all the sciences should be interconnected by mathematical links: he spent the next ten years applying this tenet to algebra.

Returning to France in 1622, Descartes sold his estate in Poitou in order to resume his travels, visiting scientists throughout France and western Europe. He finally settled in the Netherlands in 1629. Twenty years later he was invited to go to Sweden to instruct Queen Christina. On his arrival in Stockholm, he found that the somewhat whimsical queen intended to receive her instruction at 5 o'clock each morning. Unused to the cold of a Swedish winter, Descartes very shortly afterwards caught a severe chill and died on 11 February 1650. His remains were taken back to France and buried in the church of St Geneviève du Mont in Paris.

It was at the Jesuit College that mathematics became Descartes' favourite subject "because of the certainty of its proofs and the logic of its reasoning"; he was surprised at how little had been built on such firm and logical foundations. Later, with the rector of Breda – the philosopher and mathematician Isaac Beeckman – he devised a way of approaching physics generally following mathematical principles.

Descartes' great work in mathematics – most of his publications concerned either philosophy or astronomy – was his *Geometry*, published in 1637. Much of the book was revolutionary for its time but has now been long absorbed into standard textbooks of co-ordinate geometry. In it he provided a basis for analytical geometry – the geometry in which everything is reduced to numbers, so that a point is a set of numbers which are called its (Cartesian) co-ordinates, and a figure may be considered as an aggregate of points and described by formulae, equations or inequalities. Today, analytical geometry has many practical applications, such as cartography and the construction of graphs.

In establishing analytical geometry, Descartes introduced constants and variables into conventional geometry in order to enable the properties of curves to be expressed as algebraic equations. He used algebra to resolve complicated problems in geometry, and he expressed algebraic results geometrically (in graphs). Although not the first to apply algebra to geometry, he was the first to apply geometry to algebra. He was also the first to classify curves systematically, separating "geometric curves" (which can be precisely expressed as an equation) from "mechanical curves" (which cannot). The geometric curves he then further subdivided into three groups of increasing complexity according to the degree of the equation – the simplest group contained the circle, the parabola, the hyperbola and the ellipse. One of his more complex curves was the folium: $x^2 + y^2 = 3axy$, where x and y are variables and a is a constant; the result is a near loop.

Descartes' new geometry led to a concept of continuity, which in turn led to the theory of function and thence to the theory of limits.

In algebra he systematized the use of exponents (where the variable is itself a power; for example, a^x), interpreted the idea of negative

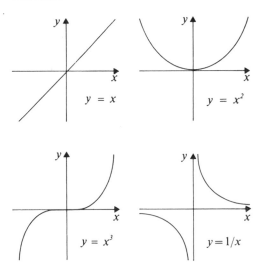

$y = x$

$y = x^2$

$y = x^3$

$y = 1/x$

The use of graphs to express algebraic functions was not new but was refined and standardized by Descartes, who gave his name to the system: cartesian co-ordinates.

quantities, and enlarged on his "rule of signs" for determining the number of negative and positive roots in (solutions to) an equation. He also resolved the long-standing problem of doubling the cube.

Descartes' work in mathematics was his greatest service to future science; his attempts to "geometrize" nature and his contributions to pure mathematics were far more permanent in their significance than all his other scientific work.

Dickson, Leonard Eugene (1874–1957), was an American mathematician who gave the first extensive exposition of the theory of fields. A prolific writer, he was also the author of a massive three-volume *History of the Theory of Numbers* (published between 1919 and 1923), now a standard work, in which he investigated abundant numbers, Diophantine equations, perfect numbers and Fermat's Last Theorem.

Dickson was born in Independence, Iowa, on 22 January 1874. He received his BA at the age of 19 from the University of Texas, where he then taught for some months. Receiving his MA in 1894, he entered the University of Chicago where in 1896 he gained his doctorate in mathematics. In 1897 he became a postgraduate student at Leipzig and in Paris. The following year, Dickson returned to the United States and - for a year at a time - was appointed Instructor in Mathematics at the Universities of California

and Texas. In 1900 he was appointed Assistant Professor at the University of Chicago; promoted in 1907 to Associate Professor, he became Professor in 1910. Apart from short periods as visiting Professor at the University of California in 1914, 1918 and 1922, Dickson remained at the University of Chicago until his retirement in 1939. He died on 17 January 1957 in Harlingen, Texas.

For his prolific work in mathematics, Dickson received many awards and honours, and became a member of many influential societies. In 1913 he was elected to the National Academy of Sciences, and in 1916 became President of the American Mathematical Society, from whom he received the Cole Prize for his book *Algebren und ihre Zahlentheorie*.

Dickson's work in mathematics spanned many topics, including the theory of finite and infinite groups, the theory of numbers, algebras and their arithmetics (for his work on which he won a \$1,000 prize), and the history of mathematics.

In his work on finite linear groups he generalized the results of Evariste Galois' studies, and those of Ernst Jordan and Jean-Pierre Serre, for groups over the field of n elements to apply to groups over an arbitrary finite field. He proved his modified version of the Chevalley theorem and published the first extensive exposition of the theory of finite fields.

During an investigation of the relationships between the theory of invariants and number theory, Dickson examined divisional algebra, particularly in the form systematized by Arthur Cayley, and he expanded the theorems of linear associative algebras formulated by Élie Cartan and Wedderburn.

Investigating the history of the theory of numbers, Dickson also studied the work of Diophantus, who lived in Alexandria in the third century. Diophantus assumed that every positive integer is the sum of four squares, a theory for which (in 1770) Waring attempted to derive an extension in the direction of higher powers. Using the results of Ivan Vinogradov, Dickson (in the 1930s) succeeded in proving Waring's theorem and made his contribution to Diophantine analysis, from which the complete criteria were obtained for the solution of $ax^2 + by^2 + cz^2 + du^2 = 0$ for any non-zero integer a, b, c or d. In addition, Dickson gave the first complete proof that $ax^2 + by^2 + cz^2 + du^2 + ev^2 = 0$ is always soluble in integers, if the non-zero integers a, b, c, d and e are not all of a like sign.

Diophantus (*fl.c.* AD 270–280) was an ancient Greek mathematician who, in solving linear mathematical problems, developed an early form of algebra. Particularly innovative was his use of a symbol for an unknown quantity.

Very little is known about him or about his life. It is probable, however, that he was born in Alexandria (now in Egypt), a great Greek cultural centre, where he certainly lived. If the evidence of what is called "Diophantus's riddle" is to be taken seriously, he lived at least to the age of 84 (which is the answer to the riddle).

To the Greeks, mathematics comprised two branches of study: arithmetic, the science of numbers, and geometry, the science of shapes. Towards the end of the Greek era - indeed, already under a declining Roman domination - Diophantus formulated his theories in a neglected field, the study of unknown quantities. His *Arithmetica*, according to its introduction, was compiled in 13 books (although the 6 that have come down to us are probably all that were completed); the work was translated by the Arabs, and it is through their word for his equations - "the re-uniting of separate parts" - that we now call the system "algebra". Diophantus would merely have thought of it as abstract arithmetic.

In the solution of equations Diophantus was the first to devise a system of abbreviating the expression of his calculations by means of a symbol representing the unknown quantity. Because he invented only one symbol for the unknown, however, in equations requiring two or more variables his work can become extremely confusing in its repetition of that single symbol.

His main mathematical study was in the solution of what are now known as "indeterminate" or "Diophantine" equations - equations that do not contain enough facts to give a specific answer but enough to reduce the answer to a definite type. These equations have led to the formulation of a system for numbers, commonly called the theory of numbers, that is regarded as the purest branch of present-day mathematics. Using his method, the possibility of determining a type of answer rather than a specific one to a given problem has allowed modern mathematicians to approach the properties of various kinds of whole numbers (such as odds, evens, primes and squares) with new insight. By then applying the use of infinite trains of numbers correlated through the Diophantine equation system, mathematicians have come to a new understanding of some of the basic rules which numbers follow.

Dirichlet, Peter Gustav Lejeune (1805–1859), was an influential German mathematician whose work in applying analytical techniques to mathematical theory resulted in the fundamental development of the theory of numbers. Also a physicist interested in dynamics, he knew many of the great scientists of his age and published a seminal book of some historic importance.

Dirichlet was born in Düren on 13 February 1805, the son of the town postmaster. Precociously interested in mathematics (it is said that at the age of 12 he used his pocket money to buy mathematical books), in 1819 he was sent to the University of Cologne - where his teachers included the physicist Georg Ohm - and completed his final examination at the very early age of 16. He was then sent to France, the country of all the contemporarily great mathematicians. Arriving at the Collège de France, in Paris, he attended lectures for little more than a year before being appointed tutor to the children of the renowned General Fay; as such, he was treated as one of the family and met many of the most prominent figures in French intellectual life, particularly Joseph Fourier (1768–1830). In 1825 Dirichlet presented his first paper to the French Academy of Sciences.

General Fay's death, however, led Dirichlet to return to Germany, where he took a research post at the University of Breslau (now Wrocław). Later he moved to Berlin, teaching initially at the Military Academy, but was soon appointed Professor also at the University of Berlin (still at the age of only 23). Dirichlet spent 27 years as a professor in Berlin, exerting a strong influence on German mathematics. He was an excellent teacher, despite being a modest and retiring man who shunned public appearances - unlike his lifelong friend Karl Jacobi (1804–1851). These two mathematicians stimulated and influenced each other, and when Jacobi's health forced him to move to Italy Dirichlet spent 18 months there with him, from 1843. Their presence caused a circle of leading German mathematicians to gather round them. In 1855, on the death of the great Karl Gauss, the University of Göttingen offered Dirichlet the prestigious vacant professorship. He accepted, but enjoyed the post for a mere three years, suffering a severe heart attack in the summer of 1858. He died the following spring, shortly after his wife had died.

Dirichlet's first interest was number theory, and much of his work was on this topic. His first paper, written in France, concerned Diophantine equations of the form $x^5 + y^5 = kz^5$. Using the methods of this paper, Adrien Legendre (1752–1833) succeeded only a few weeks later in appending a proof that Pierre de Fermat's famous equation ($x^n + y^n = z^n$) has no integral solution when $n = 5$.

Dirichlet was considerably influenced by Gauss, some of his early work being improvements on Gauss's proofs, but as his abilities developed, Dirichlet's intensive search for a general algebraic number theory substantially advanced this branch of mathematics with a number of very important papers. These included studies on quadratic forms, the number theory of irrational fields (including the integral complex numbers) and the theory of units. In 1837 Dirichlet presented his first paper on analytic number theory, giving a proof to the fundamental theorem that bears his name: any arithmetical series of integers $a \times n + b$, where a and b are relatively prime and $n = 0, 1, 2, 3 \ldots$, must include an infinite series of primes. Later papers included the analytical consideration of quadratic forms, studies of the theory of ideals and the convergence of Dirichlet series, and introduced the deceptively simple *Schubfachprinzip* (the "box principle") - a principle much used in the logic of modern number theory, which states: if in n boxes one distributes more than n objects, at least one box must contain more than one object.

In 1863 Dirichlet's *Vorlesungen über Zahlentheorie* was published posthumously by his friend and pupil Richard Dedekind (1831-1916). This summary of Dirichlet's work together with supplements by Dedekind is now considered one of the foundations on which the theory of ideals - the core of algebraic number theory - is based.

Alongside his theoretical work, Dirichlet also carried out a series of studies on analysis and applied mathematics. Important among these was an analysis of vibrating strings, in which he developed techniques now considered classic for the discernment of convergence. He also began to rewrite the vocabulary of mathematics. Whereas the mathematical concept of a function had previously been as an expression formulated in terms of mathematical symbols, Dirichlet introduced the modern concept of $y = f(x)$ as a correspondence that links each real x value with some unique y value denoted by $f(x)$.

Other papers included applications of Fourier series, a critique of Pierre Laplace's analysis of the stability of the Solar System, boundary values, and the first exact integration of the hydrodynamic equations.

Dirichlet's contributions to mathematics were both numerous and of different kinds; he made many important individual discoveries, but more important still was his method of approach - an essentially modern way of formulating or analysing mathematical problems, especially in number.

Dodgson, Charles Lutwidge (1832-1898), as Lewis Carroll is famous as the English author of *Alice's Adventures in Wonderland* and *Through the Looking Glass*, but was in fact also responsible in his publication of mathematical games and problems requiring the use of intelligent mental arithmetic for a general upsurge of interest in such pastimes. Several of his books of such puzzles suggest an awareness of the theory of sets - the basis on which most modern mathematical teaching is founded - that was being formulated by Dodgson's contemporary, Georg Cantor (1843-1918), but that did not become established until more than 20 years after Dodgson's death.

Dodgson was born in Daresbury, near Warrington, Cheshire, on 27 January 1832, the eldest son in a parish priest's family of eleven children. An acutely shy child with a pronounced stammer, he was educated at home until he reached the age of 12. He was then sent to Rugby School where, under the watchful eye of the Anglican prelate Archibald Tait (1811-1882), he displayed a natural talent for mathematics and an aptitude for divinity. He was awarded a place at Christ Church, Oxford, in 1850 and after taking courses in mathematics and classics, received his BA in 1854. The following year he was appointed Lecturer in Mathematics, and six years later he was ordained deacon in the Church of England (although he never in fact became a priest). Despite a great love of children - and particularly little girls - possibly also as a result of his shyness, Dodgson never married. Instead, he poured all his enthusiasm into writing and telling stories to the children of his friends. Under the pseudonym Lewis Carroll, he was eventually persuaded to publish two stories he had composed to amuse one little girl he especially favoured, Alice Liddell. *Alice's Adventures in Wonderland* (1865) and *Through the Looking Glass* (1872) became immensely popular, hailed as classics in the world of children's fiction. A life Fellow of Christ Church, Dodgson gave up his lectureship in 1881 and concentrated on writing, both of mathematics and of children's fantasy. After the *Alice* books, however, he never again achieved such popularity. He died at Guildford, Surrey, on 14 January 1898.

Dodgson's enjoyment of mathematics and his affection for children are both reflected in the papers he wrote on the teaching of mathematics for the young. He was particularly interested in the use of number games, and made a compilation of a wide range of puzzles and brain teasers covering all aspects of the subject (including geometry, algebra and graph work) that call for general intelligence to solve the problems rather than specialized knowledge. Number games were not a new idea (they probably originated with the ancient Greeks), but some time around the fifteenth century they had re-emerged; the Victorian society of the nineteenth century was ripe for them to regain considerable popularity. Dodgson saw their potential as teaching aids, and wrote about them as such, publishing several books including *Pillow Problems*, *The Game of Logic* and *A Tangled Tale*. The chessboard featured in some of these games. With the publisher Edouard Lucas (1868-1938), Dodgson was responsible for the continued revival of such puzzles during the latter half of the 1800s.

Nevertheless, Dodgson also wrote a considerable number of serious and advanced papers on mathematical subjects (all of which Queen Victoria was apparently dumbfounded to receive, having ordered the author's complete works after reading *Alice in Wonderland*). He produced lengthy general syllabus textbooks, quite a few books on historical mathematics (particularly on Euclid and his geometry) and a number of specialized papers (such as his "*Condensation of Determinants*").

He also showed a keen interest in photography, and has been described as having an exceptional flair for it.

E

Eilenberg, Samuel (1913-   ), is a Polish-born American mathematician whose research in the field of algebraic topology led to considerable development in the theory of cohomology. He is also well known for his work in computer mathematics.

Eilenberg was born on 30 September 1913 in Warsaw, where he grew up and completed his education, gaining his master's degree in 1934 and his PhD in mathematics two years later at the University of Warsaw. He then emigrated to the United States where, in 1940, he joined the staff of the University of Michigan as an Instructor; by 1946 he was Associate Professor of Mathematics. In that year he was appointed Professor of Mathematics at the University of Indiana, where he remained for three years. After a series of visiting professorships - some in the United States, some in Europe and the Indian subcontinent - Eilenberg became Professor of Mathematics at Columbia University, New York, where he remained for the rest of his academic life.

Eilenberg's main field of work has been that of algebraic topology - a subject on which, with N. Steenrod, he wrote a successful advanced textbook. Topology is the study of figures and shapes that retain their essential proportions even when twisted or stretched; in topology, therefore, a square is (topologically) equivalent to any closed plane figure - such as a circle - and a cube is even (topologically) equivalent to a sphere. Since Henri Poincaré first developed the subject systematically in a series of papers written between 1895 and 1905, topology theory has been elaborated at a rapid rate, and has considerably influenced other branches of mathematics. Eilenberg has carried out valuable work in the area of topology which, although generally known as the algebraic topology, is sometimes called "combinatorial" topology and which is distinctive for the extensive use of algebraic techniques to solve topological problems. The basis on which algebraic topology is founded is homology theory - the study of closed curves, closed surfaces and similar geometric arrangements in a given topological space. Much of Eilenberg's work has been concerned with a modification of homology theory called cohomology theory; cohomology groups have properties similar to homology groups but have several important advantages. It is possible to define a "product" of cohomology classes by means of which, together with the addition of cohomology classes, the direct sum of the cohomology classes of all dimensions becomes a ring (the cohomology ring). This is a richer structure than is available for homology groups, and allows finer results. Various other very complicated algebraic operations using cohomology classes can lead to results not provable in any other way - the Poincaré duality theorem, for example, is considerably easier to state precisely if cohomology groups are used.

Eisenhart, Luther Pfahler (1876-1965), was an American theoretical geometrist whose early work was concerned with the properties of surfaces and their deformation; later he became interested in Riemann geometry from which he attempted to develop his own geometry theory. The author of several books detailing his results, he also wrote two books on historical topics.

Eisenhart was born on 13 January 1876 in York, Pennsylvania, the second son of the dentist who was also the founder of the Edison Electric Light and York Telephone Company.

Educated locally, and to a high standard, he attended Gettysburg College (in southern Pennsylvania) from 1892 to 1896 where, for the last two years, he studied mathematics independently of his other work through guided reading. After a year's teaching at the College he went to Johns Hopkins University, Baltimore, in 1897, to carry out graduate studies, obtaining his PhD there three years later. He then began his life's work in mathematical research at Princeton University, retiring from there in 1945 after 45 years' successful study and teaching. Twenty years later it was there he died, on 28 October 1965.

One of Eisenhart's major achievements was to relate his theories regarding differential geometry to studies bordering on the topological. At the age of 25 he wrote one of the first characterizations of a sphere as defined in terms of differential geometry (the paper had the somewhat daunting title "*Surfaces whose first and second forms are respectively the second and first forms of another surface*"). For the next 20 years he continued to develop his research, concentrating particularly on the subject of surface deformation. The theory of the deformation of surfaces was a part of the study of the properties of surfaces and systems of surfaces that was an especially popular area for geometrical research in continental Europe at that time, but Eisenhart was (apparently) the only person in the United States to devote his attention to it. It was he, nevertheless, who managed to formulate a unifying principle to the theory. The deformation of a surface involves the congruence of lines connecting a point and its image. Eisenhart's contribution was to realize that in all known cases, the intersections of these surfaces with the given surface and its image form a set of curves which have special properties. He wrote his account of the theory in 1923, in *Transformations of Surface*.

His work on surfaces led him then to study Riemann geometry - in which the properties of geometric space are considered locally rather than in one overall framework for the whole space. Eisenhart developed a geometry analogous to Riemann geometry, which he called non-Riemann geometry (although the term has since been used for several other forms of geometry), and wrote "*Fields of Parallel Vectors in the Geometry of Paths*" in 1922; it was followed by "*Fields of Parallel Vectors in a Riemannian Geometry*" (1925) and "*Riemannian Geometry*" (1926).

Interested in history, Eisenhart also wrote several other papers, including "*Lives of Princeton Mathematicians*" (1931), "*Plan for a University of Discoverers*" (1947) and "*The Preface to Historic Philadelphia*" (1953).

Erlang, Agner Krarup (1878-1929), was a Danish mathematician who, although he was extremely knowledgeable in many fields, might never have become famous if he had not become scientific adviser - and leader - of the Copenhagen Telephone Company's research laboratory. His application of the theory of probabilities to problems connected with telephone traffic made his name known all over the world, and the "erlang" is now the unit of traffic flow. A meticulous mathematician, he published many influential papers and was also responsible for constructing a device to measure alternating electric current.

Erlang was born on 1 January 1878 in the village of Lønborg, near Tarm, in Jylland (Jutland), the son of a schoolmaster. Completing his education he studied mathematics and natural sciences at the University of Copenhagen, obtaining his MA in mathematics in 1901 (with astronomy, physics and chemistry as secondary subjects). On leaving the University he worked as a teacher in various schools. During this time he won the award for solving the mathematical prize problem set by the University of Copenhagen which, in that year, was concered with Huygens's solution of infinitesimal problems. In 1908, at the age of 30, Erlang was appointed scientific collaborator and leader of the Laboratory of the Copenhagen Telephone Company, where he remained for the rest of his life. He died suddenly on 3 February 1929, at the age of only 51. Single all his life, he devoted almost all his time to scientific study. He had a large library and collected mathematical, physical and astronomical works in particular; his knowledge in these subjects was extensive, but he was also well versed in philosophy, history and poetry. A modest man with an original mind, he was of an extremely kind and friendly disposition.

At the Laboratory of the Copenhagen Telephone Company, Erlang came under the influence of Franz Johanssen, the Managing Director of the company and another mathematician who had himself, in the year before Erlang joined, published two short essays in which he dealt with problems of telephone traffic flow - such as congestion and waiting time - and in which he introduced probability calculations. Erlang took to the work immediately. Within a year he had published his first paper on the subject, in which he was able to arrive at an exact solution to another problem posed by Johanssen previously. And over the next few years, Erlang published a number of other papers on the theory of telephone traffic which, because of their meticulous precision, became pioneer works.

It is rare for a telephone caller to get the engaged tone for any reason other than that the receiver at the call's destination is already in use. Yet it is possible through the links of the connection – the many coding selectors and digit selectors – at any one time for the call to find a selector already in use, which would automatically trip in the engaged tone. The fact that this is so rare is a result of the provision of switches in numbers based on the calculation that not more than one call in 500 at each selecting stage will fail because the equipment is engaged. To fulfil this standard, rules determining the amount of traffic to be carried per selector have been established by every telephone authority and company, following Erlang's formulae. Especially important is his formula for the probability of barred access in busy-signal systems – the so-called B-formula – and his formulae for the probability of delay and for the mean waiting time in waiting time systems. These formulae may be considered the most important within the theory of telephone traffic.

The erlang is the unit of telephone traffic flow; it is defined as "the number of calls originated during a period, multiplied by the average holding time of a call, expressed in terms of the period: one erlang is therefore equivalent to the traffic flow in one circuit continuously occupied".

Erlang also published studies of other mathematical problems. His work on logarithms and other numerical tables, in which he attempted to reduce the mean error to the lowest figure possible, resulted in the compilation of four- and five-figure tables that are now considered among the best available.

As the leader of the Laboratory of the Telephone Company, Erlang also investigated several assorted physio-technical problems that cropped up. In particular, he constructed a measuring bridge to meter alternating current (the so-called Erlang complex compensator) which was a considerable improvement on earlier apparatus of similar function. Of equal significance were his investigations into telephone transformers and telephone cable theory.

Euclid (*fl.c.* 300 BC) was an ancient Greek mathematician whose works, and the style in which they were presented, formed the basis for all mathematical thought and expression for the following 2,000 years (although they were not entirely without fault). He also wrote books on

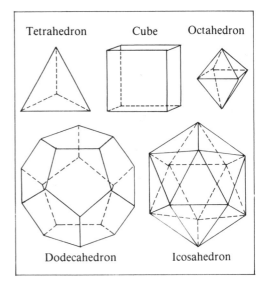

The Platonic solids are the only regular convex polyhedra. A tetrahedron is made up of four equilateral triangular faces, a cube is six squares, an octahedron is eight equilateral triangles, a dodecahedron is twelve regular pentagons and an icosahedron is twenty equilateral triangles. They are the basis for Euclidean solid geometry.

other scientific topics, but these have survived the passage of the centuries only fragmentarily or not at all.

Very little indeed is known about Euclid. No record is preserved of his date or place of birth, his education, or even his date or place of death. The influence of Plato (*c.*420–340 BC) is certainly detectable in his work – so Euclid must either have been contemporary or later. Some commentators have suggested that he attended Plato's Academy in Athens but, if so, it is likely to have been after Plato's death. In any case, it has been established that Euclid went to the recently-founded city of Alexandria (now in Egypt) in around 300 BC and set up his own school of mathematics there. Fifty years later, however, Euclid's disciple Apollonius of Perga was said to have been leading the school for some considerable time; it seems very possible, therefore, that Euclid died in around 270 BC.

Euclid's mathematical works survived in almost complete form because they were translated first into Arabic, then into Latin; from both of these they were then translated into other European languages. He employed two main styles of presentation: the synthetic (in which one proceeds from the known to the unknown via logical steps) and the analytical (in which one posits the unknown and works towards it from the known, again via logical steps). In his major work, *The Elements*, Euclid used the synthetic approach, which suited the subject matter so perfectly that the method became the standard procedure for scientific investigation and exposition for millennia afterwards. The strictly logical arrangement demanding the absolute minimum of assumption, and the omission of all superfluous material, is one of the great strengths of *The Elements*, in which Euclid incorporated and developed the work of previous mathematicians as well as including his own many innovations. The presentation was one of extreme clarity and he was rigorous, too, about the actual detail of the mathematical work, attempting to provide proofs for every one of the theorems.

The Elements is divided into 13 books. The first six deal with plane geometry (points, lines, triangles, squares, parallelograms, circles, and so on), and includes hypotheses such as "Pythagoras's Theorem" which Euclid generalized. Books 7 to 9 are concerned with arithmetic and number theory. In Book 10 Euclid treats irrational numbers. And Books 11 to 13 discuss solid geometry, ending with the five "Platonic solids" (the tetrahedron, octahedron, cube, icosahedron and dodecahedron).

Euclid favoured the analytical mode of presentation in writing his other important mathematical work, the *Treasury of Analysis*. This comprised three parts, now known as *The Data*, *On Divisions of Figures* and *Porisms*.

Euclid's geometry formed the basis for mathematical study during the next 2,000 years. It was not until the nineteenth century that a different form of geometry was even considered: "accidentally" discovered by Saccheri in 1733, non-Euclidean geometry was not in any way defined until Nikolai Lobachevsky (in the 1820s), János Bolyai (in the 1830s) and Bernhard Riemann (in the 1850s) examined the subject. It is difficult to see, therefore, how Euclid's contribution to the science of mathematics could have been more fundamental than it was.

Euler, Leonhard (or Leonard) (1707-1783), was a Swiss mathematician whose power of mental calculation was prodigious; so great was his capacity for concentrating on mathematical computation that even when he became totally blind towards the end of his life, he was able to continue his work without pause. With such ability and with true scientific curiosity, Euler - a brilliant teacher - expanded the scope of virtually all the known branches of mathematics,

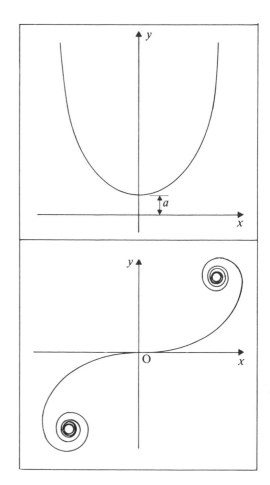

A catenary (top) is a transcendental curve that may be represented by the equation $y = (a/2)(e^{x/a} + e^{-x/a})$, where a is a constant and e is Euler's number (2.718 ...). Euler's spiral (above) is sometimes alternatively called a clothoid.

devising and formulating a considerable number of theorems and rules now named after him. He also enlarged mathematical notation.

Euler was born on 15 April 1707 in Basle, where he grew up and was educated. At the University of Basle he studied under Johann Bernoulli (of the famous scientific family), obtaining his master's degree precociously at the age of 16, in 1723. He then found it impossible - perhaps because he was so young - to gain a faculty position. Four years later, however, he was invited by his great friend and contemporary Daniel Bernoulli (nephew of Johann) to join him in Russia, at St Petersburg (now Leningrad). Euler duly arrived there, spent three years at the Naval College, and then (in 1730) was appointed Professor of Physics at the Academy of Sciences. When Bernoulli returned home in 1733, Euler succeeded him as Professor of Mathematics. Shortly afterwards, through looking at the Sun during his astronomical studies, he lost the sight of his right eye. In 1741 he travelled to Berlin at the request of the Emperor, Frederick the Great, and in 1744 became Director of the Berlin Academy of Sciences. He remained there until 1766 when the Empress Catherine the Great recalled him to St Petersburg to become Director of the Academy of Sciences there. Soon after his return he lost the sight of his other eye, through cataracts, but retained his office, competently carrying out all his duties and responsibilities for another 15 years or more, until he died on 18 September 1783.

Euler contributed to all the classic areas of mathematics, although his most innovatory work was in the field of analysis, in which he considerably improved mathematical methodology and the rigour of presentation. He advanced the study of trigonometry, in particular developing spherical trigonometry. Following the analytical work of his friend Daniel Bernoulli, Euler demonstrated the significance of the coefficients of trigonometric expansions; Euler's number (e, as it is now called) has various useful theoretical properties and is also used in the summation of particular series.

Euler also studied algebraic series and demonstrated the importance of convergence. He applied algebraic methods instead of geometric ones (as used by Newton, Galileo and Kepler previously), and improved differential and integral calculus, bringing them virtually to their modern forms. He used constant coefficients in the integration of linear differential equations and originated the calculus of partial differentials. And he became very interested in applying mathematical - and particularly analytical - principles to mechanics, especially celestial mechanics.

After his return to Russia in 1766 Euler carried out further research into the motion and positions of the Moon, and the gravitational relationships between the Moon, the Sun and the Earth. His resulting work on tidal fluctuations took him into the realm of fluid mechanics, in which he successfully analysed motion in a perfectly compressible fluid. Further astronomical work brought him an award of £300 from the British government for his development of theorems useful in navigation (he had been a member of the Royal Society since 1746).

A prolific author of influential papers detailing his methods and his results, and a teacher of outstanding authority, Euler made a number of innovations both in mathematical concept - such as Euler's constant, Euler's equations, Euler's line and Euler's variables - and in mathematical notation - he was responsible, among other things, for the use of π, e in natural (Naperian) logarithms, i for imaginary numbers, and Σ for summation. Other interests of his included acoustics and optics.

F

Feller, William (1906–1970), was a Yugoslavian-born American mathematician largely responsible for making the theory of probability accessible to students of subjects outside the field of mathematics through his two-volume textbook on the subject. He was also interested in the theory of limits, but it was his work on probability theory that brought him widespread recognition.

Feller was born on 7 July 1906 in Zagreb, where he grew up, was educated, and attended the university, earning his BA in 1925. He then continued his studies at the University of Göttingen, where he was awarded a PhD in 1926. He moved to Kiel University, and in 1929 was put in charge of the laboratory of applied mathematics there. Four years later, Feller went to the University of Stockholm, where he served as a Research Associate until 1939, working as a consultant for economists, biologists and others interested in probability theory.

At the outbreak of World War II in 1939, Feller emigrated to the United States. His first job was as executive editor of *Mathematical Reviews*, but he was soon appointed to the simultaneous post of Associate Professor at Brown University. In 1945 - by then a naturalized United States citizen - he was made Professor of Mathematics at Cornell University, New York, and in 1950 Feller became Eugene Higgins Professor of Mathematics at Princeton University, a post he held until his death in 1970.

Feller had always been fascinated by the study of chance fluctuations. He came to the conclusion, early on, that the traditional emphasis placed on averages meant that insufficient attention was paid to random fluctuations which could bear significant impact on processes under investigation. His serious study of probability theory began soon after his arrival at the University of Stockholm. Much of his effort focused on the nature and use of Markov processes (a mathematical description of random changes in a system which, for instance, can occur in either of two states). Feller used semigroups to develop a general theory of Markov processes, and was able to demonstrate the applicability of this tool to subjects in which probability theory had not usually previously been employed, for example in the study of genetics. A strong advocate of the renewal method, Feller's preoccupation with problems of methodology greatly influenced the style of his book. The work – on the introduction to and the applications of probability theory – was published in two volumes, the first in 1950 and the second in 1966, and received considerable acclaim. It may fairly be said to have been significant to the further development of study on the subject.

Feller was also keenly interested in limit theory, in which he first formulated the law of the iterated logarithm; he made a real contribution to the study of the central limit theorem.

Fermat, Pierre de (1601–1675), was a French lawyer and magistrate for whom mathematics was an absorbing hobby. He contributed greatly to the development of number theory, analytical geometry and calculus, carried out important research in probability theory and in optics, and was at the same time a competent classical scholar. Yet it is thanks only to his letters to various scientists and theoreticians that many of his accomplishments did not vanish into obscurity.

Born on 20 August 1601 in Beaumont de Lomagne, Fermat obtained a classical education locally. Between the ages of 20 and 30 he was in Bordeaux, possibly at the University of Toulouse. It was not, however, until he was 30 that he gained his bachelor's degree in civil law from the University of Orléans, set up a legal practice in Toulouse, and became Commissioner of Requests for the local parliament. In that parliament he was gradually promoted, gaining the high rank of King's Counsellor in 1648, an office he retained until 1665. In 1652, however, he suffered a severe attack of the plague after which he devoted much of his time to mathematics, being particularly concerned with reconstructing some of the missing texts of the ancient Greeks such as Euclid and Apollonius. Curiously, he refused to publish any of his achievements, which were considerable despite the occasionally eccentric style in which they were presented. In increasing isolation, therefore, from the rest of the European mathematical community, Fermat lived to an old age. He died in Castres on 12 January 1675.

While Fermat was in Bordeaux, he became fascinated by the work of the mathematician François Viète (1540–1603); it was from then that most of his mathematical achievements were attained. And it was through Viète's influence that Fermat came to regard number theory as a "lingua franca" between geometry and arithmetic, and went on to make many significant discoveries in the field. Himself responsible for the development of number theory as an independent branch of mathematics, Fermat's work on the theory was later revived by Leonhard Euler (1707–1783) and continued to stimulate further research well into the nineteenth century. In 1657 Fermat published a series of problems as challenges to other mathematicians, in the form of theorems to be proved. All of them have since been proved – except "Fermat's Last Theorem", which states that there is no solution in whole integers to the equation $x^n + y^n = z^n$, where n is greater than 2.

Fermat's technique in much of his work was "reduction analysis", a reversible process in which a particular problem is "reduced" until it can be seen to be part of a group of problems for which solutions are already known. Using this procedure, Fermat turned his attention to geometry. Unfortunately, analytical geometry was developed simultaneously both by Fermat (in letters written before 1636) and by the great René Descartes (who published his *Géométrie* in 1637). There followed a protracted and bitter dispute over priority. The discipline permitted the use of equations to describe geometric figures, and Fermat demonstrated that a second degree equation could be used to describe seven "irreducible forms", each of which gave complete descriptions for different curves (such as parabolas and ellipses). He tried to extend this system into three dimensions to describe solids (in 1643), but was unsuccessful in the attempt beyond the establishment (in 1650) of the algebraic foundation for solid analytical geometry.

In 1636 he turned to the concept of "infinitesimals" and applied it to equations of quadrature, the determination of the maxima and minima of curves, and the method of finding the tangent to a curve. All his work in these fields was superseded within 50 years through the development of calculus by Isaac Newton and Gottfried Leibniz; Newton did, however, acknowledge the importance of Fermat's work in the evolution of his own ideas.

Correspondence between Fermat and Blaise Pascal (1623–1662) resulted in the foundation of probability theory. Their joint conclusion was that if the probability of two independent events is respectively p and q, the probability of both occurring is pq.

In the field of optics, yet another disagreement with Descartes - this time on his Law of Refraction - led Fermat to investigate it mathematically. Ultimately obliged to confirm the Law - but incidentally discovering the fact that light travels more slowly through denser mediums - Fermat also derived what is now known as "Fermat's Principle", which states that light travels by the path of least duration, after making a study of the transmission of light through materials with different refractive indices.

Fibonacci, Leonardo (or Leonardo of Pisa) (*c*.1180-*c*.1250), was a mathematician of medieval Pisa whose writings were influential in introducing and popularizing the Indo-Arabic numeral system, and whose work in algebra, geometry and theoretical mathematics was far in advance of the contemporary European standards.

Fibonacci was born in Pisa in about 1180, the son of a member of the government of the Republic of Pisa. When Fibonacci was 12 years old, his father was made administrator of Pisa's trading colony in Algeria, and it was there - in a town now called Bougie - that he was taught the art of calculating, using the commercial north African medium of Indo-Arabic numerals. His teacher, who remains completely unknown, seems to have imparted to him not only an excellently practical and well-rounded fundamental grounding in mathematics, but also a true scientific curiosity.

Having achieved maturity, Fibonacci travelled extensively, both for business and for pleasure, spending time in Italy, Syria, Egypt, Greece and elsewhere. Wherever he went he observed and analysed the arithmetical systems used in local commerce, studying through discussion and argument with native scholars of the countries he visited. He returned to Pisa in about the year 1200 and began his mathematical writings. Little more is known of him, although in 1225 he won a mathematical tournament in the presence of the Holy Roman Emperor Frederick II at the court of Pisa. A marble tablet dated 1240 appears to refer to him as being awarded an annual pension following his valuable accountancy services to the state. He is assumed to have died in Pisa in about 1250.

Two years after finally settling in Pisa, Fibonacci produced his most famous book, *Liber abaci* (The Book of the Calculator). In four parts, and revised by him a quarter of a century later (in 1228), it was a thorough treatise on algebraic methods and problems in which he strongly advocated the introduction of the

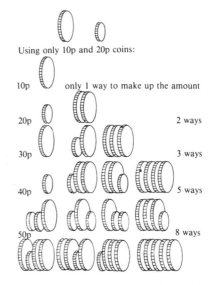

Using only 10p and 20p coins:

10p   only 1 way to make up the amount

20p   2 ways

30p   3 ways

40p   5 ways

50p   8 ways

Fibonacci numbers form a series in which, after the first and second terms (which are both 1), each term is the sum of the two preceding ones. Thus the series runs 1, 1, 2, 3, 5, 8, 13, ... It can be generated in various ways; for instance, the various numbers of ways of making up 10p, 20p, 30p, 40p, 50p, and so on using only 10p and 20p coins.

Indo-Arabic numeral system, comprising the figures 1 to 9, and the innovation of the "zephirum" - the figure 0 (zero). Dealing with operations in whole numbers systematically, he also proposed the idea of a bar (solidus) for fractions, and went on to develop rules for converting fraction factors into the sum of unit factors. (However, his expression of fractions followed the Arabic practice - on the *left* of the relevant integral.) At the end of the first part of the book, he presented tables for multiplication, prime numbers and factoring numbers. In the second part, he demonstrated mathematical applications to commercial transactions. In part three he gave many examples of recreational mathematical problems of the type enjoyed today, leading up to a thesis on series from which, in turn, he derived what is now called the Fibonacci series. This is a sequence in which each term after the first two is the sum of the two terms immediately preceding it - 1, 1, 2, 3, 5, 8, 13, 21, ... for example - and which has been found to have many significant and interesting properties. And in the final part of the book Fibonacci, a student of Euclid, applied the algebraic method. The *Liber abaci* remained a standard text for the next two centuries.

In 1220 he published *Practica geometriae*, a book on geometry that was of fundamental significance to future studies of the subject, and that (to some commentators, at least) seems to be based on a work of Euclid now lost. In it, Fibonacci used algebraic methods to solve many arithmetical and geometrical problems. In *Flos* (Flower), published four years later, he considered indeterminate problems in a way that had not properly been carried out since the work of Diophantus, and again demonstrated Euclidean methodology combined with techniques of Chinese and Arabic origin (learned during his travels many years before) in solving determinate problems. In both *Liber quadratorum* (The Book of Squares) and in a separate letter to the philosopher Theodorus, Fibonacci dealt with some problems set by John of Palermo (one of which was the one he solved in front of the Emperor); his treatments show unusual mathematical skill and originality.

The complete works of Fibonacci were edited in the nineteenth century by B. Boncompagni, and published in two volumes under the title *Scritti di Leonardo Pisano*.

Fisher, Ronald Aylmer (1890-1962), was a British mathematical biologist whose work in the field of statistics resulted in the formulation of a methodology in which the analysis of results obtained using small samples produced interpretations that were objective and valid overall. His work revolutionized research methods in many areas, and found immediate and widespread use particularly in genetics and agriculture.

Fisher was born in London on 17 February 1890. He attended Stanmore Park and Harrow schools before going to Gonville and Caius College, Cambridge, in 1909. He graduated in 1912, having specialized in mathematics and theoretical physics, and then spent an additional year at Cambridge studying statistical mechanics and researching into the theory of errors. The next six years were spent in various occupations - his poor eyesight made him unacceptable for military service during World War I - and he worked in an investment brokerage, as a teacher and even as a farm labourer. At the end of the war, however, Fisher obtained a post at the Rothamstead Experimental Station, where he formed a one-man statistics department whose main job was to analyse a huge backlog of experimental data that had built up over more than 60 years. It was while at Rothamstead that he evolved many improvements to traditional statistical methods. His textbook on the subject, which appeared in 1925, was a landmark.

At Rothamstead, Fisher was able also to indulge in his second scientific passion, genetics; he bred poultry, mice, snails and other creatures, and in his papers on the subject contributed to the contemporary understanding of genetic dominance. As a result, in 1933 he was appointed to the Galton Chair of Eugenics at University College, London. During World War II, however, his department was (ironically) evacuated to Rothamstead, and eventually disbanded. Fisher then became Balfour Professor of Genetics at the University of Cambridge in 1943. He was knighted nine years later. Officially retiring from Cambridge in 1957, he actually stayed on there until 1959 when a successor was found and when, following a first visit to the Mathematical Statistics Division of the Commonwealth Scientific and Industrial Research Organisation in Adelaide, Fisher emigrated to Australia. He died in Adelaide on 29 July 1962.

Elected a Fellow of the Royal Society in 1929, Fisher was awarded their Royal Medal in 1938, their Darwin Medal in 1948, and their Copley Medal in 1955.

Fisher's early work concerned the development of methods for the determination of the exact distributions of several statistical functions, such as the regression coefficient and the discriminant function. He improved the Helmut-Pearson χ^2- and Gosset's Z-functions, modifying the latter to the now familiar t-test for significance. He evolved the rules for "decision-making" that are now used almost automatically, and are based on the percentage deviation of the results of an experiment from the "Null Hypothesis" (which assumes that events occur on an exclusively random basis). A deviation of between 95 and 99 per cent represented only a suggestive likelihood that the Null Hypothesis was incorrect; a deviation in excess of 99 per cent indicated strongly that this was so.

Other statistical methods that Fisher originated include the analysis of variance, the analysis of co-variance, multivariate analysis, contingency tables, and more. All his mathematical methods were developed for further application, for example to the study of genetics, evolution and natural selection.

One of Fisher's first studies concerned the importance of dominant genes. A confirmed eugenicist, he looked on the study of human blood as an essential factor in his research. The department he established at the Galton Laboratories to investigate blood types made significant contributions to the final elucidation of the inheritance of Rhesus blood groups.

Fisher's methods have since been extended to

virtually every academic field in which statistical analysis can be applied.

Fontana, Niccolo (*c.*1499–1557). *See* Tartaglia.

Forsyth, Andrew Russell (1858–1942), was a British mathematician whose facility with languages enabled him first of all to keep pace with, and even surpass, mathematical developments elsewhere in contemporary Europe, and then to translate such developments into English for the benefit of British mathematicians. Having done so – in an extremely important book – he was apparently unable then to maintain his precedence. Nevertheless, it was through his influence that in Britain the subject of the theory of functions dominated mathematical research for many years.

Forsyth was born in Glasgow on 18 June 1858, and obtained his initial education at Liverpool College. From there he won a scholarship to Trinity College, Cambridge, which he entered in 1877; lectures given there by Arthur Cayley (1821–1895) had a profound influence upon him and upon his general approach to mathematics. A dissertation by Forsyth published in the *Proceedings* of the Royal Society then led to the offer of a "prize" Fellowship at Trinity College, but no subsequent offer of a faculty position was forthcoming so in 1882 he took up the Chair of Mathematics at Liverpool College instead. Two years later, however, he returned to Trinity College as Lecturer, and remained there for the next 26 years. During that time he wrote several books and translated the works of others – his crucial *Theory of Functions* appeared in 1893 – and became considerably involved with the day-to-day administration of Cambridge University. In 1895 he was appointed to the Sadlerian Chair of Pure Mathematics.

In 1910, however, at the age of 52, Forsyth left Cambridge. Much of 1912 he spent lecturing in India, returning to England the following year to become Chief Professor of Mathematics at the Imperial College, London. Determined to renew his study of languages he retired early (in 1923), but within two years had reverted to his mathematical interests. After the publication of his last mathematical work in 1935, however, he again returned to linguistic studies. He died in London on 2 June 1942.

During his lifetime Forsyth received many honours and awards. A member of the Royal Society since 1886, he was presented with its Royal Medal in 1897.

Forsyth's early work was to systematize and develop the theory of double theta functions. He succeeded in demonstrating that such functions are related to the square roots of quintic and sextic polynomials in the same way as single theta functions are related to the square roots of cubic and quadratic polynomials. He also formulated a theorem that generalized a large number of identities between double theta functions; because this work was also carried out independently yet simultaneously by Henry Smith (1826–1883), the theorem is now called the Smith–Forsyth Theorem.

Forsyth's *Theory of Functions* was intended as an advanced text that would introduce the main strands of continental mathematical study to British mathematicians who were then tending to lag behind in terms of development and innovative creativity. In fact, more importantly, the book not only served to introduce the work of the European schools, but also brought together the work of all the various schools in a single volume – and as such was of considerable importance not merely in Britain but also in continental Europe, where it also achieved success in translation. In Britain, the book led to the introduction of concepts such as symbolic variant theory, Weierstrassian elliptic functions, and many more, and completely changed the nature of mathematical thinking. The developments that the book stimulated were rapid and, sometimes, fundamental, and sadly left Forsyth – who only five years previously had been publicly acknowledged as the most brilliant pure mathematician in the country – far behind. His skills belonged to older methods. During his later years he wrote a number of books (some on ordinary, linear and partial differential equations, one or two on Einstein's General Theory of Relativity) but he never again achieved the spectacular acclaim he had once enjoyed.

Fourier, Jean Baptiste Joseph (1768–1830), was a French mathematical physicist whose particular interest was to try to describe the transfer of heat in purely mathematical terms. The formulation of equations in order to achieve this was a complex task that necessitated the development of new mathematical tools, and he was responsible in this way for the discovery of the Fourier Series and the Fourier Integral Theorem, which have together led to the evolution of the modern process now known as harmonic analysis.

Fourier was born in Auxerre on 21 March 1768, the son of a tailor. Orphaned when very young, he obtained his education at the local military academy, and it was there that his interest in mathematics was first aroused. He then went on to a Benedictine school in St Bênoitsur-Loire, but returned to Auxerre at the outbreak of the French Revolution and taught at his old school. He was arrested in 1794, only to be released a few months later after the execution of Robespierre. He next studied in Paris at the École Normale for a short period, and in 1795 was made an assistant lecturer at the École Polytechnique under Joseph Lagrange (1736-1818) and Gaspard Monge (1746-1818).

In 1798 Fourier was selected to accompany Napoleon on his Egyptian campaign, and there conducted a variety of diplomatic affairs. Returning to France in 1801 he was appointed Prefect of Isère in the south of the country. During this period he continued his mathematical studies on a part-time basis. Napoleon conferred the title of Baron on Fourier in 1808, and later made him a Count. Fourier was then made Prefect of the *département* of Rhône, but resigned the post during Napoleon's Hundred Days in protest against the activities of the régime. Soon afterwards he obtained a post at the Bureau of Statistics and was able to devote all his energies to mathematics. He was elected to the French Academy of Sciences and made joint Secrétaire Perpétuel with Georges Cuvier in 1822; he was also elected to the Academie Française and made a foreign member of the Royal Society. He died on 4 May 1830 as an indirect result of a disease he had contracted while serving in Egypt.

One of Fourier's most important contributions to both mathematics and physics was the use of linear partial differential equations in the study of physical phenomena as boundary-value problems. In order to comprehend and explain the conduction of heat under conditions of different temperature gradients, and in materials with different shapes and conductivities, Fourier developed what is now called Fourier's Theorem. This enables the equation for the description of heat diffusion to be broken up into a series of simpler (trigonometric) equations, the sum of which equals the original. The Fourier series can be used to describe complex periodic (that is, repeating) functions, and so can be applied to many branches of mathematical physics. Light, sound, and other wave-like forms of energy can be studied using Fourier's Theorem, and a developed version of this method is now called harmonic analysis. At the time, such was the creative brilliance of Fourier in using linear partial differential equations to this end, however, that for the following century or more non-linear differential equations were hardly used at all in mathematical physics.

Fourier contributed to other areas of mathematics as well; for example, he laid the groundwork for the later development of dimensional analysis and linear programming. Fascinated since the age of 16 by the theory of equations, Fourier's work at the Bureau of Statistics also stimulated him to investigate the probability theory and the theory of errors.

Fraenkel, Abraham Adolf (1891-1965), was a German-born Israeli mathematician who is chiefly remembered for his research and perception in set theory, and for his many textbooks.

Fraenkel was born on 11 February 1891 in Munich, where he grew up, was educated, and first attended University. He also studied at the Universities of Marburg, Berlin and Breslau (now Wrocław). In 1916 he became a Lecturer at the University of Marburg, and in 1922 was appointed to the position of Professor. Six years later, he taught for a year at the University of Kiel before going to Israel where, from 1929 to 1959, he taught at the Hebrew University of Jerusalem. He was a fervent Zionist, and throughout his life showed a deep interest and concern in the Jewish culture, becoming involved in many social and educational activities. Fraenkel died in Jerusalem on 15 October 1965.

From early on, Fraenkel was interested in the axiomatic foundations of mathematical theories, and some of his first work comprised an investigation into the axiomatics (universally accepted facts) of Hensel's p-adic numbers and into the theory of rings. He then became interested in the theory of sets (on which, in 1919, he wrote *Einleitung in die Mengenlehre*, a book that was well received and was reprinted several times).

Fraenkel became very involved with set theory as it had been formulated in 1908, in the axiomatic system put forward by Ernst Zermelo (1871-1953). The axioms, however, included the hitherto unexplained notion of a "definite property", and Fraenkel determined he should be the first of the several mathematicians to succeed in the attempt to overcome this difficulty.

He put forward his own proposed solution in 1922. Instead of Zermelo's notion of definite property, Fraenkel suggested the use of a notion of function introduced by definition. He also omitted entirely Zermelo's axiom of subsets, which stated that if a property E is definite in a set m, there is a subset consisting of those elements x of m for which $E(x)$ is true. To replace this axiom, Fraenkel said instead that if m is a set and ϕ and Ψ are functions, there are subsets m_E and $m_{E'}$ consisting of those elements x of m for which $\phi(x)$ is an element of $\Psi(x)$ and $\Phi(x)$ is not an element of $\Psi(x)$ respectively. Using this Axiom, Fraenkel showed that the axiom of choice – also first devised in axiomatic form by Ernst Zermelo, in 1904 – can be treated independently by referring to an infinite set of objects that are not sets themselves. It turned out to be extremely complicated to prove this without referring to an external assumption. (It was not, in fact, successfully accomplished until 1963, when P. Cohen proved it for a revised system combining the work of Zermelo, Fraenkel, and Thoralf Skolem (calling it therefore the ZFS system.)

It was however Skolem's proposal for the explanation of Zermelo's definite property, published in 1923, that was ultimately accepted. His suggestion had the advantage over Fraenkel's in that it led more directly to a logical formulation of Zermelo's axioms (which, till then, existed only as intuitive statement).

Fraenkel nevertheless actively continued his development of the theory of sets, in which he showed considerable perception, evident in his papers and books. In 1953 he published *Abstract Set Theory*, and in 1958 *Foundations of Set Theory*. His research led him to posit an eighth axiom (to follow Zermelo's seven), an axiom of replacement, which stated that if the domain of a single-valued function is a set, its counter-domain is also a set.

Later, Johann von Neumann (1903–1957) – the pioneer in computer mathematics – was to propose a ninth axiom, the axiom of foundation. It states that every non-empty set *a* contains a member *b* such that *a* and *b* have no members in common.

Fredholm, Erik Ivar (1866–1927), was a Swedish mathematician and mathematical physicist who founded the modern theory of integral equations, and in his work provided the foundations upon which much of the extremely important research later carried out by David Hilbert (1862–1943) was based. Fredholm's name is perpetuated in several concepts and theorems.

Fredholm was born on 7 April 1866 in Stockholm, where he grew up and was educated. At the age of 19 he entered the Polytechnic Institute there, studying applied mathematics; his particular interest was the solution of problems of practical mechanics. After one year, however, he transferred to the University of Uppsala where in 1888 he received his bachelor's degree. He then returned to Stockholm. After ten years of further research and work, Fredholm finally obtained his PhD from Uppsala University – for a thesis on partial differential equations – and became a Lecturer in Mathematical Physics at Stockholm University. Within the next five years he wrote his most important paper, on integral

equations; for it, in 1903, he received the Wallmark Prize of the Swedish Academy of Sciences, and the Poncelet Prize of the Académie de France. In 1906 he was promoted to Professor of Rational Mechanics and Mathematical Physics, a post he held until his death. He died in Stockholm on 17 August 1927.

Fredholm's success in deriving a theory of integral equations was in some respects a success in combining parts of the work of others with his own creative flair and a novel approach. He founded much of his theory on work carried out by the American astronomer George Hill (1838–1914) in 1877, who was investigating lunar motion. In his examination, Hill used linear equations involving determinants of an infinite number of rows and columns. In Fredholm's paper *Sur une nouvelle méthode pour la résolution du problème de Dirichlet*, published in 1900, he first developed the essential part of the theory of what is now known as Fredholm's Integral Equation; further, he went on to define and solve the Fredholm Equation of the second type, involving a definite integral.

Such equations had been under scientific consideration for some years. Niels Abel, Franz Neumann and Vito Volterra had all put forward tentative or incomplete results: Henri Poincaré had even arrived at Fredholm's solution but been unable to derive a proof of it, although in order to carry out his own work on partial differential equations (between 1895 and 1896) he had been obliged to assume that it was correct.

Fredholm's novel approach in continuing his research led to his discovery, also in 1900, of the algebraic analogue of his own theory of integral equations. It was not until 1903, however, that he completed the solution, recognizing the analogous identity between the Fredholm Integral Equation and the linear-matrix vector equation $(I + F)U = V$, and showing that the analogy was complete.

Shortly afterwards, Fredholm's results were used by David Hilbert (1862–1943), who extended them in deriving his own theories – such as the theory of eigen-values, and the theory of spaces involving an infinite number of dimensions – that finally contributed fundamentally towards quantum theory.

Frege, Friedrich Ludwig Gottlob (1848–1925), was a German logical philosopher and mathematician whose main purpose was to define once and for all an evolutionary connection between the fundamental rigour and mathematics in logic and the fundamental rigour and logic in mathematics. For this purpose he revised certain parts of mathematical notation in order to introduce total precision in logic, and he further revised philosophical vocabulary with the same intent. Publishing his work, his first books were successful – and to some extent gratifyingly revolutionary in effect. His later development of this in a two-volume work, however, was over-ambitious and was accounted a failure, unfortunately discrediting much of his earlier and his later work. Nevertheless, at this remove in time, his final system of logic is accepted as one of the greatest contributions in the field put forward in the century surrounding it.

Frege was born on 8 November 1848 in Wismar (now in East Germany), and grew up and received his early education there. He then spent two years (1869–1871) as a student in Jena before transferring to Göttingen University, where he studied physics, chemistry, mathematics and philosophy, earning his PhD in mathematics in 1873. The next year he entered the faculty of philosophy there.

Frege's studies over the following years were crystallized in a book he published in 1879 on a new symbolic mathematical language he had devised, which he called *Begriffschrift*. In that year he returned to Jena to take up a teaching post, and remained there for the rest of his working life. In 1884, Frege published another important book on the foundations of mathematics, and again relied upon his *Begriffschrift*. He attempted to develop his ideas still further in another, ill-fated, two-volume text, the first volume of which appeared in 1893, and the second in 1903. These volumes, entitled *Grundgesetze der Arithmetik*, received a severe blow when, shortly before the second volume was due to be published, Frege was sent a letter which demonstrated to him that the entire mathematical system described in the books was in fact of no value; nobly, he included a postscript to that effect in the second volume. After this personal disaster, Frege continued to study mathematics but never with the same scope or depth. He retired in 1917, still writing further material, extending some of his previous studies in the period between 1918 and 1923. He died in Bad Keinen, Germany, on 26 July 1925.

At the beginning of what was to become his life's work, Frege was correctly convinced that in terms of absolute precision ordinary language is not sufficiently strict for the expression of mathematical concepts such as the definition of "number", "object" and "function". Furthermore, he saw that the symbols already available to mathematicians were themselves not adequate for this purpose either, and so it would be necessary to create new ones – a vital step

that mathematicians before him had resisted taking.

The resultant *Begriffschrift* (which translates literally as "idea-script") was intended as a method for the analysis and representation of mathematical proofs. It has since been developed into modern mathematical symbolic logic, and Frege is generally – and only reasonably – credited as its originator. He introduced the symbols for assertions, implications, and their converse notions; he also introduced propositional logic and quantification theory, inventing symbols for "and", "or" and "if ..., then ...," and so on. Using his new "language" he was able succinctly and unambiguously to express complex logical relations, and even – when Frege applied it to the theory of sequences – to define the ancestral relation. This represented a major development in mathematical induction, and was later further explored by mathematicians such as Bertrand Russell (1872–1970) and Alfred Whitehead (1861–1947).

Frege incorporated improvements to the *Begriffschrift* into *Grundgesetze*, but was devastated to receive a letter from Bertrand Russell in 1902 – nine years after the appearance of the first volume – in which Russell asked Frege how his logical system coped with a particular logical paradox. To his chagrin, Frege's system was not able to resolve it – and since the system had been intended to be complete and contradiction-free, he was forced to acknowledge his system to be useless.

Although at the time Frege was largely discredited, his work today is seen as of considerable importance. His innovations have been useful in the development of symbolic logic, and even the problem posed by Russell was resolved by later logico-mathematicians.

Frege, nevertheless, in many ways simply stopped at that point. Despite the fact that he carried on working, and for quite a number of years, developments in early twentieth-century mathematics – such as Hilbert's axiomatics – were apparently beyond Frege's scope. He was unable to accept these new ideas, even when David Hilbert (1862–1943) himself tried to clarify the issue for him. Frege was, therefore, a mathematician with the most ambitious plans for the development of a rigorous foundation for mathematics in which, in his own eyes, he did not succeed in his own lifetime.

Frobenius, Georg Ferdinand (1849–1917), was a German mathematician who is now chiefly remembered for his formulation of the concept of the abstract group – a theory that proposed what is now generally considered to be the first abstract structure of "new" mathematics. His research into the theory of groups and complex number systems was of fundamental significance, and he also made important contributions to the theory of elliptic functions, to the solution of differential equations, and to quaternions.

Frobenius was born on 26 October 1849 in Berlin, where he received his early education. His study of mathematics began when he attended Göttingen University from 1867; in only three years he gained a doctorate. In 1870 he returned to his former school in Berlin as a teacher, where he stayed for a year before moving to a school of higher standard and status in the same city. By this time he had already presented many papers on mathematics - including the publication of his method of finding an infinite series solution of a differential equation at a regular single point, and other papers on Abel's problem in the convergence of series and Pfaff's problem in differential equations - and had earned a fair reputation. The result was that he was appointed Assistant Professor at Berlin University in 1874, and in the following year became full Professor at the Eidgenossische Polytechnikum in Zurich. Seventeen years later, in 1892, Frobenius returned to the University of Berlin in order to take up the post of Professor of Mathematics, where he remained for the rest of his working life. He died on 3 August 1917, in Charlottenberg.

It was in Berlin the first time, in a study of the work of Ernst Kummer (1810-1893) and Leopold Kronecker (1823-1891), that Frobenius became interested in abstract algebra; his major contributions to the subject were published in 1879 (*Über Gruppen von vertauschbaren Elementen*, written in collaboration with Stickelberger) and in 1895 (*Über endliche Gruppen*). Later publications contained further development of group theory, the last of which (in 1906) -*Über die reellen Darstellungen der endlichen Gruppen* - was written with Schur, together with whom Frobenius completed the theory of finite groups of linear substitutions of *n* variables.

By studying the different representations of groups and their elements, Frobenius provided a firm basis for the solving of general problems in the theory of finite groups. His methods were later continued by William Burnside (1852-1927), and his results also proved useful to the development of quantum mechanics.

Fuchs, Immanuel Lazarus (1833-1902), was a German mathematician whose work on Riemann's method for the solution of differential equations led to a study of the theory of functions that was later crucial to Henri Poincaré in

his own important investigation of function theory. Fuchs' main scientific importance may be seen, therefore, as providing a sort of link between the nineteenth- and twentieth-century ideas of mathematical development.

Fuchs was born on 5 May 1833 in Moschin (now in Poland). During his elementary education his mathematical talents were already apparent, and he went on to study at the University of Berlin, under Ernst Kummer (1810-1893) and Karl Weierstrass (1815-1897). He gained his PhD in Berlin in 1858, and began teaching at local schools. In 1865 he became a Lecturer at Berlin University, and only a year later was promoted to Professor. In 1869 he became the Professor of Mathematics at the Artillery and Engineering School at Griefswald. Later he transferred first to the University of Göttingen (in 1874) and then (in 1875) to that of Heidelberg to take up their Chairs of Mathematics. Returning to Berlin in 1882, he succeeded Weierstrass two years later as Professor of Mathematics there, and over the next 20 years held several administrative and academic posts of responsibility at the University. He died, in Berlin, on 26 April 1902.

Fuchs' interest in the theory of functions was first aroused during his student days in Berlin, but it was not until he took up his first professional appointment that he began to work seriously on his research. He produced a number of papers that were intended to develop Riemann's work on a method for solving differential equations. Fuchs' proposals were in contrast to those put forward earlier by Augustin Cauchy (1789-1857), who used power series.

The first proof for solutions of linear differential equations of order *n* was developed from this study, as were the Fuchsian differential equations and the Fuchsian theory on solutions for singular points. His work in this field was of great importance to Poincaré's work on automorphic functions. Fuchs also carried out some research into number theory and geometry.

G

Galois, Evariste (1811-1832), was a French mathematician who, building on the work of Lagrange, Gauss, Abel and Cauchy, greatly extended the understanding of the conditions in which an algebraic equation is solvable and, by his method of doing so, laid the foundations of modern group theory.

Galois was born in the village of Bourg-la-Reine, on the outskirts of Paris, on 25 October 1811. His family was of the highly respectable bourgeois class that came into its own with the restoration of the monarchy after the Napoleonic empire. His father was the headmaster of the local boarding school and mayor of the town; his mother came from a family of jurists, and it was she who gave Galois his early (chiefly classical) education. He first attended school at the age of 12, when he was sent to the Collège Louis-le-Grand in Paris as a fourth-form boarder in 1823. Another four years passed before Galois, who gained notoriety for resisting the strict discipline imposed at the school, had his mathematical imagination fired by the lectures of H.J. Vernier. He soon made himself familiar with the works of Legrange and Legendre and by 1828 he was busy mastering the most recent work on the theory of equations, number theory, and elliptic functions. He quickly came to believe that he had solved the general fifth-degree equation. Like Abel before him, he discovered his error, and that discovery launched him on his search – ultimately successful and ultimately of momentous consequence for the future of mathematics – for a solution to the problem of the solvability of algebraic equations generally. By 1829 he had progressed far enough to interest Augustin Cauchy (1789-1857), who presented Galois' early results to the Academy of Science.

In a remarkably short period of time Galois, at the age of 17, had arrived very near the apex of existing mathematical thought. Then the first of the emotional disruptions which were to darken the few remaining years of his life occurred. His father, the victim of a political plot which unjustly discredited him, committed suicide in July 1829. A month later Galois, partly from his fiery impatience with the examiners' instructions, failed to gain entrance to the *École Polytechnique*. He had therefore to be content with entering, in the autumn of 1829, the *École Normale Supérieure*.

It was then that Galois learned that the ideas which were contained in the paper presented to the Academy by Cauchy were not original. Shortly before very similar ideas had been published by Abel in his last paper. Encouraged by Cauchy, Galois began to revise his paper in the light of Abel's findings. He presented the revised version to the Academy in February 1830, with high hopes that it would gain him the *grand prix*. To his dismay the Academy not only rejected his paper, but the examiner lost the manuscript. Galois was indignant at this ill-treatment, but four months later he succeeded in

having a paper on number theory published in the prestigious *Bulletin des sciences mathématiques*. It was this paper that contained the highly original and diverting theory of "Galois imaginaires".

Thus, when the July Revolution that drove Charles X off the throne gave a shock to French society, Galois had reason to be proud of his barely acknowledged mathematical genius and cause to feel estranged, both on his own and his father's account, from the stuffy officialdom which had cast its pall over France since 1815. He joined the revolutionary movement. In the next year he was twice arrested, in May 1831 for proposing a regicide toast at a republican banquet (Louis-Philippe having taken Charles' place as king) and again in July for taking part in a republican demonstration. For the second offence Galois was imprisoned for nine months. In prison he continued his mathematical research. But shortly after his release he became involved in a duel, perhaps from political reasons, perhaps from complications arising from a love affair. The event remains mysterious. Galois, it is evident, expected to be killed. On 29 May 1832, in a letter written in feverish haste, he outlined the principal results of his mathematical inquiries. He sent the letter to his friend Auguste Chevalier, almost certainly in the expectation that it would find its way to Karl Gauss and Karl Jacobi. The duel took place on the following morning. Galois was severely wounded in the stomach and died in hospital on 31 May 1832.

So brief was Galois' life – he was only 20 when he died – and so dismissively were his ideas treated by the Academy, that he was known to his contemporaries principally as a rather headstrong republican agitator. Cauchy, who alone sensed the importance of what Galois was doing, was out of France after 1830 and did not see any of the revisions or developments of Galois' first paper. Moreover, in his letter to Chevalier, Galois had time only to put down in concise form – without demonstrations – his most important conclusions. When he died, therefore, Galois' work amounted to fewer than 100 pages, much of it fragmentary and nearly all of it unpublished.

The honour of rescuing Galois from obscurity belongs, in the first instance, to Joseph Liouville (1809-1882), who in 1843 began to prepare his papers for publication and informed the Academy that Galois had provided a convincing answer to the question whether first-degree equations were solvable by radicals. Finally, in 1846, both Galois' 1831 paper and a short notice on the solution of primitive equations by radicals were (thanks to Liouville) published in the *Bulletin*.

Galois' achievement, put tersely, was to arrive at a definitive solution to the problem of the solvability of algebraic equations, and in doing so to produce such a breakthrough in the understanding of fields of algebraic numbers and also of groups that he is deservedly considered as the chief founder of modern group theory. What has come to be known as the Galois theorem made immediately demonstrable the insolubility of higher-than-fourth-degree equations by radicals. The theorem also showed that if the highest power of x is a prime, and if all other values of x can be found by taking only two values of x and combining them using only addition, subtraction, multiplication and division, then the equation can be solved by using formulae similar in principle to the formula used in solving quadratic equations.

Galois' work involved groups formed from the arrangements of the roots of equations and their subgroups, groups which he fitted into each other rather on the analogy of the Chinese box arrangement. This, his most far-reaching achievement for the subsequent development of group theory, is known as "Galois theory". Along with other such terms - Galois groups, Galois fields and the Galois theorem - it bears testimony to the lasting influence of his rejected genius.

Gauss, Karl (or Carl) Friedrich (1777-1855), was a German mathematician, physicist and astronomer, whose innovations in mathematics proved him at least the equal of Archimedes or of Isaac Newton.

Gauss was born in Braunschweig (Brunswick) on 30 April 1777 into a poor, uneducated family. His father was a gardener and assistant to a merchant, and the treasurer of an insurance fund. Gauss taught himself to count and read - he is said to have spotted a mistake in his father's arithmetic at the age of three. At elementary school, at the age of eight, he added the first 100 digits in his first lesson. Recognising his precocious talent, the teacher persuaded his father that Gauss should be encouraged to train towards following a profession rather than learn a trade. Aged eleven, he went to high school and proved to be just as good at classics as at mathematics. At the age of 14, he was presented in court to the Duke of Brunswick in order to demonstrate his skill in computing; evidently the Duke was so impressed he supported Gauss generously with a grant from then until his own death in 1806. In 1792, with the Duke's aid, Gauss began to study at the Collegium Caro-

linum in Brunswick, and then from 1795 to 1798 he was taught at the University of Göttingen. He was awarded his doctorate in 1799 from the University of Helmstedt. At that point he had already made nearly all his fundamental mathematical discoveries. In 1801 he decided to develop his interest in astronomy; by 1807 he had gone at it so enthusiastically that not only was he Professor of Mathematics, he was also Director of the Göttingen Observatory.

At about this time, Gauss began to gain recognition from other parts of the world: he was offered a job in St Petersburg (now Leningrad), was made a Foreign Member of the Royal Society in London, and was invited to join the Russian and French Academies of Sciences. Nevertheless, Gauss remained at Göttingen for the rest of his life, and died there on 23 February 1855.

Between the ages of 14 and 17, Gauss devised many of the theories and mathematical proofs that, because of his lack of experience in publication and his diffidence, were to have to be rediscovered in the following decades. (He independently arrived at what is now called Bode's Law, for example.) The extent to which this was true was revealed only after Gauss's death. There are, nevertheless, those innovations that are ascribed directly to him during his three years at the Collegium Carolinum, including the principle of least squares (by which the equation for a curve best fitting a set of observations can be devised). At this time he was particularly intrigued by number theory, especially on the frequency of primes. This subject became a 'life's work, and he is known as its modern founder.

In 1795, having completed some important work on quadratic residues, Gauss began to study at the University of Göttingen, where he had access to the works of Pierre de Fermat, Leonhard Euler, Joseph Lagrange and Adrien Legendre. He immediately seized the opportunity to write a book on the theory of numbers, which appeared in 1801 as *Disquisitiones arithmeticae*, generally regarded as his greatest accomplishment. In it he summarized all the work that had been carried out up to that time, and formulated concepts and questions that are still relevant today.

He was still at University when he discovered, in 1796, that a regular 17-sided polygon could be inscribed in a circle, using ruler and compasses only. This represented the first discovery in Euclidean geometry that had been made in 2,000 years.

In 1799 Gauss proved a fundamental theorem of algebra, that every algabraic equation has a root of the form $a + bi$, where a and b are real numbers and i is the square root of -1. In his doctoral thesis, Gauss showed that numbers of the form $a + bi$ (called complex numbers) can be regarded as analogous to points on a plane.

The years between 1800 and 1810 were, for Gauss, the years in which he concentrated on astronomy. In mathematics he had had no collaborators, although he had inspired men such as Lejeune Dirichlet (1805-1859) and Georg Riemann (1826-1866). In astronomy, in contrast, he corresponded with many, and his friendship with Alexander von Humboldt (1769-1859) played an important part in the development of science in Germany. The discovery of the first asteroid, Ceres (and its subsequent "loss") by Giuseppe Piazzi (1746-1826) at the beginning of 1801 gave Gauss the chance to use his mathematical brilliance for another purpose. He developed a quick method for calculating the asteroid's orbit from only three observations, and published this work - a classic in astronomy - in 1809. The 1001st planetoid to be discovered was named Gaussia in his honour.

Gauss was also a pioneer in topology, and worked besides on crystallography, optics, mechanics and capillarity. At Göttingen, he devised the heliotrope, an instrument which enabled more precise trigonometric determinations of the shape of the Earth to be made. After 1831 he collaborated with Wilhelm Weber (1804-1891) in research into electricity and magnetism, and in 1833 they together invented an electromagnetic telegraph. Gauss devised logical sets of units for magnetic phenomena and the unit of magnetic flux density is therefore called after him.

There is scarcely any physical, mathematical or astronomical field in which Gauss did not work. He retained an active mind well into old age and, already an accomplished linguist, at the age of 62 taught himself Russian. The full value of his work has been realized only in the twentieth century.

Gödel, Kurt (1906-1978), was an Austrian-born American philosopher and mathematician who, in his philosophical endeavour to establish the science of mathematics as totally consistent and totally complete, proved that it could never be. This realization has been seen as fundamental to both mathematical and philosophical studies and concepts, and at the time to other scientists working in the same endeavour was devastatingly revolutionary.

Gödel was born on 28 April 1906 at Brunn in Moravia (now part of Czechoslovakia but then in Austria), where his father was a businessman. Several childhood illnesses left him with a life-long preoccupation with his health, but at school he worked hard and successfully: he is reputed never to have made a mistake in Latin grammar. At the age of 17 he went to the University of Vienna where he was at first not sure whether to read mathematics or physics, but settled for mathematics. At that time Vienna - and particularly its University - was the centre of activity in positivist philosophy and Gödel could not help but be influenced, and although he was apparently unimpressed at the meetings of the prestigious Viennese Circle of philosophers that he attended, his studies drifted from pure mathematics towards mathematical logic and the foundations of mathematics. In 1930 he was awarded his doctorate at the University, and in 1931 he published his most important paper, which was accepted by the University authorities as the thesis on which they licensed him to become an unsalaried lecturer there. Throughout the 1930s Gödel continued to work at the University of Vienna (except for a visit to Princeton in the United States in 1933-1934). Then, in 1938, when Austria became part of Germany, he was not appointed as a paid lecturer with his colleagues because it was thought, erroneously, that he was Jewish. Later the same year he married and travelled to the United States where he spent a short time at the Institute for Advanced Study, Princeton, before returning to Austria. Finally, in 1939, he went back to the United States to settle at Princeton where, in 1953, at the age of 47, he was appointed Professor. A quiet and unassuming man, Gödel was awarded many honours - although he also refused quite a number, particularly from Germany. He died at Princeton on 14 January 1978.

In 1930 Gödel was granted his doctorate for a dissertation in which he showed that a particular logical system (predicate calculus of the first order) was such that every valid formula could be proved within the system; in other words, the system was what mathematicians call complete. This research represented the way in which his studies were subsequently to take him. He then investigated a much larger logical system - that constructed by Bertrand Russell (1872-1970) and Alfred Whitehead (1865-1947) as the logical basis of mathematics, published as *Principia Mathematica*. Accordingly the title of his licensiate paper, published in 1931, was "*On Formally Undecidable Propositions of* Principia Mathematica *and Related Systems*". In it Gödel dashed the hopes of philosophers and mathematicians alike, and showed that there were systems upon which mathematics was based in which it was impossible to decide whether or not a valid statement or formula was true or false within the system. In more practical terms, it was not possible to show that such areas as arithmetic worked entirely within arithmetic; there was always the possibility of coming across something that could be either true or false.

Mathematics itself was unaffected by this bombshell. But the hopes for an absolutely perfect subject that could justify itself completely to even the most penetrating philosopher were utterly set back. Gödel himself felt that David Hilbert's Formalist School would save the day, and did not fully anticipate the effect his proof would have. Nevertheless, mathematical logic has subsequently made some progress – albeit mainly by attacking the subject from outside the logical system it embraces.

During his career Gödel made a number of other inspired contributions to the subject of mathematical logic, but none of the same importance as his earlier work. Because of his way of numbering statements in his famous proof, certain numbers were given the name "Gödel numbers" by fellow mathematicians. The other area of mathematics to which he contributed significantly was general relativity theory; this was probably due in part at least to his close friendship with Albert Einstein (1879–1955) at the Princeton Institute. Gödel solved some of Einstein's equations and constructed mathematical models of the Universe. In one of these it was theoretically possible for a person to travel into his own past, but at the cost of such a large consumption of fuel as not to make the journey feasible. (According to the model, however, it might be possible for a person to send a message into his own past.)

Gödel kept detailed diaries that record numerous interests, including the laws of nature, the evolution of life, time travel, and ghosts and demonology, as well as his preoccupation with mathematics and philosophy.

Gosset, William Sealey (1876–1937), was a British industrial research scientist, famous for his work on statistics.

Gosset was born at Canterbury on 13 June 1876 and educated at Winchester College, before going to New College, Oxford, to study mathematics and chemistry. He received a first class in his mathematical moderations in 1897 and a first class on receiving his BA in natural sciences (chemistry) in 1899. On leaving Oxford he immediately joined the Guinness brewery firm in Dublin, the firm recently having adopted the policy of hiring a number of university-trained scientists to conduct research into the manufacture of its ale. He remained with the company in Dublin until 1935, when he was posted to London to direct the operations of the new Guinness brewery there. He was appointed the company's head brewer a few months before his death, at Beaconsfield, on 16 October 1937.

When Gosset arrived in Dublin he found that there was a mass of data concerning brewing – on the relationships between the raw materials, hops and barley, and the quality of the finished product and on the methods of production – which had been almost entirely left unanalysed. After a few years with the company he was able to persuade the owners that they would profit from more sophisticated mathematical analysis of a variety of processes from the production of barley to the fermentation of yeast. Accordingly, the company sent him to University College, London, in September 1906 to study for a year under Karl Pearson (1857–1936). It was the experience of that year that turned Gosset into an outstanding statistical theorist, even though all the questions he asked were inspired directly by problems in the brewery trade.

Gosset's statistical techniques were simple: he relied on the mean, the standard deviation and the correlation coefficient as his basic tools. Through all his work ran one theme, expressed in two formulae:

$$\sigma^2_{x+y} = \sigma^2_x + \sigma^2_y + 2p\sigma_x\sigma_y$$

and

$$\sigma^2_{x-y} = \sigma^2_x + \sigma^2_y - 2p\sigma_x\sigma_y$$

Gosset's amplification of these formulae opened the door to modern developments in the analysis of variance.

When Gosset began to examine the data at the Guinness brewery, it quickly became apparent to him that what was most needed was improved knowledge of the theory of errors. In 1904 he wrote a report for the company, "Application of the Law of Error" to the brewing industry. His most famous work, published in 1908, was on the probable error of a mean. More than a century earlier Gauss had worked out a satisfactory method of estimating the mean value of a characteristic in a population on the basis of large samples; Gosset's problem was to do the same on the basis of very small samples, for use by industry when large sampling was too expensive or impracticable. For any large probability, that is one of 95 per cent or more, Gosset was able to compute the error e, such that it is 95 per cent probable that $(x - \mu) \leq e$, where x is the value of the sample, and μ is the mean. From this t-test was derived what came to be known as Student's t-test of statistical hypotheses. The name of the test comes from the fact that Gosset published all his papers under the pseudonym "Student". The test consists of rejecting a hypothesis if, and only if, the probability (derived from t) of erroneous rejection is small.

Gosset hit on the statistic which has proved to be fundamental for the statistical analysis of the normal distribution, and he went further, to make the shrewd observation that the sampling distribution of such statistics is of basic importance in the drawing of inferences. In particular it opened the way to the analysis of variance, that branch of the subject so important to statisticians who came after him.

Grandi, Guido (1671–1742), was an Italian mathematician famous for his work on the definition of curves – particularly curves that are symmetrically pleasing to the eye. It was he who devised the curves now known as the "versiera", the "rose" and the "cliela" (after Cliela, Countess Borromeo), and his theory of curves also comprehended the means of finding the equations of curves of known form. He was mainly responsible, in addition, for introducing the calculus into Italy.

At his birth, on 1 October 1671 in Cremona, his given names were Francesco Lodovico Grandi. At the age of 16 he entered the religious order of the Camaldolese and changed his christian names to Guido. In 1694 he was appointed teacher of mathematics in the order's monastery in Florence, and it was there that he first became acquainted with the *Principia Mathematica* of Isaac Newton (published in England in 1687), which inspired him to devote much of the remainder of his life to the study of geometry. Nevertheless he became Professor of Philosophy at Pisa in 1700, and seven years later was given the post of honorary mathematician to the Grand Duke. In 1714 he became Professor of Mathematics at Pisa and established a considerable reputation as a teacher. The recipient of several awards and honours – a member of the Royal Society from 1709 – Grandi died in Pisa on 4 July 1742.

In his fascination for the study of curves, Grandi was influenced first by Newton; early in his career he determined the points of inflection in the conchoid curve. He examined also the studies published by Pierre de Fermat (1601–1665), whose treatment he found somewhat limited, and by Christiaan Huygens (1629–1695), who had revealed the most important properties of logistic curves in research based on the work of Evangelista Torricelli (1608–1647). In 1701 Grandi devised a proof for Huygens's theorem.

However, Grandi's name will always be associated with the "rose", the "cliela" and the "versiera" curves; his work on the first two was presented in a paper to the Royal Society in 1723 – ten years after he had corresponded with the great Gottfried Leibniz on the subject. In 1728 he published his complete theory in *Fleores geometrica*, an attempt (among other things) to define geometrically the curves that have the shapes of flowers, particularly multi-petalled roses.

What is today known as the "rose" curve Grandi called by its Greek name *rhodonea*. The polar equation for such a curve is $r = a \sin k\theta$, where k is an integer. Depending on whether k is an odd or an even number, there are k or 2k "petals" on the rose; and depending on whether k is a rational or an irrational number, the number of petals is finite or infinite. The Cartesian co-ordinates for the curve are $(x^2 + y^2)^3 = 4a^2x^2y^2$, where a is a constant.

The "cliela" curve Grandi described as the locus of P where P represents a point on a sphere of radius a where ϕ and θ are the longitude and co-latitude of P, with P moving such that $\theta = m\phi$, where m is a constant.

Grandi defined the curve now called the "versiera" (from the Latin *sinus versus*) by stating: given a circle with diameter AC, let BDM be a straight line perpendicular to AC at B and intersecting the circumference at D; let M be a point determined by the length of BM so that $AC:BM = AB:BD$; the locus of all such points, M, is the versiera. The curve is in some places more commonly known as the "witch of Agnesi" as a result of a mistranslation and the erroneous attribution of its discovery to Maria Gaetana Agnesi in a treatise of 1748.

Although the study of curves was Grandi's joy and passion, he did make other contributions to mathematics, notably in 1703 when his treatise on quadrature – using Leibniz's methods in preference to those of Francesco Cavalieri and Vincenzo Viviani – was responsible for the introduction of the calculus into Italy.

Grandi also did some work in practical mechanics and his observations regarding hydraulics were utilized by the Italian government in such public works as the drainage of the Chiana valley and the Pontine Marshes in central Italy.

Grassmann, Hermann Günther (1809–1877), was an extremely gifted German mathematician whose methods of presentation were so unclear that his innovations were never really appreciated during his lifetime despite their importance. He had greater success with his work in a completely different field: comparative linguistics.

Grassmann was born in Stettin, German Pomerania (now Szczecín, Poland), on 15 April

1809. He studied first at home and then in local schools, before going to the University of Berlin, where he studied theology from 1827 to 1830. Instead of becoming a minister, however, he returned to Stettin and began to study mathematics and physics for an examination to enable him to teach at secondary schools. Poor marks in the examination meant that he could take classes only of younger students, from 1832. It was not until 1840 that he obtained the qualifications necessary to teach more advanced students. In 1842 he joined the staff of the Friedrich Wilhelm School in Stettin; five years later he became Senior Teacher there. Finally the Stettin high school appointed Grassmann to an important teaching post (which carried the title of Professor) in 1852. Grassmann's numerous schoolbooks and his texts on more advanced mathematics and linguistics were not uniformly successful. The international mathematical community was slow to recognize the significance of Grassmann's work in mathematics, although he received much more immediate recognition for his work in linguistics, and in particular on Sanskrit. He was elected to the Göttingen Academy of Sciences in 1871, but the honorary doctorate he received in 1876 from the University of Tübingen was for his work in linguistics. He died in Stettin on 26 September 1877. After his death his work was popularized, partly through the efforts of his children, several of whom became prominent academics.

The examination paper that Grassmann sat in 1840 in order to become eligible to teach advanced students included a paper on tides. In his research at home while framing his answer to the paper, Grassmann discovered a new calculus which enabled him to apply parts of Pierre Laplace's book on celestial mechanics to the paper on tides. The technique clearly had wider applications, so Grassmann decided to devote himself to exploring it further, and during the years from 1840 to 1844, concentrated on developing his method, which he called the theory of extension. It was one of the earliest mathematical attempts to investigate n-dimensional space, where n is greater than 3. He published the method in a book in 1844, but his vocabulary was so obscure that the book had virtually no impact at all in the short term.

Grassmann in the following year applied the method to reformulate Ampère's law, but again through poor exposition the work was ignored. (Thirty years later, Rudolf Clausius independently found a similar improvement to Ampère's law, but gave credit to Grassmann for its earlier discovery.)

The next ten years saw Grassmann investigating the subject of algebraic curves, using his calculus of extension, but the papers he published on the subject once more made little impact. He was awarded a prize for a paper in topology by the Leipzig Academy of Sciences in 1847 - but the published version needed a note of clarification because of the essay's complex format.

The poor response of the mathematical community to Grassmann's work led him also to devote considerable energy to a completely different field of study. He learned and examined many ancient languages, such as Persian, Sanskrit and Lithuanian. His books on this subject were considerably more successful, especially the glossary he published to the Hindu scriptures, the Rig-Veda, in 1873-1875. From his investigations he derived a theory of speech.

Another area of his interest was the mixing of colours. His work in this field attracted some favourable comments from Hermann Helmholtz (1821-1894) - the physiologist and expert on colour vision and colour blindness - whose work Grassmann had in fact criticized.

The book on extension theory that Grassmann published in 1844 was reprinted in a revised form in 1862, and again posthumously in 1878. Gradually it began to receive some recognition as a work of considerable value by German, French and American mathematicians. A scientist on whom it had a particularly strong effect was Josiah Gibbs (1839-1903), who made use of it in his development of vector analysis.

Green, George (1793-1841), was a British businessman whose mathematics were self-taught; nevertheless, through hard work and considerable creative and perceptive ability he made significant advances in both the physics and the mathematics of his time, although he was really achieving his proper status and recognition only at the time of his death. He is best remembered for his paper, published before he entered formal education, in which he introduced the term "potential", now a central concept in electricity.

Green was born in Nottingham on 14 July 1793. He had to leave school at an early age in order to assist at the family mill, but his mathematical interests and abilities spurred him to continue his studies on his own, through reading. The death of his father and the ensuing sale of the family firm eventually made Green financially independent. He moved to Cambridge and in 1833 (at the age of 40) became a student at Caius College in the University. Conducting his own studies in mathematics above and beyond those required by the curriculum, he graduated with honours in 1837. Further private researches led to the award to Green of a

Fellowship at Caius College – although he was not to be able to continue his work. Poor health led to his untimely death, in Sneinton, Nottinghamshire, on 31 March 1841.

Green's most famous paper was published in 1828. Only a few copies were printed, and these were circulated only privately and locally in Nottingham. It could easily have simply sunk out of sight without ever attracting the attention it deserved and eventually got. The essay dealt with a mathematical approach to electricity and magnetism. Its two outstanding features were the coining of the term "potential", and the introduction of the Green Theorem – which is still applied in the solution of partial differential equations, for instance in the study of relativity. Green demonstrated the importance of "potential function" (also known as the Green function) in both magnetism and electricity, and he showed how the Green theorem enabled volume integrals to be reduced to surface integrals.

Green went on to produce other important papers on fluids (1832, 1833), attraction (1833), waves in fluids (1837), sound (1837), and light (1837); his development of earlier work by Augustin Cauchy (1789–1857) on light reflection and refraction (1837) and on light propagation (1839) represented the best of his later work.

Green's work on electricity and magnetism might have been totally lost had it not been for William Thomson (later Lord Kelvin; 1824–1907), an undergraduate at the time of Green's death. He, after completing his studies, showed Green's 1828 essay to a number of prominent physicists whom he knew personally. It stimulated great interest, and went on to influence scientists such as James Clerk Maxwell and Kelvin himself, and was thus significant in the development of nineteenth-century theories of electromagnetism.

H

Hadamard, Jacques (1865–1963), was a French mathematician whose contributions to the subject ranged over so wide a field that he gained recognition as one of the outstanding mathematicians of modern times.

Hadamard was born at Versailles on 8 December 1865 into a family well able to perceive and to encourage his rare intellectual gifts. His father taught Latin at a lycée in Paris and his mother was an accomplished pianist and music teacher. Hadamard spent his undergraduate years at the École Normale Supérieure in Paris,

and after four years there gained his BA in mathematics in 1888. In 1890, while he was working on his doctoral thesis on function theory, he began to teach at the Lycée Buffon. He received his doctorate in 1892 and in the following year took up a teaching appointment at Bordeaux. In the next few years he was also an occasional lecturer at the Sorbonne.

In 1909 Hadamard was appointed Professor of Mathematics at the Collège de France in Paris, a Chair which he held, together with subsequent appointments at the École Polytechnique and the École Centrale, until 1937. In order to escape from the disruptions of the German occupation of France during World War II, he went to the United States in 1941, then to London, where he took part in operation research for the Royal Air Force. In 1945 he returned to France, where he lived in retirement – cultivating his tastes as an amateur musician (Einstein once played in an orchestra he assembled) and as a collector of ferns and fungi. He died in Paris on 17 October 1963.

Rare are the mathematicians who have left a heritage as rich as Hadamard did; few are the fields of mathematics which have not been touched by his influence. His first major papers, those written in the mid-1890s and growing out of his doctoral thesis, dealt with the nature of analytic functions – that is, functions which can be developed as power series that converge. Hadamard created the theory of the detection and nature of singularities in the analytic continuation of a Taylor series. He began by giving a proof of the so-called Cauchy test for convergence of a power series ($\Sigma a_n x^n$), and included the definition of an upper limit from first principles. By applying this method to Taylor series he arrived at results that are now standard textbook illustrations for the study of these series.

At about the same time he began to study the Riemann zeta function and in 1896 solved the old and famous problem relating to prime numbers of determining the number of primes less than a given number x. Hadamard was able to demonstrate that this number was asymptotically equal to $x/\log x$, which was the most important single result ever obtained in number theory.

Hadamard also became interested in the work of his friend, Vito Volterra, on the "functions of lines", numerical functions that depend upon a curve or an ordinary function as their variable. In an ordinary function such as $y = f(x)$, the variable, x, is a simple number. In the kinds of functions on which Volterra was working – Hadamard named them "functionals" – one might have, to take a simple example, $y = A(c)$, where A is the area of a closed curve, c. By asking a bold question of these functions, or functionals, Hadamard created a new branch of mathematics. He asked whether it might be possible to extend the theory of ordinary functions to the case where the variable, or variables, would no longer be a number, or numbers. This required a redefinition, or at least a new generalization, of many concepts: continuity, derivative and differential among them. In seeking to provide this new approach Hadamard gave birth to functional analysis, one of the most fertile branches of modern mathematics.

By extension from this work Hadamard came to investigate functions of a complex variable and, in so doing, to define a singularity as a point at which a function ceases to be regular. He was able to show, however, that the existence of a set of singular points may be compatible with the continuity of a function. He named the region formed by such a set a "lacunary space" and the study of such spaces has occupied mathematicians ever since.

Finally there is Hadamard's famous concept of "the problem correctly posed". Since it is often helpful, or necessary, to find an approximate solution (in physics, for example), a correctly posed problem, according to Hadamard, is one for which a solution exists that is unique for given data, but which also depends continuously on the data. This is the case when the solution can be expressed as a set of convergent power series. The idea has proved to be far more fruitful than Hadamard was able to envisage and has led mathematical analysts to consider different types of neighbourhood and continuity and so been fundamental to the development of the theory of function spaces, functional analysis.

Hadamard was a prolific mathematician. In his lifetime he published more than 300 papers on a great variety of topics. And few mathematicians influenced the growth of mathematics in so many different directions as he did.

Hall, Philip (1904–   ), is a British mathematician who has specialized in the study of group theory.

Born on 11 April 1904, in London, Hall attended Christ's Hospital until the age of 18, when he went to King's College, Cambridge. After receiving his degree, he became a Fellow of the College in 1927. Six years later he became a University Lecturer in Mathematics, a post he held until 1951, when he became Reader in Algebra at the University. Hall then became Sadlerian Professor of Pure Mathematics in 1953

and remained as such until his retirement in 1967. As Emeritus Professor, his connections with the University did not cease upon his retirement, and in 1976 he was elected Honorary Fellow of Jesus College.

In addition to his academic duties, Hall was an active participant in professional societies. The London Mathematical Society elected him to its Presidency in 1955, and awarded him the De Morgan Medal and the Lamor Prize in 1965. He was elected a Fellow of the Royal Society in 1942, and awarded its Sylvester Medal in 1961.

Hall's major contributions to mathematics have come through his work on group theory. In 1928 he extended some work on group theory done by Sylow in 1872, which led him to a study of prime power groups. From this work he developed his 1933 theory of regular groups. In that paper he also presented material which forms part of the connection between group theory and the study of Lie rings.

An investigation of the conditions under which finite groups are soluble led him in 1937 to postulate a general structure theory for finite soluble groups. In 1954 he published an examination of finitely generated soluble groups in which he demonstrated that they could be divided into two classes of unequal size.

Hall collaborated with G. Higman in 1956 in a study of p-soluble groups; their work generated results that were important to later work on the theory of finite groups, and in particular to the work of J. Thompson and W. Feit.

At the end of the 1950s Hall turned to the subject of simple groups, and later also examined non-strictly simple groups. His researches into the subject of group theory have produced many valuable results that have contributed to the further development of this area.

Hamilton, William Rowan (1805–1865), was an Irish mathematician, widely regarded in his time as a "new Newton", who created a new system of algebra based on quaternions.

Hamilton was born in Dublin, of Scottish parents, on the stroke of midnight, 3/4 August 1805. At about the age of three he was sent by his father, a solicitor, to Trim, where he was raised by his uncle (the local curate) and his aunt. He soon showed a remarkably precocious facility for languages, and made himself expert in Latin, Greek, Hebrew, French, Italian and a number of oriental languages (in which he was encouraged by his father, who wished him to get a clerkship with the East India Company). He was never to lose his interest in languages; throughout his life he wrote poetry and corresponded with Wordsworth, Coleridge and

Southey. But at the age of ten Hamilton came upon and read Euclid, and from that moment mathematics became his chief love. By the age of twelve he was reading Newton and when he went to Trinity College, Dublin, to study classics and mathematics, he had mastered the work of the great French mathematicians, including Laplace, and had begun to make experiments in physics and astronomy. In particular, he had begun to investigate the patterns produced by rays of light on reflection and refraction, known as caustics.

At Trinity College Hamilton was far and away the outstanding scholar of his generation. He gained the highest grade of *optime*, not once, which was rare in itself, but twice (in Greek and in mathematical physics), which was unprecedented. He also twice won the vice-chancellor's gold medal for English verse. In only his second year as an undergraduate he presented a paper on caustics to the Royal Irish Academy in which he showed that light travels by the path of the least action and that its path can be treated as a function of the points through which it travels and expressed mathematically in one "characteristic function" involving advanced calculus. The paper, which predicted the existence of conical refraction (later proved experimentally by H. Lloyd) was published as "The Theory of Systems of Rays" by the Academy in 1828.

This early work on caustics so impressed his contemporaries that in 1827, while he was still an undergraduate, Hamilton was appointed Andrews Professor of Astronomy at the university. With the Chair went the title of Royal Astronomer of Ireland and the charge of the Dunsink observatory. In fact, Hamilton never gave his heart to astronomy; for the rest of his life he devoted himself to mathematical research.

Throughout much of his life Hamilton was closely involved in the work of the British Association for the Advancement of Science, and at a meeting of the association in Dublin in 1835 he was knighted by the Lord-Lieutenant of Ireland. With the knighthood was awarded an annual pension of £200. Many international honours followed, and Hamilton had the distinction of being the first non-American to be elected a fellow of the National Academy of Sciences of the United States. In his latter years Hamilton became somewhat of a recluse, working tirelessly at his home (unfinished meals were found among the piles of paper in his study when he died) and drinking too heavily. He died, of gout, at Dublin on 2 September 1865.

In addition to his work on caustics, Hamilton's most important research was in the field of complex numbers and in the branch of study which he created, the algebra of quaternions. In 1833 he began to seek an improved way of handling complex numbers of the form $a + ib$ where $i = \sqrt{-1}$ and a and b are real numbers. He thought that, since a and ib were different types of quantity, it was wrong to connect them by $a + $ sign; he also considered $\sqrt{-1}$ to be meaningless. He therefore devised new rules of addition, subtraction, multiplication and division on the basis of considering $a + ib$ as a couple of real numbers represented by (a,b).

He also showed that the sum of two complex numbers could be represented by a parallelogram and that complex numbers could be used, in general, as a useful tool in plane geometry.

From couples Hamilton went on to investigate triples and this led him to his great work on quaternions. Hamilton first formally announced his definition of quaternions to the Irish Royal Academy in 1844. But it was not until he began to lecture on them in 1848 that his new algebra really began to take shape. The lectures were published in 1853. Hamilton's investigation of triples, with its obvious relevance to three-dimensional geometry, was a much more difficult task than his work on doubles. He found that many mathematical notions had to be sacrificed. Of these by far the most important was the commutative principle. Hamilton found out, during his research, that his quaternions had four components (hence the name), not three, as he had expected. They took the form $a + bi + cj + dk$ where j and k were similar to i. The fundamental formula was $i^2 = j^2 = k^2 = ijk = -1$. So delighted was Hamilton at this discovery that he scratched the formula on the stonework of a bridge under which he was passing when it came to him. The result of this formula was to reveal that for quaternions the ordinary commutative principle of multiplication (that is $3 \times 4 = 4 \times 3$) did not work, for $ij = -ji$. This was perhaps Hamilton's most important contribution to mathematics, since it forced mathematicians to abandon their belief in the commutative principle as an axiom.

Hamilton hoped that quaternions would find applications in the solution of problems in physics in the way that vectors have proved to do. Indeed, it was Hamilton who coined the word "vector" and it was he who made it possible to deal with lines in all possible positions and directions and freed them from dependence on Cartesian axes of reference. But although he wrote two large books on the subjects his hopes for quaternions were not fulfilled, and today their usefulness has been superseded, for most problems, by the development of vector and tensor analysis.

Hankel, Hermann (1839–1873), was a German mathematician and mathematical historian who, in a somewhat brief life, nevertheless made significant contributions to the study of complex and hyper-complex numbers and the theory of functions. A great innovator himself – his name is perpetuated in the Hankel functions – much of his work was also in developing that of others. In turn, his work later received considerable and useful development.

Hankel was born in Halle on 14 February 1839, but it was in Leipzig – where his father was Professor of Physics at the University – that he grew up and was educated. At the age of 21, Hankel went to Göttingen University, but transferred a year later to the University of Berlin, where he studied under Karl Weierstrass (1815–1897) and Leopold Kronecker (1823–1891), receiving his doctorate in only twelve months for a thesis on a special class of symmetrical determinates. In 1867 he was appointed Associate Professor of Mathematics at Leipzig. Taking up a similar post at Tübingen in 1869, he spent only four years there before he died, on 29 August 1873.

Hankel published many important works, the first of which was his *Theorie der complexen Zahlensysteme*, issued in 1867. The work dealt with the real, complex and hyper-complex number systems, and demonstrated that no hyper-complex number system can satisfy all the laws of ordinary arithmetic. Hankel also revised Peacock's principle of the permanence of formal laws and developed the theory of complex numbers as well as the higher algebraic systems of August Möbius, Hermann Grassmann and William Hamilton. Presenting algebra as a deductive science, Hankel was one of the original few to recognize the importance of Grassmann's work. His researches into the foundations of arithmetic promoted the development of the theory of quaternions.

In *Untersuchungen über die unendlich oft oscillerenden und unstetigen Functionen* – another of Hankel's major works, concerning in particular the theory of functions – he presented a method for constructing functions with singularities at every rational point. The method was based on a principle of his own devising, regarding the condensation of singularities. He also explicitly stated that functions do not possess general properties; this work was an important advance towards modern integration theory.

In another work on the same topic Hankel provided an example of a continuous function that was non-differentiable at an infinite number of points.

The Hankel functions provide a solution to the Bessel differential equation, which had originally occurred in connection with the theory of planetary motions. Today the equation holds more relevance to the study of wave propagation, to problems in optics, to electromagnetic theory, to elasticity and fluid motions, and to potential and diffusion problems.

Hankel was also the first to suggest a method for assessing the magnitude, or "measure", of absolutely discontinuous point sets (such as the set of only irrational numbers lying between 0 and 1). Subsequently developed by Georg Cantor, Émile Borel, Henri Lebesgue and (finally) Andrei Kolmogorov, the "measure" theory of point sets has now been extensively applied to probability, cybernetics and electronics.

Apart from his purely scientific work, Hankel was also a noteworthy historian of mathematics, concentrating on the mathematics of the classical and medieval periods. One of his assertions was that it was the Brahmins – the learned men of the highest caste – of Hindustan who were the real inventors of algebra, in that they were the first to recognize the existence of negative numbers.

Hardy, Godfrey Harold (1877–1947), was one of the foremost British mathematicians of the twentieth century; almost all his research was at a very advanced level in the fields of pure mathematics known as analysis and number theory. However, although there are few – if any – well-known results that can be directly linked with his name, his influence on early twentieth-century mathematics was enormous. His book, *A Course in Pure Mathematics*, revolutionized the teaching of mathematics at senior school and university levels, and another book, *An Introduction to the Theory of Numbers*, written in conjunction with E. Wright, was once described as one of the most often quoted in mathematical literature.

Hardy was born on 7 February 1877 at Cranleigh, Surrey, where his father was art master at Cranleigh public school. Hardy attended the school and showed no little talent in mathematics and languages. Later he obtained a scholarship on the basis of his mathematical ability to Winchester School. There, considered too able in the subject to be taught as part of the usual class, he was tutored on his own. Completing his education, Hardy then went to Trinity College, Cambridge, where in 1896 he was awarded the Smith's Prize for mathematics and elected Fellow of the College. His first results were published in 1900 and by 1906, when he became a permanent Lecturer in mathematics, he had shown himself to be an accomplished research mathematician. Two years later he published his mighty work, *A Course in Pure Mathematics*, in which his approach was based on emulation of Camille Jordan's spiritedly modern *Cours d'Analyse*. Hardy's book has ever since been a mathematical equivalent of a best-seller. By 1910, when he was elected a Fellow of the Royal Society, his reputation was world wide. He was elected to the Savilian Chair of Geometry at Oxford in 1919, but returned in 1931 to Cambridge as Sadlerian Professor of Pure Mathematics. His fame as a mathematician was universal and recognized by many honours and awards. He spent two separate years as visiting Professor at Princeton University and at the California Institute of Technology. At the age of 65 he retired from his position at Cambridge, and died on 1 December 1947.

Hardy's researches included such topics as the evaluation of difficult integrals and the treatment of awkward series of algebraic terms. Among his successes in number theory was his new proof of the prime number theorem. According to the theorem – orginally proved by the French mathematicians Hadamard and Poussin – $\pi(x)$, the number of prime numbers not exceeding x, is said to approach $x/\log_e x$ when x approaches infinity. His investigations in this area led to the discovery of further important results in the theory of numbers. Other problems on which he worked, often with John Littlewood (1885-1977), were the ways in which numbers could be partitioned into simpler numbers. (For example, $6 = 5 + 1$, $4 + 2$, and $3 + 3$, and can thus be partitioned into two numbers in three ways. It can also be partitioned into three numbers in three ways, and four numbers in two ways.) Akin to these problems were the ways in which numbers could be "decomposed" into squares and cubes, etc. Hardy also worked on the conjecture put forward by Goldbach as to whether every even number is the sum of two prime numbers. (This is still an unsolved problem.) A more geometrical problem, yet one deep in number theory, was to examine the number of points with whole number co-ordinates (or points at the vertices of an equal square lattice) inside or on the circumference of a given circle.

Apart from the books already cited, Hardy was the sole or joint author of several others, including *Inequalities* and *Divergent Series*, the latter of which was published after his death.

The purest of pure mathematicians, Hardy shunned all connections of mathematics with physics, technology, engineering – and especially with warfare. Even those branches of the subject which had peripheral applications were avoided. The only "tarnishes" on his work were a note on a problem in genetics, which described what has become known as Hardy's law, and an interest in relativity theory.

Many leading mathematicians were influenced by him and considered him a great teacher. Besides his prolific collaboration with John Littlewood, he also had a fascinating mathematical association with the largely untutored Indian mathematical genius Srinavasa Ramanujan (1887-1920).

Hausdorff, Felix (1868-1942), was a German mathematician and philosopher who is chiefly remembered for his development of the branch of mathematics known as topology, in which he formulated the theory of point sets. The author of an influential book on the subject, he wrote philosophical works too, and contributed extensively to several other fields of mathematics.

Hausdorff was born of Jewish parents in Breslau, Germany (now Wrocław, Poland), on 8 November 1868. He completed his secondary education in Leipzig and, after studying mathematics and astronomy in Berlin and Freiburg, returned to Leipzig to graduate there in 1891. For the next seven years he wrote and published a number of papers dealing with optics, mathematics and astronomy; he also produced works on philosophical and literary themes. In 1902 he was appointed Professor at Leipzig University, after which the subject of mathematics – and particularly set theory – dominated his output. Then appointed Associate Professor at Bonn University, he published his major work, *Grundzuge der Mengenlehre* (Basic Features of Set Theory). In 1913 Hausdorff took up the position of Professor at Griefswald, but eight years later returned to Bonn for the remainder of his academic life; he retired at the statutory age of 67, in 1935. Even after his retirement he continued to work on set theory and topology; all his work, however, was published outside Germany. Because of his Jewish faith, Hausdorff in 1942 was scheduled to be sent to an internment camp. Rather than let that happen he committed suicide – with his wife and her sister – on 26 January of that year.

Topology is the study of figures and shapes that retain their essential proportions despite being "squeezed" or "stretched". In this way, a square may be considered (topologically) equivalent to any closed plane figure and a cube may even be regarded as (topoloically) equivalent to a sphere. In his *Grundzuge der Mengenlehre*

Hausdorff formulated a theory of topological and metric spaces into which concepts previously advanced by other mathematicians fitted well. He proposed that such spaces be regarded as sets of points and sets of relations among the points, and introduced the principle of duality. This principle states that an equation between sets remains valid if the sets are replaced by their complements and the symbol for union is exchanged for that of intersection; and that an inequality (inequation) remains valid if each side is replaced by its complement and the symbol for union is exchanged for that of intersection, provided also the inclusion symbol is reversed.

Developing his point set theory, Hausdorff also created what are now called Hausdorff's Neighbourhood Axioms; there are four axioms.

1. To each point x there corresponds at least one neighbourhood U_x, each neighbourhood U_x containing the point x.

2. If U_x and V_x are two neighbourhoods of the same point x, their intersection contains a neighbourhood of x.

3. If U_x contains a point y, there is a neighbourhood U_y such that $U_y \subset U_x$.

4. If x is not equal to y, there are two neighbourhoods U_x and U_y such that the intersection of U_x and $U_y = 0$ (that is, such that U_x and U_y have no points in common).

From these axioms Hausdorff derived what are now called Hausdorff's Topological Spaces. A topological space is understood to be a set E of elements x and certain subsets S_x of E which are known as neighbourhoods of x. These neighbourhoods satisfy the Hausdorff axioms. Later in the book - after dealing with the properties of general space - Hausdorff introduced further axioms involving metric and particular Euclidean spaces.

Hausdorff contributed extensively to several fields of mathematics including mathematical analysis, in which he proved some very important theorems on summation methods and properties of moments. He also investigated the symbolic exponential formula which he himself derived. His main contribution to mathematics, however, was in the field of point set theory and topology, of which he is often considered the "high priest". Hausdorff's work in this area led to many results of primary importance, such as the investigation of general closure spaces, and what is now termed Hausdorff's maximal principle in general set theory.

Hawking, Stephen William (1942-   ), is a British theoretical physicist and mathematician whose main field of research has been the nature of space-time and those anomalies in space-time known as singularities.

Hawking was born in Oxford on 8 January 1942, and showed exceptional talent in mathematics and physics from an early age. At Oxford University he became especially interested in thermodynamics, relativity theory and quantum mechanics - an interest that was encouraged by his attending a summer course at the Royal Observatory in 1961. When he completed his undergraduate course in 1962 (receiving a First Class Honours degree in physics), he enrolled as a research student in general relativity at the Department of Applied Mathematics and Theoretical Physics at the University of Cambridge.

During his postgraduate program Hawking was diagnosed as having A.L.S. (Amyotrophic Lateral Sclerosis), a rare and progressive neuromotor disease which handicaps motor and vocal functions and makes it necessary for long and complex mathematical calculations to be carried out mentally. He was nevertheless able to continue his studies and to embark upon a distinguished and productive scientific career. He was elected Fellow of the Royal Society in 1974, and became Lucasian Professor of Mathematics at Cambridge University in 1980.

From its earliest stages, Hawking's research has been concerned with the concept of singularities - breakdowns in the space-time continuum where the classic laws of physics no longer apply. The prime example of a singularity is a black hole, the final form of a collapsed star. During the later 1960s, Hawking - relying on a few assumptions about the properties of matter, and incidentally developing a mathematical theory of causality in curved space-time - proved that if Einstein's General Theory of Relativity is correct, then a singularity must also have occurred at the Big Bang, the beginning of the Universe and the birth of space-time itself.

In 1970 Hawking's research turned to the examination of the properties of black holes. A black hole is a chasm in the fabric of space-time, and its boundary is called the event horizon. Hawking realized that the surface area of the event horizon around a black hole could only increase or remain constant with time - it could never decrease. This meant, for example, that when two black holes merged, the surface area of the new black hole would be larger than the sum of the surface areas of the two original black holes. He also noticed that there were certain parallels between the laws of thermodynamics and the properties of black holes. For instance, the second law of thermodynamics states that entropy must increase with time; the surface area of the event horizon can thus be seen as the entropy ("randomness") of the black hole.

Over the next four years, Hawking – with Carter, Israel and Robinson – provided mathematical proof for the hypothesis formulated by John Wheeler (1911–   ), known as the "No Hair Theorem". This stated that the only properties of matter that were conserved once it entered a black hole were its mass, its angular momentum and its electric charge; it thus lost its shape, its "experience", its baryon number and its existence as matter or antimatter.

Since 1974, Hawking has studied the behaviour of matter in the immediate vicinity of a black hole, from a theoretical base in quantum mechanics. He found, to his initial surprise, that black holes – from which nothing was supposed to be able to escape – could emit thermal radiation.

Hawking's present objective is to produce an overall synthesis of quantum mechanics and relativity theory, to yield a full quantum theory of gravity. Such a unified physical theory would incorporate all four basic types of interaction: strong nuclear, weak nuclear, electromagnetic and gravitational.

The properties of space-time, the beginning of the Universe, and a unified theory of physics are all fundamental research areas of science. Hawking has made, and continues to make, major contributions to the modern understanding of them all.

Heath, Thomas Little (1861–1940), was a British civil servant and mathematical historian of the ancient Greek mathematicians. For his considerable services to the Treasury Office he was knighted; nevertheless he received no little acclaim for his historical works – he became a Fellow of the Royal Society in 1912, and of the Royal Academy in 1932 – and for a year he was President of the Mathematical Association.

Heath was born in 1861 in Lincolnshire. As a boy he attended the Caistor Grammar School and later studied at Clifton and Trinity Colleges, Cambridge, where he obtained a First Class Classics Tripos - the first part in 1881 and the second in 1883. It was at this time that he won first place in an open competition for Home Civil Service, and was appointed a clerk in the Treasury in 1884. In 1885 he was made Fellow of Trinity College, although it was not until eleven years later that he obtained his doctorate. In 1887 he became Private Secretary to the Permanent Secretary at the Treasury, and from 1891 to 1894 held a similar post in relation to successive Financial Secretaries. He became Principal Clerk of the Treasury from 1901 to

1907, and in that year was himself appointed Assistant Secretary. In 1908 he published his first full-scale book, *Euclid's Elements*, a monumental work in three volumes. Five years later he was appointed Joint Permanent Secretary to the Treasury and Auditor of the Civil List, a post he held until 1919, when he was made Comptroller General and Secretary to the Commissioners for the Reduction of the National Debt. He remained as such till 1926, when he retired from the civil service. Meanwhile, in 1921 he produced his two-volume *History of Greek Mathematics*, which has come to be regarded as the standard work on the subject in the English language. After leaving the civil service, Heath was appointed one of the University of Cambridge Commissioners, and was also a member of the Royal Commission on National Museums and Galleries from 1927 to 1929. He died on 16 March 1940 in Ashtead, Surrey.

No doubt Heath's interest in Greek mathematics, which made him one of the leading authorities on the subject, was the result of his university training in mathematics and the Classics. He took a special interest in Diophantus, whose *Arithmetica* he edited for an English-language edition. The work, *Diophantus of Alexandria. A Study in the History of Greek Algebra*, was published in 1885, and was more in the style of an essay.

Apollonius of Perga. A Treatise on Conic Sections was published in 1896. It is particularly interesting that in this work Heath used modern mathematical notation. It was followed, a year later, by an edition of the works of Archimedes, in which Heath used the same treatment. (This was translated into German in 1914.) And Heath's version of Archimedes' *Method* appeared in 1912. In 1913, Heath produced *Aristarchus of Samos, the Ancient Copernicus*, a comprehensive account of Aristarchos and his work on astronomy.

In the great *History of Greek Mathematics*, Heath dealt with his subjects mainly according to topics and not in chronological order as others had done before him. In the Preface to the book, Heath justified such an approach by reference to the famous problem of doubling the cube, saying, "If all recorded solutions are collected together, it is much easier to see the relations ... between them and to get a comprehensive view of the history of the problem." Heath rewrote the *History* in 1931 and published it as a *Manual of Greek Mathematics*; in fact, however, it is really a mere condensed version of the original text.

Heine, Heinrich Eduard (1812–1881), was a German mathematician and a prolific author of mathematical papers on advanced topics. He completed the formulation of the notion of uniform continuity and subsequently provided a proof of the classic theorem on uniform continuity of continuous functions. This theorem has since become known as Heine's theorem.

Heine was born on 16 March 1812 in Berlin, where his father was a banker. His first education was by tutors at home, and he then attended local high schools. Eventually he went to Göttingen University and studied under Karl Gauss (1777–1855). To complete his education he returned to Berlin and became a pupil of Lejeune Dirichlet (1805–1859), Jakob Steiner (1796–1863) and the more astronomically-minded Johann Encke (1791–1865), receiving his PhD in 1842. He then spent a further couple of years at Königsberg, learning from Karl Jacobi (1804–1851) and Franz Neumann (1798–1895). Finally, at the age of 32, Heine became an unpaid lecturer at Bonn University. Four years later, in 1848, he was appointed Professor there, but in the same year he took up a similar post at Halle University. And it was at Halle he remained for the rest of his life; he died there on 21 October 1881.

During his lifetime he received few honours or awards. On the other hand, when offered the Chair in Mathematics at Göttingen University – perhaps the most prestigious appointment possible at the time – in 1875, he turned it down.

In all, Heine published more than 50 papers on mathematics. His specialty was spherical functions, Lamé functions and Bessel functions. He published his most important work – *Handbuch der Kugelfunctionen* – in 1861; it was re-issued in a second edition in 1881 and became the standard work on spherical functions for the next 50 years.

Although the name of his theory is sometimes linked with the name of Émile Borel (as the Heine-Borel theorem), it can be confidently argued that Borel's contribution was of lesser value. Borel formulated the covering property of uniform conformity, and proved it; Heine formulated the notion of uniform continuity – a notion that had escaped the attention of Augustin Cauchy (1789–1857), regarded as the innovator of continuity theory – and went on to prove the classic theorem of uniform continuity of continuous functions.

Herbrand, Jacques (1908–1931), was a French mathematical prodigy who, in a life cut tragically short, still originated some innovatory concepts in the field of mathematical logic. Interested also in class-field theory, he remains best remembered for the Herbrand Theorem.

Herbrand was born on 12 February 1908 in Paris, where he grew up and was educated, entering the École Normale Supérieure at the age of 17 already precociously talented in mathematics. Three years later he published his first paper on mathematical logic for the Paris Academy of Sciences, and in the following year – 1929, when he was 21 – for his doctorate, he produced the paper in which he formulated Herbrand's Theorem. His military service in the French army then occupied him for twelve months, at the end of which a Rockefeller scholarship enabled him to go to Berlin to study there, and then for a couple of months in Hamburg and Göttingen. He was killed in an Alpine accident on 27 July 1931.

For his doctor's degree, Herbrand introduced what is now considered to be his main contribution to mathematical logic, the theorem to which his name is attached. A fundamental development in quantification theory, Herbrand's Theorem established a link between that theory and sentential logic, and has since found many applications in such fields as decision and reduction problems.

Herbrand was also fascinated by modern algebra and wrote a number of papers on class-field theory, which deals with Abelian extensions of a given algebraic number field from properties of the field. He contributed greatly to the development of the theory which, until that time, had received scant attention since first being devised by Leopold Kronecker (1823–1891) in the middle of the nineteenth century. After Herbrand's death, however, the theory was the subject of further development by later mathematicians.

Hermite, Charles (1822–1901), was a French mathematician who was a principal contributor to the development of the theory of algebraic forms, the arithmetical theory of quadratic forms, and the theories of elliptic and Abelian functions. Much of his work was highly innovative, especially his solution of the quintic equation through elliptic modular functions, and his proof of the transcendence of e. A man of generous disposition and a good teacher, Hermite in his work showed that the brilliance of the previous generation of mathematicians – Karl Gauss, Augustin Cauchy, Karl Jacobi and Lejeune Dirichlet – was not to fade in the next.

Hermite was born the sixth of the seven children of a minor businessman in Dieuze, Lorraine, on 24 December 1822. He grew up and was educated in Nancy, however. Completing his education, he went to Paris and first studied physics at the Henry IV Collège before he went to the Lycée Louis le Grand and became fascinated by mathematics. He was always hopeless at passing examinations - but his private reading at night of the works of Leonhard Euler, Karl Gauss and Joseph Lagrange might well have distracted him from other preparation. From 1842 he studied at the École Polytechnique for a year, but because he did not pass the examinations there either (and apparently also because he was congenitally lame), he was asked not to return. So it was not until 1848, at the age of 25, that he finally graduated, although by that time he already had some reputation as an innovative mathematician. He was appointed to a minor teaching post at the Collège de France. In 1856 two things happened: he was elected to the Paris Academy of Sciences, and he caught smallpox. Recovering from the latter, he had to wait until he was 47 years old before he finally attained the status of Professor, first in 1869 at the École Normale, then a year later at the Sorbonne. An honorary member of many societies, he received numerous awards and honours during his lifetime. He died in Paris on 14 January 1901.

Throughout his life Hermite exerted great scientific influence by corresponding with other prominent mathematicians. One of his first pieces of work was to generalize Abel's theorem on elliptic functions to the case of hyperelliptic ones. Communicating his discovery to Karl Jacobi (1804-1851) in August 1844, he also discussed four other papers on number theory.

Between 1847 and 1851 he worked on the arithmetical theory of quadratic forms and the use of continuous variables. Then for ten years between 1854 and 1864 he worked on the theory of invariants.

Today he is remembered chiefly in connection with Hermitean forms (a complex generalization of quadratic forms) and with Hermitean polynomials - work carried out in 1873. In the same year, he showed that e, the base of natural logarithms, is transcendental. (Transcendental numbers are real or complex numbers which are not algebraic; we now know that most real numbers are transcendental.) It was by a slight adaptation of Hermite's proof for this that Ferdinand von Lindemann (1852-1939) in 1882 demonstrated the transcendence of π.

In 1872 and 1877 Hermite solved the Lamé differential equation, and in 1878 he solved the fifth-degree (quintic) equation of elliptic functions.

Hermite's scientific work was collected and edited by the later French mathematician Charles Picard (1856-1941).

Hilbert, David (1862-1943), was a German mathematician, philosopher and physicist whose work in all three disciplines was brilliantly innovative and fundamental to further development. An excellent teacher, unsurpassed in lucidity of exposition, his influence on twentieth-century mathematics has been enormous. He is particularly remembered for his research on the theory of algebraic invariants, on the theory of algebraic numbers, on the formulation of abstract axiomatic principles in geometry, on analysis and topology (in which he derived what is now called Hilbert's theory of spaces), on theoretical physics, and finally on the philosophical foundations of mathematics.

Hilbert was born on 23 January 1862 in Königsberg, then in German Prussia, now Kaliningrad in the Russian Republic of the Soviet Union. He grew up and was educated there, attending Königsberg University - an ancient and venerable seat of learning - from 1880 to 1885, when he received his PhD. He then studied further in Leipzig and in Paris before returning to Königsberg University to become an unsalaried lecturer. Six years later he was appointed Professor, and three years later still (in 1895) he was offered the highly prestigious post as Professor of Mathematics at Göttingen University. He accepted, and held the position until he retired in 1930. Although he developed pernicious anaemia in 1925, he recovered, and died in Göttingen on 14 February 1943.

Hilbert's first period of research (between 1885 and 1892) was on algebraic invariants; he tried to find a connection between invariants and fields of algebraic functions and algebraic varieties. Representing the rational function in terms of a square, he eventually arrived at what is known as Hilbert's irreducibility theorem, which states that, in general, irreducibility is preserved if, in a polynomial of several variables with integral coefficients, some of the variables are replaced by integers. He later investigated ninth-degree equations, solving them by using algebraic functions of only four variables. In this way, Hilbert had by the end of the period not only solved all the known central problems of this branch of mathematics, he had in his methodology introduced sweeping developments and new areas for research (particularly in algebraic topology, which he himself returned to later).

In 1897, with some help from his colleague and friend Hermann Minkowski (1864-1909), Hilbert produced *Der Zahlbericht*, in which he gathered together all the relevant knowledge of algebraic number theory, reorganized it, and laid the basis for the developing class-field theory. He abandoned this work, however, when there was still much to be done.

Two years later, having moved to another area of study, Hilbert published his classic work, *Grundlagen der Geometrie.* (It is still available in its latest edition.) In it, he gave a full account of the development of geometry in the nineteenth century, and although on this occasion his innovations were (for him) relatively few, his use of geometry, and of algebra within geometry, to devise systems incorporating abstract yet rigorously axiomatic principles, was important both to the further development of the subject and to Hilbert's own later work in logic and consistency proofs. In the related field of topology, he referred back to his previous work on invariants in order to derive his theory of spaces in an infinite number of dimensions.

In 1900, attending the International Congress of Mathematicians in Paris, Hilbert set the Congress a total of 23 hitherto unsolved problems. Many have since been solved – but solved or not, the problems stimulated considerable scientific debate, research and fruitful development.

In a study of mathematical analysis some years afterwards, Hilbert used a new approach in tackling Dirichlet's Problem, and made other contributions to the calculus of variations. In 1909 he provided proof of Waring's hypothesis (of a century earlier) of the representation of integers as the sums of powers. From that time forward, Hilbert worked on problems of physics, such as the kinetic theory of gases, and the theory of relativity – problems, he said, too difficult to be confined to physics and physicists. His deep research led finally to his critical work on the foundations of mathematical logic, in which his contribution to proof theory was extremely important by itself.

Hogben, Lancelot Thomas (1895–1975), was a British zoologist and geneticist who, somewhat surprisingly, wrote a very successful book entitled *Mathematics for the Millions.* Although he thereafter sought to use mathematical techniques in his various posts, there were in fact few opportunities to do so until he was put in charge of the medical statistics records for the British army during World War II.

Hogben was born in Southsea, Hampshire, on 9 December 1895. Growing up, he evinced a strong interest in natural history. From the Middlesex County Secondary School he won a scholarship to Trinity College, Cambridge, in 1913. Simultaneously he took an external degree course in zoology at London University. Imprisoned, however, as a conscientious objector in 1916 during World War I, he was released when his health deteriorated seriously and briefly worked as a journalist before being appointed Lecturer in Zoology at Birkbeck College, London, in 1917. Two years later, he transferred to the Imperial College and shortly afterwards received his doctorate. He then went to teach in Edinburgh for a couple of years, to Montreal, Canada, for a similar period, and to Cape Town, South Africa, for again the same duration of time. He returned to London University in 1930 to take up the post of Professor of Social Biology. In hospital in 1933, he wrote his famous *Mathematics for the Millions* partly as therapy, partly for self-education; he also became interested in linguistics. Following this latter interest, he was in Norway at the outbreak of World War II, and it was not until 1941 – after travelling through Sweden, the Soviet Union and the United States – that he got back to Britain and became a colonel in the War Office. After the war he became Professor of Medical Statistics at the University of Birmingham, where he remained until he retired in 1961. The author of many scientific papers, and the recipient of many awards and honours – a Fellow of the Royal Society since 1936 – Hogben died in Glyn Ceirog, Wales, on 22 August 1975.

It was in London in the 1930s – around the time that his popular *Mathematics for the Millions* was published – that Hogben first began to try to apply mathematical principles to the study of genetics, with particular reference to his investigation of generations of the fruit-fly *Drosophila* in relation to research on heredity in humans. He was especially concerned to evaluate the validity of statistical methods as applied in the biological and behavioural sciences, and was surprised at the apparent level of ignorance in such methods among the many scientists of those disciplines.

His desire to use mathematical principles was given considerably more scope on his appointment as colonel in charge of the War Office medical statistical records. Asked to reorganize the entire system, Hogben successfully did just that – and it was, after all, in the days when data processing was still a matter of mechanical sorting. He was subsequently promoted to Director of Army Medical Statistics. (One of his investigations into the army's clinical trials of the sulphonamide drugs proved that their indiscriminate use had favoured the selection of resistant strains of the bacteria responsible for causing gonorrhoea.)

Working at Birmingham University after the war, his attempts to reorganize civilian medical records were less successful – partly because of

resistance from some senior medical practition-
ers reluctant to change their ways.

During his last years, Hogben spent much
time revising previously published work and
writing on other aspects of philosophy and
mathematics.

J

Jacobi, Karl Gustav Jacob (1804-1851), was a
German mathematician and mathematical physicist, much of whose work was on the theory of
elliptical functions, mathematical analysis, number theory, geometry and mechanics. An influential teacher, he corresponded with many of
the other great mathematicians of his time.

Jacobi was born in Potsdam (now in East
Germany) on 10 December 1804, the second son
of a wealthy and well educated Jewish banker.
A child prodigy, he rose to the top class of his
local school within months of first entering, and
was ready to go to university at the age of 12 -
but that the authorities would not permit. He
went to Berlin University in 1821 and graduated
in the same year, with excellent results in Greek,
Latin, history and mathematics. Continuing
at the University he studied philosophy and
the Classics, reading mathematics privately
because, apart from Karl Gauss at Göttingen -
with whom he corresponded - there was simply
no one who could teach him. At the age of nine-
teen he qualified as a teacher. The following year
he received his doctorate, underwent conversion
to Christianity (as may have been professionally
advisable) and became an unsalaried lecturer at
Berlin University. After only one year there,
however, in 1826 he joined the staff at
Königsberg (now Kaliningrad) University, coming into contact there with people such as the
physicists Franz Neumann (1798-1895) and
Heinrich Dove (1803-1897), and the astronomer
and mathematician Friedrich Bessel (1784-
1846). In 1832 Jacobi was made Professor, a
post he retained for 18 years. In 1843, however,
he fell ill and went to Italy to recover, returning
to Berlin at the end of 1844. Four years later,
after an unwise and unfortunate excursion into
politics, he lost the royal pension on which he
had been living and his family was reduced to
near-destitution. Luckily, the Prussian government was not prepared to see a man of his talent
- and reputation - starve. In 1851, however, he
again fell ill, first with influenza and then with
smallpox. He died, in Berlin, on 18 February of
that year.

There are very few areas in mathematics that
Jacobi's researches at one time or another did
not cover fully. He is particularly remembered
for his work on elliptic functions, in which to
some extent he was competing against a rival in
the contemporary Norwegian mathematician
Niels Abel (1802-1829). His principal published
work on elliptic function theory was *Funda-
menta nova theoriae functionum ellipticarum*,
produced in 1829, incorporating some of Abel's
ideas and introducing his own concept of
hyper-elliptic functions. In analysis, Jacobi studied differential equations (the results of which
he applied to problems in dynamics) and the
theory of determinants. In the latter field he invented a functional determinant - now called
the Jacobian determinant - which has since been
of considerable use in later analytical investigations, and was even supportive in the development of quantum mechanics. He advanced the
theory of the configurations of rotating liquid
masses by showing that the ellipsoids now
known as Jacobi's ellipsoids are figures of equilibrium.

He had immense knowledge in every branch
of mathematics - Jacobi's PhD thesis was an
analytical discussion on the theory of partial
fractions; he was at the same time writing to
Gauss on cubic residues in number theory; his
first lecture, nevertheless, was on the theory of
curves and surfaces in three-dimensional space.
He was also always trying to link together different mathematical disciplines. For instance, he
introduced elliptic functions into number theory
and into the theory of integration, which in
turn connected with the theory of differential
equations and his own principle of the last
multiplier.

Jacobi's work, and particularly his researches
in collaboration with Franz Neumann and
Friedrich Bessel, revived an interest in mathematics generally in Germany. He therefore became a highly respected and honoured man.
After his death, his great friend Lejeune
Dirichlet (1805-1859) delivered a memorial lecture at the Berlin Academy of Sciences on 1 July
1852, in which he described Jacobi as "the greatest mathematician among members of the Academy since Joseph Lagrange".

Jordan, Marie Ennemond Camille (1838-1922),
was a French mathematician originally trained
as an engineer. An influential teacher, he was
himself strongly influenced by the work (one
generation earlier) of Evariste Galois (1811-
1832) and, accordingly, concentrated on research in topology, analysis and (particularly)
group theory. He nevertheless also made further

contributions to a wide range of mathematical topics.

Jordan was born in Lyons on 5 January 1838. Completing his education, he entered the École Polytechnique in Paris and studied engineering. He devoted most of his spare time to mathematics, however, and although he qualified as an engineer – and even began to work professionally in that capacity – it was as a mathematician that he joined the staff of the École Polytechnique at the age of 35, in 1873. He also gave lectures at the Collège de France. Eight years later he was elected to the Paris Academy of Sciences. In 1912 he retired. In 1919 – at the age of 81 – he became a Foreign Member of the Royal Society. He died in Paris on 20 January 1922.

Before he had even begun to teach mathematics, Jordan was already acknowledged as the greatest exponent of algebra in his day. Pursuing his interest in the work of the ill-fated Evariste Galois, Jordan systematically developed the theory of finite groups and arrived at the concept of infinite groups. An early result of this was the related concept of composition series, and what is now known as the Jordan-Holder theorem (which deals with the invariance of the system of indices of consecutive groups). He investigated Galois' study of permutation groups, in which Galois had considered the consequences of permutating the roots (solutions) of equations, and linked this with the problem of the solution of polynomial equations.

In 1870 Jordan published his famous *Traité des substitutions et des équations algébriques* which, for the next three decades, was to be the standard work in group theory. Following this major achievement, Jordan concentrated on his theorems of finiteness. In all he developed three, the first of which dealt with symmetrical groups. The second had its origin in the theory of linear differential equations; Immanuel Fuchs (1833–1902) had completed work on such equations of the second order, Jordan reduced the similar problem for equations of the order n to a problem in group theory. Jordan's last finiteness theorem generalized Charles Hermite's results on the theory of quadratic forms with integral coefficients.

In topology, Jordan developed an entirely new approach to what is now known as homological or combinatorial topology by investigating symmetries in polyhedra from an exclusively combinatorial viewpoint. His other great contribution to this branch of mathematics was his formulation of the proof for the "decomposition" of a plane into two regions by a simple closed curve.

Jordan's work in analysis was published in 1882 in the *Cours d'Analyse de l'École Polytechnique*, a spiritedly modern book that had a widespread influence, particularly because of Jordan's insistence on what a really rigorous proof should comprise.

Much of Jordan's later work was concerned with the theory of functions, and he applied the theory of functions of bounded variation to the particular curve that bears his name.

K

Klein, Christian Felix (1849–1925), was an extremely influential German mathematician and mathematical physicist whose unification of the various Euclidean and non-Euclidean geometries was crucial to the future development of that branch of mathematics. Equally skilled, however, in almost every branch of mathematics, Klein had as perhaps his greatest talent the ability to discover relationships between different areas of research, rather than in carrying out detailed calculations. He also possessed great organizational skills, and initiated and supervised the writing of an encyclopaedia on mathematics, its teaching and its applications. He became widely known for his lectures and his books on the historical development of mathematics in the nineteenth century. It was to a great extent due to him that Göttingen became the main centre for all the exact sciences – not just mathematics – in all Germany.

Klein was born on 25 April 1849 in Düsseldorf, where he grew up and was educated. In 1865, at the age of 16, he went to the University of Bonn to read mathematics and physics; only three years later he was awarded his doctorate there. He decided to further his education by spending a few months in different European universities, and went to Göttingen, to Berlin, and then to Paris in 1869. At the outbreak of the Franco-Prussian War he was obliged to leave Paris so he entered the military service as a medical orderly. In 1871 he qualified as a Lecturer at Göttingen University; the following year he became full Professor of Mathematics at Erlangen University. In his inaugural address there he introduced what he called his "Erlangen *Programm*" on geometries. From 1875 to 1880 he was Professor at the Technische Hochschule in Munich, and then took up a similar post from 1880 to 1886 at Leipzig. He spent the rest of his active research life at Göttingen, retiring as Professor in 1913 because of ill health. During and

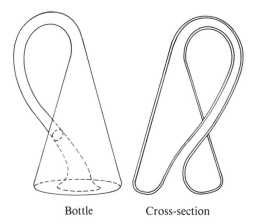

Bottle   Cross-section

*A **Klein bottle** is a "bottle" in name only because, although it would be possible to store liquids in it, it is in fact a one-sided surface which is closed and has no boundary.*

after World War I, however, he gave lectures at his home. Klein died in Göttingen on 22 June 1925.

Klein's Erlangen programme of 1872 comprised a proposal for the unification of Euclidean geometry with the geometries that had been devised during the nineteenth century by mathematicians such as Karl Gauss, Nicolai Lobachevsky, János Bolyai and Bernhard Riemann. He showed that the different geometries are each associated with a separate "collection" or "group" of tranformations. Seen in this way, the geometries could all be treated as individual members of one overall family, and from this very connection conclusions and inferences could be drawn. In the next two years, Klein developed the "programme" and published papers which demonstrated that every individual geometry could be constructed purely projectively; he produced projective models for Euclidean, elliptic and hyperbolic geometries. (Such projective models are now called Klein models.) Much later in his life, Klein returned to the Erlangen programme to apply it to problems in theoretical physics, with special reference to the theory of relativity.

Klein's early research was on topics in line geometry. In 1870, with Sophus Lie (1842-1899), who was later to succeed him at Göttingen, he discovered fundamental properties of the asymptotic lines of the "Kummer" surface, which became famous in algebraic line geometry. In his work on number theory, group theory and the theory of differential equations, Klein was greatly influenced by Bernhard Riemann. It was Klein who redefined a Riemann surface so

that it came to be regarded as an essential part of function theory, not just a valuable way of representing multi-valued functions. Borrowing concepts from physics (and especially fluid dynamics), Klein revised and developed the theory in such a way that to him it seemed the most important work he ever accomplished.

He was also interested in fifth-degree (quintic) equations, and succeeded in solving the general algebraic equation of the fifth degree by considering the icosahedron. This work led him on to elliptic modular functions.

In the 1890s he worked on mathematical physics and engineering, and wrote a textbook with Arnold Sommerfeld (1868-1951) on the theory of the gyroscope which is still an important work in this field of mechanics.

In 1900 he became interested in school mathematics, and recommended the introduction of differential and integral calculus and the function concept into school syllabuses. Eight years later, at the International Congress of Mathematicians in Rome, he was elected Chairman of the International Commission on Mathematical Instruction.

Kolmogorov, Andrei Nikolaevich (1903-   ), is a Soviet mathematician who is especially noted for his work on the theory of probability and on algorithms.

Kolmogorov was born in Tambov on 25 April 1903. Completing his education, he entered Moscow University and graduated there in 1925. He has been on the staff at that University ever since, becoming Professor in 1931, and Head of the University (at the age of 34) in 1937. A member of the USSR Academy of Sciences since 1939, he is now Chairman of the Academy of Sciences Committee on Mathematical Education, taking an active interest in the teaching of mathematics in secondary schools throughout the entire Soviet Union. He is a member also of a number of learned societies, and has received many state honours and awards.

Shortly after he graduated, Kolmogorov began researching on probability theory. By 1933 he had constructed a complete system of axioms describing the theory fully, using a rigorous and panoramic approach. The first axiomatic presentation of the theory of probability, his system still stands as the most widespread contemporary logical scheme. It involves the set U of elements, called elementary events; every event is completely described by the set of elementary events favourable to it, and so is considered as a certain set of elementary events.

From the 1930s, Kolmogorov worked on

analytical methods essential for constructing the theory of Markov processes. (Markov processes, or Markov chains, are sequences of mutually dependent random variables, where any prediction about x_{n+1}, knowing $x_1 \ldots x_n$, can be based on just x_n, without any loss.)

Kolmogorov also refined the concept of the algorithm – a basic category of mathematics that cannot be defined in any simpler concepts. (The rules of addition, subtraction, multiplication and division in elementary mathematics are examples of algorithms.) The theory of algorithms is closely related to mathematical logic in that the algorithmic concept is the basis of one of the central concepts of mathematical logic: calculus. It also forms the theoretical basis for a number of problems in computational mathematics and is closely associated with cybernetics (the theory of communication and control mechanisms). Finally, the algorithmic concept is fundamental to programmed instructions. Kolmogorov has used his research to work out the theory of conveying information along communication channels.

Some of Kolmogorov's earliest work was on the theory of a real variable. He then worked on the concept of the integral, the convergence of trigonometric series, and on sets. Later, he went back to studying the theory of functions and obtained some important results on the ways of representing functions with a number of variables, by superimposing functions with a smaller number of variables. He also worked on the theory of the approximation of functions and on functional analysis.

Kolmogorov has also contributed to constructive logic and to topology, and been the author of several textbooks.

Kovalevsky, Sonya Vasilievna (1850–1891), was a Russian mathematician and mathematical physicist who, in order to achieve first the education and then the career in which she was extremely successful, had initially to overcome the considerable disadvantage of being female. A gifted teacher – and a noteworthy writer of novels and a play – she was also an innovator in her mathematical research, and was respected and admired by many of the most well-known mathematicians of her time.

Kovalevsky was born Sonya Vasilievna on 15 January 1850 to a wealthy and cultured family of Russian aristocrats. She and her sister were brought up first on the family estate, and later in St Petersburg (now Leningrad), where the family's social circle included the novelist Dostoievsky. Her introduction to serious mathematics was early and bizarre: the walls of a room on the estate were papered with a text on differential calculus. But in 1867 she went to study at the Naval Academy in St Petersburg, where her teachers immediately recognized her great ability. Unfortunately at this time in Europe there was considerable prejudice against women's entering into higher education. In 1868, therefore, at the age of 18, Sonya entered into a formal marriage to Vladimir Kovalevsky, a young geologist, for the sole purpose of being able thereby to study at a foreign university. The following year the couple moved to Heidelberg, where Sonya was able to attend classes taught by the physicists Gustav Kirchhoff, Hermann Helmholtz and other world-famous scientists. In 1871 – by herself – she moved to Berlin to study with the leading mathematician Karl Weierstrass (1815–1897); because women were not permitted there to attend university lectures, he had to teach her privately. Three papers completed in her four years in Berlin qualified her by their very high standard for a doctorate *in absentia* from the University of Göttingen. In spite of this and the efforts of Karl Weierstrass, Kovalevsky could find no professional appointment anywhere in Europe, and was forced to return to Russia to rejoin her husband. There, because of her outspoken liberal views, she could not obtain any employment either. Matters became worse still when her husband's disgrace over certain business deals led to his suicide in 1883.

Kovalevsky was now alone but for a daughter, born five years previously. However, her acquaintance Gösta Mittag-Leffler (from her days in Berlin) had since become Professor at the University of Stockholm. He managed to persuade the University authorities to appoint her to his department, first as a Lecturer, then in 1889 as Professor of Higher Mathematics. In Stockholm she gained a reputation for brilliant teaching, and won prizes for her original papers. She also became renowned for her witty conversation and sporting talents. Besides her actively expressed liberal views, she wrote several novels, a commentary on George Eliot, and a play that was produced in Moscow. At the height of her career, however, pneumonia suddenly ended her life, on 10 February 1891.

Kovalevsky's mathematical work was centred on the then very new field of analysis. She did a considerable amount of work on partial differential equations, which she studied from an analytical viewpoint; and complex analysis featured largely in the paper she published in 1888 on the dynamics of an asymmetric gyroscope. The paper won her a French Academy of

Sciences award, and was so good that the judges nearly doubled the prize money.

What is now called the Cauchy-Kovalevsky theorem is fundamental to the study of partial differential equations. Kovalevsky was able to extend Augustin Cauchy's work on such equations to previously unconsidered cases, and to make it more general and elegant. She sought to find sufficient and necessary conditions for the solution of a partial differential equation, in particular the "boundary" conditions required for a unique particular integral. The theorem concerns these conditions for an analytic function – that is, one that can be expressed as a set of convergent power series.

Other analytical concepts – the integration of inverse functions, elliptic integrals, and Abelian functions, for example – had been developing gradually in the work of Niels Abel, Karl Jacobi, Adrien Legendre, Karl Weierstrass and others; a wealth of difficult theory remained still to be worked out. Kovalevsky made a substantial contribution to this theory, including neatly showing how to simplify certain sets of Abelian integrals (integrals of the form $\int f(x,y)dx$, where y is an algebraic function of x, and $f(x,y)$ is a rational function of x and y).

Her works in mechanics is highlighted by the brilliant paper of 1888 on the asymmetric gyroscope. Leonhard Euler, Siméon-Denis Poisson (among others) had considered rotating solid bodies in relatively simple cases. Kovalevsky took the general case of an asymmetric body and succeeded in using hyper-elliptic integrals to solve the differential equations of motion, producing a solution so general as to be unsurpassed to date.

In celestial mechanics Christiaan Huygens, James Clerk Maxwell and Pierre Laplace before her had studied Saturn's rings, but Kovalevsky generalized her investigations to examine the overall stability of a torus, or ring-shaped body, of liquid. (Others completed this work after her death.) Another major area of research for her was the study of the propagation of light through a crystalline medium.

Kronecker, Leopold (1823-1891), was a German mathematician, skilled in many branches of the subject but pre-eminent in none, who is remembered chiefly for the "Kronecker delta".

Kronecker was born at Liegnitz (now Legnica, Poland) on 7 December 1823 and attended secondary school there, where he was taught by the outstanding mathematician Ernst Kummer (1810-1893). Kummer remained a life-long friend and exercised great influence upon Kro-

necker, especially in interesting him in number theory. In 1841 Kronecker entered the University of Berlin, where he studied mathematics, chemistry, astronomy and philosophy. In 1843 he spent some time at the universities of Bonn and Breslau (where he had been appointed Professor of Mathematics), before returning to Berlin. In 1845 he received his doctorate from Berlin for a thesis on complex units.

Kronecker was then diverted from mathematical research by pressing family duties – the management of an estate near Liegnitz and the winding up of an uncle's banking business. Not until 1855, when he took up residence again in Berlin, did he begin a professional career in mathematics. Financially independent, he was able to devote himself to research without taking employment, but his election to the Berlin Academy in 1861 entitled him to give lectures at the university, an occupation which gave him such satisfaction that he turned down an invitation to take the Chair of Mathematics in Göttingen in 1868. By then his reputation had grown to such an extent that he was elected to the French Academy. In 1883 he succeeded Kummer as Professor of Mathematics at Berlin, a Chair which he held until his death, in Berlin, on 29 December 1891.

Kronecker was a gifted mathematician who never quite made the kind of discovery to place him in the very front rank of mathematical geniuses. His thesis on complex units, for example, came close to hitting upon Kummer's idea of "ideal numbers", but the actual discovery belongs to his mentor. Much of his life he was engaged in somewhat disputatious and cranky controversy. After 1855 he worked chiefly in the fields of number theory, algebra and elliptical functions, and he achieved a great deal in his endeavour to unify analysis, algebra and elliptical functions. But his progress, and his influence, were somewhat blocked by his obsession with the idea that all branches of mathematics (apart from geometry and mechanics) should be treated as parts of arithmetic. He also believed that whole numbers were sufficient for the study of mathematics – "The whole numbers has the Dear God made; all else is man's work". His refusal to grant irrational numbers equal validity with whole numbers, although it placed him in that tradition of nineteenth-century mathematical thought which attempted to define processes such as differentiation and integration in terms of simple arithmetic, led him into what we can now see as time-wasting debate.

One other controversy was more fruitful. His debate with Georg Cantor (1843-1918) and Karl Weierstrass (1815-1897) about the foundations of mathematics has been carried into the twentieth century in the form of the debate between the formalists and the intuitionists. His system of axioms, published in 1870, has also been useful. His axioms were later shown to govern finite Abelian groups and have proved to be important in the modern development of algebra.

Kronecker remains, however, most famous for his work in linear algebra, especially for the delta named after him. (It is denoted by δrs, for which $\delta rs = 0$ when $r \neq s$, $\delta rs = 1$ when $r = 1$, where r, s are 1,2,3...) Kronecker found this a useful delta in the evaluation of determinants, the r and s being concerned with a row and a column of the determinant. The delta is a fairly simple example of a tensor and Kronecker's pupil, Hensel, who edited and published Kronecker's work between 1895 and 1931, was largely responsible for popularizing the notation.

Kummer, Ernst Eduard (1810-1893), was a German mathematician, famous for his work in higher arithmetic and geometry, who introduced "ideal numbers" in the attempt to prove Fermat's Last Theorem.

He was born at Sorau (now Zary, Poland) on 29 January 1810 and was educated there before entering the University of Halle in 1828. Although his original intention was to study theology, he soon changed to mathematics and proved himself so brilliant in the subject that in 1831 the university awarded him a doctorate for his prize-winning essay on sines and cosines. From 1832 to 1842 he taught at a school at Liegnitz (now Legnica, Poland), where Leopold Kronecker (1823-1891) was one of his pupils. He was Professor of Mathematics at the University of Breslau from 1842 to 1855, when he was appointed to professorships at the University of Berlin and the Berlin War College. In 1857 he was awarded the Grand Prix of the French Academy of Sciences and in 1868 he was elected Rector for one year of the University of Berlin. In 1882 he astonished his Berlin colleagues by announcing that failing powers of memory were weakening his ability to carry out logical, coherent thought; he therefore resigned his Chair. He died at Berlin on 14 May 1893.

Kummer made an important contribution to function theory by his investigations - which surpassed those of Gauss - into hypergeometric series. But his two outstanding achievements were his introduction of "ideal number" to attempt to solve Fermat's Last Theorem and his research into systems of rays, which led to the discovery of what is now known as the Kummer surface.

Fermat's Last Theorem is one of the most famous in the history of mathematics. It states that "there do not exist integers x, y, z, none of which being zero, that satisfy $x^n + y^n = z^n$, where n is any given integer greater than 2". Fermat left merely the statement of the theorem, without proof (except for $n = 4$), in his 1637 marginal note to his copy of Diophantus. Euler later proved the theorem for $n = 3$, but no one was able to provide a generalized proof. In general what was needed was a proof that $x^l + y^l + z^l = 0$ is impossible in non-zero integers x, y and z for any odd prime $l > 3$. In the early nineteenth century Legendre proved this for $l = 5$ and Lebesgue for $l = 7$, but later attempts to find a proof for other values of l came to naught.

Kummer studied previous attempted solutions carefully and came up with one of the most creative and influential ideas in the history of mathematics, the idea of ideal numbers. With their aid he was able to prove, in 1850, that the equation $x^l + y^l + z^l = 0$ was impossible in non-zero integers for all regular prime numbers (a special type of prime numbers related to Bernoulli numbers). He was then able, by extremely complicated calculations, to determine that the only primes less than 100 which were not regular are 37, 59 and 67. For many years Kummer continued to work on the problem and he was eventually able to prove that the equation is impossible for all primes $l < 100$. It was for his work in this field, especially the introduction of ideal numbers, an invention which some mathematicians rank in importance with the invention of non-Euclidean geometry, that Kummer received the Grand Prix of the French Academy. Much work has since been done on the problem and it is now known that the equation is impossible for all primes $l < 619$.

Kummer's other great achievement was his discovery of the fourth-order surface known as the Kummer surface. It can be described as the quartic which is the singular surface of the quadratic line complex and involves the very sophisticated and complicated concept of this surface as the wave surface in space of four dimensions.

Kurosh, Alexander Genadievich (1908-), is a Soviet mathematician whose work has been chiefly in algebra and the theory of groups.

Kurosh was born on 6 January 1908. He received his BA in mathematics from the University of Smolensk in 1928 and was appointed an instructor at the University of Moscow in 1930. In 1937 he was awarded a doctorate in mathematical physics and in the same year he was made a Professor in Mathematics at the university. He continues to hold that Chair, along with the presidency of the Moscow Mathematical Society.

Kurosh has lectured widely and published prolifically on general problems in algebra. He has been a consistent advocate of the division of algebra into two categories, linear algebra and the algebra of polynomials (the study of a single equation in one unknown, but of an arbitrary degree). He is best known for his work in the theory of groups and his book, *The Theory of Groups* (1953), was widely acclaimed as the first modern text on the general theory of groups. It is notable for its emphasis on infinite groups. Kurosh has also published *A Course of Higher Algebra* (1956), *Free Sums of Multi-operator Algebra* (1960) and *Direct Expansions in Algebraic Categories* (1960).

L

Lagrange, Joseph Louis, Comte (1736-1813), was an Italian-born French mathematician who revolutionized the study of mechanics.

Lagrange was born, of a French father and Italian mother, at Turin on 25 January 1736. Almost entirely by teaching himself the subject he made himself a formidable mathematician by the age of 16, and in 1755, when he was just 19, he was appointed Professor of Mathematics at the Royal Artillery School at Turin. In 1759 he organized a mathematical society of his students and colleagues and this ultimately became the Turin Academy of Sciences. He remained at Turin until 1766 when, on the recommendation of Leonhard Euler and Jean d'Alembert, Frederick the Great of Prussia invited him to Berlin to succeed Euler as the Director of the Berlin Academy of Sciences. In 1787 he accepted the invitation of Louis XVI to go to Paris as a member of the French Royal Academy and in 1797 he was appointed Professor of Mathematics at the École Polytechnique. Five years earlier he had married a teenage girl and he lived, apparently happily, with her until his death at Paris on 10 April 1813.

Like so many brilliant mathematicians, Lagrange had his best ideas as a very young man. By the time that he began to teach at Turin in 1755, he had already conceived the heart of his great work, the *Mécanique analytique*, and was near to his first important discovery, the solution to the isoperimetrical problem, on which the calculus of variations partly depends. In 1759 he sent his solution to Euler, who had been baffled and held up by the problem for years;

Euler wrote back to express his delight at the young man's solution and delayed publishing his own work on the subject until Lagrange – whose proof had greater generality than Euler's – had published his discovery. In that year also Lagrange wrote a paper on minima and maxima and, advancing beyond Newton's theory of sound, settled a fierce dispute on the nature of a vibrating string.

In 1764 Lagrange addressed himself to the famous three-body problem on the mutual gravitational attraction of the Earth, Sun and Moon, and for his work on it was awarded the French Academy's Grand Prix. Two years later he won the award again for his work on the same problem with regard to Jupiter and its four (as were then known) satellites. When he moved to Berlin he diverted himself for a time with problems in number theory. He proved some of Fermat's theorems which had remained unproven for a century; and he solved a problem known since the time of the ancients, namely, to find an integer x so that $(nx^2 + 1)$ is a square where n is a positive integer, but not a square.

All the while, however, his chief concern was mechanics. By 1782 he had completed his *Mécanique analytique*, although it was not published until 1788, by which time Lagrange had become so uninterested in mathematics that the manuscript had lain untouched and unconsulted for two years. In his epoch-making treatise Lagrange, by considering a four-dimensional space with the aid of calculus, succeeded in reducing the theory of solid and fluid mechanics to an analytical principle. Breaking with conventional methods used since the time of the Greeks, Lagrange published his work without the aid of a single diagram or construction; his discussion of mechanics, that is to say, was entirely algebraic. Of this achievement Lagrange was justly proud, especially since he was able to reflect that the event which had, more than anything else, drawn him into mathematics was his reading, as a young boy, the work of Edmund Halley (1656-1742) in the use of algebra in optics.

Lagrange never again did anything of such significance, although his lectures at the École Polytechnique, published as the *Théorie des fonctions analytiques* (1797) and the *Leçons sur le calcul des fonctions* (1806), were of much use to Augustin Cauchy and others. But he had still one contribution to make to the world. In 1793 he was appointed president of the commission established to standardize French weights and measures and by persuading the commission to adopt 10, not 12, as the basic unit, was the father of the metric system in use throughout most of the world today. For that, perhaps, but above all for his work on mechanics he was deservedly given a final resting place in the Panthéon.

Lamb, Horace (1849–1934), was a British applied mathematician, noted for his many books on hydrodynamics, elasticity, sound and mechanics.

Lamb was born in Stockport, Cheshire, on 27 November 1849. His father was the foreman in a cotton mill; his mother died when he was young and he was brought up by his aunt, who was largely responsible for enrolling him at Stockport Grammar School. There Lamb excelled at Latin and Greek and at the age of 17 he won a classical scholarship to Queen's College, Cambridge. He spent a year at Owens College, Manchester, before going to the university, however, and having gained a scholarship to Trinity College entered there in the autumn of 1868. In 1870 he was elected a Sheepshank (astronomical exhibitioner) at the college and in 1872 he gained his BA in mathematics as second Wrangler and second Smith's prizeman. In the same year he was elected a Fellow and Lecturer at Trinity.

Cambridge still imposed celibacy upon its Fellows and in 1875, having married, Lamb went to Australia to take up the Chair of Mathematics at the University of Adelaide. He remained there until 1885, when he returned to Manchester as Professor of Mathematics at Owens College, a post which he held until his retirement in 1920. His last years were spent in Cambridge. The University established an honorary lectureship for him, called the Rayleigh Lectureship, and Trinity elected him an honorary Fellow. From 1921 to 1927 he was also a member of the Aeronautical Research Committee attached to the Admiralty and until his death he served on an advisory panel which was concerned with the fluid motion set up by aircraft.

Lamb was elected to the Royal Society in 1884 and was awarded the society's Royal Medal in 1902 and the Copley Medal, its highest honour, in 1923. He was president of the British Association in 1925. He was knighted in 1931, and he died in Cambridge on 4 December 1934.

Lamb was born a generation after men such as George Stokes (1819–1903), James Clerk Maxwell (1831–1879) and John Rayleigh (1842–1919) had begun to revive interest in the mathematical aspect of problems in physics - heat, electricity, magnetism and elasticity. His was an age of brilliant achievement in applied mathematics and he made his own mark in many fields: electricity and magnestism, fluid mechanics, elasticity, acoustics, vibrations and wave motions, seismology, and the theory of tides and terrestrial magnetism. He was particularly adept at applying the solution of a problem in one field to problems in another. His greatest achievement was in the field of fluid mechanics. In 1879 he published his best-known work, *A Treatise on the Motion of Fluids*, issued in a new edition as *Hydrodynamics* in 1895, and re-issued in five subsequent editions (the last in 1932), each of which incorporated the latest developments in the subject. The book is rightly regarded as one of the most clearly written treatises in the whole of applied mathematics.

Lamb's contributions ranged wide over the field of applied mathematics. A paper of 1882, which analysed the modes of oscillation of an elastic sphere, achieved its true recognition in 1960, when free Earth oscillations during a Chilean earthquake behaved in the way he had described. Another paper of 1904 gave an analytical account of propagation over the surface of an elastic solid of waves generated by given initial disturbances, and the analysis he provided is now regarded as one of the seminal contributions to theoretical seismology. Then, in 1915, in collaboration with Lorna Swain, he gave the first satisfactory account of the marked phase differences of the tides observed in different parts of the Earth's oceans, thereby settling a question which had been a matter of controversy since Newton's time.

Lamb made numerous important discoveries; he published widely; he was, in the words of Rutherford, "more nearly my ideal of a university professor than anyone I have known". By many people he is regarded as the finest applied mathematician of the century.

Laplace, Pierre Simon (1749–1827), was a French mathematician whose work in mathematical physics and celestial mechanics established him as one of the giants of eighteenth- and nineteenth-century science.

Laplace was born into a Normandy farming family at Beaumont-en-Auge on 23 March 1749, and between the ages of seven and 16 he attended the local school run by the Benedictines. In 1766 he went to the University of Caen to study theology. There his interest in science was awakened by one of his teachers, Pierre le Canu, and in little more than a year (having practically abandoned theological studies) he made himself thoroughly familiar with the existing body of knowledge on mechanics. He decided to leave Caen without taking a degree and in 1768, with a letter of introduction by le Canu, went to Paris. He either wrote a letter on the principles of mechanics to d'Alembert, or visited d'Alembert and a day later returned with a solution to a problem which d'Alembert had given him; whichever, d'Alembert was so struck by the promise of brilliance which Laplace gave, that he secured for him a professorship at the École Militaire. Laplace remained in Paris for the rest of his life.

Almost at once Laplace began to flood the Academy of Sciences with important papers on a host of subjects – more, the mathematician Condorcet (1743–1794) later remarked, than the Academy had ever received – and in 1773 he was elected a member. From then onwards Laplace's stock rose steadily higher not merely in mathematical circles but in French government circles. In 1784 he was appointed examiner of cadets for the Royal Artillery. When in the early 1790s the revolutionary government established the Commission of Weights and Measures he was appointed to it; he served also on the Bureau de Longitudes. In 1799, when Napoleon became first consul, he made Laplace Minister of the Interior; six weeks later he dismissed him, for "bringing the spirit of infinitesimals into administration", and raised him to the senate, where Laplace served as vice-president in 1803.

In 1814, as the French republic began to encounter difficulties, Laplace shrewdly voted for the overthrow of Napoleon and the restoration of the Bourbon monarchy. Charles X made him a marquis in 1816 and for the remainder of his life Laplace stayed true to the Bourbons, incurring the enmity of the liberals in 1826 by his refusal to sign the French Academy's declaration in favour of the freedom of the press. He died at Paris on 5 March 1827.

Laplace's first important discovery came soon after he was appointed to the École Militaire. He discovered that "any determinant is equal to the sum of all the minors that can be formed from any selected set of its rows, each minor being described by its algebraic complement". This is what is now known as the Laplace theorem.

He then turned his mind to problems in celestial mechanics, beginning in 1773 by examining the unexplained variations in the orbits of Jupiter and Saturn. Jupiter's orbit appeared to be continually shrinking, while Saturn's appeared to be continually expanding. No one had succeeded in explaining the phenomenon within the framework of Newtonian gravitation. In a brilliant three-part paper presented to the Academy between 1784 and 1786, Laplace demonstrated that the phenomenon had a period of 929 years and that arose because the average motions of the two planets are nearly commensurable. The variations, therefore, were not at odds with, but compatible with, Newton's law.

While working on that problem Laplace also published his famous paper, *Théorie des attractions des sphéroides et de la figure des planètes* (1785), in which he introduced the potential function and the Laplace coefficients, both of them useful as a means of applying analysis to problems in physics. Two years later he submitted a paper to the Academy in which he dealt with the average angular velocity of the Moon about the Earth, a problem with which Euler and Lagrange had grappled unsuccessfully. Laplace found that, although the mean motion of the Moon around the Earth depends principally on the mutual gravitational attraction between them, it is slightly reduced by the Sun's pull on the Moon, this action of the Sun depending, in turn, upon the changes in eccentricity of the Earth's orbit due to the perturbations caused by the other planets. The result (although the inequality has a period of some millions of years) is that the Moon's mean motion is accelerated, while the Earth's slows down and tends to become more circular.

Celestial mechanics remained Laplace's chief interest. In 1796 he published his *Exposition du système du monde*, a summary of existing cosmological knowledge which included a statement of the nebular hypothesis of the Solar System's origin. And between 1799 and 1825 he brought out his monumental, five-volume *Mécanique céleste*. In the middle of its publication appeared two works on probability theory, the *Théorie analytique des probabilités* (1812), a minor classic of mathematical literature, and the *Essai philosophique sur les probabilités* (1814).

For 30 years and more Laplace worked, often in close collaboration with Lagrange, on the major problems in celestial mechanics. Together they made almost all the important advances in the field at that time. Laplace's work, in particular, removed any remaining doubts about the validity of Newtonian gravitation. And he established that the number of gravitational interactions within the Solar System was large enough to allow the system to maintain itself without (as Newton had thought necessary) occasional divine intervention to keep it together. Moreover, the methods by which he achieved his results established celestial mechanics as a branch of analysis and through his work potential theory, the Laplace theorem, the Laplace coefficients, orthogonal functions and the Laplace transform (introduced in his papers on probability) became fundamental tools of analysis.

Lebesgue, Henri Léon (1875-1941), was a French mathematician who is known chiefly for the development of a new theory of integration named after him.

Lebesgue was born at Beauvais on 28 June 1875 and educated at the École Normale Supérieure in Paris between 1894 and 1897. From 1899 to 1902 he worked on his doctoral thesis while teaching mathematical science at the lycée in Nancy. He received his doctorate from the Sorbonne in 1902 and in the same year was appointed a Lecturer in the faculty of sciences at the University of Rennes. He left there to become a Professor at the University of Poitiers in 1906, remaining at Poitiers until 1910, when he was appointed Lecturer in Mathematics at the Sorbonne. In 1920 he was promoted to the Chair of the application of geometry to analysis, but he left the Sorbonne in the following year to take up his final academic post as Professor of Mathematics at the Collège de France. He died in Paris on 26 July 1941.

Lebesgue was awarded many honours, including the Prix Houllevique (1912), the Prix Poncelet (1914) and the Prix Saintour (1917). He was elected to the French Academy of Sciences in 1922 and to the Royal Society in 1934.

Lebesgue made contributions to several branches of mathematics, including set theory, the calculus of variation and function theory. With Émile Borel (1871-1956) he laid the foundations of the modern theory of the functions of a real variable. His chief work, however, was his creation of a new approach to the theory of integration.

From an early stage in his mathematicial career, Lebesgue was intrigued by problems associated with Riemannian integration and he began to get results in this field in 1902. His introduction of the Lebesgue integral was not only an impressive piece of mathematical creativity in itself, but quickly proved itself to be of great importance in the development of several branches of mathematics, especially calculus, curve rectification and the theory of trigonometric series. Later the integral was also discovered to be of fundamental significance for the development of measure theory.

Legendre, Adrien-Marie (1752-1833), was a French mathematician who was particularly interested in number theory, celestial mechanics and elliptic functions.

Legendre was born in Paris on 18 September 1752, studied mathematics and natural science at the Collège Mazarin in Paris and, despite having a private income to sustain him in independent research, took employment as a Lecturer in Mathematics at the École Militaire in 1775. He taught there until 1780 without making any impression on the mathematical world. His fortunes began to rise in 1882, when he won the prize awarded by the Berlin Academy for an essay on the path of projectiles travelling through resistant media. A year later he was elected to the French Academy of Sciences and from the year 1783 began to publish important papers. He was appointed Professor of Mathematics at the Institut de Marat in Paris in 1794, the same year in which he became head of the government department established to standardize French weights and measures. From 1799 to 1815 he served as an examiner of students of artillery and in 1813 he succeeded Pierre Laplace (1749-1827) as chief of the Bureau de Longitudes. He remained at that post until his death, in Paris, on 10 January 1833.

Legendre's first published work, a paper on mechanics, appeared in 1774, but a decade passed before his real talent showed itself. In several papers of 1783-1784 he introduced to celestial mechanics what are now known as Legendre polynomials. These are solutions to the second-order differential equation (still important in applied mathematics)

$$(1-x^2)y'' - 2xy' + n(n+1)y = 0,$$

where n is a non-negative integer. The functions which satisfy this equation are called Legendre functions.

During the 1780s Legendre worked on a number of other topics, including indeterminate analysis and the calculus of variations, but at the end of the decade his research was interrupted for a time by the outbreak of the French revolution and the suppression, in 1793, of the French Academy of Sciences. He placed himself at the service of the revolutionary government, however, to direct the project which altered the system for the measurement of angles and other decimalization projects.

His two most important contributions to mathematics were made in the 1790s, although he had begun work on both - number theory and elliptical functions - in the mid-1780s. In number theory his most significant result was the law of reciprocity of quadratic residues, although the credit for establishing the law rigorously belongs to Karl Gauss in 1801. It was Legendre alone, however, who in 1798 gave the law of the distribution of prime numbers; and very late in his career, in 1823, he proved that there was no solution in integers for the equation $x^5 + y^5 = z^5$.

Of even more use to fellow mathematicians was Legendre's long and painstaking work on elliptical functions. In 1786 he made a tentative start on the subject with a paper on the integration of elliptical curves and in 1792 he touched on the theory of elliptical transcendentals in a paper to the Academy. His great achievement, however, was the two-volume textbook on elliptical functions which he published in 1825 and 1826, in which he gave the tables of elliptical functions which he had laboriously compiled.

One other accomplishment of Legendre, of a more mundane character, ought not to be forgotten. In 1794 he published his *Eléments de géometrie*, a re-working and a clarification of Euclid's *Elements*. Among its delights was the single proof of the irrationality of π and the first proof of the irrationality of π^2. The text was translated into several languages and in many parts of the world stood as the schoolboys' basic text in geometry for the next 100 years.

Leibniz, Gottfried Wilhelm (1646-1716), was a German philosopher and mathematician who was one of the founders of the differential calculus and symbolic logic.

Leibniz was born on 1 July in Leipzig, where his father was Professor of Moral Philosophy at the university. Although he attended the Nicolai School at Leipzig, most of his early education came from his own reading, especially in the classics and the Church fathers, in his father's library. At the age of 15 he entered the University of Leipzig, where his formal training was chiefly in jurisprudence and philosophy. Privately, he read all the important scientific texts – of Bacon, Galileo, Kepler, Descartes and others. In 1663 he went to the University of Jena, where he was taught Euclidean geometry by Erhard Weigel (1625-1699). He then returned to Leipzig and after three years more study of law applied for the degree of Doctor of Law in 1666. It was refused on the ground that he was too young. He therefore went to Altdorf, where his thesis *De Casibus per plexis in jure* was accepted and the doctorate awarded.

Leibniz turned down the offer of a professorship at Altdorf and decided to travel about Europe. At the end of 1666 he entered the service of the Elector and Archbishop of Mainz; he was employed chiefly in foreign affairs, his special task being to devise plans to preserve the peace of Europe, just then emerging from the Thirty Years' War. He was invited to France by Louis XIV, to present to him his plan for a French invasion of Egypt (and so transfer war from European to African soil) and although, in the event, he never met the king, he remained

in Paris for about three years. It was in Paris that his serious work in mathematics began. He met leading scientists, including Christiaan Huygens (1629-1695), made a thorough study of Cartesianism, and began work on his calculating machine. The machine was completed in *c*.1672 and was a marked improvement on Pascal's machine, in that it was able to multiply, divide and extract roots.

The death of the Elector of Mainz in 1673 left Leibniz without an official position. He was offered the post of librarian to the Duke of Brunswick at Hanover, but went instead to London. The visit marked a turning-point in his mathematical life, for it was in London in 1673 that he became acquainted with the work of Isaac Newton and Isaac Barrow and began to work on problems which led him to his independent discovery of differential and integral calculus.

In 1676 Leibniz at last took up the appointment as librarian to the House of Brunswick. He remained in that service for the rest of his life and much of his time was spent in conducting research into the genealogy and history of the Brunswick line. He also continued to be charged with diplomatic missions and on one of his visits to Berlin he succeeded in convincing the local elector to establish an academy of science. It was founded in 1700 and Leibniz was appointed President for life. From 1712 to 1714 he was an imperial privy councillor at Vienna. In 1714 the Elector of Hanover, Georg Ludwig, Duke of Brunswick, acceded to the English throne as George I. Leibniz asked to be allowed to accompany him to London, but the request was denied. He therefore spent the last two years of his life engaged in genealogical work, embittered by the dispute with Newton over the invention of the calculus and suffering from gout. He died a neglected man – neither the Royal Society nor the Berlin Academy took any notice of the event – on 14 November 1716 in Hanover.

Just as much of his service to princes consisted in the search for a balance of power and international co-operation in Europe, just as he sought to reconcile in much of his philosophical writing Protestantism and Roman Catholicism, so did Leibniz dream of an international community of scholars, served by academies like that of Berlin, freely sharing their discoveries and continually exchanging their ideas. To this end he worked intermittently throughout his life at devising what he called a Universal Characteristic, a universal language accessible to everyone. It is therefore a matter of some sorrow that he became embroiled in a long and acrimonious dispute about the authorship of the calculus, a dispute which darkened the last 15 years of his life. In 1699 the Swiss mathematician and Fellow of the Royal Society, Fatio de Duillier, accused Leibniz of stealing the idea from Newton, a charge which the Royal Society formally upheld in 1711. Leibniz himself never sought to conceal that it was after his 1673 visit to London, by which time Newton had worked out his calculus of fluxions, that he began his investigations into tangents and quadratures, the research that eventually led to his discovery of the calculus. But Newton's discovery, probably made in 1665, was not published for many years and there is no doubt that Leibniz arrived at his calculus independently. As he put it, he, Newton and Barrow were "contemporaries in these discoveries". Leibniz always communicated his findings to fellow mathematicians; most mathematicians of the time were working on the same problems and they all knew the work that had been done on infinitesimal quantities. At any rate, to Leibniz is due the credit for first using the infinitesimals as differences. To him also is due the credit for working out, like Newton, a complete algorithm and for devising a notation so much more convenient than Newton's that it remains in standard use today.

The idea of the calculus was in the mathematical air. It was Leibniz who expressed its fundamental notions in the most effective manner. That should not be surprising, for Leibniz will always be remembered chiefly as the founder of symbolic logic. Centuries later, it has become clear that his logic, free from all concepts of space and number and hence in his lifetime not recognized as mathematical at all, was the prototype of future abstract mathematics.

Levi-Civita, Tullio (1873–1941), was an Italian mathematician skilled in both pure and applied mathematics whose greatest achievement was his development, in collaboration with Gregorio Ricci-Curbastro, of the absolute differential calculus.

Levi-Civita was born at Padua on 29 March 1873 and received his secondary education there before entering the University of Padua to study mathematics in 1890. There he came strongly under the influence of Ricci-Curbastro, one of his teachers. He was awarded his BA in 1894 and took up employment as a lecturer at the teacher-training college at Pavia. In 1897 he was appointed Professor of Mechanics at the Engineering School at Padua. In 1918 he left Padua to become Professor of Higher Analysis at the University of Rome; in 1920 he was made Professor of Rational Mechanics. He remained there until 1938, when he was forced to leave the university by the anti-Jewish laws promul-

gated by the Fascist government; he was also expelled from all Italian scientific societies. His health began to deteriorate rapidly and he died of a stroke, at Rome, on 29 December 1941.

Although Levi-Civita began to publish while he was still an undergraduate, his first important results – the fruit of several years' labour – were first published, with Ricci-Curbastro, in 1900. Together they presented to the mathematical world a completely new calculus, which became known as absolute differential calculus. One of the most important features of this new system was its remarkable flexibility – applicable, as it was, to both Euclidean and non-Euclidean spaces. Most significantly, it could be applied to Riemannian curved spaces, and the tensor system which the paper outlined was fundamental to Einstein's development of the general theory of relativity. Levi-Civita's own most important contribution to the absolute differential calculus was the publication in 1917 of a paper in which he postulated a law of parallel translation of a vector in a Riemannian curved space. This introduction of the concept of parallelism in curved space was Levi-Civita's most brilliant contribution to the history of mathematics. The discussions to which it gave rise eventually allowed absolute differential calculus to develop into tensor calculus, a tool of immense usefulness to mathematicians attempting to derive a unified theory of gravitation and electromagnetism. The idea of parallel displacement has also been of great importance in the field of the geometry of paths.

In addition to this central work, Levi-Civita also published interesting papers on celestial mechanics and hydrodynamics, and in general it may be said that his achievements in both pure and applied mathematics established him as one of the foremost mathematicians of his age.

Li, Ching Chun (1912–   ), is a Chinese-American statistician with a special interest in genetics.

Li was born in China on 27 October 1912. He graduated from the University of Nanking in agronomy in 1936 and then went to Cornell University in the United States, where he gained a doctorate in plant breeding and genetics in 1940. He returned to China to take up the Chair in Genetics and Biometry (the statistical or quantitative study of biology) in 1943. From 1946 to 1950 he was Professor of Agronomy at the National Peking University. In 1951 he went once more to the United States, this time to settle there permanently, as a research fellow at the University of Pittsburgh. He was appointed Professor of Biometry and Human Genetics there in 1975. He was president of the American Society of Human Genetics in 1960.

Li's work, which is chiefly concerned with population laws and statistics of males and females in populations, is only of the very slightest immediate interest to mathematicians, although mathematics is of essential importance to him. His investigations into haemophilia, leukaemia and other conditions have been of great value to the medical profession. His publications include *Population Genetics* (1955), *Human Genetics: Principles and Methods* (1961) and *Introduction to Experimental Statistics* (1964).

Lie, Marius Sophus (1842-1899), was a Norwegian mathematician who made valuable contributions to the theory of algebraic invariants and who is remembered for the Lie theorem and the Lie groups.

Lie was born at Nordfjordeid, near Bergen, on 17 December 1842. He received his primary and secondary schooling in Moss and then in 1859, at the age of 17, entered the University at Christiania (now Oslo) to study mathematics and science. He graduated in 1865 without, it appears, having formed a determination to become a mathematician. But in the next two or three years, while he earned money by giving private lessons, he read the works of Jean Poncelet and Julius Plücker (1801-1868) and his imagination was fired by the latter's idea for creating new geometries by using figures, not points, as elements of space. This idea stayed with Lie to influence him throughout his career.

In 1869 Lie was awarded a scholarship to study abroad and he went to Berlin, where he worked under Felix Klein, and then to Paris. In 1870 he was arrested for spying – a false charge – but was released within a month and made his way to Italy just before the German blockade of Paris in the Franco-German war of that year. In 1871 the University of Christiania awarded him a scholarship to do doctoral research and he returned to there in 1872. By the end of the year he had gained his doctorate and had a Chair of Mathematics created for him. He remained there until 1886, when he travelled to Leipzig to succeed Klein in the Chair of Mathematics at the university. His years at Leipzig, which lasted until 1898, were broken by a year in a mental hospital, caused by a kind of nervous breakdown (what was then called neurasthenia) in 1889. His last year was spent at Christiania, where another Chair of Mathematics was specially created for him. He died there of pernicious anaemia on 18 February 1899.

Lie shares with Klein the distinction of being the first mathematician to emphasize the importance of the notion of groups in geometry. By using group theory they were able to show that it was possible to decide in which kind of geometry a particular notion belonged. It was also possible to establish the relationships between different kinds of geometry, for instance of non-Euclidean geometry to projective geometry.

Lie's first great discovery, made while he was in Paris in 1870, was that of his contact transformation, which mapped straight lines with spheres and which mapped principal tangent curves into curvature lines. In his theory of tangential transformations occurs the particular transformation which makes a sphere correspond to a straight line. By 1873 Lie had turned away from contact transformation to investigate transformation groups. In this work on group theory he chose a new space element, the contact element, which is an incidence pair of point and line or of point and hyperplane. This led him to his greatest achievement, the discovery of transformation groups known as Lie groups, one of the basic notions of which is that of infinitesimal transformation.

The Lie groups provided the means to deduce from the structure the type of auxiliary equations needed for their integration, and the integration theorem which he developed (and which goes by his name) made it possible to classify partial differential equations in such a way as to make most of the classical methods of solving such equations reducible to a single principle. Moreover, the theorem led to a geometric interpretation of Cauchy's solution to partial differential equations.

The general effect of Lie's discoveries was to reduce the amount of work required in integration, although Lie's own papers on integration in the last 20 years of his life were clumsily presented and repetitive. His chief contribution to mathematics was to provide, in the Lie groups, the foundations of the modern science of topology.

Lindemann, Carl Louis Ferdinand (1852-1939), was a German mathematician who is famous for one result, his discussion of the nature of π which laid to rest the old question of "squaring the circle".

Lindemann was born at Hanover on 12 April 1852, did his undergraduate work at Göttingen and Munich, and received his doctorate from the university at Erlangen (where he studied under Felix Klein) in 1873. He then spent a couple of years travelling in England and France, meeting leading mathematicians and carrying on private research. In 1877 he was appointed a lecturer at Würzburg and in 1879 he was promoted to Professor. From 1883 to 1893 he was a professor at Königsberg; from 1893 until his death, he taught at Munich. He died on 6 March 1939.

Lindemann published papers on a number of subjects, including spectrum theory, invariant theory and theoretical mechanics (his doctoral dissertation was on the infinitely small movements of rigid bodies). He was also a highly acclaimed teacher, supervising more than 60 doctoral candidates during his career and being more than anyone else responsible for introducing the seminar method of teaching into German universities. He also translated and edited the works of Henri Poincaré and made his mathematics known in Germany.

His fame, nevertheless, rests almost entirely on the paper which he published in 1882 on the nature of π as a transcendental number. Since the time of the Greeks mathematicians had known of irrational numbers and wondered if they were algebraic; or, in other words, was it possible to define an algebraic equation with rational coefficients in which irrational numbers were the roots? In 1844 Liouville had shown, by the use of continued fractions, that a host of numbers existed which are non-algebraic. These are known as transcendental numbers. Then in 1872 Charles Hermite proved a rigorous demonstration that e, the base of "natural" logarithms, was a transcendental number. The highly interesting question, whether π was also a transcendental number, had still, however, not received a satisfactory answer.

It was Lindemann who provided, in his 1882 paper, the proof. He demonstrated that, except in trivial cases, every expression of the form

$$\sum_{i=1}^{n} A i e^{ai}$$

where A and a are algebraic numbers must be non-zero. Therefore, since i is a root of $x^2 + 1 = 0$, and since it was known that

$$1^{i\pi} + 1^0 = 0 \text{ (i.e., } 1^{i\pi} = -1)$$

then $i\pi$ and therefore π (since i is algebraic) must be transcendental.

If π cannot be the root of an equation, it cannot be constructed. Therefore the "squaring of a circle" is impossible. Lindemann had brought an end to one of the oldest puzzles in mathematics.

Liouville, Joseph (1809-1882), was a French mathematician who wrote prolifically on problems of analysis, but who is famous chiefly as the founder and first editor of the learned journal popularly known as the *Journal de Liouville*.

Liouville was born at St Omer, Pas-de-Calais, on 24 March 1809 and studied at Commery and Toul before entering the École Polytechnique in Paris in 1825. In 1827 he transferred to the École des Ponts et Chaussées, where he received his baccalaureate in 1830. For the next 50 years, beginning with his appointment to the École Polytechnique in 1831, Liouville taught mathematics at all the leading institutions of higher learning in Paris. While he was lecturing at the École Centrale des Arts et Manufactures (1833-1838), he received his doctorate in 1836 for a thesis on Fourier series. In 1838 he was elected to the Chair of Analysis at the École Polytechnique, where he remained until 1851, when he became a professor at the Collège de France. He stayed at the Collège until 1879, although in the years from 1857 to 1874 he held concurrently the post of Professor of Rational Mechanics at the Sorbonne. He was also for a time the Director of the Bureau de Longitudes. Quite unexpectedly, having shown no political ambition previously, he became infected by the revolution of 1848 and was elected as a moderate republican to the constituent assembly in April 1848. A year later he was defeated in the elections to the new Legislative Assembly and his political career closed as suddenly as it had opened. He died in Paris on 8 September 1882.

Although Liouville's early interest lay in problems associated with the study of electricity and heat, and although he was elected to the Academy of Sciences in 1839 as a member of the astronomy section, the chief mathematical interest of his career was in analysis. In that field he published more than 100 papers between 1832 and 1857. In collaboration with Charles-François Sturm (1803-1855) he published papers in 1836 on vibration which were of considerable importance in laying the foundations of the theory of linear differential equations. He also provided the first proof of the existence of transcendental functions and in a paper of 1844 laid down that the irrational numbers, e and e^2 were transcendental, since they could not be used to solve any second-degree polynomial equation. The proof of this, however, had to await Charles Hermite's demonstration in 1873.

More important than his research was Liouville's founding of the *Journal des mathématiques pures et appliqués* in 1836. Since the demise of Gergonne's *Annales de mathématiques* in 1831 French mathematicians had been deprived of a receptacle for their research papers. Liouville's journal filled the gap. He edited it from the issue of the first number in 1836 down to the thirty-ninth number in 1874. When he retired from the editorship, the mathematical spark died in him and he produced nothing more of importance.

Lipschitz, Rudolf Otto Sigismund (1832-1903), was a German mathematician of wide-ranging interests who is remembered for the so-called Lipschitz algebra and the Lipschitz condition.

Lipschitz was born at Königsberg on 14 May 1832. He does not appear to have become seriously interested in mathematics until, in 1847, he entered the University of Königsberg, where one of his teachers was Franz Neumann. After graduating from Königsberg he continued his studies at the University of Berlin, chiefly under Lejeune Dirichlet. He was awarded his doctorate in 1853. For the next few years he taught at schools in Königsberg and Elbinc, before becoming a lecturer at the University of Berlin in 1857. He moved to Breslau in 1862, but was there for only two years. In 1864 he was appointed Professor of Mathematics at the University of Bonn. He remained there for the rest of his career, so contented with his work and life there that he turned down an invitation to become a professor at the more prestigious University of Göttingen in 1873. He died in Bonn on 7 October 1903.

Lipschitz did extensive work in number theory, Fourier series, the theory of Bessel functions, differential equations, the calculus of variations, geometry and mechanics. He was also much interested in the fundamental questions concerned with the nature of mathematics and of mathematical research, and German higher education was much indebted to him for his two-volume *Grundlagen der Analysis* (1877-1880), a synthetic presentation of the foundations of mathematics and their applications. The work provided a comprehensive survey of what was then known of the theory of rational integers, differential equations and function theory.

Among his more specific contributions to mathematical knowledge, several stand out. His work in basic analysis provided a condition now known as the Lipschitz condition, subsequently of great importance in proofs of existence and uniqueness, as well as in approximation theory and constructive function theory. He has a place in the history of number theory, too, as the developer of a hyper-complex system which became known as Lipschitz algebra. In investigating the sums of arbitrarily many squares, Lipschitz derived computational rules for certain symbolic expressions from real transformations. Even more important were the investigations which he began in 1869 into forms of n differentials, for these led to his most valuable contribution to mathematics - the Cauchy-Lipschitz method of approximation of differentials. Finally, there was his work on co-gradient differentiation, which he conducted parallel to, but independently of, similar research by Elwin Christoffel (1829-1900). Lipschitz showed that the vanishing of a certain expression is a necessary and sufficient condition for a Riemannian manifold to be Euclidean, and further research into Riemann's mathematics enabled him to produce what is now the chief theorem concerning mean curvature vectors. Lipschitz's two papers on this subject, taken together with one written by Christoffel, formed a vital ingredient of what became the tensor calculus of Ricci-Curbastro and Tullio Levi-Civita.

Partly because he spread himself so wide, Lipschitz's star does not shine so brightly as some others in the mathematical firmament; but he was one of the most industrious and most technically proficient of nineteenth-century mathematicians.

Littlewood, John Edensor (1885-1977), was a British mathematician best known for his work in analysis, especially that done in collaboration with G.H. Hardy.

Littlewood was born at Rochester, Kent, on 9 June 1885, but went with his family as a young boy to South Africa, where he received his early education. In 1900 he returned to England and attended St Paul's School, London, before going to Cambridge in 1903. In 1905 he received his BA in mathematics and then remained at his college, Trinity, for a year of further study. From 1907 to 1910 he was Richardson Lecturer in Mathematics at the University of Manchester. He went back to Trinity in 1910, having been elected a Fellow of the College and awarded a Smith's Prize in 1908, and was appointed Cayley Lecturer in Mathematics. Soon thereafter he began his collaboration with Hardy, although most of their subsequent joint mathematical work was done by correspondence.

During World War I Littlewood served as a lieutenant in the Royal Garrison Artillery, working at the Woolwich Arsenal after 1916. He then returned to Cambridge, where he was appointed Rouse Ball Professor of Mathematics in 1928. He held the Chair until his retirement in 1950. After his formal retirement, he continued to give lectures at Cambridge until the age of 70. He died at Cambridge on 6 September 1977.

Although Littlewood made no startling discovery to which his name has been attached, he did much valuable work in complex analysis, function theory, number theory, trigonometric series and differential equations. With Hardy he published important papers on Diophantine approximation and number theory, also on Fourier series, which investigations he continued in the 1930s in collaboration with R.J. Paley (1907-1933). His distinction, although he remained in what Hardy would have called the "second eleven" among mathematicians, was recognized by the Royal Society, which elected him a Fellow in 1916, and awarded him the Royal Medal (1929), the Sylvester Medal (1943) and, its highest honour, the Copley Medal (1958).

Lobachevsky, Nikolai Ivanovich (1792-1856), was a Russian mathematician, one of the founders of non-Euclidean geometry, whose system is sometimes called Lobachevskian geometry.

Lobachevsky was born at Nizhni-Novgorod (now Gorki) on 2 November 1792. About eight years later, when his father died, he moved with his family to Kazan, where he was educated at the local school. In 1807 he entered the University of Kazan to study mathematics and in 1814 he was appointed to the teaching staff there. In 1822 he was made a full professor and in 1827 he was elected Rector of the university. He also took on administrative work for the government, serving as assistant trustee for the Kazan educational district from 1846 to 1855. For reasons which remain obscure (perhaps to compel him to devote himself to his government work), the government relieved him of his posts as professor and rector in 1847. Earlier it had recognized his talent by raising him to the hereditary nobility in 1837. In his later days Lobachevsky suffered from cataracts in both his eyes, and he was nearly blind when he died at Kazan on 24 February 1856.

Lobachevsky's whole importance rests on the system of non-Euclidean geometry which he developed between 1826 and 1856. Karl Gauss and János Bolyai were working on Euclid's fifth postulate and formulating their own non-Euclidean geometries at the same time; but in 1826, when Lobachevsky first gave the outline of his system to a meeting of colleagues at Kazan, neither Gauss nor Bolyai had uttered a public word, and Lobachevsky's first published paper on the subject appeared in 1829, three years before Bolyai's appendix to his father's *Tentatem*. The clearest statement of his geometry was made in the book *Geometrische Untersuchungen zue Theorie der Paralellinien*, which he published in Berlin in 1840. His last work on the subject, the *Pangéométrie*, was published just before his death.

Ever since the time of Euclid it had been believed that no geometry could be constructed without his fifth postulate, or in other words that any set of axioms other than Euclid's must, in the course of the geometry's development, produce contradictory consequences which would invalidate the geometry. Like Gauss and Bolyai, Lobachevsky abandoned the fruitless search for a proof to the fifth postulate. He came to see - this was the starting-point of his invention - that it was not contradictory to speak of a geometry in which all of Euclid's postulates *except* the fifth held true. His new geometry, by analogy with imaginary numbers, he called "imaginary geometry". By including imaginary numbers geometry became more general, and Euclid's geometry took on the appearance of a special case of a more general system.

The chief difference between the geometry of Euclid and that of Lobachevsky may be pointed up by the fact that, in Euclid's system, two parallel lines will (as a consequence of the fifth postulate) remain equidistant from each other, whereas in Lobachevskian geometry, the two lines will approach zero in one direction and infinity in the other. Another example of the difference is that in Euclidean geometry the sum of the angles of a triangle is always equal to the sum of two right angles; in Lobachevskian geometry, the sum of the angles is always less than the sum of two right angles. Lobachevskian space is such a different concept from that of Euclid's, that in the former triangles can be defined as functions of their angles, which determine the length of the sides. In Lobachevskian space, also, two geometric figures cannot have the same shape but different sizes.

The work of Lobachevsky, as of Gauss and Bolyai, demonstrated that it was useless to attempt to prove Euclid's fifth postulate by showing all other alternatives to be impossible. It demonstrated that different geometries, self-contained and self-consistent, were logically possible. The notion, prevalent since the time of Euclid, that geometry offered *a priori* knowledge of the physical world was destroyed (somewhat ironically it is the Lobachevskian model, not the Euclidean, which today seems closer to the actual world of space). Non-Euclidean geometry destroyed, once for all, the notion of empirical mathematics. It represented, William Clifford has said, a revolution in the history of human thought as radical as the revolution begun by Copernicus. Largely unrecognized in his lifetime, Lobachevsky and his fellow revolutionaries are still, outside the highest mathematical circles, too little recognized today.

M

Maclaurin, Colin (1698-1746), was a Scottish mathematician who first presented the correct theory for distinguishing between the maximum and minimum values of a function and who played a leading part in establishing the hegemony of the Newtonian calculus in eighteenth-century Great Britain.

He was born at Kilmoden in February 1698. His father died when he was six weeks old and his mother before he was ten, and he was raised by his uncle, the incumbent in the parish of Kilfinnan, in Argyllshire. In 1709 he entered the University of Glasgow to study divinity, but within a year - influenced largely by Robert Simson, the Professor of Mathematics - he abandoned divinity for mathematics. In 1713 he presented a paper entitled "On the Power of Gravity" and received his MA. Four years later, still only 19, he was appointed Professor of Mathematics at the Marischal College of Aberdeen.

On a visit to London during the vacation in 1719 Maclaurin met Isaac Newton and was elected to the Royal Academy. He visited Newton again in 1721 and a year later left Aberdeen, without official leave, to become travelling tutor to the eldest son of the English diplomat, Lord Polwarth. The next three years were spent chiefly in France and Maclaurin's paper on "The Percussion of Bodies" (later included in substance in his treatise on fluxions) won him a prize from the French Academy of Sciences. When his pupil died in the autumn of 1724 Maclaurin returned to Scotland, but having forfeited the goodwill of his colleagues at Aberdeen, moved to Edinburgh. Thanks to the kindness of Newton, who wrote a letter on his behalf and promised to provide £20 annually towards the stipend, he was appointed Deputy Professor of Mathematics at the university there. A few months later he succeeded to the Chair.

Although Maclaurin's chief work for the next 20 years was on fluxions, he was a popular lecturer on many subjects and won the admiration of Edinburgh society for his public lectures and demonstrations in experimental physics and astronomy. He also wrote a paper on the gravitational theory of tides which won a prize in 1740 from the French Academy. In 1745, during the Jacobite rebellion, he organized the defence of Edinburgh, and the exertions and exposure to cold which the effort entailed ruined his health. He died of oedema at Edinburgh on 14 June 1746.

Maclaurin's reputation rests on his great *Treatise of Fluxions*, published in 1742. It was an attempt to prove Newton's doctrine of prime and ultimate ratios and to provide a geometrical framework to support Newton's fluxional calculus. Indeed, so highly praised and so influential was the treatise, that it may be accounted one of the major contributions to the ascendancy of Newtonian mathematics which cut off Britain from developments on the continent and left it to the continental mathematicians, for the next three generations, to make the running in the establishment of those methods of analysis which are the foundation of modern mathematical analysis.

The treatise did also include, however, important solutions in geometry and in the theory of attractions. It contained Maclaurin's development of his paper on the gravitational influence on tides, and proved that an ellipsoid of evolution is formed whenever a homogeneous fluid mass under the action of gravity revolves uniformly about an axis. The treatise also included the method of defining the maximum and minimum points on a curve.

The specific theorem for which Maclaurin is most famous, and which is named after him, is a special case of the Taylor theorem. It can be used to find the series for functions such as $\log_e(1+x)$, e^x, sin x, cos x, tan x, etc., where e is the base of natural logarithms. The theorem, however, is of minor significance in the history of mathematics. Maclaurin's real distinction lies in being the first man to publish a logical and systematic exposition of the methods and principles of Newtonian mathematics.

Markov, Andrei Andreevich (1856-1922), was a Russian mathematician, famous for his work on the probability calculus and for the "Markov chains".

Markov was born into the minor gentry class at Ryazan on 14 June 1856, a somewhat sickly child who was dependent upon crutches until the age of 10. He studied mathematics at the University of St Petersburg, where he was fortunate to have Pafnuty Tchebychev as a teacher, from 1874 to 1878. His BA dissertation of 1878, on the integration of differential equations by means of continued fractions (a special interest of Tchebychev), was awarded a gold medal. He began to tutor at the university in 1880 and four years later was awarded a doctorate for his thesis on continued fractions and the problem of moments.

For the next 25 years Markov continued his research and teaching at St Petersburg, where he became an extraordinary professor at the age of 30 and a full professor in 1893. At the same time he became involved in liberal political movements and perhaps only his academic eminence saved him from punitive government measures when he protested against the Tsar's refusal to accept Maxim Gorky's election to the St Petersburg Academy in 1902. He also refused to accept Tsarist decorations and in 1907 renounced his membership of the electorate when the government dissolved the fledgling representative *duma*, or parliament. In the harsh winter famine months of 1917 he worked, at his own request and without pay, teaching mathematics in a secondary school in Zaraisk, deep in the Russian interior. Shortly afterwards his health began to fail, and he died at Petrograd (previously St Petersburg, now Leningrad) on 20 May 1922.

Markov's early work was devoted primarily to number theory - continued fractions, approximation theory, differential equations, integration in elementary equations - and to the problem of moments and probability theory. Throughout he used the method of continued fractions, most notably applying it to evaluate as precisely as possible the upper and lower boundaries of quantities such as quadratic forms.

In the latter 1890s he began to concentrate upon the probability calculus. During the middle years of the century there had been considerable development of the law of large numbers and of the central limit theorem invented by Pierre Laplace and Abraham de Moivre. But there were still no proofs with satisfactorily wide assumptions; nor had the limits of their applicability been discovered. Together, Tchebychev, Alexander Lyapunov (1857-1918) and Markov explored these problems far enough to bring about what amounted to the modernization of probability theory. Tchebychev's argument was extended by Markov in a paper of 1898 entitled "The law of large numbers and the method of least squares" (written, in fact, as a series of letters to Alexander Vassilyev). Two years later he published his book, *Probability Calculus*, which was based on the method of moments. Markov's method was less flexible than Lyapunov's, who a year later published his proof of limit theorems using a method of characteristic functions; and although Markov attempted over the next eight years to establish the superiority of his method, and did succeed in proving Lyapunov's conclusions by means of it, the method of moments remains cumbersome, more complex and less general than the method of characteristic functions.

The chief fruit of Markov's endeavours to justify his method was the discovery of the important sequence of random variables named after him, the Markov chains. Put in informal language, a Markov chain may be described as a chance process which possesses a special property, so that its future may be predicted from the present state of affairs just as accurately as if the whole of its past history were known. Markov seems to have believed that the only real examples of his chains were to be found in literary texts, and he illustrated his discovery by calculating the alteration of vowels and consonants in Pushkin's *Eugeny Onegin*. Markov chains are now used, however, in the social sciences, in atomic physics, in quantum theory and in genetics. They have proved to be his most valuable contribution to twentieth-century thought.

Menninger, Karl (1898-1963), was a German mathematician who established a reputation with his popular writings, which brought the world of mathematics to a wide audience.

Menninger was born in Frankfurt-am-Main in 1898 and studied mathematics, physics and philosophy at the Universities of Frankfurt, Heidelberg, Darmstadt and Munich. After 1924 he taught in a secondary school at Heppenheim an der Bergstrasse and, for a while, at the University of Giessen, where he was awarded the Justus Liebig Medal. Much of his time he spent travelling about Europe gathering material for a book on perspective. It was intended to be his last work, but he had not completed it when he died, at Heppenheim, in October 1963.

Menninger was a highly trained mathematician, but not an original one. He devoted little time to research. He had a talent for writing and he used it to write a number of highly entertaining books (not textbooks) on a variety of mathematical topics. His aim was to make people aware of the mathematical implications contained in their everyday life, to divert them with mathematical puzzles, and to give them some idea of the place of mathematics in human history. *Mathematik in deiner Welt* (1954) took facets of everyday life, such as flower-arrangements, lotteries, kitchen gadgets, and tried to show how the mathematical mind approaches them. His most famous book was *Number Words and Number Symbols* (1934), which was translated into many languages and which has gone through many editions, the latest in 1977.

It may be described as a cultural history of numbers, a tracing through history of the ways in which the idea of numbers has become interwoven with human activity. Other publications of Menninger include *Rechenkniffe*, a discussion of folding problems, and *Ali Baba und die 39 Kamele*, which reached its tenth edition in 1978.

Writing knowledgeably and entertainingly about mathematics for the lay public is a rare art; Menninger was one of its finest exponents.

Minkowski, Hermann (1864–1909), was a Lithuanian mathematician whose introduction of the concept of space-time was essential to the genesis of the general theory of relativity.

Minkowski was born at Alexotas, near Kaunas (now part of the Soviet Union), on 22 June 1864, but moved to Germany with his family in 1872 and settled in Königsberg. There he was educated, receiving his doctorate from the University of Königsberg in 1885. He lectured at the University of Bonn from 1885 to 1894, when he returned to Königsberg as Associate Professor of Mathematics. After only two years there, he accepted the post of Professor of Mathematics at the Federal Institute of Technology at Zurich. His last years were spent at Göttingen University, where he held the Chair created for him by David Hilbert from 1902 until his death on 12 January 1909.

Minkowski's genius first declared itself when, at the age of 19, he shared the French Academy's Grand Prix for a paper on the theory of quadratic forms with integral coefficients. Quadratic forms remained his chief interest, although he failed to find a method, like many before and after him, of generalizing Karl Gauss' work on binary quadratic forms so as to describe "*n*-ary" forms. His passion for pure mathematics led him also into problems in number theory, to which his concept of the geometry of numbers constituted an important addition. This was achieved by his use of the lattice in algebraic theory, and it was his research into that topic which led him to consider certain geometric properties in a space of *n* dimensions and so to hit upon his notion of the space-time continuum. The principle of relativity, already put forward by Jules Poincaré and Albert Einstein, led Minkowski to the view that space and time were interlinked. He proposed a four-dimensional manifold in which space and time became inseparable, a model which has not received much acceptance; but the central idea - contained in his *Raum und Zeit* (1909) - was, as Einstein allowed, necessary for the working out of the general theory of relativity.

So, in a manner not uncommon in the history of science, Minkowski, who was moved chiefly by a love of pure mathematics, made his most brilliant discovery in the field of mathematical physics.

Möbius, August Ferdinand (1790–1868), was a German mathematician and theoretical astronomer, whose name is attached to several discoveries, most notably the "barycentric calculus".

Möbius was born at Schulpforta, near Naumburg, on 17 November 1790. His father was a dancing master and his mother a descendant of Martin Luther. Until the age of 13 he was educated at home by his father and, after his father died in 1798, by his uncle. Although he showed a talent for mathematics at school (1803–1809), he went to the University of Leipzig in 1809 to study law. He soon abandoned law for mathematics and astronomy and in 1813 he went to Göttingen University to receive two semester's instruction from Karl Gauss. He received his doctorate from Leipzig in 1814 and in the following year was appointed an instructor in astronomy there. In 1816 he was promoted to Extraordinary Professor of Astronomy and was appointed as an observer at the Leipzig Observatory. He spent time in the next few years visiting observatories throughout Germany and his recommendations for the refurbishing and reconstruction of the Leipzig Observatory were carried out in 1821. In 1844 he was made a full Professor of Astronomy and Higher Mechanics and in 1848 Director of the observatory. He died at Leipzig on 26 September 1868.

Möbius made important contributions to both astronomy and mathematics. His chief astronomical work was *Die Elemente der Mechanik des Himmels* (1843), a somewhat novel book, in that it provided a thorough mathematical discussion of celestial mechanics without resort to higher mathematics. His most important mathematical work, now regarded as something of a classic, was *Der barycentrische Calkul* (1827). Möbius had formulated his idea of the barycentric calculus in 1818. The word "barycentric", formed from the Greek *barys* for "heavy", means "pertaining to the centre of gravity". Möbius began with the well-known law of mechanics that several weights positioned along a beam can be replaced by a single weight, equal to the sum of the other weights, at the centre of the beam's gravity. From that law he constructed a mathematical system in which numerical coefficients were assigned to points. The position of any point in the system could be expressed by varying the numerical coefficients of any four or

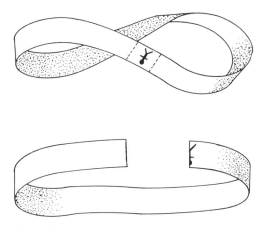

The Möbius strip has only one side and one edge. It is made by attaching one end of a strip to the other – but with a half-twist first.

more non-coplanar points. This calculus proved helpful in a number of geometrical problems.

The treatise also introduced the principle of duality and gave a thorough treatment to the cross ratio; in addition, it included a discussion of the "Möbius net", a concept later of great value in the development of projective geometry. A number of other discoveries bear his name: the Möbius tetrahedrons, two tetrahedrons which mutually circumscribe and inscribe each other, which he described in 1828; the Möbius function in number theory, published in 1832; and the Möbius strip.

The Möbius strip, presented in a paper discovered only after his death, was devised by him to illustrate the properties of one-sided surfaces, and consists of a length of paper connected at its ends with a half-twist in the middle. Credit for its discovery is shared with Johann Benedict Listing, a nineteenth-century German mathematician who is now known to have discovered it independently at the same time. The strip is one of Möbius' two contributions to the pre-natal stage of the history of topology. The other is his five-colour problem, given as a poser during a lecture of 1840. The problem he set was to find the least number of colours required on a plane map to distinguish political regions, given that each boundary line should separate two differently coloured regions. He drew maps requiring at least two, three or four colours. Neither Möbius nor anyone else has ever found a five-colour solution (though on a torus five-colour maps are easily drawn). But nor has it ever been proved that a four-colour map will always suff-

ice, even though it has been shown that for a map of up to 38 regions it will.

Monge, Gaspard (1746–1818), was a French mathematician and chemist, who was famous for his work in descriptive and analytical geometry and is generally regarded as the father of descriptive geometry.

Monge was born at Beaune, into a merchant family, on 9 May 1746, and received his first education at the local Oratory. From 1762 to 1764 he studied at the Collège de la Trinité at Lyons, where he displayed such advanced scientific knowledge and such instinctive skill that he was placed in charge of the physics course. He returned to Beaune in 1764 and never again received formal scientific education. In the summer of 1764 he made a graphic sketch of his native town, the excellence of which won the praise of an officer at the École Royale du Génie at Mézières and gained Monge his first appointment, as a draughtsman and technician, at the school. His official duties were to prepare plans of fortifications and other architectural models, but in his spare time he devoted himself to geometrical research. It was in these years, 1766 to 1771, that he made his most fruitful insights into the nature of descriptive geometry.

In 1769 Monge succeeded the Professor of Mathematics at the École Royale, although he was not given the title of Professor. A year later he was also appointed an instructor in experimental physics. In 1771 he met Condorcet and d'Alembert, by whom he was drawn into the scientific circle attached to the Academy of Sciences in Paris. In that year he submitted four papers to the Academy, of which the most significant was the "*Mémoire sur les développées les rayons de courbure et différents genres d'inflexions des courbes à double courbure*", which was read to the Academy in 1771, but which was not published until 1785. That paper was Monge's first important original work; it was followed in 1776 by another paper in infinitesimal geometry in which Monge introduced lines of curvature and the congruences of straight lines.

In 1780 Monge was elected to the Academy of Sciences and was given official duties as assistant geometer to the Academy. By then he was showing as much interest in the physical sciences as in mathematics. In 1783, independently of Lavoisier, he synthesized water. He also collaborated with J.F. Clouet to liquefy sulfur dioxide. In 1785 he was appointed examiner of naval cadets by the French government, an appointment which marked the beginning of his long participation in French public life. The burdens of the job, added to his duties at the Academy, forced him to resign his professorship at Mézières in 1784. For the next eight years Monge divided his time between inspecting naval schools throughout the country and participating in the activities of the Academy.

By the time that the French revolution broke out in 1789 Monge was one of the most celebrated of French scientists. He was an earnest supporter of the radicals and joined several revolutionary clubs and societies. In 1792 he was appointed Minister of the Navy, but as the revolution took its speedy course towards the Terror, he was discovered (despite his association with the left-wing Jacobins) to be a moderate and he resigned his post in April 1793. Thereafter he held no overt political position, although he was a member of the Committee on Arms in 1793-1794 and did important work in supervising the Paris armaments workshops and in helping to develop military balloons. He also served on the commission established to standardize French weights and measures. In March 1794 he was appointed to the commission set up to establish the École Centrale des Travaux Publics and was its instructor in descriptive geometry when the new school opened in 1795. It soon changed its name to the École Polytechnique.

In 1796 Monge's friendship with Napoleon began. Having conquered Italy, the revolutionary French government decided to plunder the country of its artistic and scientific treasures and Monge was sent, as a member of the Commission des Sciences et des Arts en Italie, to assist in the selection of objects to be removed to France. He met Napoleon briefly, but was then recalled to France in 1797 to take up a new appointment as director of the École Polytechnique. He then went back to Italy in 1798, this time as a member of a mission to inquire into the country's political organization. While he was there he was invited by Napoleon to assist in the preparation for the Egyptian campaign; he then accompanied Napoleon on the expedition to Egypt and was appointed president of the Institut d'Egypte established at Cairo in 1798. Monge also went with Napoleon on the expeditions to the Suez region and Syria in 1799, before returning to Paris at the end of the year.

He had scarcely begun to resume his duties as director of the École Polytechnique when the *coup d'état* of 18 Brumaire placed Napoleon in control of the French government. Two months later Napoleon appointed him a senator for life and he resigned the directorship of the École Polytechnique. For the rest of Napoleon's ascendancy Monge assumed the role of the foremost scientific supporter of the imperial regime. He was rewarded by being made a Grand Officer of the Legion of Honour in 1804, President of the senate in 1806, and the Count of Péluse in 1808. His creative scientific life was now a thing of the past, but in the leisure which freedom from onerous official appointments allowed, Monge brought together his life's work in a number of publications: the *Géométrie descriptive* (1799), the *Feuilles d'analyse appliquée à la géométrie* (1801), its expanded version, *Application de l'analyse à la géométrie* (1807), and several smaller works on infinitesimal and analytical geometry.

In the last decade of his life Monge was painfully afflicted by arthritis, whose ravages forced him to abandon his teaching at the École Polytechnique in 1809. Thereafter he lived in semi-retirement, although he went to the district of Liège in 1813 to organize the defence of the region against the allied armies then making their final victorious penetration into France. When Napoleon was finally overthrown in 1815, Monge was discredited. In 1816 he was expelled from the Institut (the renamed Academy of Sciences) and on 28 July 1818 he died in Paris.

Monge was one of the most wide-ranging scientists and mathematicians of his age. In the years between 1785 and 1789, for example, he submitted to the Academy of Sciences papers or notes on an astonishing variety of subjects: the composition of nitrous acid, the generation of curved surfaces, finite difference equations and partial differential equations (1785); double refraction, the composition of iron and steel and the action of electric sparks on carbon dioxide (1786); capillary phenomena (1787); and the physiological aspects of optics (1789). He holds an honoured place in the history of chemistry, not simply for his independent synthesis of water, but also for working with Lavoisier in 1785 in the epoch-making experiments on the synthesis and analysis of water. Although his own research had not led him to break entirely with the phlogiston theory, he was readily converted to the new chemistry by Lavoisier and played an energetic part in getting it accepted. Such was his standing as a chemist that he was one of the founders of the *Annales de chimie*.

It is, nevertheless, as a geometer that Monge gains his place in the scientific pantheon. Probably because he began his career as a draughtsman, he was always able to combine the practical, analytical and geometrical aspects of a problem. It was from his work on fortifications and architecture that he developed the basic principles of his descriptive geometry. The *Géométrie descriptive* was based on lectures given at the École Polytechnique in 1795. Its achievement was to translate the practical graphic procedures used by draughtsmen into a generalized technique, elegantly ordered and based upon rigorous geometrical reasoning. So popular was the book that it was quickly being used throughout Europe. It established Monge as the founder of descriptive geometry and, more, made a vital contribution to the nineteenth-century renaissance in geometry.

Throughout his life Monge's principal interest was infinitesimal geometry, especially in so far as it provided him with the opportunity to improve the rigour and enhance the status of analytical geometry. Monge broke with Cartesian tradition and asserted the autonomy of analytical geometry as a separate branch of mathematics. In particular he devoted himself to two subjects: the families of surfaces as defined by their mode of generation (which he studied in relation to their corresponding partial differential equations); and the properties of surfaces and space curves. Much of this work was a development of the theory of developable surfaces outlined by Euler in 1772, although as early as 1769 Monge had defined the evolutes of a space curve and demonstrated that such curves are the geodisics of the developable envelope of the family of planes normal to a given curve. Monge established the distinction between ruled surfaces and developable surfaces and he provided a simple method of determining, from its equation, whether a surface *is* developable. His work in analysis was less original and less rigorous, but he made valuable contributions to the theory of both partial differential equations and ordinary differential equations. He introduced the notions, fundamental to later work, of the characteristic curve, the integral curve, the characteristic developable and the characteristic cone. He also created the theory of equations of the type $Ar + Bs + Ct + D = 0$ which are now known as "Monge equations". He also introduced contact transformations, which were to be generalized by Lie a century later.

By his development of descriptive geometry and his application of analysis to infinitesimal geometry Monge not only paved the way for much of the geometrical flowering of the nineteenth century; he also proved himself to be one of the most original mathematicians of his time.

Muir, Thomas (1844–1934), was a British mathematician, who is famous for his monumental and pioneering work in unravelling the history of determinants.

Muir was born at Stonebrye, Lanarkshire, on 25 August 1844 and grew up in the nearby town of Biggar, where his father was a shoemaker. He was educated at Wishaw Public School and Glasgow University, where he excelled at Greek and mathematics. He then spent some time in Berlin, studying and book-collecting, before returning to Scotland in 1868 to take up a post as mathematics tutor at College Hall, St Andrews. From 1871 to 1874 he was Assistant Professor of Mathematics at Glasgow and from 1874 to 1891 head of the mathematics and science department at the Glasgow High School. That he chose to leave university life for secondary-school teaching revealed the deep interest he took in the general educational standards of the community. In 1891 his wife, who suffered poor health, was advised to move to a warmer climate and together they emigrated to South Africa where, in 1892, Muir accepted the post of Superintendent-General of Education in the colony. He held the post until his retirement in 1915. From 1892 to 1901 he was also Vice-Chancellor of the University of Cape Town. In addition to his mathematical work, Muir took a keen interest in geography and he was elected a Fellow of the Royal Geographical Society in 1892 and of the Royal Scottish Geographical Society in 1899. He was knighted in 1915. In 1916 he received the Gunning-Victoria Prize for his contribution to science. He died in Cape Town on 21 March 1934.

Muir earned the gratitude of South Africans for the part that he played – by far the most important part – in raising educational standards in the country and securing a proper place for science in the curriculum. In the history of mathematics he is remembered for his work on determinants, first discovered by Gottfried Leibniz in 1693. In all he published 307 papers, most of them on determinants and allied subjects, in addition to his books, *A Treatise on the Theory of Determinants* (1882), *The Theory of Determinants in its Historical Order of Development* (1890) and, above all, the magisterial five-volume treatise on the history of determinants. The first volume appeared in 1906, the last in 1930, and when it was completed it was widely acclaimed as one of the most thorough treatments of the history of any branch of theoretical knowledge. Muir's work made the results of Laplace, Cauchy, Schweins and a host of other mathematicians accessible to scholars. Muir himself was not a creative mathematician but his book lay behind many an algebraic discovery.

N

Nagell, Trygve (1895–), is a Norwegian mathematician whose most important work was in the fields of abstract algebra and number theory.

Nagell was born in Oslo on 13 July 1895 and was educated at the University of Oslo, where he received his MA in mathematics in 1920. He was appointed to the mathematics faculty of the University in that year and was awarded his PhD in 1926. He was promoted to the rank of associate professor in 1930, but a year later left Oslo to become Professor of Mathematics at the University of Uppsala, in Sweden, where he remained until his retirement in 1962. Since 1962 he has continued to live in Uppsala. For his work in mathematics he was awarded the Norwegian Order of St Olav and made Knight Commander in the Swedish Order of the North Star.

Nagell first made his name with a series of papers in the early 1920s on indeterminate equations, investigations which led to the publication of a treatise on indeterminate analysis in 1929. He also published papers and books, in Swedish and English, on number theory. From the late 1920s onwards his chief interest was the study of algebraic numbers, and his 1931 study of algebraic rings was perhaps his most important contribution to abstract algebra.

Napier, John, 8th Laird of Merchiston (1550–1617), was a Scottish mathematician who invented logarithmic tables.

Napier was born at Merchiston Castle, near Edinburgh, in 1550, into a family of influential landed nobility and statesmen who were staunchly attached to the Protestant cause. As a young boy he was educated chiefly at home, although he may have spent some time at the Edinburgh High School and, less probably, studying in France. At the age of 13 he was sent to St Salvator's College, in the Univeristy of St Andrews. There he studied mainly theology and philosophy, gained a reputation for his quick temper, and left without taking his degree. He may then have passed a few years studying on the continent. He was, at any rate, in Scotland in 1571. He built a castle at Gartnes, on the banks of the Endrick, and lived there with his wife, whom he married in 1572, until the death of his father in 1608 brought him the inheritance of Merchiston.

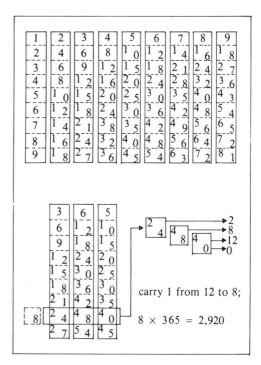

Napier's bones *consist of a set of (originally ivory) numbered rods. Using them, multiplication became merely a process of reading off the appropriate figures and minor additions. (For multipliers greater than 9, however, the user had to resort to factorization.)*

Napier was an aristocratic scientific and literary amateur. He never occupied any professional post in his life. But he became known as the "Marvellous Merchiston" for his varied accomplishments. He made advances in scientific farming, especially by the use of salt as a fertilizer; he invented a hydraulic screw and revolving axle by means of which water could be removed from flooded coalpits and obtained the patent for its sole manufacture and use in 1597; he also published, in 1593, a violent denunciation of the Roman Church entitled *A Plaine Discovery of the Whole Revelation of St John*, a popular work which ran through several editions and was translated into French, Dutch and German. He had scarcely a moment of idleness, and overwork – combined with the gout from which he suffered in his later years – brought him to his death, at Merchiston, on 4 April 1617.

Napier's favourite intellectual pursuit was astronomy, and it was via astronomy that he was led to make his great invention. He performed many calculations in the course of his observations and research. He found the lengthy calculations, involving the use of trigonometric functions (especially sines) a tiresome burden, and over the course of about 20 years the idea of logarithmic tables slowly gestated in his mind. In 1614 he explained his new invention and printed the first logarithmic table in the *Mirifici Logarithmorum Canonis Descriptio*. The word "logarithm" he formed from the Greek *logos* for "expression" and *arithmos* for "number". The best statement of his invention, however, was given in the posthumously published *Constructio* (1619).

Napier's publication was immediately recognized by mathematicians for the great advance that it was. In particular, it excited the English mathematician Henry Briggs (*c*.1556-1631), who went to Edinburgh in 1616 (and a couple of times thereafter) to discuss the new tables with Napier. Together they worked out improvements – such as the idea of using the base ten – and the result, Briggs' tables of 1617, was the production of the standard form of logarithmic tables in use until the present day (although they have largely been replaced by electronic computers and calculators).

Napier himself has a claim as the inventor of the first mechanical calculator, albeit one of a wholly primitive kind. His last work, *Rabdologia* ("numeration by little rods"), he published in 1617. In it he explained his system of multiplying and dividing by the use of rods – usually made of bones or ivory, and hence known as Napier's Bones – and showed also how square roots could be extracted by the manipulation of counters on a chessboard.

As a footnote, and a testament to the splendid practical inventiveness of the man, it should be remembered that it was Napier, too, who first used and then popularized the decimal point to separate the whole number part from the fractional part of a number.

Newman, James Roy (1907-1966), was an American lawyer who devoted a great deal of his life to making mathematics comprehensible to the lay public.

Newman was born at New York on 3 August 1907, and received his BA from Colly City, New York, in 1926 and his LLB from Columbia in 1929. He was admitted to the New York bar in 1929 and established a practice in New York city. Until 1941 he remained in private practice; during World War II he served in various government posts, including Under-secretary of War (1942-1943), Chief Intelligence Officer at the American Embassy in London (1943-1945)

and special assistant to the Under-secretary of War (1944-1945). After the war he moved more into a literary and journalistic life, becoming a consultant to the Library of Congress in literature and mathematics and acting as senior editor of the journal *The New Republic* from 1945 to 1948. For the rest of his life he combined legal practice with the writing of books on scientific subjects. He died at Washington on 29 May 1966.

Newman never displayed any original flair for mathematics himself, but he acquired a sound understanding of modern mathematical developments. He wished to convey this understanding to the public so that mathematics should not be a mysterious subject accessible only to experts. He wished also to persuade the public of the richness of mathematics, of its beauty and range. Among his publications the best known are *The Control of Atomic Energy* (1948), *What is Science?* (1955) and *The World of Mathematics* (1956).

Newton, Isaac (1642-1727), was an English natural philosopher and mathematician, the pre-eminent scientific representative of the Age of Reason, celebrated especially for his work in optics and, above all else, for his discovery of universal gravitation.

Newton was born in Woolsthorpe, near Grantham, Lincolnshire, on Christmas Day 1642 (4 January 1643 by the modern calendar). He was a premature, sickly baby whose survival defied expectations. His father died before he was born and when his mother married again he was left, at the age of three, in the charge of his grandmother at Woolsthorpe. He soon began to show a distinct skill at mechanical invention, reputedly making water-clocks, "fiery kites" and a model mill powered by a mouse. He also made innumerable drawings and diagrams. In 1654 he was sent to the grammar school at Grantham, where he remained until the age of 14, by which time he had risen to be head of the school. His mother then withdrew him from the school in order that he should become a farmer. Fortunately his uncle recognized his rare scientific ability and had him returned to the school in 1660 to prepare for university. In June 1661, having already read Kepler's *Optics*, he went to Trinity College, Cambridge. There he read widely in the scholarship of the day, paying particular attention to the works of René Descartes and John Wallis, and attended Isaac Barrow's mathematical lectures. He was elected a scholar of Trinity in 1664 and gained his BA in the following year.

The Great Plague of 1665-1666 forced the

university to close down and Newton passed 18 months in virtual seclusion at Woolsthorpe. His entire life was marked by long periods of withdrawal from society and no such period was more fruitful than this first. During this short space of time, in a miracle of intense mental activity, he laid the foundations of all his later work in mathematics, optics and astronomy. In particular, he performed his first prism experiments and he formed his basic conceptions of the law of universal gravitation and of the elements of the calculus of fluxions.

In 1667 he returned to Cambridge and was elected a Fellow of Trinity. Two years later, still only 26, he succeeded Barrow in the Lucasian Chair of Mathematics at the university. The next three decades, spent working alone for the most part, although in frequent communication with leading scientists by correspondence and through the Royal Society, were Newton's years of achievement. In 1672 the Royal Society, a year after receiving his reflecting telescope (he had become convinced that to improve the refracting telescope was impossible), elected him a Fellow. In 1687 his great work, the *Principia Mathematica*, was published. Soon afterwards his mathematical powers - or interest - began to wane. He spent more time in theological controversy and writing, became interested in politics and in 1689 was elected as a Whig to represent Cambridge University in Parliament. For a brief period the intense mental strain of the previous 25 years took its toll: in 1692 he suffered what would today be called a bout of severe depression (he was described as having "lost his reason"). In 1695 he took part in discussions about the reform of the currency, just then a question of some political importance, and a year later he was appointed Warden of the Mint. He was promoted to Master of the Mint in 1699. Newton took these new, well-paid duties seriously and, although his scientific work continued, it was greatly diminished. In 1701 he resigned the Lucasian Professorship and gave up his Fellowship at Trinity.

Thereafter Newton lived mainly in London. He became president of the Royal Society in 1703, an office to which he was annually reelected until his death, and he was knighted in 1705, the same year in which his defeat at the election for the University of Cambridge ended his spasmodic parliamentary career. The last 20 years of his life were darkened by acrimonious public disputes with John Flamsteed (1646-1719) and Gottfried Leibniz, sad reminders of an earlier public quarrel with Robert Hooke (1635-1703). He remained, however, of hearty constitution, sharp of sight and hearing and

mentally alert, until his death at London on 20 March 1727. He was buried at Westminster Abbey.

Newton's scholarly disputes were so bitterly contested and raged for such long periods that they cannot be passed over. They reveal Newton to have been unduly sensitive to criticism of his work and extremely possessive about his findings. The dispute with Hooke, who supported the wave theory of light propounded by Christiaan Huygens (1629-1695) against Newton's corpuscular theory, was relatively decorous and scholarly, although much of its cause was Newton's failure to give Hooke credit for work done in collaboration. The quarrel with Flamsteed, which lasted from 1705 to 1712, and the one with Leibniz, which lasted from 1706 to 1724, were more damaging to Newton's reputation. In the first Newton, as President of the Royal Society, saw fit to refuse to publish Flamsteed's astronomical observations in the order that Flamsteed wanted, despite the fact that Flamsteed was the Royal Astronomer. The dispute with Leibniz concerned the authorship of the calculus. Newton used the whole weight of the Royal Society publicly to deny that Leibniz had any part in its discovery, entirely ignoring that Leibniz clearly arrived at his discovery independently of, although later than, Newton and that he devised a system of notation which was almost at once recognized as being superior to Newton's.

Whatever his personal shortcomings, Newton's scientific achievements were monumental, both in their genius and in their revolutionary influence. Newton was a man of many parts. A brilliant mathematician and an exceptionally gifted optical physicist, he brought the cosmological revolution which Copernicus had begun to a triumphant close. He also conducted experiments in chemistry and alchemy and wrote prolifically and knowledgeably on matters of Biblical scholarship and theological controversy (whether he was actually anti-Trinitarian is difficult to establish).

By comparison with many mathematicians his mathematical creativity declared itself somewhat late, not until near the end of his undergraduate career. But this delay was more than made up during 1665 and 1666, of which years Newton wrote in his notebooks (*c*.1716): "In the beginning of the year 1665 I found the method for approximating series and the rule for reducing any dignity [power] of any binomial to such a series [i.e., the binomial theorem]. The same year in May I found the method of tangents of Gregory and Slusius, and in November had the direct method of Fluxions [i.e., the elements of

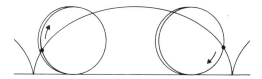

Newton proved that the cycloid – the path taken by a point on the edge of a rolling disc – is a section of the surface that a particle slides down in the least time.

the differential calculus], and the next year in January had the Theory of Colours, and in May following I had entrance into the inverse method of Fluxions [i.e., integral calculus], and in the same year I began to think of gravity extending to the orb of the Moon ... All this was in the two years of 1665 and 1666, for in those years I was in the prime of my age for invention, and minded Mathematics and Philosophy more than at any time since."

The zenith of Newton's mathematics was the *Principia Mathematica*, which was written in a mere 18 months. In this great work Newton's plan was to develop the subject of dynamics from a mathematical point of view and then to apply the results to important astronomical and physical problems. The treatise included a synthesis of Kepler's recently discovered three laws of planetary motion and of Galileo's laws of falling bodies, thus laying the foundations of modern mechanics. But although he had already developed the calculus, Newton did not use it in the *Principia*, where he preferred to prove his results geometrically.

Whether the law of gravitation first hinged itself to Newton's mind by his observing the fall of an apple remains doubtful. The story comes to us from Voltaire, who got it from Newton's step-niece, Mrs Conduitt. The idea *did* come to him in the garden at Woolsthorpe – at least the idea that the same force acted on falling objects as acted on the Moon. From there he quickly developed his general theory of gravitation as a universal attraction between any two objects in obedience to the law – here is Newton's giant step beyond Kepler – of inverse squares: the force decreases in proportion to the square of the distance between the two bodies. Newton did not complete or publish his work on gravitation until the appearance of the *Principia*. At last Aristotle was overthrown: it was shown that the planets move in ellipses according to laws discernible to man and capable of mathematical expression.

Newton's other most celebrated treatise, the *Opticks*, was published in 1704, its appearance delayed until after Hooke's death to avert the possibility of a dispute over originality. The *Opticks* presented a coherent and organized account of Newton's work on the nature and effects of light. Although Newton believed that light rays were corpuscular, he integrated into his theory the concept of periodicity, holding that "ether waves" were associated with light corpuscles, a remarkable conceptual leap, since both Hooke and Huygens, the founder of the wave theory, denied periodicity to light waves. The corpuscular theory was characteristically Newtonian: it lent itself to analysis by forces and established and analogy between the action of gross bodies and the action of light. It thus reinforced the universalizing tendency of the *Principia* and, indeed, the defining rationalism of the seventeenth-century Age of Reason.

Much of Newton's work remains little known – much of the physics and even more of the chemistry and alchemy. His papers and correspondence await thorough and expert editing. But nothing that is discovered in the future will change our basic understanding of his work nor diminish his colossal stature. His creation of the fluxional calculus and his demonstration of universal gravitation were the peaks of his achievement. The general influence of his work was to place physics on a new, anti-Aristotelian basis and to establish the supreme virtue of giving mathematical expression to explanations of physical phenomena. His place in the history of modern thought was perfectly assigned by Alexander Pope, who wrote the epitaph which appears on Newton's tombstone:

Nature and Nature's laws lay hid in night:
God said, "Let Newton be", and all was light.

Until the revolution wrought by Albert Einstein, we lived in a Newtonian Universe.

Noether, Amalie (Emmy) (1882–1935), was a German mathematician who became one of the leading figures in modern abstract algebra.

Noether was born in Erlangen on 23 March 1882, the eldest child of the famous mathematician Max Noether, Professor of Mathematics at the University of Erlangen. After completing her secondary education, she came up against the rule then prevailing in Germany which barred women from becoming fully fledged students at a university. She was, however, allowed to attend lectures in languages and mathematics without student status for two years from 1900 to 1902; eventually she was accepted as a student and awarded a doctorate in 1907 for a thesis on algebraic invariants.

Once more the rules blocked her way, this time barring her from a post in the university faculty. She nevertheless persisted with her research independently and at the request of David Hilbert (1862-1943) was invited to give lectures at Göttingen University in 1915-1916. There she worked with Hilbert and Felix Klein (1849-1925) on problems arising from Einstein's theory of relativity, and thanks to Hilbert's constant nagging the university eventually, in 1919, gave her the status of "unofficial associate professor". In 1922 her position was made official, and she remained at Göttingen until the Nazi purge of Jewish university staff in 1933. The rest of her life was spent as Professor of Mathematics at Bryn Mawr College in Pennsylvania, where she died from a post-surgical infection on 14 April 1935.

Noether first made her mark as a mathematician with a paper on non-commutative fields which she published in collaboration with Schmeidler in 1920. For the next few years she worked on the establishment, and systematization, of a general theory of ideals. It was in this field that she produced her most important result, a generalization of Dedekind's prime ideals and the introduction of the concept of primary ideals. Modern work in this field dates from her papers of the early 1920s. After 1927 she returned to the subject of non-commutative algebras (in which the order in which numbers are multiplied affects the result), her chief investigations being conducted into linear transformations of non-commutative algebras and their structure.

No other woman has achieved the mathematical eminence of Emmy Noether and for that reason, as also for her breaking down the male grasp on German universities, her life had an importance stretching beyond the history of mathematics.

Noether, Max (1844-1921), was a German mathematician who contributed to the development of nineteenth-century algebraic geometry and the theory of algebraic functions.

Noether was born at Mannheim on 24 September 1844 and educated locally until the age of 14, when he contracted polio, which left him permanently handicapped and for two years deprived him of the use of his legs. He was tutored at home until he entered the University of Heidelberg in 1865 to study mathematics. He was awarded his doctorate in 1868 and was appointed to the Heidelberg faculty. In 1874 he became an associate professor, but a year later

he moved to the University of Erlangen, where he was promoted to a Professorship in 1888. He retired, with an emeritus professorship, in 1919 and died at Erlangen on 13 December 1921. His daughter Amalie (Emmy) also became a famous mathematician.

Noether published books on algebraic curves (1882) and algebraic functions (1894), as well as several biographies of mathematicians, but his reputation rests principally on his work in the early 1870s. Much of his initial inspiration came from the work of Antonio Cremona (1830-1903). In 1871 he published a proof (independently found at about the same time by William Clifford and J. Rosanes) that a Cremona transformation can be constructed from quadratic transformations. Then, two years later in 1873, he published his one outstanding result, the theorem concerning algebraic curves which contains the "Noether conditions". The theorem runs as follows. Given two algebraic curves, $\phi(x, y) = 0$ and $\psi(x, y) = 0$, which intersect at a finite number of isolated points, the equation of an algebraic curve that passes through all the points of intersection may be expressed as

$$A\Phi + B\Psi = 0,$$

where A and B are polynomials

in x and y

if, and only if, certain conditions (the "Noether conditions") are satisfied.

Noether said that his result could be extended to surfaces and hypersurfaces, but he never succeeded in demonstrating this. It was left to Julius König to generalize the theorem to n dimensions in 1903.

O

Ore, Oystein (1899–   ), is a Norwegian mathematician whose studies, researches and publications have concentrated on the fields of abstract algebra, number theory and the theory of graphs.

Ore was born on 7 October 1899 in Oslo, where he grew up and was educated, entering Oslo University in 1918; he received his BA in 1922. He then paid a fleeting visit to the University of Göttingen - that great centre of mathematics - where he met the influential mathematician Emmy Noether (1882-1935) who was at that time building up an active research group in abstract algebra. The work being done at Göttingen undoubtedly exercised a strong influence over Ore.

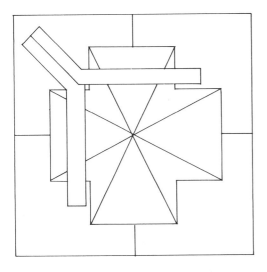

The four-colour problem was studied by Oystein Ore. To date, nobody has managed to invent a plane design that needs more than four colours in order to avoid the same colour bordering itself. Even the complicated pattern shown here can, with some thought, be shaded using only four colours.

Returning to Scandinavia, he worked from 1923 until 1924 at the Mittag-Leffler Mathematical Institute in Djursholm, Sweden, at the end of which time he was awarded his PhD in mathematics by the University of Oslo. Two years later (and after another short visit to Göttingen), Ore was appointed Professor of Mathematics at Oslo University. Only twelve months later, however, he moved to take up an equivalent position at Yale University in the United States; there, he was rapidly promoted to Associate (1928) and then to full Professor (1929), serving as Chairman of his department from 1936 to 1945. He then returned to Norway, although he maintains his connections with Yale to this day. A Knight of the Order of St Olav, Ore is the author of many books on mathematical subjects.

During the 1920s and 1930s Ore's primary research interest was abstract algebra. Among other topics, he investigated linear equations in non-commutative fields; most of his work on this subject was summarized in a book he published in 1936 on abstract algebra. He then turned to an examination of number theory, and in particular of algebraic numbers. His investigations in this subject were contained in a text on number theory and its origins which he published in 1948.

Much of Ore's later research has dealt with the theory of graphs. He took a special interest in the four-colour problem, the theory that maps require no more than four colours for each region of the map to be coloured but with no zone sharing a common border with another zone of the same colour. Ore is the author of a book detailing his investigations into the problem; it appeared in 1967.

Another of Ore's interests has been the history of mathematics. He has written biographies of the sixteenth-century Italian Gerolamo Cardano and of his fellow Norwegian, the ill-starred Niels Abel; they were published in 1953 and 1957 respectively.

P

Pappus of Alexandria (*fl.*AD 300–350), was a Greek mathematician, astronomer and geographer whose chief importance lies in his commentaries on the mathematical work of his predecessors.

Nothing is known of his life and many of his writings survive only in translations from the original Greek. According to the *Suda Lexicon*, he lived in the time of the emperor Theodosius I (who reigned from AD 379 to 395), but the compiler of the *Suda Lexicon* was notoriously unreliable and from other sources it appears that Pappus lived rather earlier. The most important piece of evidence is found in his commentary on Ptolemy, in which he writes of an eclipse of the Sun that took place in AD 320 in language which strongly suggests that he himself witnessed the event as a grown man. It is usual, therefore, to place Pappus in the first half of the fourth century.

Pappus' chief works are the *Synagogue* (more commonly referred to as the *Collection*), the commentary on Ptolemy's *Syntaxis* or *Almagest*, and the commentary on Euclid's *Elements*. He wrote also a commentary on Euclid's *Data* and one on the *Anelemma* of Diodorus; neither of these works, however, survives. Pappus may also have written the section from the fifth book onwards of the commentary on Ptolemy's *Harmonica* which was chiefly the work of Porphyry. More convincingly established is Pappus' authorship of the *Description of the World*, a geographical treatise which has come down to us only in the form of a book written in Armenian and bearing the name of Moses of Khoren as its author. That the treatise does not exist in Greek is no hindrance to attributing it to Pappus because, of all his works, only the *Collection* and the commentary on the *Almagest* survive in their original form. Some scholars believe that the *Description* should be attributed to Anania Shirakatsi, but the consensus is that the work is either a direct translation or a very close paraphrase of Pappus. It should also be mentioned, in a list of Pappus' work, that a twelfth-century Arabic manuscript attributes to Pappus the invention of an instrument to measure the volume of liquids. If Pappus did invent such an instrument – and there seems to be no good reason to doubt it – he may have written a treatise on hydrostatics that has been lost to posterity.

By far the most important of Pappus' works is the *Collection*. Without it, much of the geometrical achievement of his predecessors would have been lost for ever. The *Collection* is written in eight parts, of which the first two have never been found; Pappus may have intended it to extend to twelve parts and, indeed, may have done so. The *Collection* deals with nearly the whole body of Greek geometry, mostly in the form of commentaries on texts which it is assumed the reader has to hand. It reproduces known solutions to problems in geometry; but it also frequently gives Pappus' own solutions, or improvements and extensions to existing solutions. Thus Pappus handles the problem of inscribing five regular solids in a sphere in a way quite different from Euclid, gives a broader generalization than Euclid to the famous Pythagorean theorem, and provides a demonstration of squaring the circle which is quite different from the method of Archimedes (who used a spiral) or that of Nicomedes (who used the conchoid).

Perhaps the most interesting part of the *Collection*, measured by its influence on modern mathematics, is Book VII, which is concerned with the problems of determining the locus with respect to three, four, five, six or more than six lines. Pappus' work in this field was called "Pappus' problem" by René Descartes, who demonstrated that the difficulties which Pappus was unable to overcome could be got round by the use of his new algebraic symbols. Pappus thus came to play an important, if minor, role in the founding of Cartesian analytical geometry. And it is another mark of his originality and skill that he spent much time working on the problem of drawing a circle in such a way that it will touch three given circles, a problem sophisticated enough to engage the interest, centuries later, of both François Viète and Isaac Newton.

For his own originality, even if his chief importance is as the preserver of Greek scientific knowledge, Pappus stands (with Diophantus) as the last of the long and distinguished line of Alexandrian mathematicians.

Pascal, Blaise (1623-1662), was a French mathematician, physicist and religious recluse who was not only a scientist anxious to solve some of the problems of the day but also a gifted writer and a moralist. He is remembered not so much for his original creative work – as are his contemporaries René Descartes (1596-1650) and Pierre de Fermat (1601-1665) – but for his contributions to projective geometry, the calculus of probability, infinitesimal calculus, fluid statics, and his methodology in science generally. Much of his work has become appreciated only during the last 150 years.

Pascal was born on 19 June 1623 at Clermont-Ferrand, the son of a civil servant in the local administration. His mother died when he was only three, and his father – also a respected mathematician – looked after the family and saw to the education of the children. In 1631 they all moved to Paris, where Pascal's sister Jacqueline showed literary talent and Pascal himself displayed mathematical ability. By 1639, when Pascal was 16, he was already participating in the scientific and philosophical meetings run at the Convent of Place Royale by its Director, Father Marin Mersenne (1588-1648); some of these meetings were attended also by Descartes, Fermat and other celebrated figures (such as Thomas Hobbes). The illness and eventual death of his father led Pascal to commit himself to a more spiritual mode of life, one from which he was at times terrified of lapsing. Converted to the rigorous form of Roman Catholicism known as Jansenism in 1646, he finally experienced a fervently spiritual "night of fire" on 23 November 1654, and from then on wrote only at the direct request of his spiritual advisers, the order of monks at Port Royal. Five years later his health had become poor enough to prevent him from working at all. He died from a malignant ulcer of the stomach on 19 August 1662 in Paris, aged only 39.

Pascal's first serious work was actually on someone else's behalf. In 1639 Gérard Desargues (1593-1662) published a work entitled *Brouillon project d'une atteinte aux evenements des rencontres du cone avec un plan* ("Experimental project aiming to describe what happens when the cone comes in contact with a plane"), but its content baffled most of the mathematicians of that time because of its style and vocabulary, and the refusal of Desargues to use Cartesian algebraic symbols. Pascal became Desargues' main disciple, and in the following year published his *Essai pour les coniques* in explanation

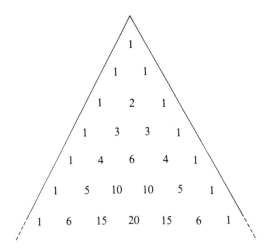

Pascal's triangle is an array of numbers in which (a) each is the sum of the two immediately above, left and right; (b) each is the sum of all those in each diagonal, starting from either immediately above, left or right; and (c) each diagonal constitutes an arithmetical series.

of the subject. The paper was an immediate success in the mathematical world; that in itself, coupled with the fact that his own algebraic notational system now had strong competition, left René Descartes smarting rather, and he thenceforward regarded Pascal as something like an opponent.

Grasping the significance of Desargues' work, Pascal used its basic ideas - the introduction of elements at infinity, the definition of a conic as any plane section of a circular cone, the study of a conic as a perspective of a circle, and the involution determined on any straight line by a conic and the opposite sides of an inscribed quadrilateral - and went on to make his first great discovery, now known as Pascal's mystic hexagram. He stated that the three points of intersection of the pairs of opposite sides of a hexagon inscribed in a conic are collinear. By December 1640 he had deduced from this theorem most of the propositions now known to have been contained in the *Conics* of the ancient Greek mathematician Apollonius. It was not until 1648, however, that Pascal found a geometric solution to the problem of Pappus (which Descartes had used in connection with demonstrating the strength of his new analytical geometry in 1637). Pascal's solution was important because it showed that projective geometry might prove as effective in this field as the Cartesian analytical methods.

The full treatise that Pascal wrote covering the whole subject was never published; the manuscript was seen later only by Gottfried Leibniz (1646-1716). And in fact, because the work of Desargues was so complicated, it was not until the nineteenth century, with the researches of Jean-Victor Poncelet (1788-1867), that attention was drawn to the work of Pascal.

In 1642, to help his father in his work, Pascal decided to construct an arithmetical machine that would mechanize the processes of addition and subtraction. He devised a model in 1645, and then organized the manufacture and sale of these first calculating machines. (At least seven of these "computers" still exist. One was presented to Queen Christina of Sweden in 1652.)

For much of the 1640s Pascal concentrated on his work in physics, focusing particularly on the statics of gases and liquids, and repeating Evangelista Torricelli's experiments with enclosed vacuums and barometric measurements.

Pascal kept up a long correspondence with Fermat on the subject of the calculus of probabilities. Their main interest was in the study of two specific problems: the first concerned the probability that a player will obtain a certain face of a dice in a given number of throws; and the second was to determine the (portion of the) stakes returnable to each player of several if a game is interrupted. Pascal was the first to make a comprehensive study of the arithmetical triangle (called the Pascal triangle) that he then used to derive combinational analysis. Together with Fermat, he provided the foundations for the calculus of probability in 1657. In 1658 and the next year, Pascal perfected what he called "the theory of indivisibles" (which he had first referred to in 1654). This was in fact the forerunner of integral calculus, and enabled him to study problems involving infinitesimals, such as the calculations of areas and volumes.

After 1661, when his sister died, Pascal became even more solitary and his health deteriorated further. His last project was to design a public transport system for Paris. The system was actually inaugurated in 1662, the year Pascal died.

Peano, Giuseppe (1858-1932), was an Italian mathematician who applied the rigorous and axiomatic methods used in mathematics to his study of logic. He is chiefly remembered for his concise logical definitions of natural numbers, devised - not entirely by himself - in order to derive a complete system of notation for logic, and for his discovery in analysis of a curve that fills topological space.

Peano was born on 27 August 1858 in Spinetta, near Cuneo. Living on a farm he was educated locally until the age of 12 or 13, when he was sent to Turin to receive private lessons. In 1876 he won a scholarship to the Collegio delle Provincie, Turin University. On graduating, he joined the staff of the University and remained there for the rest of his life, first becoming a professor there in 1890. By that time he had already held a professorial appointment for four years teaching at Turin Military Academy; he retired from this concurrent post in 1901. During his lifetime he received several honours and awards, and participated actively within the Turin Academy of Sciences. He died of a heart attack on 20 April 1932 and, by his request, was buried in Turin General Cemetery; his remains, however, were removed to the family tomb in Spinetta in 1963.

Peano was a pioneer in symbolic logic and a fervent promoter of the axiomatic method – but he himself considered that his work in analysis was more important. It was carried out mainly in the 1880s while Peano was investigating the integrability of functions. In 1886 he was the first to show that the first order differential equation $y' = f(x,y)$ was solvable using only the one assumption that f is continuous. In 1890 he generalized this result, and in his published study gave the first explicit statement of the axiom of choice.

His first work in logic was published in 1888. It contained his rigorously axiomatically-derived postulates for natural numbers which received considerable acclaim, although he studiously acknowledged his debt for some of the work to Richard Dedekind (1831–1916) who had also published during the same year. The postulates are nevertheless now known as the Peano Axioms. They formed the basis on which Peano went on to found his system of mathematical notation for logic; *Formulario Mathematico*, comprising his work and that of collaborators, was published between 1895 and 1908, and contained 4,200 theorems. Later, Bertrand Russell was to say that he reached a turning point in his own life on meeting Peano; part of Peano's work was used in Russell's *Principia Mathematica*.

Peano also applied the axiomatic method to other fields, such as geometry, first in 1889 and again in 1894. A treatise on this work contained the beginnings of geometrical calculus.

His name is in addition particularly associated with the discovery of the "Peano curves" that fill a space (such as a square), and that are used in topology. He provided new definitions of the length of an arc of a curve and of the area of a surface. He determined an error term in Simpson's formula and became interested in errors in numerical calculations. And he developed a theory of gradual operations which led to new methods for resolving numerical equations.

After 1900, he changed his interests slightly, and created an international language that never really caught on. Between 1914 and 1919 he organized conferences for secondary mathematics teachers in Turin. Finally he became a mathematical historian and recorded many exact origins of mathematical terms and first applications of symbols and theorems.

Pearson, Karl (1857–1936), was a British mathematician and biometrician who is chiefly remembered for his crucial role in the development of statistics as applied to a wide variety of scientific and social topics.

Pearson was born in London on 27 March 1857. He was tutored at home, except for a period between 1866 and 1873 when he attended the University College School. He began his university studies at King's College, Cambridge, in 1875, where an indication of Pearson's somewhat uncompromising and unconventional spirit is found in his successful pressuring of the authorities to abolish the mandatory classes in divinity for undergraduates. Pearson graduated with high honours in 1879, and was awarded a Fellowship at the College from 1880 to 1886 that gave him financial independence without obligation and enabled him to travel and study as he pleased. He visited universities in Germany, took a degree in law in 1881 (although he never practised), and was awarded his master's degree in 1882. In 1884 – still officially a Fellow at King's College – Pearson was named Goldsmid Professor of Applied Mathematics and Mechanics at University College, London; he was to hold this post until 1911 although his most productive work during the period was carried out elsewhere. He was also appointed Lecturer in Geometry at Gresham College, London, in 1891, which required him to give a short series of lectures each year. And it was from them on that Pearson became interested in the development of statistical methods for the investigation of evolution and heredity. His efforts in this aim were most fruitful, and were recognized by his election as Fellow of the Royal Society in 1896 (which awarded him its Darwin Medal in 1898). He then founded and became Editor (until his death) of *Biometrika*, a journal established to publish work on statistics as applied to biological subjects. His work on eugenics led to his appointment as Head of the Laboratory of Eugenics at London University upon Francis Galton's retirement in 1906. In 1911 he became the first Galton Professor of Eugenics, a post he retained until 1933, when he retired to become Emeritus Professor. (His department was then split into two sections, one of which was headed by Pearson's son.) Pearson continued to work in his department until his death in Cold-harbour, Surrey, on 27 April 1936.

During the early years of Pearson's career he did little work in mathematics, concentrating instead on law and political issues. His appointment to the Goldsmid Chair required him to focus his attentions on academic duties and on writing. A further marked change overtook his life in the early 1890s with the publication of Francis Galton's book *Natural Inheritance*, and with Pearson's exposure to the ideas of Walter Weldon, the newly appointed Professor of Zoology at University College.

Weldon was interested in the application of Galton's methods for correlation and regression to the investigation of the validity of Darwin's model of natural selection. Pearson threw himself into this project with great vigour, examining graphical methods for data presentation, studying probability theory and concepts such as standard deviation (a term he himself introduced in 1893, although the idea was by then nearly a century old), and more complex distribution patterns. He submitted many papers on statistical methods to the Royal Society of London, but encountered some stiff opposition to his mathematical approach to biological material. This prompted him to launch his own journal, *Biometrika*.

The major achievement in the early part of his investigation was the elucidation of a method for finding the values for the parameters essential for the description of a particular distribution, and also the classification of the different types of curves produced in the plotting of data into general types. This contributed to putting the Gaussian (or "normal") distribution into more realistic perspective.

Pearson's discoveries included the Pearson coefficient of correlation (1892), the theory of multiple and partial correlation (1896), the coefficient of variation (1898), work on errors of judgement (1902), and the theory of random walk (1905). The last theory has since been applied to the study of random processes in many fields. In addition, Pearson's *Biometrika* for 1901 is a book of tables of the ordinates, integrals and other properties of Pearson's curves, and was of great practical use in rendering accessible statistical methods to a large number of scientists.

Perhaps the most familiar of Pearson's achievements was his discovery in 1900 of the χ^2 (chi-squared) test applied to determine whether a set of observed data deviate significantly from what would have been predicted by a "Null Hypothesis" (that is, totally at random). Pearson also demonstrated that it could be applied to examine whether two hereditary characteristics (such as height and hair colour) were inherited independently.

Weldon's death in 1906 dealt a severe blow to Pearson's work in the field of mathematics as applied to biology; Pearson himself lacked the biological background to keep up with the increasingly sophisticated developments in the field of genetics. A great controversy had grown up around the approach of Weldon – who believed in gradual but continuous evolution – as against that of the followers of Gregor Mendel, such as William Bateson – who believed in intermittent variation. Pearson felt that Mendel's results were not incompatible with a statistical approach, although many Mendelians were convinced that it was. But it was the equally celebrated statistician Ronald Fisher (1890-1962) who was ultimately able to bring about the beginnings of a reconciliation between the two approaches.

During the rest of Pearson's career he concentrated on the establishment of a thriving department dedicated to the training of postgraduate students so that statistical techniques might be applied to subjects in many areas of academic study. He also worked on eugenics, examining the relative importance of environment and heredity in disorders such as tuberculosis and alcoholism, and in the incidence of infant mortality.

Picard, Charles Emile (1856-1941), was a distinguished French mathematician whose work in analysis – and particularly in analytical geometry – brought him deserved fame. Responsible for the formulation of "Picard's little theorem" and "Picard's big theorem", he was also an excellent teacher, interested to apply mathematical principles as much as possible to other branches of science, particularly physics and engineering.

Picard was born on 24 July 1856 in Paris, where his father was the Director of a silk factory. He showed talent as a pupil at the Lycée Henry IV, where his excellent memory contributed to his outstanding results. Completing his education, he entered the École Normale Supérieure in 1874. Within three years he had already made some important algebraic discoveries, been placed consistently first among his contemporary fellow-students, and had earned his doctorate. He was then retained as an assistant instructor at the École between 1877 and

1878. In 1879 he was appointed professor (at the age of 23) in Toulouse. Two years later, however, he returned to Paris as Lecturer in Physics and Experimental Mechanics at the Sorbonne and, simultaneously, again at the École Normale Supérieure. Also in 1881 his name was put forward for election to the Paris Academy of Sciences (although his election did not actually occur until 1889). In 1885 he took the Chair of Differential and Integral Calculus at the Sorbonne, and served as his own assistant until he reached the prescribed age of 30, at which he was officially able to hold the post. In 1897, at his own request, he exchanged this post for the Chair of Analysis and Higher Algebra because he wanted a position in which he could train students for research. He was made a member of the Académie Française in 1924, and received the Grande Croix de la Légion d'Honneur in 1932. He also won the Mittag-Leffler Gold Medal from the Swedish Academy of Sciences, received honorary degrees from five foreign universities, and was a member of 37 Academies and learned societies. Highly respected for his administrative capability, and an excellent teacher, Picard died on 11 December 1941 in the Palais de l'Institut in Paris, where he was living as permanent secretary.

Picard's work was mainly in the fields of mathematical analysis and algebraic geometry. In 1878 he studied the integrals of differential equations by making successive substitutions with equations having suitable partial derivatives. A year later, he proved the theorem now known by his name, that an integral function of the complex variable takes every finite value, with one possible exception. He expressed it in this way:

> Let $f(z)$ be an entire function. If there exist two values of A for which the equation $f(z) = A$ does not have a finite root, then $f(z)$ is a constant. From this it follows that if $f(z)$ is an entire function that is not a constant, there cannot be more than one value of A for which $f(z) = A$ has no solution.

In the following year he stated a second theorem:

> Let $f(z)$ be a function, analytic everywhere except at a where it has an essential isolated singularity; the equation $f(z) = A$ has in general an infinity of roots in any neighbourhood of a. Although the equation can fail for certain exceptional values of the constant A, there cannot be more than two such values.

From these results, generalizations were worked out that are now known as "Picard's little theorem" and "Picard's big theorem".

Picard created a theory of linear differential equations analogous to the Galois theory of algebraic equations. (This work was later extended by his pupil, Ernest Vessiot (1865–1952).) His work on the integrals attached to algebraic surfaces, together with the associated topological questions, developed into an area of algebraic geometry that had applications in topology and function theory. Much of Picard's work was recorded in a three-volume book entitled *Traité d'Analyse*.

He also applied his method of analysis to the theories of elasticity, heat and electricity, in theoretical physics, and produced a solution to the problem of the propagation of electrical impulses along a cable. At an age of more than 80 he presented a paper to the Academy of Sciences on questions of homogeneity and similarity encountered by physicists and engineers.

Poincaré, Jules Henri (1854–1912), was an innovative French mathematician and prolific mathematical writer. His interests and achievements were wide-ranging, although he is probably best known for his introduction of automorphic functions in pure mathematics, of ergodicity in the theory of probability, and of some of the understanding of the dynamics of the electron later attributed to Albert Einstein in the theory of relativity. He was also renowned for his study of celestial mechanics.

Poincaré was born on 29 April 1854 in Nancy, the son of a doctor. A brilliant student, he won first prize in an open competition between lycée students from throughout France. Completing his education, he entered the École Polytechnique in Paris in 1873, where he graduated. He then studied engineering at the École des Mines, but it was in mathematics that in 1879 his doctoral thesis was successfully composed. Immediately afterwards, Poincaré was appointed to a teaching post at the University of Caen, and only two years later he became Professor of Mathematics at Paris University. In 1887 he was elected to the Academy of Sciences, and during the remainder of his lifetime he received many other honours and awards. He died in Paris on 17 July 1912.

Poincaré's first great work was in pure mathematics, where he generalized the idea of functional periodicity in his theory of automorphic functions that are invariant under a denumerably infinite group of linear fractional transformations. He showed how these functions could be used to express the co-ordinates of any point of an algebraic curve as uniform functions of a single parameter, and could also be used to integrate linear differential equations with rational algebraic coefficients. Developing his investigations, he found that one class of automorphic functions - which he called Fuchsian, after the German mathematician Immanuel Fuchs (1833-1902) - were associated with transformations arising in non-Euclidean geometry. The originator of the study of algebraic topology, Poincaré has sometimes been compared with Karl Gauss in terms of the innovatory nature of his discoveries and the genuine desire for rigorous and precise presentation of data.

Poincaré contributed to the theory of the figures of equilibrium of rotating fluid masses and discovered the pear-shaped figures used in the researches of George Darwin (the great Charles's second son) and others. But perhaps his greatest contribution to mathematical physics was his paper on the dynamics of the electron, published in 1906, in which he obtained many of the results of the theory of relativity later credited to Albert Einstein (1879-1955). Poincaré worked quite independently of Einstein; his treatment was based on the full theory of electromagnetism and limited to electromagnetic phenomena, whereas Einstein developed his theory from elementary considerations involving light signalling. Poincaré's studies of mathematical physics led him inevitably to investigations in the field of celestial mechanics. He made important contributions to the theory of orbits, particularly with the classic three-body problem - the mutual gravitational and other effects of three bodies close together in space - which he generalized to a study of n bodies. In the course of his work he developed powerful new mathematical techniques, including the theories of asymptotic expansions and integral invariants. He made important discoveries about the behaviour of the integral curves of differential equations near singularities, and wrote a massive three-volume treatise on his new mathematical methods in astronomy. From his theory of periodic orbits he developed the entirely new subject of topological dynamics.

Poincaré wrote on the philosophy of science. He believed that some mathematical ideas precede logic, and made an original analysis of the psychology of mathematical discovery and invention in which he stressed the role played by convention in scientific method.

He was said, very early in his career, to be a "mathematical giant". Certainly Poincaré's output of writings was gigantic - he produced, in all, more than 30 books and 500 papers. But one outstanding quality of his authorship was that it appealed not merely to scientists but to educated people in all walks of life. When he was elected to the Académie Française in 1908, it was to fill the position left vacant following the death of the poet René Sully Prudhomme - a writer, not a scientist.

Poisson, Siméon-Denis (1781-1840), was a French mathematical physicist who was also a great educationist. More an analyser and a developer of other people's work than an innovator, Poisson nevertheless made many fundamental contributions to contemporary knowledge of electricity and magnetism; he is also known for the Poisson ratio, used in the mathematical theory of elasticity, and for his work on the theory of probability.

Poisson was born on 21 June 1781 in Pithiviers, Loirel, where his father was a civil servant in the local administration. Initially training as a surgeon, but discovering he had neither the manual dexterity for nor any interest in the profession, he entered the École Centrale in Fontainebleau in 1796 to study mathematics. Two years later he continued his studies in Paris at the École Polytechnique (coming first in the entry examination), where he studied under Pierre Laplace (1749-1827) and Joseph Lagrange (1736-1813). After only twelve months there, in 1799 he submitted a paper on the theory of equations that enabled him not only to graduate in 1800 but to begin teaching at the École himself. Two years later he was named Deputy Professor and, in 1806, became Professor. In 1808 he was appointed Astronomer at the Bureau des Longitudes, and the following year he was appointed Professor of Mechanics at the Faculty of Sciences. In 1815 he became an examiner at the École Polytechnique. Nominated Conseil Royal de l'Université in 1820, he became an administrator at the highest level in France's educational system and, as such, played a particularly prominent part in the "defence" of science against the conservative policies of the government of the day. Seven years later, he was appointed Mathematician at the Bureau des Longitudes in succession to Laplace. And in 1837 Poisson became a nobleman on accepting the offer of a baronetcy. He died in Paris on 25 April 1840.

Much of Poisson's work involved applying mathematical principles in theoretical terms to contemporary and prior experiments in physics, particularly with reference to electricity and magnetism but also with special regard to heat and sound. Quite early in his career, Poisson adopted the "two-fluid" theory of Jean Nollet (1700-1770), according to which the like fluids of electricity repelled and the unlike fluids attracted, and showed that Joseph Lagrange's potential function would be constant over the surface of an insulated conductor. He went on to give an ingenious proof of the formula for the force at the surface of a charged conductor.

Charles Coulomb (1736–1806) had already carried out experimental work involving the surface densities of charge for two spherical magnets placed any distance apart. Poisson produced theoretical results which were in agreement with those obtained experimentally by Coulomb and, in 1824, gave a very complete theory of magnetism using Coulomb's model – again incorporating two "fluids". Poisson derived a general expression for the magnetic potential at any point: the sum of two integrals due to volume and surface distribution of magnetism respectively.

In his own experiments on the elasticity of materials, Poisson deduced the ratio between the lateral and longitudinal strain in a wire; this is now known as Poisson's ratio.

His significant work in probability theory was considered at first to be a mere popularization of the work of Laplace. Poisson's formula for the great asymmetry between opposite events, such that the prior probability of either event is very small, was not used until the end of the nineteenth century, when its importance was finally recognized. Poisson was also responsible for a formulation of the "law of large numbers", which he introduced in his important work on probability theory, *Recherches sur la probabilité des jugements* (1837).

In his few but significant studies of pure mathematics, Poisson made noteworthy contributions to the calculus of variations, to differential geometry and to complex analysis. Although he is remembered as an analyst rather than as an innovator, Poisson's work nevertheless was such that it motivated in others an experimental approach. It could be said that without him, much of the progress achieved in French science in the early nineteenth century would not have occurred.

Polya, George (1887–), is a Hungarian mathematician, one of the founders of the Hungarian School of Mathematics, who is best known for his work on function theory, probability and applied mathematics.

Polya was born in Budapest on 13 December 1887. He studied at the Eotvos Lorand University and was awarded his PhD in mathematics by the University of Budapest in 1912. While there he was a member of a thriving community of mathematicians, but he then chose to devote two years to postgraduate study abroad. He attended courses at the University of Göttingen and in Paris before in 1914 accepting the offer of a

position as Assistant Professor of Mathematics at the Swiss Federal Institute of Technology in Zurich. He was promoted to Associate Professor and in 1928 to Full Professor of the Institute. He served as Dean and Chairman of the Mathematics Department from 1938, but in 1940 left to go to the United States. Brown University in Providence, Rhode Island, offered him the post of Visiting Professor which he held for two years before moving to Smith College, Northampton, Massachusetts, as Professor of Mathematics. In 1946 Polya became Professor of Mathematics at Stanford University, Palo Alto, California, where he remained until his retirement as Emeritus Professor in 1953. He frequently made lecture tours to universities throughout North America and Europe after his "retirement". From 1963 he also served on the Research Council of Greater Cleveland.

Polya is a member of numerous scientific and mathematical organizations, including the National Academy of Sciences, the American Academy of Arts and Sciences, and the London Mathematical Society. He has been awarded several honorary degrees and is the author of numerous books.

One of Polya's best known achievements was his discovery in 1920 of the theorem since named after him. Polya's theorem is a solution of a problem in combinatorics theory and method. Much of his other early work was on function theory, and he published studies on analytical functions in 1924 and on algebraic functions in 1927. He also worked on linear homogeneous differential equations (1924) and transcendental equations (1930). One of his studies in mathematical physics was an investigation into heat propagation published in 1931. He extended some of the previous results obtained by Andrei Markov (1856–1922) on the limit of probability, and probability theory became one of Polya's major research areas.

Other subjects he has examined include the study of complex variables, polynomials and number theory. His contributions to mathematics can thus be seen to be notable both for their breadth and their depth.

Poncelet, Jean-Victor (1788–1867), was a French military engineer who, to pass the time during two years as a prisoner of war, revised all the mathematics he could remember and went on to make fresh discoveries, particularly in projective geometry. He was among the leaders of those who initiated and developed the concept of duality.

Poncelet was born in Metz on 1 July 1788, the illegitimate (although later recognized) son of Claude Poncelet, a rich land-owner and an *advocat* at the *Parlement* of Metz. He was sent to live with a family in Saint-Avold, and they were responsible for his earliest education. At the age of 16 he returned to Metz and attended the lycée. In 1807 he went to the École Polytechnique in Paris, and stayed there for three years. He then fell behind with his studies, however, because of ill health, and in 1810 joined the Corps of Military Engineers. He graduated from the École d'Application in Metz in February 1812, and went to work on the fortification of the Dutch island of Walcheren. In June of the same year he became lieutenant of engineers and, attached to the staff of the Engineer-General, took part in the campaign against the Russians. He was captured at the Battle of Krasnoy, and was imprisoned in Saratov, a city on the Volga, until 1814. He then returned to France in September of that year and became Captain of the Engineering Corps in Metz. From then until 1824 he was engaged on projects in military engineering there. At the end of that time he was appointed Professor of Mechanics applied to machines at the École d'Application de l'Artillerie et du Génie in Metz, six years later becoming a member of Metz Municipal Council and Secretary of the Conseil-Général of the Moselle. He was elected to the Mechanics section of the Académie in 1834, and from 1838 to 1848 was Professor to the Faculty of Science at Paris. From 1848 to 1850 he was Commandant of the École Polytechnique with the rank of General. He died in Paris on 22 December 1867.

Poncelet's first great work was done while he was imprisoned at Saratov. With no textbooks at his disposal, he reconstructed the elements of pure and analytical mathematics (specifically geometry) from memory before undertaking some original research on the systems and properties of conics. It was projective geometry that interested him most, and it was his study of this aspect of conics that established the basis for his later important work, the treatise entitled *Traité des propriétés projectives des figures* published in 1822 (with a second edition of two volumes, published in 1865-1866). Poncelet had been a pupil of Gaspard Monge (1746-1818), who was the originator of modern synthetic geometry – synthetic geometry's viewing of figures as they exist in space is an alternative mathematical tool to the equation in the analytical method – but was equally conversant with either discipline. In fact, he used both methods and ranks as one of the greatest of those who contributed to the development of the relatively new synthetic (projective) geometry.

Poncelet became the centre of controversy over the principle of continuity. He also discovered the circular points at infinity, although the concept of points at infinity goes back to Gérard Desargues (1591-1661), and many of the individual ideas of projective geometry go back considerably further. But it was Poncelet who first developed them as a distinct branch of the mathematical science. His rather forceful presentation – and his occasionally wild accusations of plagiarism by other geometrists – antagonized the young German, Julius Plücker (1801-1868), to such an extent that he turned from using synthetic methods and became himself one of the greatest of analytical geometrists.

The principle of duality was first recognized and publicized by Poncelet in the *Journal für Mathematik* of 1829, although previously formulated by Joseph Gergonne in 1825-1827. (It can be illustrated by considering a statement capable of two meanings, both true, one obtained from the other simply by interchanging two words. In projective geometry, in two dimensions, this is achieved by interchanging the words "point" and "line". In three-dimensional geometry, there is a corresponding duality between points and planes; in this case the line is self-dual, in that it is determined by any two distinct points on it or by any two distinct planes through it.) Much of higher geometry is concerned with duality, and every new application practically doubles the extent of existing knowledge.

His engineering skills were much used between 1814 and 1840, for the first ten years of which he was engaged on projects in topography and the fortification and organization of an engineering arsenal. In 1821 he developed a new model of a variable counterweight drawbridge, which he described and publicized in 1822. His most important technical contributions were concerned with hydraulic engines, such as Poncelet's waterwheel, with regulations and with dynamometers, as well as in devising various improvements to his own previous fortification techniques. In applied mechanics he worked in three interrelated fields: experimental mechanics, the theory of machines, and industrial mechanics.

Pythagoras (*fl.c.*530 BC) was an ancient Greek religious philosopher, part of whose mystic beliefs entailed an intense study of whole numbers, the effect of which he sought to find in the workings of nature. He founded a famous school which lived as a cultic community governed by what might now be considered eccentric – if not downright primitive – rules, but which during and after his lifetime discovered an astonishing number of facts and theorems, some immortal.

Very little is known about the life of Pythagoras, other than that he was born on the island of Samos and (possibly) obliged to flee the despotism of its ruler, Polycrates, he (probably) travelled extensively. His work seems to show the influence of contemporary ideas in Asia Minor; nevertheless, Pythagoras is next authoritatively recorded in southern Italy, in the Dorian colony of Crotona, in about 529 BC. There he became the leader of a religious community that had political pretensions to being an association for the moral reform of society. The Pythagorean brotherhood flourished; as a mathematical and philosophical community it was extending science rapidly, and as a political movement it was extending its influence over several western Greek colonies. More distant colonies put up some physical resistance, however, and it was probably one act of suppression in particular - led by one Cylon - that saw Pythagoras exiled (yet again) to Metapontum until he died, possibly around 500 BC. The school continued for something like another 50 or 60 years before being finally and totally suppressed.

Pythagoras was all but obsessed by numbers. He and his community looked for numerical values in all they saw around them, and strove to create relationships in the values they found. In elementary pure mathematics they studied the

properties of the numbers themselves, and their practice of representing numbers as lines, triangles or squares of pebbles has given us our word calculate (from *calculus*, the Greek for pebble). It also led directly to a firm basis for geometrical considerations. In this way, they established that the addition of each successive odd number after 1 to the preceding ones results in a square ($1 + 3 = 2^2$; $1 + 3 + 5 = 3^2$, and so on) and Pythagoras himself is supposed ultimately to have arrived at the theorem to which his name is attached, regarding right-angled triangles. (In fact he is supposed to have proved it from a more general equation he is said also to have formulated:

$$m^2 + \{\tfrac{1}{2}(m^2 - 1)\}^2 = \{\tfrac{1}{2}(m^2 + 1)\}^2$$

and to have noted that if the triangle in question is isosceles, the ratio of the hypotenuse to either side is the irrational number $\sqrt{2}$.)

Using geometrical principles, the Pythagoreans were able to prove that the sum of the angles of any regular-sided triangle is equal to that of two right-angles (using the theory of parallels), and to solve any algebraic quadratic equations having real roots. They formulated the theory of proportion (ratio), which enhanced their knowledge of fractions, and used it in their study of harmonics upon their stringed instruments: the harmonic of the octave was made by touching the string at $\tfrac{1}{2}$ its length, of a fifth at $\tfrac{2}{3}$ its length, and so on. Pythagoras himself is said to have made this the basis of a complete system of musical scales and chords.

He is said also to have taken a keen interest in astronomy, seeking numerical consistency among the celestial movements and objects.

Triangular numbers	Square numbers
1 ○	○ 1
3 ○ ○ ○	○ ○ ○ ○ 4
6 ○ ○ ○ ○ ○ ○	○ ○ ○ ○ ○ ○ ○ ○ ○ 9
10 ○ ○ ○ ○ ○ ○ ○ ○ ○ ○	○ ○ ○ ○ ○ ○ ○ ○ ○ ○ ○ ○ ○ ○ ○ ○ 16

Triangular numbers and square numbers were part of the foundations of number theory investigated by the Ancient Greeks who noted, for example, that the sum of two adjacent triangular numbers always equals a square.

R

Ramanujan, Srinavasa Ayengar (1887-1920), was an Indian mathematician who, virtually unaided and untaught, by his own independent endeavour reached an exceptionally high standard in particular aspects of mathematics. His work and his evident desire for further study impressed the Cambridge mathematician Godfrey Hardy (1877-1947) so much that he was offered a scholarship to Trinity College. Despite the brevity of the remainder of his life, Ramanujan established a world-wide reputation.

Ramanujan was born in Erode, near Kumbakonam, in Tanjore, Madras, on 22 December 1887. His family was poor, although of the high Brahmin caste. At school Ramanujan did himself and his teachers credit until, at the age of

15, he read and became fascinated by Carr's textbook *A Synopsis of Elementary Results in Pure and Applied Mathematics* (published in 1880). Obsessed by the section on pure mathematics – which he soon learned by heart – he won a scholarship to the state college at Kumbakonam, but failed at the end of his first year because he had devoted such a disproportionate amount of his time and energy to mathematics, to the neglect of other subjects (English in particular). Unemployed, he nevertheless developed his own theorems and hypotheses from the mathematics he knew.

Finances became even worse in 1909 when he got married. In the next three years, however, he was given a small grant by Ramachaudra Rao that enabled him to maintain his mathematical investigations and begin publishing his results, and he found work as a clerk in the offices of the Madras Port Trust. Then began his correspondence with Godfrey Hardy at Cambridge University. Deeply impressed both by the results of Ramanujan's work to date, and by the surprising gaps in his knowledge of certain aspects (later found to be gaps in Carr's textbook), Hardy eventually managed to persuade the somewhat relectant Indian to take up the scholarship offered. Ramanujan arrived in 1914, and published 25 papers in European journals over the next five years. During that time, however, he contracted tuberculosis, and although the pleasure afforded him by his election as Fellow of the Royal Society in 1918 temporarily alleviated his condition, he was obliged to return to the more favourable climate of India in the following year. But although he kept on working, his health deteriorated further, and he died in Chetput, near Madras, on 26 April 1920. His collected papers were edited by Godfrey Hardy and published in 1927.

Carr's textbook, and particularly the section on pure mathematics, was the firm foundation on which Ramanujan based all his original work. In fact, he first scrutinized the book in detail from start to finish, checking its theorems and examples. From the knowledge he gained he was able to proceed beyond the material published and develop his own results in many fields, but particularly in function theory and number theory. When he arrived at Cambridge, Hardy was amazed at the standard he had reached in these areas – although Ramanujan knew nothing of subjects that had not been covered in Carr's book. Hardy was thus obliged to ensure that Ramanujan was given a speedy, but thorough, grounding in (for example) doubly periodic functions, the techniques of rigorous mathematical proofs, Cauchy's theorem and

other items that were all new ground. Hardy was also astonished to find that Ramanujan did much of his calculation mentally, and had achieved many of his creditable results by working through a large number of examples to check correlation.

It was perhaps in number theory that Ramanujan made his most enduring contribution. With Hardy he published a theory on the methods for partitioning an integer into a sum of smaller integers, called summands. In function theory he found accurate approximations to π, and worked on modular, elliptic and other functions. Because of his background, much of his work was of extraordinary originality – although he had the tendency also, unwittingly, to "discover" theorems and statements first formulated by other notable mathematicians from Pythagoras onwards.

Ricci-Curbastro, Gregorio (1853–1925), was an Italian mathematician who is chiefly remembered for his systematization of absolute differential calculus (also now called the Ricci calculus), which later enabled Albert Einstein (1879–1955) to write his gravitational equations, to express the principle of the conservation of energy, and thereby fully to derive the theory of relativity.

Although his complete surname was Ricci-Curbastro, he is often known simply as Ricci. He was born on 12 January 1853 in Lugo, Romagna, where he grew up and was educated at home by private tutors. At the age of 16 he went for a year to Rome University to study mathematics and philosophy, before returning to Lugo. Two years later he enrolled at the University of Bologna. After a year there, in 1872 he enrolled at the Scuola Normale Superiore in Pisa. In 1875 he received his doctorate in the physical and mathematical sciences. After winning a scholarship to travel and study, he spent a year (1877–1878) at Munich, where he met Felix Klein (1849–1925) and Enrico Betti (1823–1892). During 1879, Ricci stayed in Pisa and worked as an assistant to the mathematician U. Dini.

In December 1880 Ricci was appointed Professor of Mathematical Physics at the University of Padua, and stayed there for the remainder of his life. He published his major work – on the absolute calculus – between 1888 and 1892, but after being asked in 1891 to teach other aspects of mathematics in addition to those he was appointed to, he also published works on higher algebra, infinitesimal analysis and the theory of real numbers. He received many honours and awards, and was elected to membership of a surprising number of Academies. He also made valuable contributions to his local administration: as a magistrate and councillor he was not only concerned with problems of water supply, swamp drainage and public finance, he was also able to encourage the close collaboration of the government with science and its use in the service of the state. He died in Bologna on 6 August 1925.

Ricci's invention of absolute differential calculus was the result of ten years of research from 1884 to 1894. By introducing an invariant element – an element that can also be used in other systems – Ricci was able to modify the existing differential calculus so that the formulae and results retained the same form regardless of the system of variables used. Starting with the idea of co-variant derivation formulated by Elwin Christoffel (1829–1900), the work of Bernhard Riemann (1826–1866) on the theory of invariants of algebraic form, and with Rudolf Lipschitz's work on quadratic forms, Ricci realized that the methods used by these mathematicians could be generalized. In 1893 he published his *Di alcune applicazione del calculo differenziale assoluto all teoria delle forme differenzial quadratiche*, in which he gave a specific form to his ideas.

In 1896 he applied the absolute calculus to the congruencies of lines on an arbitrary Riemann variety; later, he used the Riemann symbols to find the contract tensor, now known as the Ricci tensor (which plays a fundamental role in the theory of relativity). Ricci also discovered the invariants that occur in the theory of the curvature of varieties.

Later still, he collaborated with a former pupil of his, Tullio Levi-Civita (1873–1941), to produce *Méthodes de calcul différentiel absolu et leurs applications*. This work contains references to the use of intrinsic geometry as an instrument of computation dealing with normal congruencies, geodetic laws and isothermal families of surfaces. The work also shows the possibilities of the analytical, geometric, mechanical and physical applications of the new calculus. In application to mechanics, Ricci solved the Lagrange equations with respect to the second derivatives of the co-ordinates. The application to physics includes equations in electrodynamics, the theory of heat and the theory of electricity.

Although for some time, however, the new calculus found few applications, when Albert Einstein came to formulate his General Theory of Relativity Ricci's method proved to be an apt means. Einstein's use of it has since encouraged the intensive study of differential geometry based on Ricci's tensor calculus.

Ricci continued to take an active part in mathematical studies into his very last years. His final major contribution was in 1924, when he presented a paper to the International Congress of Mathematicians held in Toronto, Canada; his subject then was the theory of Riemann varieties.

Riemann, Georg Friedrich Bernhard (1826–1866), was a German mathematician whose work in geometry – both in combining the results of others and in his own crucal and innovative research – developed that branch of mathematics to a large degree. His concepts in non-Euclidean and topological space led to advances in complex algebraic function theory and in physics; later Albert Einstein (1879–1955) was to make use of his work in his own theory of relativity. Riemann's study of analysis was also fundamental to further development. Despite the brevity of his life, he knew most of the other great mathematicians of his time, and was himself a famed and respected teacher.

Riemann was born on 17 September 1826 in Breselenz (in Hanover), one of the six children of a Lutheran pastor. From a very early age he showed considerable talent in mathematics. Nevertheless, on leaving the Lyceum in Hanover in 1846 to enter Göttingen University, it was to study theology at the behest of his father. However, he soon obtained his father's permission to devote himself to mathematics and did so, being taught by the great Karl Gauss (1777–1855). Riemann moved to Berlin in 1847 and there came into contact with the equally prestigious teachers Lejeune Dirichlet (1805–1859) and Karl Jacobi (1804–1851); he was particularly influenced by Dirichlet. Two years later he returned to Göttingen and submitted a thesis on complex function theory, for which he was awarded his doctorate in 1851.

During the next two years Riemann qualified as an unsalaried lecturer, preparing original work on Fourier series, and working as an assistant to the renowned physicist Wilhelm Weber (1804–1891). At Gauss's suggestion, Riemann also wrote a paper on the fundamental postulates of Euclidean geometry, a paper that was to open up the whole field of non-Euclidean geometry and become a classic in the history of mathematics. (Although Riemann first read this paper to the University on 10 June 1854, neither it nor the work on Fourier series was published until 1867 – a year after Riemann's death.) Riemann's first course of lectures concerned partial differential equations as applied to physics. The course was so admired by physicists that it was reprinted as long afterwards as in 1938 - 80 years later. He published a paper on hypergeometric series and in 1855-1856 lectured on his (by now famous) theory of Abelian functions, one of his fundamental developments in mathematics which he published in 1857. When Karl Gauss died in 1855, Dirichlet was appointed in his place, and Riemann was appointed Assistant Professor in 1857. On Dirichlet's untimely death in 1859 Riemann became Professor. Three years later, Riemann married; but in the same year he fell seriously ill with tuberculosis and he spent much of the following four years trying to recover his health in Italy. But he died there, in Selasca, on 16 June 1866 at the age of 39.

Riemann's first work (his thesis, published when he was already 25) was a milestone in the theory of complex functions. Augustin Cauchy (1789-1857) had struggled with general function theory for 35 years, had discovered most of the fundamental principles, and had made many daring advances - but some points of understanding were still lacking. Unlike Cauchy, Riemann based his theory on theoretical physics (potential theory) and geometry (conformal representation), and could thus develop the so-called "Riemann surfaces" which were able to represent the branching behaviour of a complex algebraic function.

He developed these ideas further in a paper of 1857 which continued the exploration of Riemann surfaces as investigative tools to study complex function behaviour, these surfaces being given such properties that complex functions could map conformally onto them. In the theory of Abelian functions there is an integer p associated with the number of "double points" - a double point may be represented on a graph as where a curve intersects itself. Riemann formed, by extension, a multiconnected many-sheeted surface that could be dissected by crosscuts into a singly connected surface. By means of these surfaces he introduced topological considerations into the theory of functions of a complex variable, and into general analysis. He showed, for example, that all curves of the same class have the same Riemann surface. Extensions of this work become highly abstract - the genus p was in fact discovered by Niels Abel in a purely algebraic context; it is not simply the number of double points. Not until much more work had followed, by Henri Poincaré (1854-1912) in particular, did Riemann's ideas in this field reach general understanding. However, his work considerably advanced the whole field of algebraic geometry.

Often his lectures and papers were highly philosophical, containing few formulas, but dealing in concepts. He took into account the possible interaction between space and the bodies placed in it; hitherto space had been treated as an entity in itself, and this new point of view - seized on by the theoretical physicist Hermann von Helmholtz (1821-1894) among others - was to become a central concept of twentieth-century physics.

Riemann's most profound paper on the foundation of geometry (presented in 1854), also had consequences for physics, for in it he developed the mathematical tools that later enabled Albert Einstein to develop his theory of relativity. The three creators of "hyperbolic geometry" - Karl Gauss, Nikolai Lobachevsky and János Bolyai - all died in the 1850s with their work unacknowledged, and it was Riemann's paper that initiated the revolution in geometry. In 1799 Gauss had claimed to have devised a geometry based on the rejection of Euclid's fifth postulate, which states that parallel lines meet at infinity. Another way of expressing this is to consider a parallelogram in which two opposite corners are right-angled - but in which the other two angles are less than 90°; this is "hyperbolic" geometry.

One possible case for the two angles to be less than 90° would come about according to two-dimensional geometry on the surface of a sphere. Straight lines are in those circumstances sections of great circles, and a "rectangle" drawn on the surface of the sphere may have angles of less than 90°. In this way, Riemann invented "spherical" geometry, which had previously been overlooked (and which can be more disconcerting than hyperbolic geometry). In 1868 Eugenio Beltrami developed this, considering "pseudo-spheres" - surfaces of constant negative curvature which can realize the conditions for a non-Euclidean geometry on them.

Many other ideas were contained in Riemann's paper. He took up the discussion - and returned again to it later in life - of the properties of topological variabilities (manifolds) with an arbitrary number of (n) dimensions, and presented a formula for its metric, the means of measuring length within it. He took an element of length ds along a curve, and defined it as

$$\mathrm{d}s^2 = \Sigma g_{ij}\mathrm{d}x^i\mathrm{d}x^j \ (i, j = 1, 2, \dots n).$$

The structure obtained by this rule is called a Riemann space. It is in fact exactly this sort of concept that Einstein used to deal with time as a "fourth dimension", and to talk about the "curvature of space". Euclidean geometry requires the "curvature" to be zero. The definition of the curvature of a directed space curve at a point was introduced in this same paper, and implicitly introduces the concept of a tensor.

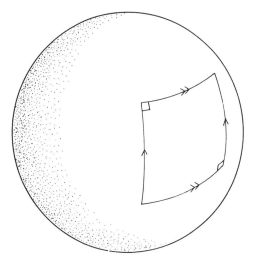

In spherical geometry, although a parallelogram may have two opposite angles at 90°, it does not necessarily follow that the other two angles are also 90°, as pointed out by Riemann.

From generalization of this work, and despite opposition at the time, *n*-dimensional geometries began to be used, especially to examine the properties of differential forms with more than three variables.

Riemann's career was short, and not prolific, but he had a profound and almost immediate effect on the development of mathematics. Everything he published was of the highest quality, and he made a breakthrough in conceptual understanding within several areas of mathematics: the theory of functions, vector analysis, projective and differential geometry, non-Euclidean geometry and topology. Twentieth-century mathematics bears witness to the extreme fruitfulness of Riemann's ideas.

Robinson, Abraham (1918-1974), was a German-born mathematician and educationist who travelled widely and lived in several countries. Most of his research was in the development of work first carried out by David Hilbert (1862-1943) in pure mathematics and in logic. He also wrote a number of popular modern textbooks.

Robinson was born in Waldenburg on 6 October 1918, of Jewish parents. Political pressures interrupted his academic studies, and he served with the Free French forces for the first part of World War II, and then became Assistant Scientific Officer at the Royal Aircraft Establishment at Farnborough, before he received his master's degree from the Hebrew University of Jerusalem in 1946. He then became a Senior Lecturer in Mathematics at Cranfield, where he was also elected to the Fluid Motion Committee of the National Aero-Research Council. In 1951 he went to Toronto, Canada, to become Associate Professor and then Professor of Applied Mathematics at the University there. Six years later he was appointed Professor of Mathematics at the Hebrew University of Jerusalem. He remained there until 1962, and then for five years he was Professor of Mathematics and Philosophy at the University of California at Los Angeles. As such he wrote most of his textbooks, although for much of his time he was actually in Europe as Visiting Professor at various universities. And from 1967 onwards he was Professor of Mathematics at the University of Yale. He died suddenly in April 1974.

Robinson had a very varied career, in a number of different countries. Although his early work was on aerodynamics and applied mathematics, in later years he was more interested in logic and philosophy. Most of his work, in both stages, was inspired by the work of the great mathematician David Hilbert. In pure mathematics Robinson studied – and attempted to extend – Hilbert's research into systems in which infinitesimals – numbers that are not zero but that are less than any finite number of magnitude – can occur. (Until the nineteenth century it was generally thought that infinitesimals were necessary to the development of differential and integral calculus, but once adequate definitions for irrational numbers were formulated and an arithmetical theory of limits had been worked out, it was possible to show that no real number is infinitesimal with respect to any other, and that calculus could be based on real numbers and the arithmetical theory of limits. It was the proof of the absence of infinitesimals from the system of real numbers that led Hilbert to look for systems in which infinitesimals could occur.) It was in fact on this same quest that Robinson was engaged at the time of his death: his contribution to a symposium on the subject was published posthumously.

Robinson was also concerned with the construction of mathematical and logical models. The theory of models involves the relationships between systems of sentences – frequently the "lower predicate calculus" (a term used in logic) – and systems of mathematical structures that satisfy such sentences. According to the theory, the problem is to determine a structure M which satisfies a given finite or infinite set of sentences. In his published study on the subject, Robinson used Hilbert's term "metamathematics" to describe the intuitive part of the rigorous logical process. But although he gained some renown for his work, he did not actually extend Hilbert's results.

Roth, Klaus Friedrich (1925-   ), is a British pure mathematician whose main field of study has been in the development and extension of the ideas of Ivan Vinogradov (1891-   ) concerning number theory. Always interested particularly in prime numbers, Roth's most significant published work - apart from translations of Vinogradov's research - has been his book, *Sequences* (1966).

Roth was born on 29 October 1925. Completing his education in London, he then attended Peterhouse College, Cambridge, where he received his BA in 1945. After a year as an assistant teacher at Gordonstoun, Australia, Roth joined the staff at University College, London, on receipt of his master's degree there in 1948. He remained at University College until 1966, by which time he had already been elected a Fellow of the Royal Society (in 1960) and been appointed a professor (in 1961). He then became Professor of Pure Mathematics at the Imperial College, London, a post he still holds.

The theory of numbers has always fascinated Roth, and he has achieved some renown in trying to widen the scope of the field. In fact *Sequences* was acclaimed on publication for its development of the subject. The book represents a study of various specific integer sequences, such as sequences of prime numbers and sequences of squares. The aim is to determine the distribution of elements of some important sequence, as in the case of prime number theory; to investigate the representation of integers as sums of elements of given sequences or to look at other arithmetical properties. Sometimes the results of one special sequence can hold for a wide class of sequences, or even for all integer sequences. Roth has studied integer sequences with a view to finding properties common - or laws related - to extensive classes of such sequences. Using a mathematical device called the Selburg sieve in connection with certain special sequences, he has made interesting studies which hinge on the multiplicative structure of integers. He has worked on arithmetical progressions and used van der Waerden's theorem, which states: that if the natural numbers are subdivided into a finite number of classes by any means whatever, at least one of these classes contains arbitrarily long arithmetical progressions. (This raises many questions that remain largely unanswered.)

Since 1934, analytic number theory has been virtually transformed by the work of Ivan Vinogradov, through his use of trigonometrical sums. Roth, too, has been influential in this area, not only through his translations and interpretations of Vinogradov's research, but also by means of his own investigations. He has been particularly intrigued in his work involving trigonometrical sums by the problem of considering points whose co-ordinates satisfy certain inequalities, or whose co-ordinates are themselves prime numbers.

Ruffini, Paolo (1765-1822), was an Italian mathematician, philosopher and doctor who made valuable contributions in all three disciplines. In his mathematical work he is remembered chiefly for what is now known as the Abel-Ruffini theorem.

Ruffini was born on 22 September 1765 at Valentano, Viterbo. While he was very young his family moved to Modena, and it was there that he grew up and remained for the rest of his life. Studying medicine, philosophy, mathematics and literature at the University, Ruffini was an exceptional student. During his own final year of instruction, he also taught one of the courses in mathematics. In 1788 he obtained degrees in philosophy, medicine and mathematics, and was appointed Professor of the Foundations of Analysis. Three years later he became Professor of the Elements of Mathematics.

Napoleon entered Modena in 1796, and Ruffini found himself obliged to take up an appointment as an official of the Republic, until permitted to return to his teaching two years later. Then, however, he refused to swear the oath of allegiance to the Republic and was immediately barred from teaching or holding any public office. He busied himself with his medical work and other research, and was soon recalled to the University. After the fall of Napoleon, Ruffini held the Chair of Applied Mathematics as well as the Chair of Clinical Medicine, and in 1814 he was also appointed Rector. Three years later he contracted typhus during an epidemic in the city, but with true scientific detachment he observed the progress of the disease and afterwards wrote a paper on the symptoms and treatment of typhus. He died, in Modena, on 9 May 1822.

In the year of his return to the University from being barred, Ruffini published a theorem - later to become known as the Abel-Ruffini theorem - which stated that it was impossible to give a general solution to equations of greater than the fourth degree using only radicals (such as square roots, cube roots, and so on). To try to clarify this, he published a demonstration of the theorem in a paper entitled *The General Theory of Equations;* it was not well received. In 1813 he published it in revised form, again to little avail. His methods of proof were regarded as lacking in scientific rigour. In 1824 the Norwegian mathematician Niels Abel (1802-1829) demonstrated more convincingly the same theorem, having come independently to the identical conclusion.

Ruffini also made a substantial contribution to the theory of equations, developing the so-called theory of substitutions which was the forerunner of modern group theory. His work became incorporated into the general theory of the solubility of algebraic equations developed by the ill-starred Evariste Galois (1811-1832).

In addition, Ruffini brought his mathematical insight to bear on philosophical and biological matters, publishing a number of papers between 1806 and 1821. He considered the possibility that living organisms had come into existence as the result of chance, thus anticipating more modern work on probability.

Russell, Bertrand Arthur William (1872-1970), was a British philosopher and mathematician who, during a long and active life, made many contributions to mathematics and wrote about morals and politics, but is best remembered as one of the founders of modern logic. He was a prolific writer and was awarded the 1950 Nobel Prize in Literature.

Russell was born in Trelleck, Monmouthshire, on 18 May 1872 into a family that had long been prominent in British social and political life. His grandfather was Lord John Russell, who introduced the 1832 Reform Bill in Parliament and went on to serve twice as Prime Minister. Russell's parents died when he was still a child and it was his grandfather who, disapproving of arrangements made by his parents, undertook to bring up Russell and his brother Frank. Instead of being educated by the Nonconformist thinkers his parents had nominated, he was educated at home until he was 18 by governesses and tutors.

In 1890 Russell entered Trinity College, Cambridge, to study mathematics and philosophy. Two years later he was elected to the Apostles – a small informal group that regarded itself as being made up of the best minds in the university. Another member, Alfred North Whitehead (1861-1947), was then a Lecturer in Mathematics. Russell was elected to a Prize Fellowship at Trinity in 1895 and in 1910 to a Lectureship in Logic and the Philosophy of Mathematics.

Russell was a pacifist at the outbreak of World War I in 1914, a stand that was bitterly resented by many people of his class. A leaflet published in 1916, in which he protested at the harsh treatment of a conscientious objector, led to his prosecution and dismissal from the Trinity lectureship. Two years later Russell was imprisoned for six months when his article in *The Tribunal*, a pacifist weekly, was judged to be seditious. While serving the sentence in Brixton Prison, he wrote *Introduction to the Philosophy of Mathematics.*

In 1922, after World War I, Russell stood as a Labour Party candidate in the General Election, but was defeated (two other attempts at entering Parliament were also unsuccessful). Soon afterwards he wrote two books that reflected contemporary developments in science: *The ABC of Atoms* (1923) and *The ABC of Relativity* (1925). In 1931 he succeeded his brother and became the 3rd Earl Russell. He was appointed to the staff of City College, New York in 1940, but was dismissed by a State Supreme Court Order following a wave of protest against the liberal views on sex expressed in his book *Marriage and Morals*. He did, however, lecture in philosophy at other American universities in Chicago and Philadelphia.

During the Cold War that followed World War II Russell even more vehemently expressed his views on pacifism, and in 1958 he was the president of the Campaign for Nuclear Disarmament. He was briefly imprisoned once more in 1961, when he was aged 89.

Russell received many honorary degrees, was elected a Fellow of the Royal Society in 1908 and made a member of the Order of Merit in 1949. He married four times, three of his marriages ending in divorce. He died in Plas Penrhyn, Merionethshire, on 2 February 1970.

Russell published the first volume of *Principles of Mathematics* in 1903, expounding his belief that the basic principles of mathematics can be founded on fundamental logical concepts so that all the propositions of pure mathematics can be deduced from this basis using only a few of the most important logical principles. This work was indebted to a symbolic calculus developed by George Boole (1815-1864).

But Russell's most significant publication concerning mathematical logic, derived from his collaboration with Whitehead, was the three-volume *Principia Mathematica* (1910, 1912, 1913), whose title reflected that of Isaac Newton's fundamental work. The arguments proposed in the *Principia* were explained, without the use of technical logical symbolism, in *Introduction to the Philosophy of Mathematics.* The book is a model of clarity and of the lucid expression of complex and abstract ideas. It was followed by a second edition of the *Principia* which incorporated an introduction that set out how the system must be modified as a result of the work of other mathematicians such as Leon Chwistek (1884-1944) and Ludwig Wittgenstein (1889-1951).

S

Seki Kowa (*c*.1642-1708) was a Japanese mathematician who did much to change the role of mathematics in his society; from being an art form indulged in by intellectuals at leisure, he made it a science. To do this he not only created a basic social paradigm embodying scientific curiosity, he even found himself obliged to create a new mathematical notation system. Using his new techniques, Seki discovered many of the theorems and theories that were being – or were shortly to be – discovered in the West. It is likely, for example, that he derived the determinant (part of a method to solve linear equations) before Gottfried Leibniz (1646-1716) did in 1693. In his own country Seki is sometimes referred to as "the sacred mathematician".

Seki was born probably in Huzioka in about the year 1642 – the exact date is unknown, and even his birthplace is the subject of some doubt. His father's name was Nagaakira Utiyama, but he was adopted by the Seki family and was known either as Seki Kowa or Seki Takakazu. Nothing is known about his life, other than his efforts to popularize mathematics, except that the date of his death has been definitely established as 24 October 1708; he died in what is now called Tokyo.

Much of Seki's reputation stems from the social reform he introduced in order to develop the study of mathematics in Japan. By the time of his death, anyone could take an interest in the subject, and could teach others – although the books available for instruction were still couched in the formal (and possibly condescending) terms of the *literati* of society. Seki himself was much influenced by the book of Chu Shih-Chieh, which dealt with the solution of problems by transforming them into a one-variable algebraic equation. The challenge of the book was that it contained problems which the author declared to be unsolvable; Seki solved many of these using methods of his own devising. He introduced Chinese ideograms to represent un-

knowns and variables in equations, and although he was obliged to confine his work to equations up to the fifth degree – his Tenzen Zyutu algebraic alphabet was not suitable for general equations of the nth degree – he was able to create equations with literal coefficients of any degree and with several variables, and to solve simultaneous equations.

In this way he was able to derive the equivalent of $f(x)$, and thereby to arrive at the notion of a discriminant – a special function of the root of an equation expressible in terms of the coefficients.

Another of Seki's important contributions was the mathematically rigorous definition (rectification) of the circumference of a circle; he obtained a value for π that was correct to the eighteenth decimal place. Further work included the rectification of a circular arc and the cubature of a sphere. He established a theorem relating to the solid resulting from the revolving of a segment of a circle about a straight line that is in the same plane as the segment. (This theorem was substantially the same as the well known theorem of Pappus.)

Seki is also credited with major discoveries in calculus. He developed a method of finding the approximate value of the root of a numerical equation and also evolved a method of determining the coefficients of an expression in the form

$$y = a_1 x + a_2 x^2 \ldots \ldots a_n x^n$$

which was similar to the method of finite difference.

Shannon, Claude Elwood (1916-   ), is an American mathematical engineer, whose work on technical and engineering problems within the communications industry led him to fundamental considerations on the nature of information and its meaningful transmission. His mathematical theory to describe this process was sufficiently general for its applications to other areas of communication to be immediately appreciated. He is therefore regarded as one of the founders of information theory.

Shannon was born in Gaylord, Michigan, on 30 April 1916. He earned his bachelor's degree at the University of Michigan in 1936, and then continued his studies at the Massachusetts Institute of Technology (MIT). There he became a Bowles Fellow in 1939, and a year later was awarded both his master's degree and his doctorate in mathematics. Shannon then worked for a year as a National Research Fellow at Princeton University before becoming in 1941 a staff member at the Bell Telephone Laboratories. The

117

work that he carried out during the 1940s led him to postulate a theory for communication, which he published in book form in 1949 (*The Mathematical Theory of Communication*). This theory brought him considerable acclaim, and he was presented with several notable awards and honours. In 1956 Shannon - still technically working for Bell Telephone - became Visiting Professor of Electronic Communications at the Massachusetts Institute of Technology; a year later he became Professor of Communications Science and Mathematics there; and in 1958 he finally and officially left Bell Telephone to become Donner Professor of Science. A member of a number of prestigious scientific associations, Shannon now lives in Winchester, Massachusetts.

As early as in 1938 Shannon was examining the question of a mathematical approach to language. At the laboratories of Bell Telephone he was given the task of determining which of the many methods of transmitting information was the most efficient, in order to enable the development of still more efficient methods. For this Shannon produced a model in which he reduced a communications system to its most simple form, so that it included only the most essential components. He also reduced the notion of information to a binary system of a series of Yes/No choices, which could be presented by a 1/0 binary code. Each 1/0 choice, or piece of information, he called a "bit" (now a technical term in talking of computers). In this way complex information could be organized according to strict mathematical principles.

An important feature of Shannon's theory was the prominence given to the concept of entropy, which he demonstrated to be equivalent to a shortage in the information content (a degree of uncertainty) in a message. One consequence of this work was the demonstration of the redundancy in most messages constructed using ordinary language; it became evident that many sentences could be significantly shortened without losing their meaning.

His methods, although devised in the context of engineering and technology, were soon seen to have applications not only to computer design but to virtually every subject in which language was important, such as linguistics, psychology, cryptography and phonetics; further applications were possible in any area where the transmission of information in any form was important.

Simpson, Thomas (1710-1761), was a British mathematician and writer who, after a somewhat erratic start in life, contributed greatly to the development of mathematics in the eighteenth century. He is particularly remembered for Simpson's Rule, which simplifies the calculation of areas under graphic curves.

Born at Market Bosworth, Leicestershire, on 20 August 1710, Simpson was the son of a weaver. Uninterested in his studies, he left home and lodged at the house of a widow in Nuneaton, whom he married in 1730 (although she was twenty years older than he was). A few years later, following an eclipse of the Sun, Simpson became obsessed by astrology and gained a reputation in the locality for divination. But after he had apparently frightened a girl into having fits by "raising a devil" from her, he was obliged to flee with his wife to Derby. In 1735 or 1736 he moved to London and worked as a weaver at Spitalfields, teaching mathematics in his spare time. It was there that he published his first mathematical works, which created a better sort of reputation and even won some acclaim. Soon after 1740 he was elected to the Royal Academy of Stockholm. And in 1743 he was appointed Professor of Mathematics at the Royal Academy at Woolwich, largely through the interest of William Jones (1675-1749). Finally, on 5 December 1745 he was elected Fellow of the Royal Society. From then on he was a constant contributor to *The Ladies' Diary*, acting as its Editor from 1754 to 1760. He died in Market Bosworth on 14 May 1761, and was buried at Sutton Cheynell, Leicestershire. (Mrs Simpson survived him and received a pension from the Crown after her husband's death, until she herself died in 1782 - at the age of 102.)

Simpson's first mathematical work, in 1737, was to study Edmund Stone's translation of L'Hôpital's *Analyse des infiniements petits*, and from it to write a new treatise on "fluxions" (calculus). This was an important contribution to the subject - although it also showed up the defects in the mathematical training that Simpson had received. In 1740 he wrote *The Nature and Laws of Chance*, and some essays on several subjects in speculative and general mathematics providing a solution to Kepler's Problem. In 1742 *The Doctrine of Annuities and Reversions* appeared; in 1743, *Mathematical Dissertation on a Variety of Physical and Analytical Subjects. A Treatise of Algebra* followed in 1745, and in its appendix contained some extremely ingenious solutions to algebraic problems. Ingenuity also distinguished his *Elements of Geometry*, published in 1747. His next works were *Trigonometry, Plane and Spherical* (1748) and *Select Exercises in Mathematics* (1752). In a paper he produced in 1755, Simpson proved that the arithmetic mean of n repeated measurements (which was already in limited use) was preferable to a single measurement in a precisely specifiable case. His final major publication was *Miscellaneous Tracts on Some Curious Subjects in Mechanics, Physical Astronomy and Special Mathematics* (1757). He also contributed several papers to the *Transactions* of the Faraday Society, most of which have been republished.

Simpson is most famous for having devised a method for determining approximately the area under a curve, known as Simpson's Rule. The method is to join the extremities of the ordinates by parabolic segments. In a general parabola whose axis is parallel to the y-axis between two co-ordinates (for example) $x = -h$ and $x = h$ each side of zero, and whose equation is (for example) $y = ax^2 + bx + c$, Simpson found that the approximate area under the curve between those ordinates is

$$\int_{-h}^{h} (ax^2 + bx + c)dx = \left[\frac{ax^3}{3} + \frac{bx^2}{2} + cx \right]_{-h}^{h}$$

which he then reduced to $\frac{h}{3}[y_1 + y_3 + 4y_2]$. This result gives the area under a quadratic curve exactly, and gives an approximation to the area under a curve which is not parabolic. Greater accuracy can be obtained by dividing the range of integration into a larger number of intervals and successively applying the rule for three ordinates.

On another occasion, Simpson worked out a way to calculate the volume of a prismoid, a solid bounded by any number of planes, two of which are parallel and contain all the vertices. The two parallel faces are called the bases. He said that the volume $V = \frac{1}{6}h(B + B' + 4M)$, where M is a section made by a plane parallel to the bases B and B', and midway between them, and h is the distance between the bases. This formula can be used to find the volume of any solid bounded by a ruled surface and two parallel planes.

Skolem, Thoralf Albert (1887–1963), was a Norwegian mathematician who did important work on Diophantine equations and who helped to provide the axiomatic foundations for set theory in logic.

Skolem was born at Sandsvaer on 23 May 1887 and was educated at the University of Oslo, where he studied mathematics, physics and the life sciences. He graduated with the highest distinction in 1913, having written a dissertation on the algebra of logic. By that time he had for four years been working as an assistant to Otto Birkeland, with whom he published

his first papers, on the subject of the "northern lights". In 1918 he was made an Assistant Professor of Mathematics at Oslo, eight years before he finally submitted, in 1926, at the age of 40, a doctoral thesis. From 1930 to 1938 Skolem was able to conduct his research, without teaching duties, as a fellow of the Chr. Michaelsons Institute in Bergen. In 1938 he was appointed Professor of Mathematics at Oslo, where he lectured on algebra and number theory to the virtual exclusion of mathematical logic, his area of specialization. He retired in 1957, but continued to do research until his death at Oslo, just before a projected lecture tour of the United States, on 23 March 1963.

Skolem was a retiring man, devoted almost entirely to mathematical research. He wrote 182 scientific papers and, unusually for a mathematician, most of them were written after he had reached the age of 40. It was not, indeed, until he was 33 that he published his first papers in mathematical logic, but those papers of 1920 elevated him at once to a leading place in the field. To the chagrin of his foreign colleagues Skolem published chiefly in Norwegian journals (a number of which he edited) and so were inaccessible; lectures given on his frequent visits to the United States went some way to break down this barrier.

Skolem's early work was in the highly abstruse field of formal mathematical logic. From papers published in the 1920s emerged what is now known as the Löwenheim–Skolem theorem, one consequence of which is Skolem's paradox. It takes the following form. If an axiomatic system (such as Ernst Zermelo's axiomatic set theory, which intends to generate arithmetic, including the natural numbers, as part of set theory) is consistent (i.e. satisfiable), then it must be satisfiable within a countable domain; but Georg Cantor had shown the existence of a never-ending sequence of transfinite powers in mathematics (i.e. uncountability). How to resolve this paradox? Skolem's answer was that there *is* no complete axiomatization of mathematics. Certain concepts must be interpreted only relatively; they can have no "absolute" meaning.

In this work Skolem was ahead of his time, so much so that in the 1930s he had to take pains to summarize his work of a decade earlier in order to bring it to the attention of mathematicians. As his papers remained largely unread (admittedly partly because they were written in Norwegian), he became somewhat dispirited and turned away from mathematical logic to more conventional topics in algebra and number theory. In particular, he began to work on Diophantine equations, publishing what was for many years the definitive text on the subject.

Nevertheless, his main field remained the logical foundations of mathematics. Before such subjects as model theory, recursive function theory and axiomatic set theory had become separate branches of mathematics, he introduced a number of the fundamental notions which gave rise to them.

Sommerville, Duncan MacLaren Young (1879–1934), was one of the leading geometers of the early twentieth century who made significant contributions to the study of non-Euclidean geometry.

Sommerville was born on 24 November 1879 at Beawar, Rajasthan, India, the son of Scottish parents. He was educated in Scotland, first at Perth Academy and then at the University of St Andrews. From 1902 to 1904 he was a lecturer in the mathematics department there. In 1911 he became President of the Edinburgh Mathematical Society, which he had helped to found.

In 1915 Sommerville went to New Zealand as Professor of Pure and Applied Mathematics at Victoria University College, Wellington. He also became the first executive secretary of the Royal Astronomical Society of New Zealand, of which he was a founder-member. He presided over the mathematical section of the Australasia Association for the Advancement of Science in 1924 and four years later was awarded the Hector Medal of the Royal Society of New Zealand. He retained his post of Professor of Mathematics in Wellington until he died there on 31 January 1924.

Sommerville wrote numerous papers, nearly all of them on geometrical topics. The first appeared in 1905 under the title "Networks of the Plane in Absolute Geometry", which was followed by "Semi-regular Networks of the Plane in Absolute Geometry" (1906). He also wrote two other papers in that year which gave a pure mathematical treatment to the questions of a statistical nature that arose from the biometric researches of Karl Pearson (1857–1936).

Sommerville was an accomplished teacher and taught in both Scotland and New Zealand. His contribution to this area was enhanced by the publication of four textbooks on non-Euclidean geometry. Two of these indicated his major research specialties: *Elements of non-Euclidean Geometry* and *An Introduction to the Geometry of n Dimensions*, which included concepts that Sommerville himself had originated. He explained how non-Euclidean geometries arise from the use of alternatives to Euclid's postulate of parallels, and showed that both Euclidean and non-Euclidean geometries – such as hyperbolic and elliptic geometries – can be considered as sub-geometries of projective geometry. He stated that projective geometry is the invariant theory associated with the group of linear fractional transformations. He studied the tessellations of Euclidean and non-Euclidean space and showed that, although there are only three regular tessellations in the Euclidean plane, there are five congruent regular polygons of the same kind in the elliptical plane and an infinite number of such patterns in the hyperbolic plane. The variety is even greater if "semi-regular" networks of regular polygons of different kinds are allowed (because the regular patterns are topologically equivalent to the non-regular designs). In his later work on n-dimensional geometry, Sommerville generalized his earlier analysis to include "honeycombs" of polyhedra in three-dimensional spaces and of polytopes in spaces of 4, 5, ... n dimensions – including both Euclidean and non-Euclidean geometries.

Sommerville also studied astronomy, anatomy and chemistry. His interest in crystallography played a significant part in motivating him to investigate repetitive space-filling geometric patterns. He was also a skilful artist, as was exhibited in the models he constructed to illustrate his abstract conceptions.

Steiner, Jakob (1796–1863), was a Swiss mathematician, the pre-eminent geometer of the nineteenth century and the father of modern synthetic, or projective, geometry.

Steiner was born at Utzenstorf, near Bern, on 18 March 1796. Because he had to help out in the family business his early education was neglected and colleagues in later years were astonished to discover that he did not learn to read and write until the age of 14. When he was 18 he left home to enrol at the Pestalozzi school in Yverdon; it was run on the monitorial system and in a very short time Steiner was employed as an instructor in mathematics. For a while he maintained himself by teaching and in 1821 received a teacher's certificate in Berlin. He had also attended some mathematical lectures at Heidelberg and acquired sufficient skill and knowledge to be given a place as a student at the University of Berlin in 1822. By 1825 he was teaching at the university and in 1834 a Chair of Geometry was created for him; he held the Chair for the rest of his life. His health began to deteriorate in the 1850s and he died at Bern on 1 April 1863.

When Steiner began to publish his epoch-making geometrical discoveries in the 1820s, mathematics was in that exciting transitional stage which has produced the modern explosion in mathematics. Steiner played an important role in the transition. His first published paper, which appeared in *Crelle's Journal* in 1826, contained his discovery of the geometrical transformation known as inversion geometry. His most important work, the *Systematische Entwicklung der Abhängigkeit geometrischer Gestalten von Einander* appeared in 1832. The work was notable for its full discussion and examination of the principle of duality and for the wealth of fundamental concepts and results in projective geometry which it contained. In it are to be found the two discoveries to which he had lent his name, the Steiner surface (also called the Roman surface), which has a double infinity of conic sections on it, and the Steiner theorem. The theorem states that two pencils (collections of geometric objects) by which a conic is projected from two of its points are projectively related. The book also included a supplement listing problems to be solved, and it remained a rich quarry for geometers for the next 100 years.

Steiner's other principal result was the theorem now known as the Steiner-Poncelet theorem, an extension of work done by Jean Poncelet in 1822. Steiner proved that any Euclidean figure could be generated using only a straight rule if the plane of construction had drawn on it already a circle with its centre marked. (In 1904 it was shown by Francesco Severi (1879–1961) that only the centre of the circle and a small arc of its circumference were necessary.)

Steiner's consistent aim was to discover fundamental principles from which the rest of geometry could be derived in an orderly and coherent manner. His work, in general, was marked by his disdain of using analysis and algebra; he preferred to rely on entirely synthetic methods. It is for that reason that whether he was, as some believe, the finest geometer since Apollonius of Perga, he is universally recognized as the great progenitor of projective geometry.

Stieltjes, Thomas Jan (1856–1894), was a Dutch mathematician who contributed greatly to the theory of series and is often called the father of analytical theory.

Stieltjes was born at Zwolle on 29 December 1856, the son of a distinguished civil engineer. Almost all his scientific and mathematical training was received at the École Polytechnique in Delft. He graduated the school in 1877 and was appointed to a post at the Leiden Observatory. He remained there until 1883, and though little is known of his mathematical doings in those years, it seems probable that he continued to do research, since in 1884 he was

appointed to the Chair of Mathematics at the University of Groningen. In that year also he was awarded an honorary doctorate by the University of Leiden. Two years later he was elected to the Dutch Academy of Science. In 1886 he went to France, became a naturalized French citizen, and for the rest of his short life taught mathematics at the University of Toulouse. Although he was never elected to the French Academy (despite being nominated in 1892), he won the Academy's Ormoy prize in 1893 for his work on continued fractions. He died in Toulouse on 31 December 1894.

In a short working life Stieltjes studied almost all the problems in analysis then known – the theory of ordinary and partial differential equations, Euler's gamma functions, elliptic functions, interpolation theory and asymptotic series. But his lasting reputation rests on his investigations into continued fractions. The fruit of those researches is contained in his last memoir, *Recherches sur les fractions continues*, completed just before he died. The memoir was a milestone in mathematical history. Before its appearance only special cases of continued fractions had been considered. Stieltjes was the first mathematician to give a general treatment of continued fractions as part of complex analytical function theory. He did so, moreover, in a book of exemplary clarity and beauty.

A continued fraction is derived from a sequence of ordinary fractions, a_1/b_1, a_2/b_2, a_3/b_3, which are called partial quotients, by adding each fraction to the denominator of the preceding fraction. In such series, a_1, a_2, a_3 etc. are called partial numerators; b_1, b_2, b_3 etc. are called partial denominators. They may be real or complex numbers. To this day one of the most important continued fractions in analytic theory remains the Stieltjes-fraction, or S-fraction.

In this fraction the values of k are constants other than zero and z is a complex variable. Taking the values of k as real and positive, Stieltjes was able to solve what is known as the Stieltjes moment problem – that is, the problem of determining a distribution of mass which has pre-assigned moments. His solution has been very fruitful, as has the very problem itself, extended as it has been into many fields.

Stieltjes' researches also raised the mathematical status of discontinuous functions and divergent series. He advanced the theory of Riemann's function, especially by the appearance, in his last great paper, of the integral

$$_a\int^b f(u)\delta g(u)$$

which is a generalized form of the Riemann integral and is now known as the Stieltjes integral. Stieltjes came upon it in his search for a way to express the limit of a certain sequence of analytic functions. What he did was to replace lengths of intervals (in the approximating sums for Riemann integration) by masses spread on them. He introduced this distribution of masses by means of a non-decreasing function, g, which gives the increment $g(b) - g(a)$ of the function g to every interval $[a,b]$. From this he was able to obtain his integral.

Stieltjes' analysis of continued fractions has had immense influence in the development of mathematics. His ideas greatly helped David Hilbert in his working out of the theory of quadratic forms in infinitely numerous variables. They were also used by Felix Hausdorff in his work on divergent series. Indeed, so varied are the fields which have profited from Stieltjes' creative imagination – number theory, the theory of equations, the theory of integration, infinite matrices, the theory of functions and, in the physical sciences, dynamics and the construction of electrical networks – that he well deserves to be known as the chief progenitor of modern analysis.

Sylow, Ludwig Mejdell (1832–1918), was a Norwegian mathematician who is remembered for his fundamental theorem on groups and for the special type of sub-groups which are named after him.

Sylow was born at Christiania (now Oslo) on 12 May 1832 and attended the cathedral school there until 1850, when he entered the University of Christiania to study mathematics. After graduating, he trained to become a teacher and received his certificate in 1856. For the next 40 years he taught in a school at Halden, although he travelled around Europe on a scholarship in 1861 and lectured at the University of Christiania in 1862. From 1873 to 1877 he was given a leave of absence from his teaching duties to collaborate with Sophus Lie on producing an edition of the works of Niels Abel. A year earlier Sylow had published his theorem, the first major advance in group theory since Cauchy's work of the 1840s and still regarded as essential for work on finite groups. At the same time he introduced the concept of sub-groups, now known by his name. The edition of Abel's work prepared by Sylow and Lie was published in 1881; it was followed by Sylow's edition of Abel's letters in 1901. Through Lie's influence, Sylow was rewarded with a Chair of Mathematics at the University of Christiania in 1898, where he remained until his death on 7 September 1918.

Sylvester, James Joseph (1814–1897), was a British mathematician, one of the pre-eminent algebraists of the nineteenth century and the discoverer, with Arthur Cayley, of the theory of algebraic invariants.

Sylvester was born at London on 3 September 1814, the sixth of nine children in the family of Abraham Sylvester, a Jew from Liverpool. He was educated at a school for Jewish boys in north London and in 1828 entered the new University of London, founded especially for Dissenters who were still unable to take degrees at the ancient universities and dedicated to establishing the sciences on a finer basis in the university curriculum. After only five months there he was expelled for attempting to wound a fellow student with a table knife. In 1829 he enrolled at the Royal Institution school at Liverpool, where he won a prize of £250 for a paper on arrangements before running away to Dublin, apparently to escape from anti-Semitic persecution. He was sent back to England by a cousin of his mother and in 1831 entered St John's College, Cambridge. In the Tripos of 1837 he emerged as second Wrangler but, unable to subscribe to the Thirty-nine Articles of the Church of England, he was unable to compete for the Smith's Prize or to take his degree. He therefore went to Trinity College, Dublin, where he gained his BA in 1841.

In the meantime he had been appointed to the Chair of Natural Philosophy at University College, London, in 1837 and elected to the Royal Society in 1839. In 1841 he went to the United States to become Professor of Mathematics at the University of Virginia, but after some sort of personal squabble (the truth has never been established) resigned the Chair and returned to England in 1845. For the next ten years he abandoned academic life, although he took in private pupils, including Florence Nightingale. He worked for the Equity and Law Life Assurance Company from 1845 to 1855, entered the Inner Temple in 1846 and was called to the bar in 1850. At about this time he also founded the Law Reversionary Interest Society.

In 1855 he returned to academic life, becoming Professor of Mathematics at the Royal Military Academy at Woolwich and editor of the *Quarterly Journal of Pure and Applied Mathematics*, over which he presided from its first number in 1855 to 1877. He remained at Woolwich until 1877, when he again went to the United States to become Professor of Mathematics at the newly founded Johns Hopkins University at Baltimore. During his tenure there he founded, in 1883, the American *Journal of Mathematics*. In that year he took up his last academic post as Savilian Professor of Geometry at Oxford University, where he was elected a fellow of New College. He died at London, three years after his retirement, on 15 March 1897.

Sylvester was a prolific writer of mathematical papers, but he was unmethodical, and his brilliant inventiveness was somewhat dulled by his failure to provide rigorous proofs for the ideas which, born of his creative intuition, he was confident in asserting. He is remembered chiefly for his algebra, especially for laying the foundations with Arthur Cayley (with whom he did not collaborate) of modern invariant algebra. He also wrote two long memoirs (1853 and 1864) on the nature of roots in quintic equations and did brilliant work on the theory of numbers, especially in partitions and Diophantine analysis. He introduced the concept of a denumerant and he coined the term "matrix" (in 1850) to describe a rectangular array of numbers out of which determinants can be formed. His high achievements were acknowledged by the Royal Society, which awarded him the Royal Medal in 1861 and the Copley Medal in 1880.

T

Tartaglia (*c*.1499–1557) was a medieval Italian mathematician, mathematical physicist and writer who, despite an unpromising youth, worked hard eventually to find fame for his work in mathematics, topography and mechanical physics.

Tartaglia was born Niccolò Fontana in Brescia, Lombardy, in either 1499 or 1500. His father was a postman and his family was very poor. When he was 12, the French marched in and sacked Brescia, seriously injuring the boy in the process. Only the careful nursing by his mother of the savage sword-thrust wound in his mouth saved his life, but ever thereafter he was called Tartaglia – "stammerer" – because of the speech defects the wound caused. Virtually self-educated, Tartaglia developed a true scientific curiosity and absorbed knowledge from every source he could find, particularly in mathematics and physics. In 1516 he moved to Verona and became a teacher of the abacus. Later he took charge of a school there from 1529 to 1533. After that he went on to Venice, a city in which he was to remain for the rest of his life. Although he gained a position of Professor of Mathematics, and published many papers on his work during the later stages of his life, he never made much money from his skills and died

alone and poor in humble dwellings near the Rialto Bridge on 15 December 1557.

With the coming of the sixteenth century, a revival took place in most branches of science, and Tartaglia was perhaps one of the more important contributors to it. Mathematics, in particular, had made little progress since the Greek scholars set down the basic rules; succeeding generations had evidently been content with simple counting and the ability to undertake elementary explanations to problems. Capable of applying his mind to most things, Tartaglia read all he could and then chose – among other enquiries – to explore the complexities of third-degree equations, to investigate the cubic. (Solutions had by then already been found for the linear and quadratic equations.) He was only one among many concerned with the task, however, most of the others also being Italian. There was keen rivalry, and Tartaglia more than once entered into a public contest of skills with another mathematician. In one particular confrontation with a certain Antonio Fior, Tartaglia emerged the victor by applying his methods and solving all the problems set for him by Fior, whereas Fior could not solve those set by Tartaglia.

He next turned his attention to solving the problem of calculating the volume of a tetrahedron from the length of its sides. Successful in that endeavour, he attempted Malfatti's problem – to inscribe within a triangle three circles tangent to one another, and managed to do that too.

Although Tartaglia spent much of his time teaching mathematics, he was also responsible for translating Euclid's *Elements* into Italian (1543) – the first translation of Euclid into a contemporary European language.

His greatest love, however, appears to have been in using his mathematical (and other relevant) skills to solve military problems. He delighted in planning the disposition of artillery, surveying the topography in relation to the best means of defence, and in designing fortifications. He also attempted a study of the motion of projectiles, and formulated what is now generally known as Tartaglia's theorem: the trajectory of a projectile is a curved line everywhere, and the maximum range at any speed of its projection is obtained with a firing elevation of 45°.

A practical man and a colourful character, Tartaglia fired the imagination of many in an age when imagination and scientific curiosity were beginning once more to bloom.

Thales of Miletus (*fl.*585 BC), was a Greek mathematician and natural philosopher, the first known Greek scientist of note.

Little is known of Thales' life and what we do know (or think we know) of his work comes from the writing of later scholars, especially from Proclus' commentary on Euclid of the fifth century AD. He was born at Miletus, in Ionia (now part of Greece), into a distinguished family, some time between 640 BC and 620 BC and died some time between 550 BC and 540 BC. His *floruit* is traditionally given as 585 BC, for no better reason than that is the year in which he is supposed to have predicted an eclipse of the Sun, a prediction which in its turn is supposed to have been the foundation of his scientific reputation.

The degree of sophistication which Thales reached in his thought, as well as the authenticity of the specific beliefs and discoveries ascribed to him, is a matter of controversy. For instance, it has generally been thought that in order to make his prediction of the Sun's eclipse in May of 585 BC Thales used a "Babylonian saros", a cycle of 223 lunar months. Recently writers have argued that the saros was the invention of Edmund Halley, the seventeenth-century British astronomer and mathematician. Most of Thales' natural philosophy is contained in passages in Aristotle's *Metaphysics* and *De Caelo*. Aristotle says that Thales believed water to be the primary element out of which all matter was made; also that he believed the Earth to float upon water. On this premise he built an explanation of earthquakes. That his notion was false is evident. What matters, so long as it is Thales, not Aristotle, doing the thinking, is that the explanation is sought in natural causes, not divine activity. It is for that reason that Thales is looked upon as the precursor of the modern scientific attitude.

The same may be said of his practical engineering feats, again known to us only by not altogether reliable anecdotes. One of the most famous of these feats is recounted by Herodotus. Thales is said to have diverted the River Halys to enable Croesus' army to cross it, a manoeuvre which was possible only if the imagination had ceased to think of the movement of water as divinely ordained and controlled.

Thales' greatest achievement (again, be it remembered, a matter for doubt) was his geometry. If Proclus' account is right, Thales was an important innovator in geometry, particularly for introducing the notion of proof by the deductive method, whereas his Babylonian and Egyptian predecessors had not progressed beyond making generalizations from experience on a rough-and-ready inductive principle. In five fundamental propositions Thales laid down the foundations on which classical geometry was raised. (1) A circle is bisected by its diameter.

(2) In an isosceles triangle the two angles opposite the equal sides are themselves equal to each other. (3) When two straight lines intersect, four angles are produced, the opposite ones being equal. (4) The angle in a semi-circle is a right angle. (5) Two triangles are congruent if they have two angles and one side that are respectively equal to each other.

Thales' proofs were not always very rigorous. But they had the nub of logical unassailability in them. Consider the proof of the proposition that the angle in a semi-circle is a right angle.

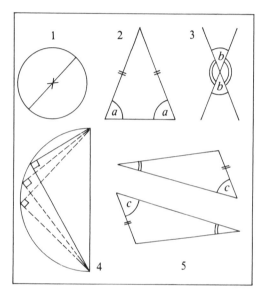

Some of the basic rules of geometry *were first laid down by Thales: (1) a circle is bisected by its diameter; (2) in an isosceles triangle, the two angles opposite the equal sides are themselves equal; (3) when straight lines cross, opposite angles are equal; (4) the angle in a semicircle is a right-angle; and (5) two triangles are congruent if they have two angles and one side identical.*

It is obvious that the diagonals of a rectangle are of equal length and that they bisect one another. It is obvious, also, that any quadrilateral possessing these properties is a rectangle. If we draw two diameters, AOC and BOD, of a circle with centre O, we therefore get a rectangle. Omit the dotted lines in the figure and we are left with the proposition that, if A is any point on the arc of a semi-circle with the diameter BD, then the angle BAD is necessarily a right angle. Without this method of reasoning – so like Euclid's – the original proposition would not appear obvious.

It is abstract reasoning of this kind that makes Thales such an important figure in the history of European thought. It is entirely in the proper spirit that Thales, on making his discovery of his fourth proposition, sacrificed a bull to the gods in thanks.

Thom, René (1923-   ), is a French mathematician who is a leading specialist in the fields of differentiable manifolds and topology and is famous for his model popularly known as "Catastrophe Theory".

Thom was born at Montbéliard on 2 September 1923. He studied in Paris at the École Normale Supérieure, where he received a degree in mathematical sciences, from 1943 to 1946 and then spent four years at the Centre National de la Recherche Scientifique. In 1951 he was awarded a doctorate by the University of Paris for his thesis on algebraic topology. From 1954 to 1963 he was a professor in the faculty of science at the University of Strasbourg and since 1963 he has been a professor at the Institute of Advanced Scientific Studies at Bures-sur-Yvette. He was awarded the Fields Medal at the Edinburgh Congress of 1958, the Brouwer Medal of the Academy of Sciences of the Netherlands in 1970, and the Grand Prix of Science by the city of Paris in 1974.

Since his student days Thom's major interest has been in problems of topology. Much of his early work was done just at the time that the operations of the American mathematician, Norman Steenrod, had been discovered. In his doctoral thesis he related Steenrod's definition of powers to the action of a cyclic group of permutations. From there he went on to write, with the help of H. Cartan, to formulate a precise series associated with "space spherical bundles" and to demonstrate that the fundamental class of open spherical bundles showed topological invariance and formed a differential geometry. This led him to his famous theorem, the Theorem of Signature, which states that in order that a directed form M^{4K} of dimension 4K may become cuspal, it is necessary that the quadratic curve defined by the cusp produced on H^{2K} (M^{4K}, Q) contain as many positive points as negative points (in order to be of zero index). In his work on the theory of forms Thom has shown that there are complete homological classes that cannot be the representation of any differential form. He was able to improve the understanding of this Steenrodian problem (although it is far from being completely understood) by formulating auxiliary spaces. These are now known as "Thom spaces".

In 1956 Thom developed the theory of transversality, and contributed to the examination of singularities of smooth maps. This work laid the ground for his later statement of the "catastrophe theory", which he first published in 1968. The theory is, in fact, a model (not yet an explanation) for the description of processes which proceed by sudden changes, so that their action is not continuous, but discontinuous. They are thus not able to be described by means of mathematical tools derived from calculus. Catastrophe theory seeks to describe sudden changes from one equilibrium state to another and to do so Thom proposed seven "elementary catastrophes" which he hoped would be sufficient to describe processes within man's own experience of space-time dimensions. The seven elementary catastrophes are the fold, cusp, swallow-tail, butterfly, hyperbolic, elliptic and parabolic. Of these the cusp is both the simplest and the most likely to provide immediate applied use.

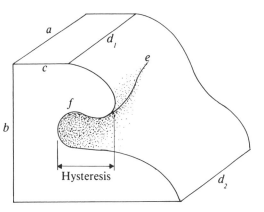

The cusp is one of seven elementary catastrophes in catastrophe theory: a, b and c are axes describing interacting factors in a process; d is a folded sheet with an upper zone (d_1) and a lower zone (d_2) describing the behaviour under investigation. At e there is a bifurcation, beyond which d_1 and d_2 are separate; f is the intermediate zone. The region of overlap is called hysteresis.

The important features of the cusp are the following:

a, *b* and *c*: axes which describe interacting factors in a process
d: a folded sheet, divided into an upper zone, d_1, and a lower zone, d_2, which describes the behaviour of a substance, person or group under investigation

e: the bifurcation point, a singularity, beyond which d_1 and d_2 separate

f: the intermediate zone between d_1 and d_2

The region of overlap between d_1 and d_2 is called the hysteresis. It is the existence of this overlap which makes possible sudden and dramatic changes from the equilibrium state d_1 and the equilibrium state d_2.

Thom is perhaps best known for his book published in 1972, *Structural Stability and Morphogenesis*. It is there that he introduced the notion of the "universal unfolding" of a singularity. The book itself is not so much a mathematical treatise as a discussion of how the concept of structural stability may be applied to the appearance and evolution of natural forms in physics and the life sciences. In particular, the book attempts to use the model of catastrophe theory to analyse embryogenesis. The model has been used also to study nerve transmission and the heart beat, to analyse change of phase in physics (for example, from liquid to gas), and, even, by sociologists, to study human events such as the outbreak of riot or war. Whether the catastrophe theory will ultimately prove of great moment in the history of mathematics (it is, after all, fundamentally simply an argument by analogy) may be doubtful, but Thom's work has been of central importance to research in topology since 1945.

Turing, Alan Mathison (1912–1954), was a British mathematician who worked in numerical analysis and played a major part in the early development of British computers.

Turing was born at London on 23 June 1912 into a family distinguished by its diplomats and engineers, three of whom had been elected to the Royal Society. He was educated at Sherborne School from 1926 to 1931, when he went to King's College, Cambridge, to study mathematics. After receiving his BA in 1935, he was elected a Fellow of the college on the strength of his paper "On the Gaussian Error Function", which won a Smith's Prize in mathematics in 1936. The paper was a characteristic example of the headstrong, but brilliant, nature of Turing's mathematical method throughout his life. He "discovered" the central limit theorem in utter ignorance of the fact that it had already been discovered and proved.

In 1936 Turing went to the United States for two years to work at Princeton University with the mathematical logician, Alonso Church. There he worked on the theory of computation and in 1937 he presented to the London Mathematical Society the paper, "On Computable Numbers", which was his most famous contribution to mathematics. It constituted a proof that there exist classes of mathematical problems which are not susceptible of solution by fixed and definite processes, that is to say, by automatic machines. He returned to King's in 1938 and after the outbreak of World War II in 1939 was employed by the government Code and Cipher School at Bletchley Park. For his work in designing machines to break the German Enigma Codes he was awarded an OBE in 1946.

After the war Turing joined the mathematics division of the National Physical Laboratory at Teddington, where he began immediately to work on the project to design the general computer known as the Automatic Computing Engine, or ACE. Although he left the project in 1947 to return to Cambridge, Turing played an important part in the theoretical work for the production of the ACE; a pilot version of the machine was in operation by 1950 and the mature version (like most computers of the time quickly rendered obsolete by newer machines) by 1957.

In 1948 Turing was appointed reader in the theory of computation at the University of Manchester and was made assistant director of the Manchester Automatic Digital Machine (MADAM). Two years later he published in *Mind* his trenchant discussion of the arguments against the notion that machines were able to think, "Computing Machinery and Intelligence". His conclusion was that, by his definition of "thinking", it was possible to make intelligent machines.

In his last years at Manchester much of his work was done at home. All his life he had been concerned with mechanistic interpretations of the natural world and he now devoted himself to attempting to erect a mathematical theory of the chemical basis of organic growth. In this he was partly successful, since he was able to formulate and solve complicated differential equations to express certain examples of symmetry in biology and also certain phenomena such as the shapes of brown and black patches on cows. He died from taking poison at his home on 7 June 1954, either deliberately, which was the coroner's verdict, or by accident, as his mother (knowing that he kept poisons in unmarked containers such as tea-cups and sugar bowls) believed.

Turing's place in the history of mathematics rests on the theory of computation which he worked out in 1936 and 1937. He suggested a basic machine which was not a mechanical device, but an abstract concept representing the operation of a computer. Quite simply, it was a paper tape, divided into squares, with a head for erasing, reading or writing on each square and a mechanism for moving the tape to either the left or the right. The tape could have instructions already written on it and it was of either limited or unlimited length. So Turing's concept contained, in embryonic form, the now familiar notions of program, input, output and, by implication, the processing of information. Turing machines were therefore of two types: machines designed to carry out a specific function and process information in a specified way and machines of a universal function capable of carrying out any procedure.

V

Vandermonde, Alexandre-Théophile (1735–1796), was a French musician and musical theorist who wrote original and influential papers on algebraic equations and determinants.

Vandermonde was born in Paris on 28 February 1735. Being a somewhat sickly child he was educated privately – at first chiefly in music, the sphere in which he was expected to make his career. But the tuition of the famous French geometer, Alexis Fontaine des Bertins (1705–1771), awakened his mathematical interest, and although he later wrote some skilful papers on musical composition, the early years of his maturity were devoted to mathematics. Fontaine introduced him to leading members of the French Academy of Sciences and in 1771, before he had written a single scientific paper or made any very remarkable discovery, he was elected to the Academy. In the next two years he presented to the Academy the only four mathematical papers he ever wrote. He played a part in the founding of the Conservatoire des Arts et des Métiers and served as its Director after 1782. In the 1780s he also collaborated with his close friend Gaspard Monge (1746–1818), and with the chemist Claude Berthollet (1748–1822) in an analysis of the difference between pig iron and steel, published in 1786. He died in Paris on 1 January 1796.

Of Vandermonde's four mathematical papers, the most celebrated are the first and the fourth. The first, regarded by some mathematicians as his best, considered the solvability of algebraic equations. Vandermonde found formulae for solving general quadratic equations, cubic equations and quartic equations. Lagrange published similar results at about the same time, but Vandermonde's two methods of solution for solving lower order equations – called substitution and combination – were independently worked out by him. In addition he found the solution to the equation, $x^{11} - 1 = 0$, and stated, without giving a proof, that $x^n - 1 = 0$ must have a solution where n is a prime number.

The fourth paper occupies a controversial place in the history of mathematics. Some mathematicians regard it as a decisive moment in the establishment of the theory of determinants; others consider that, although it might be the first coherent statement of the theory, its content had mostly already been published in other forms. Whatever the truth of the matter, the paper did include the Vandermonde determinant, his best-known contribution to mathematics.

The second paper may have influenced Gauss in his work on electrical potentials; the third was a relatively unimportant work on factorials. It is really on the strength of two papers, written within a year of each other, that Vandermonde (who subsequently contributed nothing at all to mathematics) earned a permanent place in the subject's history.

Veblen, Oswald (1880–1960), was an American mathematician who made fertile contributions to *analysis situs*, or early topology, and to differential geometry.

Veblen was born at Decorah, in Iowa, on 24 June 1880, the son of a Professor of Physics and the nephew of the political economist, Thorsten Veblen. He gained his BA at the University of Iowa in 1898 and then, after working briefly as a technician in the physics laboratory there, a second BA from Harvard in 1900. He then went to the University of Chicago, where he first undertook serious research into the foundations of geometry and received his PhD for a thesis in that field in 1903. He taught mathematics at Chicago until 1905, when he was appointed Lecturer at Princeton University. He spent the rest of his academic career at Princeton, as Professor of Mathematics at the university until 1932, and thereafter as a professor at the Institute for Advanced Studies. During World War I he served as a captain, then as a major, in the Ordnance Department of the army, with special responsibility for conducting ballistic tests. During World War II he again took part in ballistics work and participated in the development of the ENIAC computer. He retired from the Princeton Institute as Professor Emeritus in 1950, the year in which he served as President of the International Congress of Mathematicians at Harvard. He died at Brooklin, Maine, on 10 August 1960.

Veblen's doctoral dissertation was an ambitious entry into the world of advanced mathematics, consisting of a new axiomatic presentation of Euclidean geometry put forward as an alternative to the system published by David Hilbert in 1899. The full development of this early work was published in his two-volume *Projective Geometry* (1910, 1918). Veblen next became interested in *analysis situs*, the branch of geometry initiated by Henri Poincaré (1854–1912). Veblen's treatise, called *Analysis Situs* (1922) was the first full book-length discussion of topology. It stimulated a burst of activity among American mathematicians and was thus of great significance in the early development of topology. Veblen's third major research interest, differential geometry, was inspired by the discovery of relativity. In *The Invariants of Quadratic Differential Forms* (1927) he provided a thorough examination of the central tenets of Riemannian geometry and in *Foundations of Differential Geometry* (1932), written with John Whitehead (1904–1960), he extended Tullio Levi-Civita's work on the parallel translation of vectors in curved space, thereby advancing work on the geometry of paths.

Veblen believed that geometry could be usefully studied only if it were regarded as a branch both of mathematics and of physics. It was therefore entirely natural that his mind should be drawn to problems in relativity theory and that he should seek to find for the theory a geometric structure which could form a field theory to unify gravitation and electromagnetism. In this regard his most valuable result, worked out in reference to the Kaluza-Klein field theory, was his physical interpretation (the first offered) of the 5th co-ordinate.

Venn, John (1834–1923), was a British logician whose diagram, known as the Venn diagram, is much used in the teaching of elementary mathematics.

Venn was born at Drypool, Hull, on 4 August 1834 into a prominent Anglican family. When he was a young boy his father moved to London to take up an appointment as honorary secretary to the Church Missionary Society and he was educated first at Sir Roger Cholmley's School (now Highgate School). In 1853 he matriculated at Gonville and Caius College, Cambridge. He was elected a mathematical scholar in 1854 and gained his BA in 1857. In the same year he was elected a Fellow of the College; he remained a Fellow all his life.

Given his family background it was no sur-

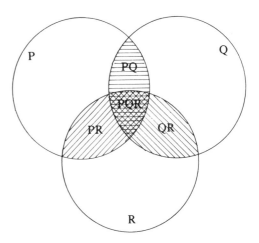

A Venn diagram shows a relationship between sets of which some members appear in more than one set. For example, if circle P represents all the students in one group, circle Q represents all those who are left-handed, and circle R those with brown hair, the central shaded region (PQR) represents all the left-handed students with brown hair.

prise that Venn was ordained as a deacon at Ely in 1858 and as a priest in 1859. He then held curacies at Cheshunt, Hertfordshire, and Mortlake, Surrey, before returning to Cambridge in 1862 as a college lecturer in moral sciences. For the next 30 years his chief interest was in logic, the subject to which he contributed a trilogy of standard texts: *The Logic of Chance* (1866), *Symbolic Logic* (1881) and *The Principles of Empirical Logic* (1889). While he was pursuing his logical research, Venn became infected by the crisis of belief prevalent in high Victorian, post-Darwinian England and, although he never lost his faith, he found himself unable any longer to subscribe to the Thirty-nine Articles of the Church of England and abjured his clerical orders in 1883. In the same year he was elected to the Royal Society and awarded a ScD by the University of Cambridge. After publishing his third volume of logic, he turned increasingly to the history of the university and the three-volume biographical history of Gonville and Caius (1897) was almost entirely his work. He died at Cambridge on 4 April 1923.

Venn is remembered chiefly for his logical diagrams. The use of geometrical representations to illustrate syllogistic logic was not new (they had been used consistently by Gottfried Leibniz), and Venn came to be highly critical of the various diagrammatic methods prevalent in the nineteenth century, in particular those of George Boole and Augustus de Morgan. Neither Boole's algebraic logic nor Morgan's formal logic satisfied him and it was largely in order to interpret and correct Boole's work that he wrote his *Symbolic Logic*. In it appeared the diagrams which have since become universally known as Venn's diagrams.

Before publishing the *Symbolic Logic*, Venn had adopted the method of illustrating propositions by means of exclusive and inclusive circles; in the new book he added the new device of shading the segments of the circles to represent the possibilities which were excluded by the propositions at issue. It was these diagrams, more than his attempt to clarify what he considered to be inconsistencies and ambiguities in Boole's logic, which constituted the real merit of the book. His diagrams were based on his belief that those which merely represented the relations between two classes or two propositions were not sufficiently general; later, he extended his method by proposing a series of circles dividing the plane into compartments, so that each successive circle should intersect all the compartments already existing. It was this idea, taken up and refined by Charles Dodgson (1832-1898), which led to the use of the closed compartment enclosing the whole diagram to define the universe of discourse – or, what is now known as the universal set.

Viète, François (1540-1603), was a French mathematician, the first extensively to use letters of the alphabet to represent numerical quantities and the foremost algebraist of the sixteenth century.

Viète was born at Fontenay-le-Comte, in the Poitou region, in 1540. He was educated locally until 1556, when he entered the University of Poitiers to study law. He graduated in 1560 and for the next four years or so practised law at Fontenay, studying cryptography and mathematics in his spare time. From *c.*1566 to 1570 he was tutor to Catherine of Oarthenay at La Rochelle. In 1570 he moved to Paris and entered the service of Charles IX. He remained in the royal employment until 1584, when persecution of the Huguenots forced him to flee to Beauvoir-sur-Mer. The years at Beauvoir provided him with the opportunity to devote himself to serious mathematical work and it was in these years that his most fruitful algebraic research was carried out. On the accession of Henry IV in 1589, Viète returned to the royal service, and in the succeeding years of the continued war against Spain he gave valuable service to the French crown by deciphering letters

of Phillip II of Spain. He was dismissed from the court in 1602 and died at Paris on 13 December 1603.

Although his stock of astronomical knowledge was slight, Viète's mathematical achievements were the result of his interest in cosmology. One of his first major results was a table giving the values of six trigonometrical lines based on a method originally used by Ptolemy. The table, which worked out the values of trigonometric lines from degree to degree and the length of the arc expressed in parts of the radius, appeared in his *Canon mathematicus seu ad triangula* (1579), almost certainly the first book to treat systematically of plane and spherical triangle solution methods by means of all six trigonometric functions. Viète was the first person to use the cosine law for plane triangles and he also published the law of tangents. He was, above all, eager to establish trigonometry as something more than a poor relation of astronomy and his work went a good way towards doing so.

Viète is most celebrated for introducing the first uniformly symbolic algebra. His *In artem analytica isogoge* (1591) used letters for both known and unknown quantities, an innovation which paved the way for the development of seventeenth-century algebra. More specifically, his use of vowels for unknown quantities and consonants for known ones was a pointer to the later development of the concepts of variables and parameters.

In 1593 Viète gave the first explicit explanation of the notion of "contact". He asserted that "the circle may be regarded as a plane figure with an infinite number of sides and angles, but a straight line touching a straight line, however short it may be, will coincide with that straight line and will not form an angle". His last important work, *De aequationum recognitione et emandatione*, appeared in 1615, more than a decade after his death. In it Viète gave solutions to the lower-order equations and established connections between the positive roots of an equation and the coefficients and the different powers of the unknown quantities. He is credited with introducing the term "coefficient" into algebra to denote either of the two rational factors of a monomial.

Mathematics to Viète was little more than a hobby, yet by providing the first systematic notation and, as a general tendency, substituting algebraic for geometric proofs in mathematics, he gave algebra a symbolic and analytical framework.

Volterra, Vito (1860-1940), was an Italian

mathematician whose chief work was in the fields of function theory and differential equations.

Volterra was born at Ancona on 3 May 1860, but after his father's death, when he was two, he lived at Florence with his mother and her brother. He attended the Scuola Tecnica Dante Alighieri and the Istituto Tecnico Galileo Galilei. As a young boy he gave signs of a distinct flair for mathematics and physics and by the time he had reached his early teens he had studied a number of sophisticated mathematical texts, including Legendre's Éléments de géométrie. Not only was he able to solve difficult problems, he set himself interesting new ones. So, at the age of 13, after reading Jules Verne's *From the Earth to the Moon* (published eight years before), he became interested in projectile problems and came up with a plausible determination for the trajectory of a spacecraft which had been fired from a gun. His solution was based on the device of breaking time down into small intervals during which it could be assumed that the force was constant. The trajectory could thus be viewed as a series of small parabolic arcs. This was the essence of the argument which he developed in detail 40 years later in a series of lectures at the Sorbonne.

When Volterra was still at school, his mother wished him to abandon his academic studies and become a bank clerk, in order to supplement the small family income. His teacher, Antonio Roiti, averted this by finding him a job as an assistant at the physics laboratory of the University of Florence. He was thus able to continue at the Istituto and in 1878 he entered the University of Florence to study natural sciences. Two years later he entered the Scuola Normale Superiore at Pisa, and there he began to work with Enrico Betti (1823–1892), who was to have a profound influence on his career. It was Betti who turned him in the direction, first of function theory (while still a student, Volterra published papers offering solutions to functions previously believed to be non-derivable), then on mechanics and mathematical physics.

In 1882 Volterra was awarded a doctorate and in the following year he was appointed Professor of Mechanics at the University of Pisa. He remained there until 1892, when he moved to the University of Turin. In 1900 he succeeded Eugenio Beltrami (1835–1899) in the Chair of Mathematical Physics at the University of Rome. During World War I he established the Italian Office of War Inventions, where he played an important part in designing armaments for airships. He also proposed that helium be used in place of hydrogen dirigible airships.

After the war he became increasingly involved in politics, speaking in the Senate and openly voicing his opposition to the Fascist regime. For his views he was eventually dismissed from his Chair at Rome in 1931 and banned from taking part in any Italian scientific meeting, although he was elected to the Pontifical Academy of Sciences in 1936 on the nomination of Pope Pius XI. From 1931 onwards, although deprived of an official post, he continued to write papers and to lecture abroad, principally at the Sorbonne. He died in Rome on 11 October 1940.

Volterra's achievements were numerous, but most of them involved function theory and differential equations. He contributed especially to the foundation of the theory of functionals, the solution of integral equations with variable limits, and the integration of hyperbolic partial differential equations. His chief method, hit upon as a young boy, was based on dividing a problem into a small interval of time and assuming one of the variables to be constant during each time-period. Thus his papers on partial differential equations of the early 1890s included the solution of equations for cylindrical waves:

$$\frac{d^2u}{dt^2} = \frac{d^2u}{dx^2} + \frac{d^2u}{dy^2}$$

He also brought his knowledge of mathematics to bear on biological matters. One example of this is his construction of a model for population change, in which the prey, x, and the predator, y, interact in a continuous manner expressed in these differential equations;

$$\frac{dx}{dt} = x(g - ky) \text{ and } \frac{dy}{dt} = y(-d + kx)$$

Volterra's mathematics was given its broadest statement in his two most important publications, *The Theory of Permutable Functions* (1915) and *The Theory of Functionals and of Integral and Integro-differential Equations* (1930).

Von Mises, Richard (1883–1953), was an Austrian mathematician and aerodynamicist, who made valuable contributions to statistics and the theory of probability.

Von Mises was born on 19 April 1883 at Lemberg (now Lvov, in the Soviet Union). He was educated at the University of Vienna, where he received his doctorate in 1907, and was Professor of Applied Mathematics at the University of Strassburg (now Strasbourg, in France) from 1909 to 1918. In 1920 he was appointed Professor of Applied Mathematics and Director of the Institute for Applied Mathematics at the University of Berlin. With the coming to power of

Adolf Hitler in 1933, he emigrated to Turkey and taught at the University of Istanbul until 1939. In that year he went to the United States to join the faculty of Harvard University. He was made Gordon McKay Professor of Aerodynamics and Applied Mathematics in 1944, the Chair which he held until his death, at Boston, on 14 July 1953.

Von Mises looked upon himself principally as an applied mathematician and was especially proud of having founded in 1921, and edited until 1933, the journal *Zeitschrift für angewandte Mathematik und Mechanik*. His first interest was fluid mechanics, especially in relation to the new and exciting field of aerodynamics and aeronautics. He learned to fly and in the summer of 1913 gave what is believed to be the first university course in the mechanics of powered flight. In the next year or so he made significant improvements in boundary-layer-flow theory and aerofoil design and, in 1915, built a 454-watt (600hp) aeroplane for the Austrian military. During World War I he served as a pilot in the air-arm of the army and in 1916 published a book on flight which formed the basis of his later book, *Theory of Flight*, published with scientists in England towards the end of World War II.

Von Mises' chief contribution to pure mathematics was in the field of probability theory and statistics. He was drawn into this subject by his association (from 1907 until the 1920s) with the Viennese school of logical positivism. The development of the frequency theory of probability had proceeded slowly, in opposition to the classical theory of Laplace, during the second half of the eighteenth century and the first half of the nineteenth century. It then took a leap forward with John Venn's imaginative stroke in equating probability with the relative frequency of the event "in the long run". Venn introduced the concept of a mathematical limit and the infinite set, but von Mises came to the conclusion that a probability cannot be simply the limiting value of a relative frequency. He added the proviso that any event should be irregularly or randomly distributed in the series of occasions in which its probability is measured. This emphasis on the idea of random distribution, in other words bringing the notion of the Venn limit and that of a random sequence of events together, was von Mises' outstanding contribution to the frequency theory of probability.

Von Mises' ideas were contained in two papers which he published in 1919. Little noticed at the time, they have come to influence all modern statisticians. The consistency of the mathematics of von Mises' theory has been called into ques-

tion by a number of mathematicians, but it seems doubtful that any of the proposed alternatives will prove to be more satisfactory. After 1919 von Mises achieved very little of a highly creative or original nature, but his *Probability, Statistics and Truth* (1928) is both historically sound and, for the lay reader, stimulating.

Von Neumann, Johann (John) (1903–1957), was a Hungarian-born American mathematician and physicist, famous for his pioneering work in computer theory and for his invention of the branch of mathematics known as "Games Theory".

Von Neumann was born in Budapest on 28 December 1903 and was given private tuition at home before 1914, when he entered the local secondary school. Because of the exceptional mathematical skill which he had already displayed, he continued to receive private teaching from university professors. He left Hungary in 1919 to study at the Universities of Berlin and Zurich, and received his BA in chemical engineering from the Zurich Institute in 1925 and his PhD in mathematics from the University of Budapest in 1926. Between 1927 and 1930 he taught mathematics at the Universities of Berlin and Hamburg.

In 1930 von Neumann emigrated to the United States. Until 1933 he was Professor of Mathematics at Princeton University; he was then invited to become the youngest member of the newly established Institute of Advanced Studies at Princeton. He remained there for the rest of his career. During World War II he worked on the government's atomic bomb project at Los Alamos, and he continued to be associated with the project until 1955, when he was appointed a member of the Atomic Energy Commission. He died at Washington on 8 February 1957.

Von Neumann was primarily interested in pure mathematics at the outset of his career and his early work was chiefly in the fields of mathematical logic, set theory and operator theory. His theory of the rings of operators is, in particular, highly regarded. But he gradually became increasingly drawn to applied mathematics and he is best known for his work in three fields: games theory, quantum mechanics and computing.

When von Neumann read a paper on games theory to a scientific meeting at Göttingen he was introducing an entirely new branch of mathematics. Games theory consists of constructing mathematical models for determining the best strategy to play a game, that is to achieve optimal results with minimal losses. The fullest statement of it was given in Neumann's *The Theory of Games and Economic Behaviour* (1944), but its applications stretch far beyond the world of business to warfare, the social sciences and the behavioural sciences. It was also used by the scientists working on the H-bomb project in the early 1950s.

In theoretical physics von Neumann's chief contribution was the axiomatization of quantum mechanics. He began to work on this subject in 1927 and in 1932 he published his results in his book *The Mathematical Foundations of Quantum Mechanics*. It was his knowledge of quantum theory, together with his powerful insight into the practical applications of nuclear energy, which allowed von Neumann to play a central role in the development of the atomic bomb.

After his attachment to the atomic research project in 1943, von Neumann did not absolutely abandon pure mathematics. In the late 1940s he did a considerable amount of work on non-commutative algebras. And his interest in computers, which chiefly occupied the last 12 years of his life, was rooted in his knowledge of mathematical logic and number theory. The chief impetus to his computer research, however, was new problems which came to light during the atomic research. The need to produce approximate models quickly for complex physical problems led von Neumann to seek ways of improving the existing computer machines. In 1945 he was appointed director of the Electronic Computer Project at Princeton, the project which developed a number of new computers, most notably MANIAC (mathematical analyser, numerical integrator and computer). Completed in 1952, it was the first computer able to use a flexible stored programme. He also drew analogies between computers and neurological networks and proposed one of the first theories of a self-producing machine.

As a pure mathematician von Neumann was neither as wide-ranging nor as creative as mathematicians of the stature of David Hilbert. His special talent was rather for organizing and axiomatizing complex subjects and for bridging gaps between pure and applied mathematics, and his achievements were lavishly recognized in the year before his death, when he was awarded the Medal of Freedom, the Albert Einstein Award and the Enrico Fermi Award.

W

Wallis, John (1616–1703), was an English mathematician who made important contributions to the development of algebra and analytical geometry and who was one of the founders of the Royal Society.

Wallis was born in Ashford, Kent, on 23 October 1616. He began his education at Ashford, but was sent to boarding school at Ley Green, near Tenterden, on the outbreak of plague at Ashford in 1625. In the years 1630 to 1631 he attended the Martin Holbeach School in Felsted, Essex. There he learned Greek, Latin and Hebrew and was introduced to the elements of his logic. It was his brother who, in the Christmas vacation of 1631, instructed him in the fundamentals of arithmetic. In 1632 he went to Emmanual College, Cambridge, to study physics, medicine and moral philosophy. He received his BA in 1637. In 1640 he was ordained in the Church of England and for the next four years earned his living as a private chaplain in Yorkshire and later in Essex. On his mother's death in 1643 he came into a large inheritance which left him financially independent.

In 1644 Wallis was elected a Fellow of Queen's College, Cambridge, but was compelled to relinquish the fellowship a year later when he married. He moved to London and assisted the parliamentary side by deciphering captured coded letters during the Civil War. In gratitude for that work Oliver Cromwell overlooked Wallis' signature on the 1648 remonstrance against the execution of Charles I and, in 1649, appointed him Savilian Professor of Geometry at Oxford University. It was then that Wallis began to study mathematics in earnest. In 1655 he published his most famous work, the *Arithmetica Infinitorum*, which immediately raised him to international scientific eminence. In 1658 he was appointed Keeper of the University Archives. In 1660 Charles II chose him as his royal chaplain. In the meantime Wallis had, ever since 1649, been meeting regularly with other lovers of science, notably Robert Boyle (1627–1691), at the discussions that led to the founding of the Royal Society in 1660.

In the second half of his life Wallis' chief publications were his *Mechanica* (1669–1671), which was the fullest treatment of the subject then existing, and his *Algebra* (1685). He also became involved in a long and acrimonious dispute with Thomas Hobbes over what he considered to be the anti-Christian tendencies of Hobbes' philosophy - a quarrel which lasted for 25 years and ended only with Hobbes' death in 1679. He also conducted experiments in speech and attempted to teach, with some success, deaf-mutes to speak. His method was described in his *Grammatica Linguae Anglicanae* (1652). After the revolution of 1688-1689 which drove James II from the throne, he was employed by William III as a decipherer. He held the Savilian Chair until his death, at Oxford, on 28 October 1703.

Wallis' two great works established him as one of the foremost mathematicians of the seventeenth century. The *Arithmetica* was the most substantial single work on mathematics yet to appear in England. In it he applied Cartesian analysis to Torricelli's method of indivisibles and (in an appendix) applied analysis for the first time to conic sections as curves of the second degree. The treatise also introduced the symbol ∞ to represent infinity, the germ of the differential calculus and, by an impressive use of interpolation (the word was Wallis' invention), the famous value for π and the celebrated formula.

$$\frac{4}{\pi} = \frac{3 \times 3 \times 5 \times 5 \times 7 \times 7}{2 \times 4 \times 4 \times 6 \times 6 \times 8} \ldots$$

The *Algebra* was the first treatise ever to attempt to combine a full exposition of the subject with its history and was important for introducing the principles of analogy and continuity into mathematics.

Weaver, Warren (1894-1978), was an American mathematical physicist who was Director of the Natural Science Division of the Rockefeller Foundation from 1932 to 1955.

Weaver was born at Reedsburg, in Wisconsin, on 17 July 1894. He was educated at the University of Wisconsin, where he received his BS in 1916. In the following year he gained another first degree in civil engineering. In 1917 and 1918 he served as a second lieutenant in the Army Air Service. On his discharge he was appointed Assistant Professor of Mathematics at the California Institute of Technology, and in 1920 he was appointed to the same rank in the mathematics department at Wisconsin. In 1921 he was awarded his PhD in mathematical physics and in 1925 he was made a full Professor of Mathematics.

Weaver gained a reputation as a brilliant mathematician in his early career, especially for his insight into the applications of mathematics to engineering, probability, diffusion and electromagnetics. In 1932, however, he left the academic world to become Director of the Natural Science Division of the Rockefeller Foundation.

He had published no outstanding mathematical results and for the rest of his career his energies were chiefly devoted to administration. In addition to his post at the Foundation, he was a member of a host of national advisory councils, including the National Science Board (1956-1960) and the National Advisory Cancer Council (1957-1960). He was also involved in the work of a number of government agencies during World War II and was credited with making fighter bombers more effective and with revolutionizing anti-aircraft fire control. For his work during the war he was awarded the Medal of Merit by the United States government and the King's Medal for Service in the Cause of Freedom by the British government.

After the war he played a part in the development of computers. In collaboration with Claude Shannon (1916-) he wrote several papers, including "The Mathematical Theory of Communication" (1949) which, in suggesting ways in which computers could be used beyond simple calculation, contributed to the birth of cybernetics. He also, in the latter part of his life, became increasingly eager to create a numerate, scientifically informed general public. One of his more popular publications was *Lady Luck - The Theory of Probability* (1963). For his work in bringing scientific issues to the people - especially his work as chairman of a committee to report on the biological effects of atomic radiation to the genetics panel of the National Academy of Sciences - he was awarded the Kalinga Prize by UNESCO in 1965.

Weaver's last contribution to the public administration of science in the United States was to serve as the Director (1963-1967) of a body which he was instrumental in founding, the Scientists' Institute for Public Information. He died on 28 November 1978.

Weber, Heinrich (1842-1913), was a German mathematician whose chief work was in the fields of algebra and number theory.

Weber was born in Heidelberg on 5 May 1842. He entered the university there to study mathematics and physics and, with a year's interval at the University of Leipzig, received his doctorate in 1863. He then went to Königsberg, where for three years he worked with Franz Neumann (1798-1895) and Friedrich Richelot (1808-1875). He began to teach at the University of Heidelberg in 1866 and was made an Extraordinary Professor in 1869. Thereafter he taught at a number of institutions - the Zurich Polytechnic, the University of Königsberg, the Technical High School at Charlottenburg and the universities of Marburg and Göttingen - before taking up his last post at Strasbourg in 1895. He died in Strasbourg on 17 May 1913.

The three years that Weber spent at Königsberg as a young man had a decisive influence on his mathematical career. The influence of Karl Jacobi (1804-1851) was then very powerful there and much of Weber's work shows his solid grounding in Jacobian methods. His early work was based on the theory of differential equations, and he was encouraged by Neumann to apply his knowledge to problems in physics. Yet it was not until late in his career that Weber's work in such subjects as heat, electricity and electrolytic dissociation was published. Most of it was contained in his *Die partiellen Differentialgleichungen der mathematischen Physik* (1900-1901), which was essentially a reworking of, and a commentary upon, a book of the same title, based on lectures given by Bernhard Riemann and written by Karl Hattendorff.

In the decades before that book appeared Weber produced most of his important work, especially his most outstanding contribution to mathematics, his demonstration of Abel's theorem in its most general form. Another brilliant result was his proof of Kronecker's theorem that the absolute Abelian fields are cyclotomic - that is, that they are derived from the rational numbers by the adjunction of roots of unity. This work on Abel's mathematics reflected the influence of Richelot, under whose guidance Weber became an expert in the manipulation of algebraic functions.

In the 1890s Weber produced several important results, chief among them his demonstration of the critical importance of linking analysis and number theory in investigating problems involving complex multiplication. In 1896 there appeared his culminating work in algebra, the two-volume *Lehrbuch der Algebra*, which for a generation was the standard algebra text. That book, as also his editorship of the three-volume *Enzylopädie Elementär-Mathematik* (1903-1907), commended Weber not just to higher mathematicians but also to the humbler host of teachers and students who came after him.

Wedderburn, Joseph Henry (1882-1948), was a British mathematician who opened new lines of thought in the subject of mathematical fields and who had a deep influence on the development of modern algebra.

Wedderburn was born at Forfar, Scotland, on 26 February 1882 and was educated at the University of Edinburgh, which he entered in 1898. He received a degree in mathematics in 1903 and in the following year was awarded a Carnegie fellowship to study at the University of Chicago.

In 1905 he returned to Scotland, where he was appointed a Lecturer in Mathematics at the University of Edinburgh and editor of the *Proceedings of the Edinburgh Mathematical Society*. In 1908 he was awarded a doctorate and in 1909 he went back to the United States to teach at Princeton University. During World War I he saw active duty in France as a soldier in the British army. He then returned to Princeton, where he remained until his retirement in 1945. For the last 20 years of his life he was in poor health and he stopped publishing in 1938. He died at Princeton on 9 October 1948.

The first paper that Wedderburn published, "Theorem on Finite Algebra" (1905), was a milestone in algebraic history. Before it appeared little was known about hyper-complex numbers and their roles in algebra. The classification of semi-simple algebras had been investigated only for fields composed of real or complex numbers. Wedderburn was able to show, by introducing new methods, that it was possible to arrive at a complete understanding of the structure of these algebras over any field.

From that foundation he went on to derive the two theorems to which his name has become attached. The first was contained in his paper, "On Hyper-Complex Numbers" (1907), in which he demonstrated that a simple algebra consists of matrices of a given degree with elements taken from a division of algebra. This paper marked the beginning of a new approach to this type of algebra. The first Wedderburn theorem states that "if the algebra is a finite division algebra (that is, that it has only a finite number of elements and always permits division by a non-zero element), then the multiplication law must be commutative, so that the algebra is actually a finite field".

Wedderburn's second theorem states that a central-simple algebra is isomorphic to the algebra of all $n \times n$ algebras. He arrived at it by an investigation of skew fields with a finite number of elements. When he started, all commutative fields with a given number of elements had been classified; but it was assumed that no non-commutative field existed, because none had ever been found. Wedderburn's discovery that every field with a finite number of elements is commutative under multiplication thus led to a complete classification of all semi-simple algebras with a finite number of elements.

The modern study of mathematical fields owes an enormous debt to Wedderburn, who may rightly be regarded as one of the creative geniuses of his age.

Weierstrass, Karl Theodor Wilhelm (1815-1897),

was a German mathematician who is remembered especially for deepening and broadening the understanding of functions.

Weierstrass was born at Ostenfelde, Westphalia, on 31 October 1815. Because of his family's frequent change of residence he attended many schools as a young boy and it was not until he entered the Roman Catholic School at Paderborn in 1829 that he began to reveal his mathematical ability. In deference to his father's wish that he should pursue a "respectable career", he entered the University of Bonn in 1834 to study law, administration and finance. By 1837 he was certain that mathematics alone interested him and in that year he left Bonn, without taking a degree, to enter the Theological and Philosophical Academy at Münster, with the dual intention of gaining a teacher's certificate and devoting himself to the study of advanced mathematics.

He received his teaching certificate in 1841. From 1842 to 1848 he taught at a secondary school in Deutsch-Krone, in west Prussia, then moved to Braunsberg, where he became a lecturer at the Roman Catholic School. In his spare time he did his mathematical research and in 1854 he published in *Crelle's Journal* a paper on Abelian integrals that established his reputation and earned him the award of an honorary doctorate from the University of Königsberg. The strain of combining his research with a heavy teaching load (physics, botany and history in addition to mathematics) told on his health. From 1850 he suffered from debilitating attacks of vertigo and for the rest of his life he was rarely in good health. He was therefore happy to be given a leave of absence in 1855 to complete his work on function theory, begun in the 1854 paper.

That paper marked a turning-point in his academic life. Down to the age of 40 Weierstrass had worked in isolation. Then, in 1856, he was appointed Professor of Mathematics at the Royal Polytechnic School in Berlin and, jointly with it, Associate Professor at the University of Berlin, although he did not begin actually to lecture at the university until 1864. In 1861 he suffered a complete physical breakdown, and although a year of convalescence brought an end to the attacks of vertigo, he thereafter suffered from bronchitis and phlebitis. By 1894 he was confined to a wheelchair; he died of pneumonia in Berlin on 19 February 1897.

Weierstrass' most important work was in function theory, the subject which he first treated seriously in the examination paper for his teacher's certificate in 1841. This was followed up by the 1854 paper, which solved the inversion of hyperelliptic integrals, and a second paper of 1856. His greatest achievement was the demonstration, published in 1871, that there exist continuous functions in an interval which have derivatives nowhere in the interval. In fact, he published very little. Much of his reputation rested on his lectures at Berlin, which ranged over the whole of mathematics and which became famous for their "Weierstrassian rigour". In particular, Weierstrass did much (again more in lectures than in publications) to clarify the meaning of basic concepts such as "function", "derivative" and "maximum". His development of the modern theory of functions was described in his *Abhandlungen aus der Funktionlehre* (1886), a text derived chiefly from his students' lecture notes. In the 1890s Weierstrass planned the publication of his life's work, again to be compiled from lecture notes. Two volumes were published before his death and five more appeared during the next three decades. Three volumes of the projected 10-volume set remain unpublished, but even the incomplete work remains a rich quarry for the present-day mathematician.

Weil, André (1906–   ), is a French mathematician whose main field of activity has been number theory, group theory and algebraic geometry.

Weil was born on 6 May 1906 in Paris, where he grew up, was educated, and attended the University, receiving his doctorate in 1928. In 1930 he went to India for two years as Professor of Mathematics at Aligarh Muslim University. Returning to France, he took up a similar post at Strasbourg University and remained there until 1940. Then, after a year's lecturing in the United States, he moved to Brazil where in 1945 he became Professor of Mathematics at the University of São Paolo. From 1947 to 1958 he was Professor of Mathematics at the University of Chicago, and then transferred to a similar post at the School of Mathematics at the Institute of Advanced Studies of the University of Princeton. Although now retired, he still maintains links with Princeton.

One of Weil's earliest contributions to number theory came in 1929, when he extended some earlier work by Henri Poincaré (1854–1912). This resulted in the postulation of what is now called the Mordell-Weil theorem, a theorem that is closely connected to the theory of Diophantine equations.

Weil worked on quadratic forms with algebraic coefficients and extended Émil Artin's work on the theory of quadratic number fields. He also contributed to the generalization of algebraic geometry.

In addition, he was a founder member of that secretive and esoteric club called the Bourbaki Group, which until recently was still very much in existence, and which has published brilliant and entertaining mathematical papers under the blanket pseudonym Nicolas Bourbaki. (Although there was no limit to the number of members in the Group, its membership was always changing because retirement was compulsory on reaching the age of 50.)

Weil's own major work, *Foundations of Algebraic Geometry*, was published in 1946.

Welchman, William Gordon (1906-   ), is a British mathematician who, with Philip Milner-Barry, worked as a cryptographer during World War II. The two men contributed greatly to the British war effort by deciphering German military codes.

Welchman was born in 1906 and educated at Marlborough College. He went to Trinity College, Cambridge, to study mathematics in 1925, in the same year as Milner-Barry (who was also born in 1906). He graduated in 1928 and, after a year as an Assistant Master at Cheltenham College (Milner-Barry's old school), he was elected a Research Fellow of Sidney Sussex College, Cambridge, in 1929. During the 1930s he was the Junior Dean and Mathematical Tutor there, and during World War II (1939-1945) he worked for the Foreign Office. In 1945 he took up the appointment as Director of Research and Planning with John Lewis & Company. Three years later he went to the United States in the employ of Ferranti of London and spent some time at the Massachusetts Institute of Technology. He moved to Washington in 1952 and returned to London two years later. In the 1970s, still with Ferranti, he was again in Massachusetts.

Philip Stuart Milner-Barry was born on 20 September 1906 and educated at Cheltenham College, before entering Trinity College, Cambridge, in 1925. (He was British Boy Chess Champion in 1923.) From 1929 to 1938 he worked for a firm of stockbrokers, and was Chess Correspondent of *The Times* from 1938 to 1945, while being temporarily employed by the Foreign Office (1940-1945) during World War II. After the war he worked for the Treasury, first as Principal and then from 1947 as Assistant Secretary until 1954, when he became Director of Organization and Methods. He held a similar position in the Ministry of Health from 1958 to 1960. He was Under-Secretary of the Treasury until 1966. Milner-Barry was a member of the British International Chess team between 1937 and 1961 and President of the British Chess Federation (1970-1973). He was knighted in 1975.

Welchman and Milner-Barry came together again at the beginning of World War II to help with decoding operations. In the autumn of 1938 Welchman had attended a brief cryptological course run by the Government Code and Cipher School at the London Headquarters of the British Secret Service. By 1939 it had moved to Bletchley, Buckinghamshire, and Welchman reported there on 3 September 1939, the day war was declared. Milner-Barry was recruited in 1940, together with Hugh O'Donel Alexander, another British chess champion, and the computer pioneer Alan Turing.

Together this team was set the task of cracking the codes used by the German *Enigma* enciphering machine. By January 1940 they had established the key for the *Enigma* settings of the previous October, and by the following April they were able to decipher the German messages. They went on to use an electromechanical device to check possible wheel and rotor settings of the *Enigma* machine (which had 17,576 possible wheel settings for each of 60 possible wheel orders). For their vital contributions, each man was awarded an OBE at the end of the war.

Weyl, Hermann (1885-1955), was a German mathematician and mathematical physicist whose range of research and interests was remarkably wide, and found expression also in published works on philosophy, logic and the history of mathematics. A one-time pupil of the renowned David Hilbert (1862-1943) and colleague of Albert Einstein (1879-1955), it was probably inevitable that Weyl is remembered chiefly for his studies on topological space and Riemannian geometry.

Weyl was born in Elmshorn on 9 November 1885. Attending the high school in Altona (now a suburb of Hamburg), he evinced a strong interest in mathematics and in philosophy. At the age of 18 he entered Göttingen University where, four years later, he received his doctorate for a dissertation on singular integral equations. Until 1913 he then became an unsalaried lecturer at the University, but at that time turned down a professorship in order to take up the Chair of Mathematics at the Technische Hochschule in Zurich. He held the post until 1930 - despite temporary conscription into the German army during World War I and a year as Visiting Professor at Princeton University in the United States in 1928. He then succeeded David Hilbert to the Chair of Mathematics at the University of Göttingen, but the unfavourable political climate of Nazi Germany prompted him to move to the Institute of Advanced Studies back at Princeton, where he then held a permanent post as Professor of Mathematics. After his retirement in 1951, Weyl divided his time between Princeton and Zurich. During his lifetime Weyl's mathematical talents and contributions were recognized by the award of many honorary degrees and his election to the membership of prestigious scientific societies such as the National Academy of Sciences and the Royal Society. In addition to his many articles published in various journals, Weyl also wrote 15 books that were published in both the United States and Europe. He died in Zurich on 8 December 1955.

Weyl's early university days were strongly influenced by two great mathematicians in his department at Göttingen: David Hilbert and Herman Minkowski (1864-1909). Weyl was to develop interests in fields that included and went beyond those of these two important men.

The whole of Weyl's mathematical career is permeated by his abilities in analysis, but it was during his earliest years, from 1908 to around 1915, that these interests were dominant. He first examined the problems of singular eigenvalues for differential equations, and then turned his attention to oscillations in structures such as membranes and elastic bodies.

As a colleague of Albert Einstein during 1913, he became interested in the developing general theory of relativity and differential geometry. He lectured on both topics, and consolidated these lectures into a book he published in 1918 entitled *Raum-Zeit-Materie* ("space-time-matter"), which in five years ran to five editions. Weyl's interest in relativity theory took him to the point where he believed (erroneously) that he had found a way to a grand unification of gravitation and electromagnetism - something towards which Einstein was to strive for the rest of his life (and which is still being sought). Also in theoretical physics, Weyl was able to anticipate the non-conservation of parity, which has now been found to be characteristic of weak interactions between leptons (a class of subatomic particles which obeys Fermi-Dirac statistics).

Weyl's lectures on Riemann surfaces prompted him to write a book on the subject which was first published in 1913 (and then republished in 1955). His most important work in this field was the definition of the complex manifold of the first dimension, which has been important in all later work on the theory of both complex and of differential manifolds. This work demanded skills in topology, geometry and other areas quite different from those he had previously applied in his work in analysis.

The number of papers Weyl produced on the subject of number theory was small - but their impact was great. In 1916 he published one of his best papers, on the definition of the uniform distribution modulo 1, which was to be of great significance in the later work of Godfrey Hardy (1877-1947) and John Littlewood (1885-1977) on number theory. Other productive research areas during Weyl's fruitful tenure at the Technische Hochschule in Zurich included calculus, continuous groups and Lie groups. He applied his work on group theory to the analysis of the atom in a book on quantum mechanics he published in 1928.

During the rest of Weyl's career he returned to these subjects and explored them further. He published books on classic groups in 1939 and on number theory in 1940. His interest in the philosophy of mathematics led him to write a book on this theme as well, in 1949. A mathematician of profound and diverse talents, Weyl made significant contributions to several fields of both mathematics and mathematical physics.

Whitehead, Alfred North (1861-1947), was a British mathematician and philosopher whose research in mathematics involved a highly original attempt - incorporating the principles of logic - to create an extension of ordinary algebra to universal algebra, a meticulous re-examination of the relativity theory of Albert Einstein (1879-1955) and, in work carried out together with his friend and collaborator Bertrand Russell (1872-1970), the production of what is probably one of the most famous mathematics books of the century, *Principia Mathematica*. This book endeavoured to show that logic could be regarded as the basis of mathematics.

Whitehead was born in Ramsgate, Kent, on 15 February 1861, son of a school headmaster who, when Whitehead was aged 6, became the vicar of a large parish near Ramsgate. From 1875 to 1880 the boy went to Sherborne School; he then went to Trinity College, Cambridge. Receiving his doctorate in 1884, he was elected to a Fellowship of the College, and was appointed Lecturer. One of his pupils there was Bertrand Russell; the two struck up a friendship and together attended the 1900 International Congress of Philosophy in Paris. The result of this excursion was the publication of their joint work, *Principia Mathematica*, in 1910. In that year, however, Whitehead left Cambridge and held a number of positions at University College, London, before being appointed Professor of Applied Mathematics at the Imperial College in 1914. There he produced his book on relativity theory. It gave a thorough, but obscure, analysis and projected further development of the subject. But his interests were already turning more and more to actual philosophy, and the book is a complicated mixture of mathematics, physics and philosophy. In 1924 - at the age of 63 - he was invited to become Professor of Philosophy at Harvard University in New York. During his subsequent years in the United States he produced many fine contributions to philosophy but very little in the way of mathematics. At Harvard he still considered himself an Englishman, and his services to his home country were recognized in the presentation to him of the country's highest award, the Order of Merit, in 1945. A Fellow of the Royal Society since 1903, Whitehead died at Harvard on 30 December 1947.

Even in his mathematical studies, Whitehead preferred to think of the philosophical aspects; he was convinced that to regard the various branches of mathematics in a theoretical way, as manifestations of human intellectuality, was far preferable to considering them as real, concrete structures, as was the prevailing fashion at the turn of the century. It was from this viewpoint that he produced his first major work *A Treatise of Universal Algebra* (published in 1898), an attempt at a total expansion of algebraic principles that also demonstrated his growing interest in philosophy itself.

At the International Congress of Philosophy in 1900, Whitehead and Russell heard Giuseppe Peano (1858-1932) describe the rigorously axiomatic method by which he had arrived at the axioms concerning the natural numbers - for which, despite the acknowledged prior work by Richard Dedekind (1831-1916), Peano is now famous. He was using logical methods to derive mathematical instruments. It occurred, apparently first to Bertrand Russell, that similar methods to those of Peano could be used to deduce mathematics from logic in a general and fundamental way. The collaboration of the two on the project lasted ten years, and culminated in the publication of the very complicated three-volume treatise *Principia Mathematica*. The book did not quite accomplish its objectives - in fact, in some ways, some of it was nullified by events of its own instigation - but it did have a momentous influence on mathematical thought about the foundations of the subject. It had a considerable effect on many individual branches, from the development of Boolean algebra finally to Kurt Gödel's work in which he demonstrated - devastatingly - that arithmetic,

and hence mathematics, can never be proved to be consistent.

There was to have been a fourth volume, by Whitehead alone, devoted entirely to geometry, but it was never completed.

John Whitehead (1904-1960), the pure mathematician, was Alfred North Whitehead's nephew.

Whitehead, John Henry Constantine (1904-1960), was a British mathematician who achieved eminence in the more abstract areas of diffential geometry, and of algebraic and geometrical topology.

Whitehead was born on 11 November 1904 in Madras, India, where his father was the Anglican Bishop; he was the nephew of Alfred North Whitehead (1861-1947). Educated first in Oxford, then at Eton, he entered Balliol College, Oxford, and gained a BA degree in mathematics. After graduating he joined a firm of stockbrokers, but left after 18 months to return to Oxford. For his mathematical researches he was in 1929 awarded a scholarship to the University of Princeton, New Jersey, where he met and worked with Oswald Veblen (1880-1960). Four years later he returned again to Oxford and was elected Fellow of Balliol College; he took up the Wayneflete Chair of Pure Mathematics there in 1947. On a visit to Princeton in 1960, he suffered a heart attack and died in May of that year.

Whitehead's early research was on differential geometry, and the application of differential calculus and differential equations to the study of geometrical figures. It was the results of his years of study in these fields that he took with him to Princeton, to meet a man he had already known by reputation for some considerable time, Oswald Veblen. Yet Veblen's primary interest at the time was in topology - the study of shapes and figures that retain their essential properties despite being "stretched" or "squeezed". Nevertheless, each mathematician influenced the other. Veblen learned so much about differential geometry that he and Whitehead wrote a textbook together on the subject: *Foundations of Differential Geometry* was published in 1932.

Whitehead, in turn, learned a great deal about topology. Combining his interests thereafter, much of his mathematics became very complex and advanced. Some of his most significant work, however, was in the study of knots. In geometry a knot is a two-dimensional representation of a three-dimensional curve that because of its dimensional reduction (by topological distortion) appears to have nodes (to loop onto itself).

Wiener, Norbert (1894-1964), was an American statistician whose main interest lay in devising the means to describe continuously changing conditions and phenomena. His work in a number of fields involving such random processes led him to develop, and later to popularize, the theory of cybernetics, and to contribute fundamentally towards an understanding of the concept of decision-making.

Wiener was born in Columbia, Missouri, on 26 November 1894. A child prodigy, he was put under pressure by his father to excel academically. He was reading fluently at the age of three, entered high school when only nine, and completed the four-year high school course in two years. He went on to take his bachelor's degree at Tuft's College at the age of fourteen. The following year, Wiener began postgraduate studies at Harvard University, intending to concentrate on zoology; he transferred to Cornell University in 1910, but returned to Harvard in 1911 having finally chosen to specialize in the philosophy of mathematics. He earned his master's degree in 1912, and his PhD a year later. A travelling Fellowship then enabled Wiener in 1913 to visit England and go to Cambridge University, where he studied logic under Bertrand Russell (1872-1970), and afterwards to go to the University of Göttingen, Germany, to work with David Hilbert (1862-1943).

On his return to the United States, Wiener took up successive teaching posts at Columbia, Harvard and Maine Universities; worked for a year as a staff writer for the *Encyclopedia Americana* in Albany, New York; spent another year working as a journalist for the *Boston Herald;* and then took up his first appointment at the Massachusetts Institute of Technology (MIT). He worked first as an Instructor in the mathematics department (from 1919 to 1924), then as an Assistant Professor (from 1924 to 1928), as Associate Professor (from 1928 to 1932), and finally as full Professor from 1932 until his retirement in 1960 as Emeritus Professor.

Many professional awards were bestowed on Wiener in recognition of the value of his contribution to mathematics; a member of prestigious international mathematical and scientific organizations, he was also the author of both academic and popular texts. He died in Stockholm, Sweden, on 18 March 1964.

Wiener's commitment to pure mathematics developed somewhat slowly, and it was only in 1918 (at the age of 24) that he began to take a serious interest in integral and differential equations. From the beginning, he worked in areas that had some application to physical processes. His results on the Lebesgue integral are important in the study of wave mechanics. He produced a mathematical theory for Brownian motion (1920), and the enthusiasm of the engineering department at MIT spurred him then to examine problems in harmonic analysis. This led him to make certain deductions about information flow along a wave.

Newtonian analytical methods are not amenable to the investigation of continuously changing processes, so Wiener devoted much of his efforts to methodology, developing mathematical approaches that could usefully be applied to such phenomena. During the 1930s he carried out some work in collaboration with others on Fourier transformations, on Tauberian theorems, on radiation equilibrium, and on the application of mathematics to the study of physiology.

During World War II, Wiener worked on the control of anti-aircraft guns (which required him to consider factors such as the machinery itself, the gunner, and the unpredictable evasive action on the part of the target's pilot), on filtering "noise" from useful information for radar, and on coding and decoding. His investigations stimulated his interest in information transfer and processes such as information feedback. He related the occurrence of these processes in, for instance, for firing of anti-aircraft weapons and in mental processes.

The statistically random (stochastic) components of this process made it familiar material for Wiener. He published a book in 1948 about his ideas on the communication of information and its control. He thereby established and named a new branch of science: cybernetics, the theory of which involves a mathematical description of the flow of information. It is applied to many areas outside mathematics, including neurophysiology, computer design and biochemical regulation. Wiener's book had an immediate impact; the common usage of such terms as "input", "feedback" and "output" in everyday speech is, to a large measure, thanks to him.

A revised edition of the book, *Cybernetics*, was published in 1961. But soon after it was first produced, Wiener stopped doing research and decided to devote the rest of his life to awakening world leaders to the inevitable prospect of automation in many spheres of ordinary life.

Wilks, Samuel Stanley (1906-1964), was an American statistician whose work in data analysis enabled him to formulate methods of deriving valid information from small samples.

He also concentrated on the developments and applications of techniques for the analysis of variance.

Wilks was born on 17 June 1906 in Little Elm, Texas. Educated locally, he studied architecture at the North Texas State College, obtaining his bachelor's degree there in 1926, and his master's two years later at the University of Texas. A two-year scholarship then took him to Iowa University, where he studied statistics and received his doctorate in 1931. Three further scholarships enabled him to continue studying, in New York, London, and Cambridge (England), before he finally joined the staff of Princeton University. Initially an Instructor, he became Assistant Professor in 1936, Associate Professor in 1938, and Professor of Mathematical Statistics in 1944. Active as a government advisory panellist, he received a number of awards and honours; he was also the author of several textbooks on statistics. He died in Princeton on 7 March 1964.

Much of Wilks's early work concerned problems associated with the statistical analysis of data obtained from small samples, such as those derived from experiments in psychology. His investigations of the analysis of variance were devoted especially to multivariate analysis. Two of his most original contributions were the Wilks Λ criterion and his multiple correlation coefficient.

He was particularly interested in the application Board, which carry out extensive educa- The United States College Entrance Examination Board, which carries out extensive educational tests, found his assistance invaluable in analysing their results. Seeking also to apply these methods to industrial problems, Wilks did fundamental work in the establishment of the theory of statistical tolerance.

Wittgenstein, Ludwig Josef Johann (1889–1951), was an Austrian mathematician and philosopher who is best known for his philosophical theories of language.

Wittgenstein was born in Vienna on 26 April 1889, the youngest boy of eight children. His father was prominent in the iron and steel industry, and his mother was the daughter of a banker. He was educated at home until he was 14, and then in 1903 went to school in Linz to study mathematics and the physical sciences, going on to the Technische Hochschule at Charlottenburg in Berlin to study engineering. He went to Britain in 1908 and registered as a research student in aeronautical engineering at the University of Manchester.

On the advice of Friedrich Frege (1848–1925),

Wittgenstein moved to Trinity College, Cambridge, in 1912 to study philosophy under Bertrand Russell (1872–1970). In late 1913 he went to live on a farm in Skjolden, Norway, to have seclusion in which to develop his ideas on logic. On the outbreak of World War I in 1914 Wittgenstein volunteered for the Austrian Army and saw service on the eastern front and in southern Tyrol. He continued his philosophical work, however, and when he was captured in 1918 he had with him the completed manuscript of *Tractatus Logico-Philosophicus*. Through a mutual friend, the economist John Keynes (1883–1946), the manuscript was delivered to Russell in Cambridge and eventually published in 1921.

After the war Wittgenstein abandoned philosophy - saying his mind was "no longer flexible" - and he became a schoolteacher in various Austrian villages. Then in January 1929 he returned to Cambridge, his interest in philosophy having apparently been rekindled by a lecture given in Vienna by Luitzen Brouwer (1881–1966) on the foundations of mathematics. From 1930 to 1936 he gave lectures in Cambridge, and then spent a year in Norway, returning to Britain in 1937. Two years later he succeeded G.E. Moore as Professor of Philosophy.

During World War II Wittgenstein worked first as a hospital porter in Guy's Hospital, London, and then as a laboratory assistant at the Royal Victoria Infirmary in Newcastle-upon-Tyne. He went back to Cambridge in 1944 and following his retirement in 1947 moved to Ireland to live. Two years later he was found to have cancer and during his last days he returned to Cambridge, to his doctor's house, where he died on 24 April 1951.

Wittgenstein's *Tractatus* is concerned with the presuppositions and conditions of ordinary everyday language. He argued that a sentence literally represents the world in such a way that any significant proposition in language can be "logically analysed" into simple "elementary propositions" which are a nexus of names that stand for definite objects. The structuring of the parts of a proposition depicts a possible real combination of elements. Logical and mathematical propositions are exceptions - lacking reference to real or possible states of affairs and yet not being nonsensical.

Wittgenstein began work on his *Philosophical Investigations* in 1936, although it was not published until 1953, after his death. It took a more subtle and complex view than the *Tractatus*, retaining an interest in the problem of meaning but arguing that the meanings of words depends on their role within particular "language games". He postulated that no single feature may be supposed to be present in all forms of language, just as no single definitive feature is common to all of the practices we call games. The unity of language games is like a family resemblance, and to understand the workings of a language we must understand the complex of usages present in language games: words are used to do things rather than merely stand for objects, and the meaning of a concept depends on how it is used in a particular language game. So that in mathematics, the force of a proof – the necessity of mathematical proof – is based on convention or agreement about what is to count as following a rule in the language game of mathematics. But we do not agree *because* the proof follows a rule; rather, agreement with a mathematical calculation fixes its meaning as a proof or a rule, and human practice determines what the rules shall be.

Z

Zassenhaus, Hans Julius (1912–   ), is a German mathematician whose main area of study has been in the field of group therapy and number theory. Perhaps, however, his life has been more concerned with teaching than with publishing his own results.

Born in Coblenz on 28 May 1912, Zassenhaus completed his education by entering the University of Hamburg, from which he received his doctorate in 1934, qualifying as a lecturer there in the same year. For 15 years he worked there and at Rostock University; then he spent 10 years as Redpath Professor of Mathematics in Montreal, Canada. Transferring to the United States, he finally became Professor of Mathematics at Ohio State University in 1964, a post he still holds.

Zassenhaus's research work has concentrated on group theory – the study of systems in which the product of any two members of a system results in another member of the same system (for example, even numbers) – and on number theory. His most significant results have been obtained in his investigations into finite groups, a class of which has been named Zassenhaus groups and forms part of the basis for the contemporary development of finite group theory. The work of Zassenhaus and Schur on group extensions led to the postulation of what has become known as the Schur-Zassenhaus theory.

Zassenhaus has also made contributions to the study of Lie algebra, the geometry of numbers, and applied mathematics.

Zeeman, Erik Christopher (1925–   ), is a British mathematician noted for his work in topology and for his research into models of social behaviour that accord with the relatively recent formulation of catastrophe theory.

Born on 4 February 1925, Zeeman was educated at Christ's Hospital, Sussex. At the age of 18, during World War II, he joined the Royal Air Force and became a Flying Officer. After the war he took up a scholarship to Christ's College, Cambridge, receiving his bachelor's degree in 1948, his master's degree in 1950, and a doctorate in 1954. From then for ten years he was a Fellow of Gonville and Caius College, Cambridge, and a Lecturer there. Thereafter he became Professor of Mathematics at the University of Warwick, where he founded – and became Director of – the Mathematics Research Centre. He has held visiting Professorships in various countries in Europe, in the United States and in Brazil. Elected a Fellow of the Royal Society in 1975, the following year he was made Senior Fellow of the Science Research Council.

Between 1951 and 1958 Zeeman researched into algebraic topology; between 1958 and 1967 he studied geometric topology and brain modelling; and his interests since then have been concerned with catastrophe theory and its applications to the physical, biological and behavioural sciences, and with dynamical systems.

Probably Zeeman's most significant work has been on the recently formulated catastrophe theory. Mathematical analysis cannot easily be used for things that change suddenly, or that have intermittent fits and starts. Where the change is smooth and continuous, it can be described in terms of differential equations. (Newton's laws of motion and gravitation, and James Clerk Maxwell's theory of electromagnetism, can all be described in terms of differential equations. Even Albert Einstein's General Theory of Relativity culminates in a set of differential equations.) A mathematical method for dealing with discontinuous and divergent phenomena was developed only in 1968, and derived from topology – the branch of geometry concerned with the properties of shapes and figures that remain unchanged even when the shape or figure is deformed. This method, the catastrophe theory, has great potential; it can describe the evolution of forms in all aspects of nature and so has great generality. It can be applied to situations where gradually changing forces lead to abrupt changes in behaviour. Many events in physics have now been identified as examples of catastrophe theory, but ultimately its most important applications may be in the "inexact" sciences - biology and social science.

The theory was first devised by René Thom (1923-   ), who saw it as a development of topology in that the underlying forces in nature can be described as the smooth surfaces of equilibrium, and when equilibrium breaks down, catastrophe occurs. The problem for catastrophe theory then is to describe shapes of all the possible equilibrium surfaces. Thom showed that for processes controlled by not more than four factors, there are two elementary catastrophes. His proofs are very complicated, but the results are easier to understand and can be applied to scientific problems without reference to the proof.

If the two elementary catastrophes (two conflicting behavioural drives, for example) are plotted as axes on the horizontal plane - called the control surface - and the complementary result (the resulting behaviour, to carry the example further) is plotted on a third axis perpendicular to the first two, from most likely result to next most likely, and so on, resultant points can be plotted for the entire control surface, and when connected form a surface of their own. Concerning behavioural results, the application in which Zeeman was particularly interested, this surface is known as the behaviour surface. Catastrophe theory reveals that in the middle of the surface is a pleat, without creases, which becomes narrower towards the back of the surface, and it is this pleat which gives the model its most interesting characteristics. For Zeeman, all the points on the behaviour surface represent the most probable behaviour, with the exception of those on the pleated middle part, which represent the least likely behaviour. At the edge of the pleat, the sheet on which the behaviour points have been travelling folds under and is wiped out. The behaviour state falls to the bottom sheet of the graph and there is a sudden change in behaviour. In an argument, for instance, an aggressive protagonist may waver in his opinion, abandon his position and apologize; the timid opponent may make repeated concessions, then lose his temper and become aggressive.

Zeeman, with J. Hevesi, a psychotherapist, has in particular worked on the problems of anorexia nervosa, an illness especially common in adolescent girls, which involves sudden changes from dieting to obsessive fasting. Catastrophe theory has been able to predict behaviour patterns in this disorder and help towards treating the sufferers.

The theory is still a young offshoot of science. But it has already been applied to the propaga-

tion of shock waves, the minimum areas of surfaces, to non-linear oscillations, to scattering and to elasticity. Zeeman has constructed catastrophe models of heartbeat, the propagation of nerve impulses, and the formation of the gastrula and of somites in an embryo. There remains considerable research on the subject still to be done.

Zermelo, Ernst Friedrich Ferdinand (1871-1953), was a German mathematician who made many important contributions to the development of set theory, particularly in developing the axiomatic set theory that now bears his name.

Zermelo was born on 27 July 1871 in Berlin, the son of a university Professor. Educated locally, he passed his final examinations in 1889 and went to study mathematics, physics and philosophy first at Halle University, then at Freiburg University. Among his teachers were Georg Frobenius (1849-1917), Immanuel Fuchs (1832-1902) and Max Planck (1858-1947). Zermelo received his doctorate at Berlin in 1894 and went to Göttingen where, five years later, he was appointed as an unsalaried lecturer. In 1904 he supplied a proof of the well-ordering theorem, and in the following year he was appointed Professor. A few years later he moved to Zurich after accepting a Professorship there; poor health forced him to resign this post in 1916. A gift of 5,000 marks from the Wolfskehl Fund enabled him to live quietly in the Black Forest for the next ten years, restoring himself once more to full health. In 1926 he was appointed honorary Professor at the University of Freiburg in Breisgau. He stayed there for nine years, but in 1935 resigned his post once more, this time in protest against the Nazi regime. He was reinstated in 1946 at his own request, and remained in Freiburg until he died, on 21 May 1953.

Zermelo's first research was on the applications of the theorem formulated by Henri Poincaré (1854-1912). He detected some apparent anomalies in kinetic theory, following Poincaré's research, notably that the recurrence theorem arising from Poincaré's work in mechanics seems to make any mechanical model such as the kinetic theory incompatible with the second law of thermodynamics.

It was in 1900 that Zermelo turned his attention to set theory. He provided an ingenious proof to the well-ordering theorem, which states that every set can be well ordered (that is, can be arranged in a series in which each subclass - not being null - has a first term).

He said that a relation $a < b$ (a comes before b) can be introduced such that:

for any two statements a and b, either $a = b$, or

$$a < b \text{ or } b < a;$$

if there are three elements a, b and c, then if

$$a < b \text{ and } b < c, \text{ then } a < c.$$

This gave rise to the Zermelo axiom that every class can be well ordered.

Zermelo subsequently pointed out that for any infinite system of sets, there are always relations under which every set corresponds to one of its elements. Because of a storm of criticism from other mathematicians, however, he felt obliged to produce a second proof.

In 1904 Zermelo defined the axiom of choice, the use of which had previously been unrecognized in mathematical reasoning. The first formulations of axioms for set theory – an axiom system for Georg Cantor's theory of sets – were made by Zermelo in 1908. This system has since proved of great value in the development of mathematics. There are seven axioms (which found written formulation rather later), in which only two terms are used: the set, and the element of the set. Every set except the null set is an object of B for which there is another object b of B such that $a\mathcal{E}b$. The axioms state:

(1) that $m = n$ if, and only if, $a\mathcal{E}m$ is equivalent to $a\mathcal{E}n$;

(2) that there is a null set;
(3) that if a property E is definite for the elements of a set m, then there is a subset m_E of m consisting of exactly those elements of m for which E holds;
(4) that for any set m there is a set $P(m)$ that has the subsets of m for its elements;
(5) that for any set m there is a set Um (the union of m) consisting of the elements of m;
(6) that if m is a set of disjoint non-void sets, then Um contains a subset n that contains exactly one element from every set of m;
(7) and that there is a set A that has the null set as an element and has the property that, if x is an element of A, then $\{x\}$ is also an element of A.

However, Zermelo's axioms involved an unexplained notion of a "definite property". This difficulty was overcome later by Abraham Fraenkel (1891–1965). Fraenkel had criticized Zermelo's conclusions, particularly axiom 7, because of weakness. Zermelo afterwards improved on them by describing the set of definite properties as the smallest set containing the basic relations of the domain B and satisfying certain close conditions. A logical formulation of Zermelo's axioms was later achieved by Thoralf Skolem in 1923.

Glossary

Abelian functions Functions of the form $\int f(x,y)dx$, where y is an algebraic function of x, and $f(x,y)$ is an algebraic function of x and y.

abstract algebra Generalization of ALGEBRA; the word "abstract" merely draws attention to the level of generality.

abstract group Generalization of a GROUP; the word "abstract" merely indicates that a group is to be considered with reference not to a specific example but to its more general properties (which are shared therefore by other examples).

abundant number A natural number of which the sum of its divisors exceeds twice the number itself.

algebra Study of structural or manipulative properties in mathematics. At an elementary level, algebra investigates the properties of such operations as addition or multiplication in the general context of real numbers, and recognizes similarities between this context and, for example, the addition of vectors.

algebraic curve. Geometrical curve that can be precisely described by an (algebraic) equation.

algebraic numbers Numbers that satisfy a polynomial equation with rational coefficients: e.g. $\sqrt{2}$ solves $x^2 - 2 = 0$. REAL NUMBERS that are not algebraic are called TRANSCENDENTAL NUMBERS. Although there is an infinity of algebraic numbers, there is in fact a "larger" infinity of transcendental numbers.

algebraic topology Study of SURFACES and similar but more general objects in higher dimensions, using algebraic techniques. It is based upon HOMOLOGY.

algorithm Any basic mathematical operation or method of calculation; e.g. in elementary mathematics, the rules for addition, subtraction, multiplication or division. Almost the same as a computer program, an algorithm may be described as a scheme of calculations commonly designed to be applied repeatedly, so that the result of a first calculation is used as the starting point of another calculation which uses identical procedures. A further example is thus Euclid's algorithm for finding the highest common factor of two natural numbers.

analogue In mathematics, part or all of a second statement that can be proved to correspond in operation or effect, though in a different context, with part or all of the original statement, theorem or hypothesis.

analysis Historically came to mean referring to operations that deal with numbers, or that convert other systems so that they can be considered numbers – e.g. analytical geometry reduces figures in two or more dimensions to co-ordinates of points, and thus formulae or equations. By extension, analysis now includes the branch of mathematics in which the central tools are defined by LIMIT processes such as differentiation and integration, or expansion by infinite series (e.g.

$$\sin x = x - \frac{x^3}{3!} + \frac{x^5}{5!} - \ldots).$$

analytical geometry See ANALYSIS.

analytical method In geometry, investigation carried out using a co-ordinate system. (In other mathematical contexts the term merely implies the application of ANALYSIS.)

angle of parallelism In non-Euclidean geometry involving the application of classical geometrical principles to non-flat surfaces, the angle at which a line perpendicular to one of two parallel lines meets the other – which may also be 90°, or may be less.

Apollonius's problem Problem set by Apollonius of Perga, to describe a circle touching three other given circles.

approximation Common mathematical device, deriving instead of the desired result one that is "close enough", i.e. differing by less than a specified amount. Iterative techniques proceed by calculating approximations successively closer to the required answer, and will approach it in LIMIT.

Argand diagram Method of representing COMPLEX NUMBERS geometrically, in which the real and imaginary parts of a complex number form respectively the first and second co-ordinate.

asymptote In geometry, the asymptote to a curve may be represented by a straight line which the curve approaches more and more closely. By extension, "asymptotic" describes curves or calculations approaching a specific value but not achieving it, although finally attaining a limit value in the difference.

automorphic function Function that in relation

to a GROUP of TRANSFORMATIONS has a value on the transformed point identical with the value on the original point.

axiom, axiomatic principles In a rigorous treatment of an area of mathematics, an axiom is a statement that is assumed without proof. Generally, axioms describe the basic properties of a concept in terms of an established "working definition".

axiom of choice In set theory, an assumption that amounts to the possibility of an infinite number of choices to be made. Formally, the axiom states that for a family of non-empty sets X_i, there is a set A such that A meets each X_i in precisely one point.

barycentric calculus Co-ordinate geometry calculations using a co-ordinate system devised by August Möbius in which numerical coefficients are assigned to points on a plane, giving the position of a general point by reference to four or more non-co-planar points. Described in this way, the general point thus represents a centre of gravity for a distribution of mass at the four (or more) points proportional to the assigned numbers.

Bernoulli numbers Sequence of RATIONAL NUMBERS that may be represented by the symbolic form $B_n = (B+1)^n$, corresponding to the sequence

$B_0 = 1,$	$B_1 = -\frac{1}{2},$	$B_2 = \frac{1}{6},$
$B_3 = 0,$	$B_4 = -\frac{1}{30},$	$B_5 = 0,$
$B_6 = \frac{1}{42},$	$B_7 = 0,$	$B_8 = -\frac{1}{30}$
		etc.

B numbers (as they are called) of odd order (except B_1) are zero; B numbers of even order alternate in sign.

Betti numbers Numbers characterizing the connectivity of a VARIETY.

binary system Simplified form of numeration specifically appropriate for use by computers, involving only two distinct digits; the system is thus to base 2, as opposed to the ordinary standard base 10. Commonly, the two digits are represented by 0 and 1, and the system begins.

decimal 0	is represented by binary	0
1		1
2		10
3		11
4		100
5		101
6		110
7		111
8		1000
		and so on.

binomial coefficients Coefficients that appear in the expansion of the expression $(x+y)^n$, commonly written in the form $\binom{n}{k}$. According to the BINOMIAL THEOREM, these may be calculated according to the formula

$$\binom{n}{k} = \frac{n(n-1)(n-2)\ldots(n-k+1)}{1 \times 2 \times 3 \times \ldots k} \text{ for } n \geq k \geq 1.$$

binomial theorem Statement of the rule by which the expansion of the bionomial $(a+b)^n$ proceeds:

for $n=1$ $(a+b)^1 = a+b$
for $n=2$ $(a+b)^2 = (a+b)(a+b)$
$\qquad = a^2 + 2ab + b^2$
for $n=3$ $(a+b)^3 = (a+b)(a+b)(a+b)$
$\qquad = (a+b)(a^2+2ab+b^2)$
$\qquad = a^3 + 3a^2b + 3ab^2 + b^3$

and so on. This is commonly expressed in the general form

$$(a+b)^n = a^n + \binom{n}{1}a^{n-1}b + \binom{n}{2}a^{n-2}b^2 + \ldots$$
$$\ldots + \binom{n}{n-1}ab^{n-1} + b^n.$$

In this theorem $\binom{n}{1}$, $\binom{n}{2}$ etc. are BINOMIAL COEFFICIENTS.

biquaternions Type of QUATERNIONS devised by William Clifford to use specifically in association with linear algebra to represent motions in three-dimensional non-Euclidean space.

B numbers *See* BERNOULLI NUMBERS.

Bode's law Sequence of the form $\frac{0+4}{10}$, $\frac{3+4}{10}$, $\frac{6+4}{10}$, $\frac{12+4}{10}$, $\frac{24+4}{10}$ and so on. Devised first in 1772, it was then found to represent fairly accurately the distances from the Sun of the then known planets of the Solar System, measured in astronomical units. It is sometimes known alternatively as the Titius–Bode rule.

Boolean algebra Algebraic structure formulated by George Boole initiating algebraic study of the rules of logic. His basic process was to subdivide objects into separate classes, each with a different property.

boundary value In applied mathematics a natural phenomenon in a given region may be described by functions that satisfy certain differential equations in the interior of the region and take specific values on the boundary of the region. The latter are referred to as boundary values.

Bourbaki group Group of predominantly French mathematicians who published collectively under the pseudonym Nicolas Bourbaki from the 1930s onward. The group consisted of an ever-changing 20 or so members, and was centred at the École Normale Supérieure in Paris.

braid theory Part of the study of NODES in three-dimensional space, first devised by Emil Artin.

Burali-Forte's antimony Paradox stating that to every collection of ORDINAL NUMBERS there corresponds an ordinal number greater than any element of the collection. In particular it would follow that the collection of all ordinal numbers is itself an ordinal number. This contradiction demonstrated the need for a rigorous exposition of set theory in which not all collections may be accepted as valid subjects of discourse. There is thus no such thing as a "set of all sets", nor a "set of all ordinals" (indicating that the FOUNDATION OF MATHEMATICS cannot be expressed in purely logical terms). One therefore distinguishes between sets which may be manipulated and CLASSES which may not (except in the simplest of circumstances).

calculus General term for a body of useful calculatory procedures. *See* DIFFERENTIAL CALCULUS *and* INTEGRAL CALCULUS; *see also* CALCULUS OF VARIATIONS.

calculus of variations Method of calculation for solving problems in which one of the unknowns cannot be expressed as a number or a finite set of numbers, but is representable as a curve, a function or a system of functions. (A classic problem in the subject is to show that a circle, among all curves of fixed length, encloses the maximum area.)

catastrophe theory Theoretical model devised in an attempt to investigate processes which are not continuous but subject to sudden - and possibly violent - changes (catastrophes). The model consists of, for example, a SURFACE that incorporates some kind of discontinuity or fold so that a point travelling on it continuously under gravity may suddenly come off it in a manner much like "falling off a precipice" and land again on the surface. Plotted by René Thom, the seven elementary catastrophes are: the fold, cusp, "swallow-tail", butterfly", hyperbolic, elliptic and parabolic.

catenary A TRANSCENDENTAL CURVE that can be represented by an equation of the general form

$$y = \frac{a}{2}(e^{\frac{x}{a}} + e^{\frac{-x}{a}})$$

where a is a constant and e is EULER'S NUMBER. It is the shape assumed by an ideal chain suspended from two points that are not immediately vertical one above the other.

caustic curve Curve formed by the points of intersection of rays of light reflected or refracted from a curved surface.

χ^2 function (chi-squared function) Function that in PROBABILITY THEORY provides a test for deviation from a NULL HYPOTHESIS. It is usually represented as being made up of

$$\frac{(\text{Observed frequency} - \text{Expected frequency of result})^2}{\text{Expected frequency of result}},$$

in which the top line indicates the (squared) deviation from the expected.

class Notion used in set theory to distinguish between collections of objects made up solely with regard to a "collecting property", and those which may validly be manipulated without risk of inconsistency. *See also* BURALI-FORTE'S ANTIMONY.

class field theory Theory involving the mathematical structure known as a FIELD, dealing specifically with those that extend a given field in a special kind of way.

closed curve Curve of which the end point coincides with the initial point, e.g. a circle or an ellipse.

coefficient of correlation *See* CORRELATION COEFFICIENT.

cohomology, cohomology theory Algebraic study, using group theory, of geometric objects with specific reference to the operation of finding a boundary. Cohomology theory represents a modification of HOMOLOGY in which it is possible both to add and to multiply CLASSES.

collinear On a single straight line.

commutation, commutative principle Principle obeyed by the operations of ordinary addition and multiplication, to the effect that $a + b = b + a$, and $ab = ba$. This principle need·not hold true in certain structures, e.g. quaternions.

compact (and bicompact) spaces Special kinds of topological space exhibiting the property that, internally, every family of open sets whose union is the whole space necessarily contains a finite subfamily whose union is already the whole space. An alternative definition, first formulated with regard to a special class of such spaces, requires every sequence of points to have a converging sub-sequence. Russian mathematicians initially used the word "bicompact" (not now used in the West) to distinguish between the specialized and the general definitions.

complement Of an angle in geometry, the number of degrees that with it would make a right-angle. In set theory, all those elements of a fixed set not belonging to a specified subset.

complex number The sum of a REAL and an IMAGINARY NUMBER (the latter being a multiple of $\sqrt{-1}$). Complex numbers may be represented geometrically by means of an ARGAND DIAGRAM, and are useful in the study of differential equations.

complex variable A VARIABLE representing a COMPLEX NUMBER.

concentric Having the same centre.

conchoid curve An ALGEBRAIC CURVE represented by an equation of the general form

$$x^2 y^2 = (x-a)^2 (c^2 - x^2).$$

congruence In geometry two sets are congruent if either can be transformed by translations and rotations into the other.

conics, conic sections Study initiated by Apollonius of Perga of how a cone can be "cut" so as to produce circles, ellipses, parabolas and hyperbolas; he stated "a conic section is the locus of a point which moves so that the ratio of its distance f from a fixed point, to its distance d from a straight line, is constant". Whether the constant c is greater than, equal to, or less than 1 determines the type of curve the section represents.

contingency tables Tables listing information classified as variable according to two or more independent attributes. Such tables are used commonly in commerce, notably by insurance companies.

continued fraction Development of any REAL NUMBER in the form of a sequence of integers from which approximations to the number may be calculated successively; e.g.

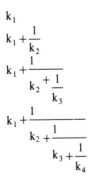

and so on. The sequence can be finite or infinite. The development will be finite in the case of a rational number, and the calculation will then terminate on reaching the rational number. In the case of an irrational number, a termination will be reached only as the LIMIT of the sequence of values calculated.

continuous function(s), continuity Of TRANSFORMATIONS, represents continuous motion, uniform variation. More precisely, a function f is said to be continuous at an argument value x if the function value for arguments close to x can be held down to a value as near to $f(x)$ as required by keeping the argument close enough to x.

convergence Of a sequence or series, describes its approaching to a LIMIT; it is the opposite of divergence.

correlation coefficient In statistics and PROBABILITY THEORY, a measure of how closely two variables, generally within the same numerical framework, can be related or identified. For complete lack of similarity, the correlation coefficient (commonly expressed as $r) = 0$; for perfect positive linear correlation, $r = 1$; for perfect but negative (opposite) linear correlation, $r = -1$.

cosecant (cosec) *See* TRIGONOMETRIC FUNCTIONS.

cosine (cos) *See* TRIGONOMETRIC FUNCTIONS.

Cramer's paradox That although two different cubic curves intersect at nine points, part of the definition of a single cubic curve is that it is itself determined by nine points.

Cramer's rule Method of solving a simultaneous system of linear equation by using DETERMINANTS.

cross ratio In projective geometry, a ratio expressing a relationship between two other ratios determined by four points on a given line, namely the ratio

$$\frac{CA}{CB} : \frac{DA}{DB}.$$

For the purposes of projection, the "point at infinity"" may be any one of A, B, C or D; if the given line is then projected onto another, the cross ratio of the projected points will remain the same – hence the importance of the cross ratio.

cubic curve Geometrical curve in three-dimensional space. It may be parametrized after a change of variables as $(x,y,z) = (at^3, bt^2, ct)$ and may thus be said to be determined by nine points. *See also* CRAMER'S PARADOX.

cybernetics Study of control systems, involving the input of "power" and "information" that effects the desired and/or correct result.

decomposition General term with its meaning set by its context: e.g. in number theory, the FACTORIZATION of an integer into other integers which are of the second or third degree (squares or cubes); in PLANE geometry, the dividing of a plane into two regions by a simple CLOSED CURVE.

Dedekind's cuts Mathematical device by which IRRATIONAL NUMBERS can be referred to by means of sets of fractions (rational numbers).

Δ, δ (delta) As a capital, the term means "difference"; Δx represents the difference between consecutive x values according to context. Leopold Kronecker's delta is a symbol used in the evaluations of DETERMINANTS (in MATRIX THEORY), to the effect that $\delta(i,j) = 1$ if $i = j$, and is 0 otherwise. (It thus measures whether i and j are different.) The d used by Gottfried Leibniz in his notation for differential calculus, as in dy/dx, was based on an intended association with the delta. As a lower-case (small) letter, another delta (∂) commonly represents a partial DERIVATIVE in PARTIAL DIFFERENTIAL CALCULUS.

de Moivre's equation Statement that for integers n $(\cos z + i \sin z)^n = \cos nz + i \sin z$ where $i = \sqrt{-1}$.

denominator In an ordinary division operation, the number or expression by which the numerator is divided.

derivative A FUNCTION derived from another by the application of differentiation or of partial differentiation. A derivative of a derivative is called a derivative of the second order.

descriptive geometry Branch of mathematics in which three-dimensional objects are represented as two-dimensional (plane) figures, using any of many types of projection.

determinant In solving linear equations, a number corresponding in a specified way within a square-shaped array of numbers arranged in rows and columns; e.g.

$$\begin{vmatrix} a & b \\ c & d \end{vmatrix} = ad - bc$$

determinates "Known" values, as opposed to indeterminate, unknown, values.

diacaustic A CAUSTIC CURVE formed by refraction.

difference equation Equation which relates the value of a function at time t to its values at a specified number of past times, from among $t-1$, $t-2$, $t-3$, etc.

differential calculus, differentiation Branch of mathematics concerned with the behaviour of a function in the f vicinity of a point. The central operation is the evaluation of the derivative (written dy/dx or $f(x)$) of the function at the point x. The derivative gives the slope of the tangent to the graph of f at x, and may be calculated as

limit, as h tends to 0, of $\dfrac{f(x+h) - f(x)}{h}$.

The importance of the tangent is that it is the straight line which best approximates to the graph in the vicinity of the point $(x, f(x))$. Higher order approximations may then be obtained by repeated use of the limit process above. Generalizations to functions of several variables involve similar calculations made separately for each variable (partial differentiation); the overall process of obtaining the derivative is called differentiation; and the reverse of differentiation is called integration, a process which represents the calculation of area under a graph.

differential equations Equations involving DERIVATIVES (see DIFFERENTIAL CALCULUS). In a linear differential equation, the unknown function and its derivatives never appear in a power other than 1. Partial differential equations involve unknown functions of several variables, and partial derivatives do therefore appear.

differential geometry Investigation of geometrical surfaces using DIFFERENTIAL CALCULUS.

differentiation See DIFFERENTIAL CALCULUS.

Diophantine equations Algebraic equations involving one or more unknowns (indeterminates) with INTEGERS as coefficients, to which one or more solutions are sought, also in integers. The classic form is $ax + by = c$. Part of the significance of this is that even if not enough information is given to derive a single solution, enough is given to reduce the answer to a definite type. Diophantus, who lived in the third century AD, thus began the investigations into NUMBER THEORY that still continue.

Dirichlet's principle Part of Bernhard Riemann's solution to DIRICHLET'S PROBLEM, stating that there is a mathematical means of defining and accounting for a decrease in heat flow. But that is all it does state.

Dirichlet's problem Problem in physics involving PARTIAL DIFFERENTIAL EQUATIONS in evaluating heat flow and electrostatics.

Dirichlet's theorem States that any series of integers $a \times n + b$, where a and b are relatively prime and $n = 0, 1, 2, 3 \ldots$, includes an infinite series of primes. (There are other theorems also named after Lejeune Dirichlet.)

discriminants Special functions of the coefficients of an equation, used to find roots of a polynomial equation.

disjoint sets See SET THEORY, UNIVERSAL SET.

distributive law, distributivity Expresses the principle operative in the equation

$$a(b + c) = ab + ac.$$

divergent Of a sequence or series, describes the fact that there is no LIMIT for it to approach; it is the opposite of convergent.

domain Set of objects within a mathematical structure on which operations are to be performed. In a simpler context it is the set of arguments (inputs) for which a function is defined.

double theta functions ELLIPTIC FUNCTIONS in the form of THETA FUNCTIONS of higher degree.

doubling the cube Ancient Greek problem in geometrical construction, to derive a cube of exactly twice the volume of another cube of given measurement, using ruler and compass only.

duality, the principle of duality Principle that a law or theorem remains valid if one particular element within that law is exchanged for another equally pertinent element. In projective geometry, a statement of a two-dimensional proposition remains valid if the word "point" is exchanged for "line" (and vice versa); a three-dimensional proposition likewise if "point" is exchanged for "plane".

dy/**dx** *See* DIFFERENTIAL CALCULUS.

e See EULER'S NUMBER.

eigen-value For a matrix A, the number λ is said to be an eigen-value of the matrix if there is a non-zero VECTOR x such that $Ax = \lambda x$. Eigen-values are used to derive a change of base to simplify the matrix to one which has entries only on its diagonal. More generally, the number λ is an eigen-value of a linear transformation T if there is a non-zero vector x so that $T(x) = \lambda x$.

Elements Title of the major mathematical work by Euclid. Various other mathematical authors have since also used the title.

elements In set theory, the members of a set.

ellipse A CLOSED CURVE in PLANE geometry which, instead of a single focus (or centre, as in a circle) has two foci. Its typical form is represented by the equation

$$\frac{x^2}{a^2} + \frac{y^2}{b^2} = 1.$$

elliptic functions Integrals of the general form $\int f(x, \sqrt{R})dx$, where f is any rational function of x and R is a quartic polynomial corresponding to

$$a_0x^4 + a_1x^3 + a_2x^2 + a_3x + a_4$$

with no multiple roots. Adrien Legendre proved that any elliptic integral can be reduced to the sum of an elementary function and of scalar multiples of three special functions. ABELIAN FUNCTIONS and THETA FUNCTIONS are both extensions. Elliptic functions are used in the integration of the square root of a cubic or a QUARTIC, and are thus important to many mathematical operations.

elliptic geometry System of NON-EUCLIDEAN GEOMETRY developed as the initial form of RIEMANN GEOMETRY, and regarding all geometrical operations as carried out in "curved" space, e.g. as though on the surface of an ellipsoid or sphere. A "straight line" is thus defined (then) as the shortest curve (geodesic) on the curved surface joining two points.

elliptic modular functions Functions defined in the upper half of an Argand plane which are automorphic relative to a group of modular transformations, i.e. transformations T such as

$$T(z) = \frac{az + b}{cz + d}, \text{ subject to the condition that}$$

$ad - bc = 1$.

epicycle Circular orbit round a point that is itself in a circular orbit round a focus.

ergodics In dynamics, study of the mathematical principles involved in the kinetic theory of gases.

Erlangen programme Expression used by Felix Klein to denote his unification and classification of geometries Euclidean and non-Euclidean as "members" of one "family", corresponding to the transformations found in each.

error theory, theory of errors In statistics and PROBABILITY THEORY, method of evaluating the effects and the significance of errors, for example when obtaining a mean value from a small sample.

Euclidean geometry *See* GEOMETRY.

Euclid's fifth postulate Stated that parallel lines meet only at infinity.

Euler's number (e) The limit of the sequence

$$a_n = 1 + \frac{1}{1!} + \frac{1}{2!} + \frac{1}{3!} + \ldots + \frac{1}{n!}.$$

An irrational number introduced originally by Leonhard Euler, *e* may be represented to the sixth decimal place as 2.718282; it has useful theoretical properties in differential calculus and serves as a natural base for logarithms (known as "natural logarithms").

excluded middle, law of the Law in logic, that a statement is either true or false, leaving no room for any further alternatives. There are non-classical systems of logic which distinguish between true = proven true and false = proven false, and so allow intermediate values (such as "possibly true"). Boolean-valued logic systems attach probability values to statements which may therefore also have intermediate values other than merely true or false; the values form a BOOLEAN ALGEBRA.

exponent Power to which a number is raised, commonly represented as the unknown variable x; e.g. 4^x.

factorial (!) Involving the product of all positive whole integers up to and including the one quoted; factorial 5 (or 5!) thus represents $1 \times 2 \times 3 \times 4 \times 5$; $n!$ represents the series extended to n.

factorization Reduction into constituent factors (which when multiplied together produce the original number or expression).

Fermat's last theorem States that the equation $a^n + b^n = c^n$ is not solvable in integers if n is greater than 2. The theorem has never been proved (Fermat's own alleged proof has never been found) for all values of n, although for a very large number of values the theorem has been verified.

Fibonacci series Sequence in which each term after the first two is the sum of the two terms immediately preceding it; it begins 1, 1, 2, 3, 5, 8, 13, 21 ... and has a variety of important applications (e.g. in search algorithms).

field theory Theory involving the mathematical structure known as a field, which displays the operations of addition and multiplication and their inverses (subtraction and division). An elementary example other than the real numbers is constituted by the rational numbers; there are many other types. A RING is much like a field but does not include the inverse operations. A GROUP is a more restricted concept still.

finite In mathematics generally, may be labelled by the natural numbers; not infinite. Of a set, may be arranged in a (finite) list that can therefore be labelled with the natural numbers less than some fixed number. Of a real number, not plus or minus infinity. Of a line segment, of finite length.

(of the) first order In differential equations, involving only the first DERIVATIVE.

fluxions See CALCULUS.

foundations of mathematics, foundations of arithmetic Subject of attempts to derive the basic precepts of elementary mathematics from a standpoint of pure logic (thence to derive the more complex principles).

Fourier analysis See FOURIER THEOREM.

Fourier series Series in which the terms comprise multiples of the cosine and/or sine of multiple angles. Represented by the formula

$$\tfrac{1}{2}a_0 + \Sigma a_n \cos nx + b_n \sin nx,$$

it is used to analyse periodic functions (i.e. functions whose graph repeats itself preriodically).

Fourier theorem Adaptation of the process developed by Joseph Fourier as the FOURIER SERIES to the investigation of energy propagated in the form of waves (particularly heat, sound and light). A further developed version of this method is known as harmonic analysis. Use of the theorem in investigating wave forms is known as Fourier analysis.

fraction Ratio describing as one integer above another the number of parts (the top figure) of the whole (the bottom figure, in the same units); a number over itself thus represents unity, and a top figure higher than a bottom figure represents more than unity.

function In mathematics, dependence of a quantity or number on one or more other constituent variable quantities or numbers; y is a function of x if a value of y can be calculated for each value of x. The classic form is thus $y = f(x)$, in which x is called the argument and f the function.

functional analysis See FUNCTION THEORY.

functions of complex variables, theory of Involves FUNCTIONS of which the arguments are COMPLEX NUMBERS.

functions of real variables, theory of Involves FUNCTIONS of which the arguments are REAL NUMBERS.

function theory, theory of functions Use of FUNCTIONS, primarily in order to denote mathematical relationships, but also in application to other sciences. Functional analysis, for example, considers problems in which an unknown function is to be found; at this stage VARIABLES may represent functions as opposed to numerical values.

game theory Construction of mathematical models for determining the best strategy to win a game, i.e. to achieve optimal results with minimal losses. Devised first by John von Neumann, the theory has many applications to the behavioural sciences.

Gaussian distribution See NORMAL DISTRIBUTION.

General Theory of Relativity Final form of the theory of RELATIVITY formulated by Albert Einstein. In his prior Special Theory, Einstein had outlined a four-dimensional structure of space-time (much helped by his knowledge of RIEMANN GEOMETRY). The General Theory further provided an understanding of gravitation as a curvature within that four-dimensional structure, of defined mathematical properties.

geodesic A "straight line" (i.e. the shortest curve) between two points lying on a curved surface, in NON-EUCLIDEAN GEOMETRY.

geometric curve Curve that can be precisely expressed by an equation (unlike a mechanical curve); e.g. a circle, parabola or hyperbola.

geometry Study of the properties and relations of lines, surfaces and solids in space. The basic elementary geometry is Euclidean, involving two or three dimensions only, and in which lines may be straight, curved, parallel, finite or infinite; in which surfaces are two-dimensional, corresponding to regular co-ordinates; and in which solids are three-dimensional. Other modern considerations in geometry include ELLIPTIC GEOMETRY and HYPERBOLIC GEOMETRY.

graph Pictorial plot of a function f, consisting of points on the plane of the form $(x, f(x))$. Such a representation provides the means of solving for x equations of the form $y = f(x)$ for given y value(s). Points of intersection of the graph with the horizontal line corresponding to the ordinate value y give solutions to the equation. It is commonly convenient, however, to rewrite $y = f(x)$ as, for example, $g(x), = h(x)$ so as to have two separate functions of x, one on each side of the equation and so that y is involved in the constitution of g and h; where the graphs of g and h then meet again give the required solution(s).

group theory Investigation and classification of the properties of the mathematical structures known as groups. A group possesses two operations – "multiplication" and "inverting of an element" – and a further designated element called "unity". An example is provided by the set of non-zero real numbers with ordinary multiplication and reciprocation (i.e. being multiplied or becoming reciprocals). Another example is provided by the integers for which the operation of multiplication ($n \times m$), is to be addition ($n + m$), with the inverse of n being $-_n$, and the "unity element" is in fact zero. A third example is provided by a collection of TRANSFORMATIONS of the plane where $S \times T$ effectively means applying transformation T and then S; such a collection is a group if it includes the identity transformation I (the transformation which leaves all points unchanged) and for each transformation T its inverse, T^{-1} (the transformation of which the effect is to return each point to its original positon before it was transformed by T).

harmonic analysis *See* FOURIER THEORUM.

homology Branch of TOPOLOGY involving the study of CLOSED CURVES, closed surfaces and

similar geometric arrangements in two- to n-dimensional space, and investigating the ways in which such spatial structures may be dissected. The formulation of the homological theory of dimensionality led to several basic laws of DUALITY (relating to topological properties of an additional part of space).

hyperbola Double-branched plane curve; i.e. a curve consisting of two separate but similar and related (infinite) pieces. The equation for the general form is represented by

$$\frac{x^2}{a^2} - \frac{y^2}{b^2} = 1,$$

where a and b are two real numbers.

hyperbolic geometry System of NON-EUCLIDEAN GEOMETRY developed by Bernhard Riemann, complementary to ELLIPTIC GEOMETRY and comprising the geometry of GEODESICS in the neighbourhood of a point on the (curved) surface at which a tangential plane intersects the surface in a hyperbolic curve.

hyper-complex numbers Numbers that expand on COMPLEX NUMBERS, e.g. QUATERNIONS.

ideal In projective geometry and algebra, describes a point (one on every line) at infinity in such a way that the point has a co-ordinate position. In number theory, the term describes a collection of elements in a RING that has specific properties within a UNIVERSAL SET, i.e. that form a closed system under addition (among themselves) and under scaling by any element from the universal set. For example, the even numbers form an ideal within the universal set of integers in that when added (or multiplied) together, even numbers result.

image (points) *See* TRANSFORMATION.

imaginary number That part of a COMPLEX NUMBER which is a multiple of $\sqrt{-1}$.

indeterminate problems Problems involving one or more unknown or variable quantities. *See also* DIOPHANTINE EQUATIONS.

infinite In mathematics, having no specified end, no highest or lowest value; not FINITE.

infinitesimal calculus Original terminology for "calculus", i.e. DIFFERENTIAL and INTEGRAL CALCULUS, and so called because it was thought to rely on "infinitely small" quantities. (It is now seen to be based upon a precise theory of LIMITS.)

infinitesimals Numbers that are not zero but that are less than any finite number. These clearly do not exist in the conventional system of real numbers, but it is of interest to know that modern developments in logic allow the use of an extended system of numbers which includes infinitesimal numbers. Calculations with these adhere to certain restrictions and require a good understanding of LIMITS.

infinity Term with a number of precise uses that, in naive contexts, corresponds to placing some kind of object at the "end" of a mathematical object which is INFINITE. For example, there may be a point on a line at infinity, or a conventional number (written ∞) to follow all real numbers; orders of infinity occur in set theory (*see* TRANSFINITE).

integer A signed (plus or minus) whole number.

integral *See* INTEGRAL CALCULUS.

integral calculus, integration Method of calculation corresponding to a means of determining the area under the graph of a function $f(x)$, a basic problem in analysis.

Suppose $f(x) \geqslant 0$, the integral $\int_a^b f(x)dx$ of f

between points a and b (area) is defined by a limiting process through approximate sums representing the sum of rectangles inscribed beneath the curve, all of whose horizontal width grow progressively thinner. It can be shown

that if $f(x) = \dfrac{dF(x)}{dx}$ for some function F (known

as the primitive), then the integral equals the change in between a and b. Integration is thus the opposite of DIFFERENTIATION.

integral equations Equations involving integrals of the unknown function.

integral number An INTEGER.

integration *See* INTEGRAL CALCULUS.

intrinsic geometry Study of a surface without reference to any point, condition or space outside it. All measurements and operations carried out on the surface are therefore in terms of its own (intrinsic) form.

intuitional mathematics, intuitionism An alternative foundational basis for mathematics that adopts a stricter logic in its approach to proofs concerning the infinite. For example, it dismisses the law of the EXCLUDED MIDDLE, and so disregards "proofs" derived by double negatives if the relevant positive statement has not actually been demonstrated to be true. Although this may be considered a sort of philosophical puritanism, the outlook leads to a more refined classification of proof material than merely "true" or "false". The fact that such a critical attitude can itself be formalized in a mathematically sound system is an important achievement. Nevertheless, most practising mathematicians remain unconcerned by this logical analysis.

invariant As a general term, describes a property that is preserved through specified mathematical operations.

inverse function For a function $f(x)$, a function $g(y)$ such that $g(f(x)) = x$, i.e. which inverts the transformation f.

irrational numbers Those REAL NUMBERS which cannot be represented as fractions; e.g. $\sqrt{2}$, π. *See also* ALGEBRAIC NUMBER and TRANSCENDENTAL NUMBER.

isoperimetry Branch of geometry involving the study and measurement of figures with equal perimeters.

knot In two- and three-dimensional geometry, a CLOSED CURVE that loops over or through itself; representations of such structures are commonly presented as congruency problems.

(laws of) large numbers Theorems in probability theory that predict that the observed frequencies of events for a large number of repeated trials are more and more likely to approach their theoretical probability as the number of repetitions increases.

lattice, lattice theory A mathematical structure consisting of objects within an order corresponding to size or value, such that any two possess an element that is the largest smaller than both (i.e. a minimum) and similarly an element that is the smallest larger than both (i.e. a maximum). For example, if there is a point on a plane with integer co-ordinates (n,m), and if (k,l) is larger than (n,m) in that k > n and l > m, joining these points by horizontal and vertical lines creates a "lattice" pattern, from which the theory gets its name.

(method of) least squares Method of deriving as exact an average value as possible from a set of approximate or inaccurate values by introducing the errors as unknown variables and requiring the sum of their squares to be minimized. The method was devised by Karl Gauss as a precise way of best fitting a straight line through a set of plotted data points that are not collinear.

Legendre functions Functions that satisfy the second-order differential equation

$$(1 - x^2)y'' - 2xy' + n(n+1)y = 0.$$

lemniscate Curve represented by the equation

$$(x^2 + y^2)^2 = a^2(x^2 - y^2),$$

where a is constant and x and y are variables.

Lie groups, Lie rings Collections of mathematical objects in groups or rings that have further (topological) structure under which the collective operations are CONTINUOUS, e.g. vectors in the plane (where open discs define a topological structure).

limit An important general term, of which the intuitive content may be summed up as "the end value towards which a process proceeds, which it may or may not ever achieve". Its importance lies in giving a rigorous basis for any mathematical calculations that involve approximation. Examples are: for the sequence 0.9, 0.99, 0.999, 0.9999 and so on, the terms are closer and closer to unity the further they are taken - and unity is thus the limiting value; regular polygons inscribed in a circle approach the shape of the circle as the number of sides is increased - and the limiting shape of the polygons is thus a circle. A proper mathematical definition of the term "limit" involves a notion of indexing in an ordered fashion (corresponding to discrete steps, as for instance in calculations of better and better approximations, or to continuous processes, as for example the movement of a point in space with time), an association of some value to each index, and a measurement of closeness.

linear differential equations *See* DIFFERENTIAL EQUATIONS.

linear function, linear transformation In its simplest context, a transformation such as $y = mx$ which may be depicted as a line through the origin. More generally, a transformation T defined on a vector space with the property that $T(\alpha x + \beta y) = \alpha T(x) + \beta T(y)$ for x, y vectors and α, β scalars.

Lipschitz condition For a function f the condition that for some constant (number) K,

$$|f(x) - f(y)| \leqslant K|x - y|$$

no matter what the arguments are. It is useful in proving the existence or uniqueness of a solution to a differential equation.

ln Expression for NATURAL LOGARITHMS.

logarithms A method of reducing multiplication to addition (used extensively before the introduction of electronic calculators). The logarithm to base 10 of a number a greater than zero is that power b such that $10^b = a$. If $a_1 = 10^{b_1}$ and $a_2 = 10^{b_2}$, then

$$a_1 a_2 = 10^{b_1} . 10^{b_2}$$
$$= 10^{b_1 + b_2}$$

and it becomes obvious that to multiply a_1 and a_2 it is sufficient to add their logarithms. By consulting tables the number of which the logarithm is $b_1 + b_2$ can be discovered. The first logarithm tables were produced by Henry Briggs in 1617.

logic Systematic study of the laws and uses of reasoning. From very early times logic has been considered closely associated in methodology - if not by effectively parallel derivation - with the science of mathematics.

logistic curves. Curves that represent logarithmic functions, from which logarithms

of ordinary numbers can be read off.

Malfatti's problem Medieval European problem, to inscribe within a triangle three circles tangent to one another.

manifold In two-dimensional space, a regular SURFACE that locally looks like a flat plane slightly distorted. It can be represented by differentiable functions. There are analogues in spaces of more dimensions.

mapping *See* TRANSFORMATION.

Markov processes, Markov chains Random, but mutually dependent, changes within a system that exists in potentially more than one state. As part of PROBABILITY THEORY, they are defined as sequences of mutually dependent random variables for which any prediction about x_{n+1}, knowing $x_1 \ldots x_n$, can be based on just x_n without any loss.

mathematical logic View of mathematics and logic that relates the two disciplines, and to do so uses mathematical or similar notation in the expression of axiomatic statements. BOOLEAN ALGEBRA was the original form, and led to Gottlob Frege's SYMBOLIC LOGIC.

mathematical philosophy *See* PHILOSOPHY OF MATHEMATICS.

mathematical structure Collection of objects that display a) one or more relationships, and b) one or more operations of which the properties may be summarized as a list of AXIOMS; for example, a GROUP, VECTOR, SPACE or RING.

Matrix In algebra, a rectangular array of numbers, used for example to represent the coefficients of a system of simultaneous linear equations, each row of the array corresponding to one equation. Matrices may be multiplied following specific rules relating to the change in coefficients of the simultaneous equations when a change of variables is effected.

mean value Average value of a number of values, obtained by totalling the values and dividing by the number of values. *See also* the method of LEAST SQUARES.

measure theory Extension of the notion of length, area or volume (as appropriate) to general sets of points on the line, plane or in space. Used commonly in analysis (especially integration theory), functional analysis, probability theory and game theory (in the assessment of the size of coalitions), its definitive form was derived by Henri Lebesgue.

mechanical curve. Curve that cannot be precisely expressed as an equation (unlike a geometric curve).

method of least squares *See* LEAST SQUARES, METHOD OF.

metric In special mathematical structures, a

means of measuring distance or discrepancy. It has the characteristic property of satisfying the triangle inequality: i.e. that the distance x to y does not exceed the distance x to z plus the distance z to y for any z.

minor In the theory of DETERMINANTS, smaller determinant obtained by deleting one of the rows and one of the columns of a MATRIX.

modulo In number theory, two numbers are said to be equivalent modulo a fixed number if their difference is divisible by the fixed number.

moments In statistics and probability theory, are generalizations to higher powers of the mean. The rth moment of a random variable is the expected value of the rth power of the variable less its mean.

monotone, monotonic Of a sequence, that its terms are increasing or decreasing along the sequence.

Mordell's equation Is represented by $y^2 = x^3 + k$.

n Undefined positive whole number larger than 3, usually representing the unknown variable at the end of a series or sequence.

$n!$ Factorial n, i.e. $1 \times 2 \times 3 \times 4 \times \ldots xn$.

Napier's Bones Primitive mechanical calculation device created by John Napier and consisting of a set of little bone rods with which to multiply or divide.

natural logarithms System of logarithms based on EULER'S NUMBER instead of the (more elementary) base 10. In place of the abbreviation "log", the expression "ln" is used unless the context itself makes clear what base is intended.

natural (integral) numbers Whole, positive integers.

n-dimensional Having an unstated but finite number of dimensions. A typical example is the set of all runs of n-numbers (i.e., $x_1 \ldots x_n$), which is the basis of a co-ordinate geometry generalizing three-dimensional coordinates (x_1, x_2, x_3).

neighbourhood In topology, subsets of points in a TOPOLOGICAL SPACE defining a "locality" round a specific point, which includes an open set to which the specific point belongs. Axioms describing neighbourhoods were first formulated by Felix Hausdorff.

nodes In two- and three-dimensional geometry, where a curve intersects itself.

non-commutative In which the principle of COMMUTATION does not apply.

non-Euclidean geometry, non-Euclidean space Study of figures and shapes in three- or more-dimensional (or curved) space, in which Euclid's postulates may not apply fully or at all (*see* GEOMETRY). There are now many forms

of non-Euclidean geometry, probably the best known being those propounded by Bernhard Riemann; the first proponents of such systems, however, were Karl Gauss, Nikolai Lobachevsky and János Bolyai.

normal (or Gaussian) distribution Special probability density function, ordinarily represented as a graph that it symmetrically bell-shaped, starting with a near-zero value low on the left, rising to a smooth-domed peak of probability in the centre, and sinking again to low on the right. Devised first by Abraham de Moivre, it is now fundamental to PROBABILITY THEORY. *See also* STANDARD DEVIATION.

Null Hypothesis In probability theory, assumes that events occur on a purely random (chance) basis.

null set Conventional SET which has no members.

null vector Is also known as the zero VECTOR.

number theory, theory of numbers Branch of pure mathematics concerned with numbers: algebraic, complex, even, irrational, natural, negative, odd, positive, prime, rational, real and transcendental, in sequence or in series, in any operation and expressed even in other forms.

ordinary numbers *See* SET THEORY.

orthogonal In geometry, having a right-angle, right-angled or perpendicular.

parabola In plane geometry, an infinite open curve about a single line known as its axis. The equation for the general form is represented by $y^2 = 2px$, where p is a positive real number.

parallels, parallelism In Euclidean geometry, describes two (or more) lines in a plane that neither approach nor diverge from each other, however far extended, but remain at a constant distance; a perpendicular drawn to one crosses the other also at $90°$. Such lines, according to Euclid, meet only at infinity. For the non-Euclidean analogue, however, *see* ANGLE OF PARELLELISM.

partial differentiation Form of DIFFERENTIAL CALCULUS in which instead of a function $y = f(x)$ which has one variable, a function of two or more variables e.g. $z = f(x,y)$ which represent a surface in three-dimensional space is considered. The rate of change of z may be calculated in two independent directions – parallel to the x-axis or parellel to the y-axis. At a point x,y these are calculated according to the formulas

$$\text{limit, as } h \text{ tends to } 0, \frac{f(x+h,y) - f(x,y)}{h}$$

and

limit, as k tends to 0, $\dfrac{f(x,y+k)-f(x,y)}{k}$

In the first case, this reduces to ordinary differentiation relative to a constant value of y. The corresponding symbols are $\dfrac{\partial z}{\partial x}, \dfrac{\partial z}{\partial y}$.

partitioning Of an integer in number theory, breaking the integer down into its constituent parts in as many ways as possible; e.g. the number 6 can be partitioned in three ways: $5+1, 4+2$ and $3+3$. Each of these contributory numbers is known as a summand.

Peano axioms Axioms that formally introduce the properties of the positive whole numbers (originally devised, despite the term, by Julius Dedekind).

perfect number Number that comprises the sum of all its factors except itself; e.g. 6 is a perfect number, being $1+2+3$.

permutation group GROUP consisting of all the transformations (operations) permutating a fixed number of objects among themselves. Such groups were studied first by Evariste Galois in connection with permutations (solutions) of roots (solutions) of a polynomial equation.

philosophy of mathematics Has three main aspects: the logical (in which mathematics is simply a branch of logic), the formalist (involving the study of the structure of objects and the property of symbols), and the intuitional (grounded on the basic premise of the possibility of constructing an infinite series of numbers).

pigeon-hole principle See SCHUBFACHPRINZIP.

plane In mathematics, either two-dimensional (as in plane geometry) or a two-dimensional (flat) surface of the "thickness" of a point.

Platonic solids Five regular three-dimensional polyhedra that can be bordered by other, congruent polyhedra (i.e. that can pack with identical others into an overall solid shape). They are: the tetrahedron (a pyramid with base and three sides as equilateral triangles), the hexahedron (a cube), octahedron (an 8-faced solid), the dodecahedron (12-faced) and the icosahedron (20-faced). Each can be inscribed and circumscribed by concentric spheres. As two-dimensional figures in profile, they have similar properties.

point sets In geometry or topology, sets comprising some or all of the points of the space under study.

polar planimeter Device invented by Jakob Amsler–Laffon to measure area on a curved surface; it could be used to determine Fourier coefficients and was thus particularly valuable to ship-builders and railway engineers.

polyhedron, polyhedra Many-sided three-dimensional figure(s). About them, Leonhard Euler stated that the number of vertices $v+$ the number of faces $f=$ the number of edges $E+2$, so long as the figures are regular or at least simple (otherwise the constant 2 needs to be amended).

porisms Old-fashioned term for conclusion or hypotheses following directly upon a statement or proposition.

power, powers Ordinarily, an indication of the number of times a number (or equivalent term) is multiplied by itself, expressed as a superior figure after the principal; e.g. $2^1=2$, $2^2=2\times 2$, $2^3=2\times 2\times 2$, and $2^n=2\times 2\times \ldots n$ times. The power 0 represents unity; i.e. $x^0=1$. Minus powers represent reciprocal positive powers; i.e. $2^{-1}=\frac{1}{2}$, $2^{-2}=\frac{1}{2}^2=\frac{1}{4}$. Fractional powers represent roots; i.e. $2\frac{1}{2}=\sqrt{2}$ and $2\frac{4}{3}=\sqrt[3]{2^4}$.

power series An infinite series of the general form $a_0+a_1x^1+a_2x^2+a_3x^3+\ldots+a_nx^n+\ldots$ This is called a power series in x. Examples of power series are the exponential series –
$$e^x=1+x+\frac{x^2}{2!}+\frac{x^3}{3!}+\ldots$$– the logarithmic series, and the series for the trigonometric functions (sine, cosine and tangent).

predicate calculus In logic, part of the theory of devising models involving deduction and the use of variables and negatives in systems of sentences; the term occurs commonly in MATHEMATICAL LOGIC.

primary factors Most reduced (lowest) form of numbers which, when multiplied together, produce the principal numbers or expression.

prime number Any whole integer of which the only whole-number factor less than itself is 1.

Principia Mathematica Title (in part and wholly, respectively) of two works: the first, by Sir Isaac Newton, published in 1687, was a compilation of mathematics combined with physics, and was a landmark in both disciplines; the second, by Bertrand Russell and Alfred North Whitehead, was an attempt to derive the FOUNDATIONS OF MATHEMATICS, published in 1910–1913.

probability theory Mathematical tool for assessing the likelihood of an event's occurrence. Its practical significance is its ability to predict outcomes often enough (as opposed to always). Its framework is usually initially described by defining the (irreducible) "atomic" events of a given application – known as the population – of which it is customarily assumed that each member possesses one or more numerical characteristics (e.g. the height of an individual, or the number of dots on the face of a dice) which is well defined. It is also assumed that a selection process randomly picks an element of the population (e.g. the throw of the dice). Such randomness is modelled by a prior assessment of the likelihood of an individual's being selected, generally an equal likelihood unless there is reason to expect otherwise; the practical judgement that one choice is as likely as another has the accepted mathematical translation that the observed frequency of occurrence of the events (provided the selective mechanism is allowed to operate an appropriate number of times) is roughly equal for each. The mathematical theory thereafter considers more complex events (*see* laws of LARGE NUMBERS). One of the most remarkable discoveries in relation to probability theory is the central limit theorem, which defines a LIMIT (as sample size increases) in terms of the NORMAL (GAUSSIAN) DISTRIBUTION graph. *See also* the NULL HYPOTHESIS, the χ^2 TEST and STANDARD DEVIATION.

product The result after multiplying one quantity by another.

projective geometry Form of two- and three-dimensional geometry concerned with the geometrical properties that remain constant (invariant) under projection, i.e. extended on a single plane, or projected from one plane on to another. Perspective – two-dimensional representation of three-dimensional reality – uses the basic theory of projective geometry.

proof Rigorously defined and complete demonstration using accepted and specific AXIOMS of the correctness of a statement, law, theorem, etc. In mathematics, the expression of the proof may sometimes be even more useful and constructive than the original assertion, in that it may lend itself to further application.

Pythagoras's theorem States that in a right-angled triangle, the square on the hypotenuse is equal to the sum of the squares on the other two sides. Named after Pythagoras (6th century BC) who provided a proof for it, the effect was nevertheless known to the Babylonians up to a millennium earlier.

quadratic Involving second powers, e.g. x^2.

quadratic equations Equations involving an expression of the second degree; the classic form is represented by $x^2 + px + c = 0$.

quadratic extension Extension of a FIELD to a larger field by adjoining the root of a quadratic equation, e.g. the set of all $p + q\sqrt{2}$ with both p and q as rational numbers is a quadratic extension of the field of rationals.

quartic To the power 4; it is occasionally replaced by the word "biquadratic".

quaternions Extended system of COMPLEX NUMBERS, representable in the generalized form $a + bi + cj + dk$, where a, b, c and d are real numbers, and in which i, j and k are additional objects that multiply according to specific rules such that $i^2 = j^2 = k^2 = -1$, $ij = -ji = k$, $jk = -kj = i$, and $ki = -ik = j$.

quintic To the power 5.

quotient The result after dividing one quantity by another.

radical Operation principle in the extraction of roots; i.e. square roots, cube roots etc.

rational numbers Fractions; the ratios of integral numbers.

real numbers Types of number expressible using a decimal point: NATURAL (or positive) INTEGRAL NUMBERS, ALGEBRAIC NUMBERS, RATIONAL NUMBERS, IRRATIONAL NUMBERS and TRANSCENDENTAL NUMBERS. The COMPLEX NUMBERS are a QUADRATIC EXTENSION of the real numbers; *see also* IMAGINARY NUMBERS.

recursive In mathematics, a very general description of a function with NATURAL NUMBERS as arguments, corresponding to the intuitive notion of computability. The basic recursive functions are $x + y$, xy, $f(x,y,z, \ldots) = x$, $g(x,y,z, \ldots) = y$, and a restricted form of the taking of a minimum.

relativity Concept explained by Albert Einstein first in his Special Theory, comprising two basic yet very original postulates contrary to Newtonian physics – that a ray of light (in a vacuum) passes an observer at the speed of light no matter how uniformly fast nor in what direction the observer is travelling, and that time is not an absolute quantity (with the implication that all observers therefore possess co-ordinate systems that incorporate their own time reference). Among the consequences of the theory is the condition that measurement of a variety of other physical quantities depends on the observer – e.g. the observed contraction of a fast-moving body, and the fact that a magnetic force may appear as an electrical force in a different frame of reference. The unifying concept is the principle of conservation of energy, educed mathematically by Einstein as $E = mc^2$, where c is the speed of light. Ten years later, Einstein produced his GENERAL THEORY OF RELATIVITY.

Riemann geometry System of NON-EUCLIDEAN GEOMETRY devised by Bernhard Riemann, developed primarily as ELLIPTIC GEOMETRY, but then extended to HYPERBOLIC GEOMETRY.

Riemann hypothesis Statement that has as yet not been proved (or disproved), that the ZETA FUNCTION takes the value zero in the right-half plane of the ARGAND DIAGRAM only for complex numbers of the form $\frac{1}{2}+ia$, where $i=\sqrt{-1}$ and a is real.

Riemann space A non-Euclidean geometry, using $n=$ dimensional co-ordinates $(x_1 \ldots x_n)$ and calculating length according to the formula

$$ds^2\sum g_{ij}dx^i dx^j,$$

where ds is the limiting incremental length along a curve, dx^i is "a limiting increment in the i co-ordinate", and i,j run through the values 1, 2, 3, ... n.

Riemann surface In non-Euclidean geometry, a multi-connected many-sheeted SURFACE that can be dissected by cross-cuts into a singly connected surface. Such a representation of a complex algebraic function is used to study the "behaviour" of other complex functions as they are mapped conformally (transformed) onto it. A Riemann surface has been described as topologically equivalent to a box with holes in it.

ring A mathematical structure that constitutes a restricted form of FIELD in which division might be unavailable.

root Either the solution to an (algebraic) equation in connection with equations involving a real or complex unknown, or, of a number, another number which when multiplied by itself to an indicated extent, provides the first number as product.

rose (curve) Symmetrical curve represented by the equation $(x^2+y^2)^3=4a^2x^2y^2$, where a is constant.

scalar *See* VECTOR SPACE.

Schubfachprinzip Principle (ordinarily called the pigeon-hole principle, in English) which states that if in n boxes one distributes more than n objects, at least one box must contain more than one object. The principle is used in the logic of number theory.

secant (sec) *See* TRIGONOMETRIC FUNCTIONS.

(of the) second order Of a differential equation, involving only first and second DERIVATIVES. The term is occasionally used in algebraic contexts to mean "of the second degree", i.e. involving expressions raised to at most the power of 2 (squares).

sequence A list of mathematical objects indexed by the natural numbers, following one another in some defined relationship (but with no mathematical operation implied). Sequences are said to increase (to higher values) or decrease (to lower), and may be finite (if the list terminates), convergent (to a limit) or divergent. If the values increase or decrease along the sequence, the sequence is said to be monotonic or monotone.

series An expression that denotes the addition of a list which constitutes a SEQUENCE. Series may be represented in an abbreviated form using the summation sign - e.g. the series $a_1 + a_2 + a_3 + \ldots + a_n$ to infinity may be represented as $\sum_{k=1}^{\infty}a_k$. The word "series" is for historical reasons occasionally misused to mean "sequence", as in the Fibonacci series. Strictly speaking, however, a series is the limit of the sequence of partial sums.

set, set theory, theory of sets Rigorous manifestation of the notion of collecting together various objects into one new entity if they all possess some property of interest – for instance, P. The resultant object is referred to as the set of all objects possessing P, commonly expressed as $\{x: x$ has property $P\}$. The description $x\varepsilon S$ means that x belongs to the set S. Difficulties may arise if restrictions are not placed on the collecting process, although the process can be continued beyond the finite numbers, giving "transfinite" numbers characterized by the fact that each consists of all the numbers preceding it. Because these numbers may be used as a standard for indexing purposes, they are called ordinal numbers. Cardinal numbers are those ordinals whose members cannot be indexed by means of a smaller set of ordinals, and the cardinality of a set is the smallest ordinal that can be used to index a set. Its existence is guaranteed by the AXIOM OF CHOICE. Set theory provides a foundation for mathematics – and is the basis for most modern elementary mathematical education – yet is known to be incomplete (so that, for example, the cardinality of the set of real numbers may be assumed to be either a large or small order of infinity). Two sets are said to be disjoint if they contain no common elements although their elements are part of the same UNIVERSAL SET. A null set has no members and is written ø or {}.

sextic To the power 6.

$\sum$ **(sigma)** *See* SUMMATION SYMBOL.

simplex method In linear computer-programming, an algorithm designed to find the optimum solution in a finite number of steps.

sine (sin) *See* TRIGONOMETRIC FUNCTIONS.

soluble group Notion introduced to extend theorems concerning commutative groups to a wider class of groups which, in an intuitive sense, can be constructed out of commutative "pieces". Given a group G, the commutator subgroup C is introduced (generated by elements of the form $xyx^{-1}y^{-1}$); G can then be "collapsed" to an Abelian group by a process that reduces C to the identity element; C is then collapsed in an identical fashion, and the process continually repeated. If the process, through a finite number of steps, eventually leads to a last group that is already commutative, G is said to be soluble.

space Collection of mathematical objects (referred to as points) with an associated structure resembling (or analogous to) the properties of the space of everyday experience.

space constant Term characterizing the line in NON-EUCLIDEAN GEOMETRY that relates the ANGLE OF PARALLELISM of two lines – a concept formulated by János Bolyai.

spherical geometry System of non-Euclidean geometry devised by Bernhard Riemann as an extension of ELLIPTIC GEOMETRY and comprising two-dimensional geometry as effected on the outer surface of a sphere.

squaring the circle Ancient Greek problem in geometrical construction, to describe a square of exactly the same area as a given circle, using ruler and compass only. Ferdinand von Lindemann established that π was a TRANSCENDENTAL NUMBER; unable thus to be the root of an equation, it cannot be constructed by ruler and compass – and the problem is therefore not solvable.

standard deviation parameter (σ) In PROBABILITY THEORY, a numerical assessment of the amount by which an event is likely to deviate from the expected. It is measured as the square root of the average (either summed or integrated) of the squares of all possible deviations.

subset In SET THEORY, set that is completely contained in another set. It is generally written using the symbol $\subset$, e.g. $C \subset D$ (the set C is contained in the set D).

sum The result after the addition of one quantity and another.

summation symbol ($\sum$) Sign representing the sum taken over all instances that accompany the sign, indicated above and below it. Thus

$$\sum_{i=1}^{n} a_i$$

means $a_1 + a_2 + a_3 + \ldots + a_n$. The symbol is the capital form of the Greek letter sigma.

surface In three-dimensional geometry, the equivalent in three dimensions to an area in two dimensions.

tangent (tan) *See* TRIGONOMETRIC FUNCTIONS.

(Brook) Taylor's theorem Expands a function of x as an infinite power series in powers of x.

tensor calculus Position in ordinary space usually requires specification of three co-ordinates, singly indexed, e.g. x_1, x_2, x_3. In describing mathematical objects more complicated than position, a generalized type of co-ordinate system may be employed: e.g. x_{ijk} where i,j,k can take values 1, 2 or 3 each. Tensor calculus is a systematized use of such awkward objects.

tessellation Covering of a plane surface by regular congruent quadrilaterals in a side-by-side pattern; the first quadrilateral is derived by joining the mid-points of the sides of a given (regular or irregular) quadrilateral.

tetrahedron, tetrahedra Four-sided figure.

theory of fields *See* FIELD THEORY.

theory of functions *See* FUNCTION THEORY.

theory of groups *See* GROUP THEORY.

theory of limits *See* LIMIT.

theory of numbers *See* NUMBER THEORY.

theta functions Four types of ELLIPTIC FUNCTION devised by Carl Jacobi. Each function is defined as a Fourier series, and written θ_1, θ_2, θ_3 and θ_4; any θ can be converted by translation of the argument into another θ multiplied by a simple factor. (The quotient of any two θs is then periodic twice.)

three-body problem Mathematical problem in astronomy, to describe the gravitational effects of three interacting celestial bodies on each other, and the shape of their orbits round each other.

topological equivalence *See* TOPOLOGY.

topology Study of figures and shapes (and other mathematical objects) with particular regard to the properties that are retained even when the figures or shapes are "stretched" or "squeezed". For example, if a solid ball is stretched and squeezed back into the form of an identical ball (so that effectively the ball has been transformed onto itself) there is a point which is transformed into itself. Fixed point theorems like this are important in the study of differential equations. Furthermore, in topology, two objects are regarded as identical (topologically equivalent) if either can be transformed into the other by a transformation that is continuous and that has a continuous inverse - for example, a cube and a solid ball (of which both have at least 8 identical co-ordinate points).

torus, toroidal Three-dimensional solid resembling a ring doughnut or an inflated inner-tube.

transcendental curves Curves for which there are no representative algebraic equations; examples are logarithmic curves and trigonometric curves.

transcendental numbers REAL NUMBERS that are not ALGEBRAIC NUMBERS, and can therefore not be expressed as roots (solutions) of an algebraic equation with integral coefficients; and example is EULER'S NUMBER (*e*).

transfinite *See* SET THEORY.

transformation Operation between two spaces, particularly between two VECTOR SPACES, also defined as an operation allotting to each point *P* of one space a point (usually written as *P'*) of the other space. *P* is then known as the argument, and *P'* the image point. A transformation is also often called a mapping.

trigonometric functions Represent the relationships between the sides and angles of a right-angled triangle, such that of an angle *a*,

$$\text{sine } a = \frac{\text{opposite side}}{\text{hypotenuse}}$$

$$\text{cosine } a = \frac{\text{adjacent side}}{\text{hypotenuse}}$$

$$\text{tangent } a = \frac{\text{opposite side}}{\text{adjacent side}}$$

$$\text{secant } a = \frac{\text{hypotenuse}}{\text{adjacent side}}$$

$$\text{cosecant } a = \frac{\text{hypotenuse}}{\text{opposite side}}$$

trigonometric series Expression of the sine and cosine TRIGONOMETRIC FUNCTIONS as convergent POWER SERIES.

unit theory, theory of units In a FIELD or RING, involves an element which possesses an inverse. In a field, every non-zero element is a unit; in a ring, 1 and -1 represent a unit.

universal set In set theory, with regard to a MATHEMATICAL STRUCTURE, a set of objects in the structure. More generally, it represents the "universe of discourse" appropriate to the discourse – for example, the set of vowels and the set of consonants are disjoint sets within the universal set comprising the alphabet.

variable In mathematics, an expression representing either a general point taken from a specific set of values which may therefore be substituted by any selected point of the specified set, or a name for an unknown point to be found within a specified set of possible values. It is often regarded as fixed at least through the duration of a mathematical train of thought.

variance In probability theory, the square of the STANDARD DEVIATION.

variety In algebra, the set of solutions of a simultaneous system of equations with a fixed number of variables. In two dimensions, examples are a circle, an ellipse, a parabola, etc. In three dimensions, a variety is a surface, e.g. the surface of a sphere.

vector In the elementary sense, a directional line of finite length in a plane or in three-dimensional space, emanating from the origin. The (degenerate) case of zero length is referred to as the zero (or null) vector. More generally, a vector is an element of a VECTOR SPACE.

vector space Also called linear space, a mathematical structure comprising two types of objects: vectors and scalars. Vectors can be added by themselves; scalars lengthen or shorten them (i.e. scale the vector length up or down) and are commonly either real or complex numbers. In general, scalars of a vector space comprise a FIELD. The prime example of a vector space is the collection of elementary vectors (*see* VECTOR) in the two- or three-dimensional space of everyday experience. (The operation of addition follows the parallelogram law: to add two vectors, complete the parallelogram defined by the two lines – the sum is given by the diagonal through the common origin.) Vector spaces provide a framework for the study of LINEAR TRANSFORMATIONS – which can in finite dimensional spaces be represented by MATRICES – and are important in mathematical modelling of complicated systems (engineering, biological, etc.) where general transformations are approximated by linear ones, with recourse to the apparatus of DIFFERENTIAL CALCULUS.

Venn diagrams In elementary set theory, use of overlapping (or similar closed curves) to illustrate how some members of one set may also be members of another set.

zero vector *See* VECTOR.

zeta function Function that may be represented as the value of the infinite series

$$\zeta(s) = 1 + \frac{1}{2^s} + \frac{1}{3^s} + \frac{1}{4^s} + \dots$$

where s is a complex number. The function was significant in Leonhard Euler's study of prime numbers. *See also* the RIEMANN HYPOTHESIS.

Index

161